W9-BDT-116

A HISTORY OF INNER ASIA

Geographically and historically Inner Asia is a confusing area which is much in need of interpretation. Svat Soucek's book offers a short and accessible introduction to the history of the region. The narrative, which begins with the arrival of Islam, proceeds chronologically, charting the rise and fall of the changing dynasties, the Russian conquest of Central Asia and the fall of the Soviet Union. Dynastic tables and maps augment and elucidate the text. The contemporary focus rests on the seven countries which make up the core of present-day Eurasia, that is Uzbekistan, Kazakstan, Kyrgyzstan, Tajikistan, Turkmenistan, Sinkiang, and Mongolia. Since 1991, there has been renewed interest in these countries which has prompted considerable political, cultural, economic, and religious debate. While a vast and divergent literature has evolved in consequence, no short survey of the region has been attempted. Soucek's history of Inner Asia promises to fill this gap and to become an indispensable source of information for anyone studying or visiting the area.

SVAT SOUCEK is a bibliographer at Princeton University Library. He has worked as Central Asia bibliographer at Columbia University, New York Public Library, and at the University of Michigan, and has published numerous related articles in *The Journal of Turkish Studies*, *The Encyclopedia of Islam*, and *The Dictionary of the Middle Ages*.

A HISTORY OF INNER ASIA

SVAT SOUCEK

Princeton University

CAMBRIDGE
UNIVERSITY PRESS

PUBLISHED BY THE PRESS SYNDICATE OF THE UNIVERSITY OF CAMBRIDGE
The Pitt Building, Trumpington Street, Cambridge, United Kingdom

CAMBRIDGE UNIVERSITY PRESS
The Edinburgh Building, Cambridge CB2 2RU, UK
40 West 20th Street, New York, NY 10011–4211, USA
477 Williamstown Road, Port Melbourne, VIC 3207, Australia
Ruiz de Alarcón 13, 28014 Madrid, Spain
Dock House, The Waterfront, Cape Town 8001, South Africa

http://www.cambridge.org

© Cambridge University Press 2000

This book is in copyright. Subject to statutory exception
and to the provisions of relevant collective licensing agreements,
no reproduction of any part may take place without
the written permission of Cambridge University Press.

First published 2000
Reprinted 2001, 2002

Printed in the United Kingdom at the University Press, Cambridge

Typeset in 11/12.5 Monotype Baskerville in QuarkXPress™ [SE]

A catalogue record for this book is available from the British Library

Library of Congress Cataloguing in Publication data

ISBN 0 521 65169 7 hardback
ISBN 0 521 65704 0 paperback

Contents

Maps

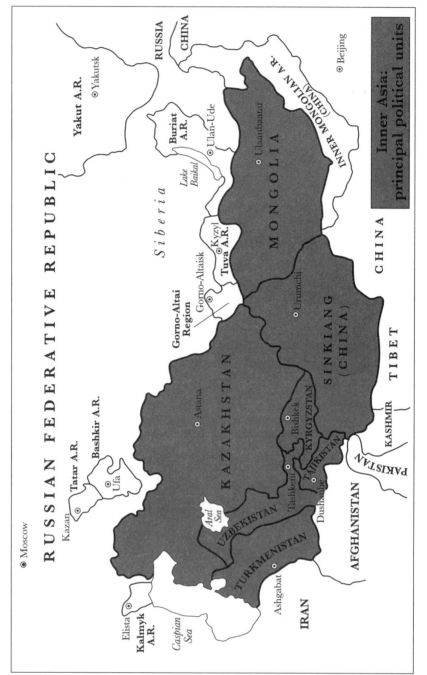

Map 1 Inner Asia: principal political units

Preface

This book is an attempt to offer the reader a historical and topical introduction to several countries in the core of Eurasia which until recently were little noticed except by a small community of scholars or people who had special reasons to do so. One result of this neglect has been a lack of adequate literature of the kind presented here: a general survey of the past and present of this part of the world.

Almost overnight, a few years ago, these countries – Uzbekistan, Kazakhstan, Kyrgyzstan, Tajikistan, Turkmenistan, Sinkiang, and Mongolia – began to attract considerable attention from politicians, journalists, businessmen, and academicians. The reason was the collapse of the Soviet Union in 1991. Since the formation of that Union in the early 1920s, the first five of the group had been almost sequestered by the rulers of the Soviet empire. The outside world was barred from unhindered access and communication with them, and their own citizens found contact with that world both difficult and risky. Mongolia was officially independent, but its membership in the family of Soviet satellites had imposed on it similar strictures. For the same reason, the Soviet Union's demise affected it almost as profoundly as it did the five Union republics. We are also including Sinkiang, although the course of its recent history has followed a somewhat different path. The inclusion is justified, we think, because the province is geographically as well as historically an integral part of the group, and because the evolution occurring among its members is likely to affect Sinkiang as well.

The historic change rather unwittingly set in motion by Mikhail Gorbachev but then gaining its own momentum has thus generated a sudden surge of interest in these countries, an interest that spans the broad spectrum of political, cultural, economic, and even religious spheres, and that emanates from countries as divergent as the United States, China, Turkey, Iran, Saudi Arabia, and Israel. This in turn has begun to produce a rapidly growing volume of literature, ranging from newspaper reports to financial analyses, statistical yearbooks, specialized periodicals, and learned articles and monographs. Paradoxically but perhaps understandably, however, a comprehensive survey of the kind attempted here has so far not been published. Our book is meant to fill this gap.

The principal focus of this study, we have said, is on seven countries: the republics of Kazakhstan, Kyrgyzstan, Tajikistan, Turkmenistan, and Uzbekistan; the Sinkiang Uighur Autonomous Region of the People's Republic of China; and the Republic of Mongolia. The first five units have also been known collectively as Western or Russian Turkestan, or, more recently, as Soviet Central Asia; the sixth unit, as Eastern or Chinese Turkestan, or High Tartary; and the seventh, as Outer Mongolia.

It is not customary to discuss the three groups together when they are approached as specific political units, or when the historical narrative includes the modern period after the formation of these units. The reasons for this reside more in the different academic, journalistic, or political backgrounds of the observers than in any intrinsic justification for such a separation. Our treatment of the subject will demonstrate, we hope, that the bonds unifying Western and Eastern Turkestan are stronger than the differences between them, and that without Mongolia the historical picture would be incomplete.

INNER ASIA: PRINCIPAL POLITICAL UNITS

The "centrality" of Inner Asia as the landlocked core of the Eurasian continent is graphically brought out by the brackets which Moscow and Beijing form to encompass the seven countries under discussion.

The seven countries are Kazakhstan (capital: Astana), Kyrgyzstan (capital, Bishkek), Tajikistan (capital: Dushanbe), Turkmenistan (capital: Ashkhabad), Uzbekistan (capital: Tashkent), Sinkiang (capital: Urumchi), and Mongolia (capital: Ulan Bator).

Area: Kazakhstan, 2,717,300 sq. km. (1,048,000 sq. miles); Kyrgyzstan, 198,500 sq. km. (76,641 sq. miles); Tajikistan, 143,100 sq. km. (55,251 sq. miles); Turkmenistan, 488,100 sq. km. (188,455 sq. miles); Uzbekistan, 447,400 sq. km. (173,591 sq. miles); Sinkiang, 1,646,000 sq. km. (635,829 sq. miles); and Mongolia, 1,565,000 sq. km. (604,247 sq. miles). Their order in terms of size is thus Kazkhstan, Sinkiang, Mongolia, Turkmenistan, Uzbekistan, Kyrgyzstan, Tajikistan.

Population: (approximate figures, due to the evolving situation; based on data from 1981–94): Kazakhstan, 17,200,000; Kyrgyzstan, 4,600,000; Tajikistan, 5,700,000; Turkmenistan, 4,000,000; Uzbekistan, 21,900,000; Sinkiang, 15,200,000; Mongolia, 2,400,000. Their order according to the size of the population is thus Uzbekistan, Kazakhstan, Sinkiang, Tajikistan, Kyrgyzstan, Turkmenistan, Mongolia. In ethnolinguistic terms, the principal nationalities of these countries are Turkic (Uzbekistan, Kazakhstan, Sinkiang, Kyrgyzstan, Turkmenistan), Iranian (Tajikistan), and Mongol (Mongolia).

In addition to the seven principal countries, Map 1 also shows eight other units based on ethnolinguistic and historical principles that relate them to our theme. Seven of these are in the Russian Federation, the eighth is in China. Those in the Russian Federation are the autonomous republics of Tatarstan (capital: Kazan), Bashkiria or Bashqurtistan (capital: Ufa), Kalmykia (capital: Elista), the autonomous region of Gorno-Altai (capital: Gorno-Altaisk), and the autonomous republics of Tuva (capital: Kyzyl), Buriatia (capital: Ulan-Ude), and Yakutia (capital: Yakutsk). The one in China is the Inner Mongolian Autonomous Region (capital: Hohhot). The determinant nationalities of five of these units speak Turkic languages (Tatarstan, Bashqurtistan, Gorno-Altai, Tuva, and Yakutia), and of three, Mongol languages (Kalmykia, Buriatia, Inner Mongolia).

Moreover, a strict focus on the seven distinct units makes sense only for the present and recent situation. For times farther back, we shall treat the subject as a history of Inner Asia, whose core will still be the aforementioned countries but whose area will retain a certain flexibility, with the centers of gravity shifting or dividing or multiplying according to the flow of events; and we shall thus frequently pay attention to places well beyond the seven units' modern political boundaries.

Finally, yet another qualification is necessary. The past as we have conceived of it for the purposes of this book starts in the seventh century with the arrival of Islam in Central Asia. There are two reasons for this decision. One is the academic background of the author, the other the fact that for Central Asia, earlier periods are the domain of the archaeologist rather than of the historian.

In addition to "Central Asia," we also use the term "Inner Asia." *Inner Asia,* somewhat of a neologism and limited to scholarly parlance, designates the whole area in its historical and geographical sense; *Central Asia,* as used in English, means the western portion of Inner Asia, roughly

Western Turkestan and the western part of Eastern Turkestan, together with such adjacent areas as northeastern Iran and northern Afghanistan. For the present political configuration we shall use the names of the six republics (Kazakhstan, Kyrgyzstan, Tajikistan, Turkmenistan, Uzbekistan, and Mongolia), while Sinkiang will stand for its unwieldly and long official name, Sinkiang Uighur Autonomous Region of the People's Republic of China.

TRANSLITERATION AND GEOPOLITICAL TERMINOLOGY

This book deals with an area and history where several language families and alphabets have existed, often coexisting or replacing one another or going through natural or imposed transformations. Transliteration of the multitude of names and terms is a daunting and expensive (if a profusion of diacritical marks is used) challenge, and perfection is impossible. Even when writing for the reduced audience of scholars, an author must explain the compromise he has chosen and apologize for the shortcomings.

We have followed, with some modifications, the transliteration system used by the *Encyclopaedia of Islam*. The main exception is dispensation with diacritical signs and special letters. In a book of this kind an array of such features would be pointless or even disruptive. The general reader, we think, would find no use for scrupulously marked Arabic or Turkic words, while the specialist, if he chooses to read the book, will not need such additional help. We have thus limited the use of diacritics to their occurrences in the languages using the roman alphabet – in our book chiefly French, German, and Turkish. For Chinese, we follow the Wade-Giles system, except for names that have become familiar in their *pinyin* form (the official transliteration now used in China).

A different type of compromise has also been imposed by practical considerations. While we have endeavored to avoid anachronisms when referring to specific regions, complete consistency has not been attempted. Sinkiang received this name only in 1758, yet we freely avail ourselves of this name even when discusssing earlier periods, simply because using (or creating) other names would cause needless confusion. Similarly, Mongolia was from the sixth to the ninth centuries the core of Inner Asian Turkic empires. Should we call it, when discussing that period, Turkestan (or Turkey, for that matter)? Or again southern Russia and Ukraine were in antiquity the home of the Iranian Scythians, and in the early Middle Ages of Kipchak Turks. Referring to them as Scythia or Kipchakia would sound rather pedantic in our book.

The author wishes to express warmest thanks to the following friends and colleagues who took pains in reading the manuscript and making numerous helpful suggestions: Thomas Allsen, Michael Cook, Mark Farrell, Peter Golden, Norman Itzkowitz and Jacob Landau.

Introduction

Inner Asia is marked by three distinct features: (1) a belt of steppes and, to a lesser degree, deserts, which extend in a general latitudinal direction. This belt is delimited on the north by the Eurasian forest zone (the "taiga" of Siberia); on the south the limits are a variety of features, chiefly mountain chains but also transition to different climatic zones (notably in China) and bodies of water such as the Caspian and Black Seas; (2) several of these mostly latitudinal mountain chains that separate the steppe belt from South Asia, besides demarcating important segments within the area; and (3) a number of rivers, many of which drain into interior lakes or seas or disappear in the deserts through evaporation. All these features have affected the type and history of human presence, but some have in turn been modified by man's intervention, since the dawn of sedentary civilization but especially in recent decades.

The steppe belt, an immense swath of landlocked grassland, made possible the appearance of a unique historical phenomenon: the horse-breeding, highly mobile Eurasian nomad. To be sure, nomads have also existed in other parts of the world, but the scale of the habitat, the role of the horse, and the relative and paradoxical proximity of great agricultural or urban civilizations made it possible for the Inner Asian nomad to play a historical role as unique and often as grandiose as was his homeland. In historical times, these nomads have been Turks and Mongols: these peoples had earlier seized primacy from the Indo-Europeans, some of whom they absorbed and some of whom migrated to India, the Middle East, or Europe.

Despite or perhaps partly because of their vastness, the Eurasian steppes and deserts have not been known by any comprehensive name. Those portions which have received generally accepted and well-known appellations owe them to historical circumstances or to special geographical features. Leading this roster are the Orkhon valley in Central

1

Mongolia, the Jungarian plain in northern Sinkiang, the Ili valley and Semireche in northwestern Sinkiang and southeastern Kazakhstan, and various deserts – the Gobi of southern Mongolia and eastern Sinkiang, Taklamakan in western Sinkiang, Betpak Dala ("Plain of Misfortune") in southern Kazakhstan, Kyzyl Kum ("Red Sand") in Uzbekistan, and Kara Kum ("Black Sand") in Turkmenistan. The great expanse of the steppe of Kazakhstan, southern Russia and southern Ukraine, known to medieval Muslim authors as Dasht-i Kipchak ("The Steppe of the Kipchak [Turks]"), has since the political and demographic transformations of recent centuries become nameless, or has come to be known by the names of new administrative apportionments.

In contrast, the mountains and rivers of Inner Asia more easily catch our eye and retain evocative names: the Altai, Tianshan, and Pamirs are the most prominent ranges from among a number of lesser but still impressive systems; their location makes them central to our story, but the Kunlun, Karakoram, and Himalayas of Tibet, and the Urals of northern Eurasia also deserve mention. The Kunlun, Karakoram, and Himalayas, the highest mountain complexes in the world, allowed trade and religion to circulate through their passes between India and Inner Asia, but they impeded the southward expansion of the nomads' steppe empires. The Urals attract our attention with the contrast they offer to the centrally located latitudinal Tianshan, for example: this extended longitudinal chain divides the Eurasian continent's forest zone into its European and Asian parts, or, expressed in political terms, into European and Siberian Russia. Its southern outcroppings protrude into the northernmost part of the Kipchak Steppe, dividing it too into two approximate halves, a task then taken over by the Ural river, which rises in the Urals and eventually flows into the Caspian Sea.

Both rivers and mountains affected the nomads' lives. Mountains played a role whose importance was second only to that of the steppes. First of all, the positive role: such ranges as the Tianshan encouraged through the pastures on their northern slopes and in their valleys a sea-sonal, vertical migration of the transhumant type that is a counterpart to the equally seasonal but horizontal (often south–north) migration in the steppes. Thus the Kyrgyz became almost exclusively mountain nomads, in contrast to their closest kinsmen the Kazakhs who were steppe nomads, or to the Mongols. The mountains also often functioned as places of refuge and starting points for the nomads' political regrouping: the Altai, Hangai, and Hentei ranges of Mongolia have all played such roles in the history of the Turks and Mongols. Certain peaks even acquired a magic aura where rituals and burials were performed or where a leader would go into seclusion in order to communicate with *tengri*, the nomads' celestial deity, at such crucial moments as the eve of an important battle. To this should be added the likelihood that such mineral-rich ranges as the Altai facilitated the early Turks' metallurgy and weapon production. As for their negative role: mountains, we have suggested, could not but act as barriers to vaster movements of nomads in search of new habitats or empires to build; indeed, when they built empires, the latter were steppe empires, to use a term made classic by René Grousset.

If nomads occupied the most characteristic place of human presence in Inner Asia, they were by no means its only inhabitants, and agriculture as well as urban life have flourished in many parts of it. Settlements usually owed their existence to mountains, but indirectly: agriculture was mostly of the irrigated and oasis type, dependent on rivers or underground conduits whose sources feed from the rainfall and glaciers of Inner Asian mountains. Dry farming depending on rainfall was not absent, but it in turn occurred chiefly in the higher elevations and foothills of the mountains or, more recently, in the northern latitudes of the steppe belt.

The part of Inner Asia where settled agricultural and urban civilization had appeared in protohistory and soon reached an especially developed and intensive level lay between the Caspian and Aral Seas on the west and the Tianshan and Pamir mountains on the east. This is the core of Central Asia, an area of plains and rivers, with no daunting mountain ranges until faced by the historic range of Hindukush; and it lies at the crossroads between the steppe world of Inner Asia to the north and the different regions of the Middle East and India to the south. The two worlds, the steppes of Inner Asia of the north and the subtropical regions of the south, were too distant to be encompassed by either the steppe empires of Inner Asia or the great monarchies of Iran or India. However, human migration through Central Asia was feasible, and the area became an important gateway through which in protohistory and antiquity peoples of Inner Asia moved south to Iran or India.

HISTORICO-GEOGRAPHICAL SURVEY

In the course of our narrative, names of regions, cities, and natural phenomena will appear that may be unfamiliar to the reader. Good maps or atlases – such as *The Times Atlas of the World*, *The Times Atlas of China*,

An Historical Atlas of Islam edited by W. C. Brice and published under the patronage of the Encyclopaedia of Islam, *The Historical and Commercial Atlas of China* by K. Herrmann, and *The Times Atlas of World History* – can help, as should, we hope, the accompanying maps throughout this book. A preliminary survey may also be worthwhile.

Let us start with the historical core of Central Asia, a region called Transoxania (or Transoxiana). The scholars who coined this name did so because the area lies beyond the River Oxus as one approaches it from the classical world of Iran, more specifically from its northeastern province of Khurasan. The Oxus, a Latinized form of an ancient Iranian word, was known to the Arabs as Jayhun, and is now called Amu Darya ("the Amu river"; this too may be an originally Iranian name, based on a local variant, Amu, and the Persian word for lake or sea, *darya*, borrowed by Central Asian Turkic with the connotation of river). The name indicates where Transoxania begins on the south, but does not say where it ends on the north, west, or east. There we have to use history's indirect evidence and its possible interpretations, while admitting that this matter is less relevant than the question of why Transoxania was important, and where its center of gravity lay. The latter can be sought along another river, the Zarafshan ("gold-strewing" in Persian), which like the Amu Darya originates farther east in the Pamir mountains; it then flows west, first in its valley between the protrusions of the Pamirs called here Turkestan and Zarafshan ranges, then through the central lowland of Uzbekistan, and ultimately makes a lunge for the Amu Darya but disappears, exhausted, in the sands of Uzbekistan's Kyzyl Kum desert. Irrigation derived from the Zarafshan has since antiquity supported dense agricultural and urban settlements, and cities like Panjikent in Tajikistan, or Samarkand and Bukhara in Uzbekistan are only the best remembered or most famous examples. Moreover, the Zarafshan is only the principal among the streams in Transoxania and adjacent areas that have made irrigation possible and through it settled and urban life. One of these, the Kashka Darya, rises in the southern watershed of the Zarafshan range. It then flows southwest and westward, in a manner somewhat parallel to that of the Zarafshan, toward the Bukharan oasis, but disappears before reaching it. Among the settlements it has nourished are such historical places as Shahrisabz, earlier known as Kesh and remembered as the birthplace of Timur (Tamerlane), and Karshi, the former Nasaf which was renamed in the Mongol period after the palace (*karshi*) built there by one of the Mongol rulers. The Zarafshan range is paralleled on the south by the Hisar range (often written Hissar or

Gissar, for no good reason except that this echoes Russian spelling), the last of these chains as we proceed southward. From then on we descend toward the valley of the Amu Darya. If we cross this river and continue, we eventually approach the mighty Hindukush mountains of Afghanistan. These two ranges, the Hisar on the north and Hindukush on the south, bracket the core territory of historical Bactria, the later Tokharistan; today this territory corresponds to northern Afghanistan, southern Tajikistan and southeastern Uzbekistan and Turkmenistan. The delimitation of Bactria on the east and west is less clear-cut, but one feature deserves mention: the "Iron Gate," a defile about half-way between Balkh and Samarkand that breaks the low mountain range extending from the Hisar range southward toward the Amu Darya. The Iron Gate was a historic passageway between Bactria and Sogdia, used by conquerors, ambassadors, pilgrims and merchant caravans, and its name was more than just a legend: an actual gate reinforced with iron used to exist there.

The people who inhabited the area along the Zarafshan river as well as adjacent regions at the time of the Arab conquest were the Sogdians, hence the historical name for this central part of Transoxania, Sogdia or Sogdiana. They spoke an Iranian tongue, for Sogdia, like much of Central Asia, was then an Iranian-speaking area. One trace of that is toponymy, which includes many towns whose names end in -*kent*, -*kand*, -*kat* or other variants of this Iranian word meaning "town": Panjikent, Uzgend, Samarkand, Numijkat (the original name of Bukhara), Tashkent, Yarkand, or simply Kat for example. Another vestige is the fact that a sizable component of the population is still Iranian-speaking or bilingual Iranian–Turkic (although some time after the Islamic conquest a shift occurred from Sogdian to Farsi, the language of Fars, a province in southern Persia, which developed into modern Persian). Muslim geographers of the tenth century (remarkable for the florescence of Islamic geography written in Arabic) called the country Bilad al-Sughd, Land of the Sogdians, and the Zarafshan, Wadi al-Sughd, Sogd river.

Historical Sogdia was thus the core of Transoxania, as it is today of modern Uzbekistan. For Transoxania the Arabs used the term Mawarannahr, "That which is beyond the river [Jayhun]," thus following the same psycholinguistic process. By contrast, the name Uzbekistan, "country of the Uzbeks," came into official usage only in 1924 with the creation of the republic of that name. The second part of this compound, the Indo-European -*stan* (place of abode, sojourn, camp, tent;

cognate of the English verb to stand), met with prodigious fortunes in the entire Orient that was either Iranian or Iranian-inspired, whether Turco-Mongol or Indian: the ubiquitous suffix appeared in the Arabs' Turkistan and in a myriad other names of regions from Kazakhstan to Hindustan and Pakistan, besides existing independently as the term for each of the provinces of modern Iran, *ustan* (and even as a suffix forming associative rather than geographical concepts: thus *Gulistan*, "Place of Roses" and *Bustan*, "Place of Fragrance," titles of two famous collections of poems composed by the fourteenth-century Persian poet Sadi).

Khurasan, Mawarannahr, and Tokharistan were thus the standard terms for Central Asia to the south and north of the Jayhun river (Oxus, Amu Darya) in early Islamic civilization as formulated through its principal medium, the Arabic language. Once the Iranian element of the Islamic empire reasserted its identity, however, two other terms appeared that harkened back to the times of rivalry between the sedentary inhabitants of pre-Islamic Persia and the nomadic ones of Inner Asia: Iran and Turan. These concepts were more symbolic and political than expressions of ethnic difference, for the population on both sides of the Oxus was at that time Iranian; to the north of this river, however, suzerainty belonged ever more to the nomadic Turks of the steppe, so that pre-Islamic Persians thought of it as Turan, a place or abode (*an*) of the Turks (*Tur*; this interpretation, however, is very dubious), in contrast to Iran. This usage remained limited to classical Persian poetry, but the awareness of the Oxus as the great demarcation line between two different worlds – that of the Middle East, and that of Inner Asia – remained pervasive throughout the Middle Ages.

To the northwest of Transoxania lay Khwarazm (also spelled Khwarizm, Khawarazm, Kharazm, Khorazm and Latinized as Chorasmia), a region which, like the former, can be better defined by its core than by its limits, besides the fact that its northeastern portion was technically also Transoxania. The core is the lowermost course of the Amu Darya and its sprawling delta estuary fringing the southern shore of the Aral Sea. Here too it was the river, this time the Amu itself, that made possible a flourishing agricultural and urban civilization which was, since protohistory, Iranian. In pre-Islamic and early Islamic times two kingdoms tended to divide up Khwarazm: one in the southeast, with the city of Kat by the right, northern bank of the Amu Darya, as its capital; the other in the northwest, with the city of Urgench as the ruler's residence. Both are archaeological sites today, with the qualification that another town called Urgench arose in the seventeenth century farther upstream, while the original site came to be known as Kunya Urgench, "Old Urgench" (from the Persian *kuhna*, "old"). Even the name Khwarazm has disappeared from current usage except in the rather artificial administrative parlance introduced after the upheavals of the Russian Revolution and establishment of the Soviet regime (the short-lived "Republic of Khorazmia," and then the Khorazmian Region of the Uzbek SSR and now of Uzbekistan; the Region, whose administrative center is the aforementioned "new" Urgench, is only a fraction of historical Khwarazm, whose greater part corresponds to the present Karakalpak Autonomous Republic and the Dashhovuz Region of Turkmenistan). Other cities, names, and formations have developed in Khwarazm through the centuries; from among these Khiva, on the southern side of the delta's apex, rose to prominence in the seventeenth century, and gave its name to a khanate that survived until 1919. A peculiar feature of the Amu Darya is the fact that all of its water did not always flow into the Aral Sea. At certain periods one branch swerved, shortly after having reached the apex of the delta, northwest and then southwest, passing by medieval Urgench. Called Uzboy, this branch then pursued the southwesterly course all the way to the Caspian Sea, which it entered through a wide coastal plain south of Krasnovodsk (Turkmenbashy). Before entering this plain, this arm of the Amu Darya flowed through a valley between two low mountain ranges, Greater Balkhan on the northwest and Lesser Balkhan on the southeast; a noteworthy feature of the foothills of the Greater Balkhan is the town of Nebit Dag with the now famous deposits of natural gas in its vicinity. In 1576 the river swerved back toward the Aral Sea, and the definitive decline of Old Urgench, thus deprived of its water supply, is by some historians attributed more to this natural cause than to devastations wrought by the armies of Genghis Khan and Timur.

The damages done to irrigation by warfare, especially at the time of the Mongol invasion, are painful episodes in Central Asia's past. An incalculably more terrible devastation – destruction of the environment and people's health – was visited on the region in the heyday of Russian rule, and grew in intensity right down to the collapse of the Soviet empire. This devastation was brought about by irrigation undertaken by the Russian masters to suit the imperial metropolis at the expense of Central Asia. We shall return to this theme in the final chapters of our book. Here the case of the Amu Darya changing its course and thus causing the definitive demise of Old Urgench is an opportunity for mentioning a paradox characteristic of the Soviet period: the catastrophic destruction of Central Asia's environment caused by *excessive* irrigation. Irrigation, we have seen, was not a novelty here; in antiquity and the Middle Ages it enabled man to turn this part of the world into a flourishing region of gardens, orchards, fields growing varieties of cereals, and of prosperous towns. The Soviet government, however, turned this earthly paradise into a monster megafarm by ordering it to deliver cotton for Russia's textile industry, and in addition to turning grainfields and orchards into water-thirsty cottonfields it undertook the construction of supercanals to irrigate vast tracts of steppe or even desert land in order to produce still more of that raw material. One such project was the 1,266 kilometer long Karakum canal, which traverses almost the whole length of Turkmenistan. It starts in the republic's east by tapping the Amu Darya a few kilometers after this river has left Afghan territory, and proceeds all the way to the town of Kazanjik not far from the Caspian Sea. The Karakum canal, proudly boasting the epithet "Imeni V. I. Lenina" ("In the name of V. I. Lenin," a favorite Soviet mark of distinction), was inaugurated in 1959, but its construction, begun before the war, still went on in the 1970s beyond Kazanjik. The Amu Darya is the lifeblood of man, beast, and plant that live and grow downstream, and it used to be the chief provider of water that kept the Aral Sea alive. The Karakum canal became a leech sucking this lifeblood from the beneficial river. The canal is of course only the most dramatic example of the violence perpetrated against man and nature in Soviet Central Asia; the Amu Darya – like its sister river the Syr Darya and other streams – was being tapped in many other parts of its course, and for the same principal purpose: ever more cotton for Russia's textile industry. The dwindling – we might almost say desertification – of the Aral Sea, and the catastrophic consequences of excessive irrigation, seem to have escaped the notice of most observers, Soviet and foreign alike, before *glasnost*. Since the late 1980s, by contrast, a flood of articles and books on this crisis has drawn the attention of both the domestic and international audience, and generated a search for a solution which, the Central Asians hope, will be facilitated through massive international technical and financial aid. One aspect seldom given attention by either expert or journalistic observers is the destruction of a once-flourishing wildlife. The Amu Darya delta as well as other riparian regions of Central Asia used to shelter such animals as tigers, besides their principal prey, Bukhara deer and wild boar, and a multitude of waterfowl, while the Aral Sea teemed with fish supporting a lively fishing industry. All that is gone, the Aral has since 1965 dwindled by more than a half, and some predict its complete disappearance by 2005.

Medieval Khwarazm also functioned as an important commercial link between the Middle East and Russia, for it was through it that the most important trade routes between these two worlds passed. The trade was further stimulated by the Islamization of the Middle East, and the rise of Urgench as the chief Khwarazmian city from the tenth century onwards was partly due to this conjuncture. The caravans struck out across the broad plateau between the Aral and Caspian Seas known as Üst-yurt ("elevated ground" in Turkic), and headed toward the Volga river. Some of the traffic may also have headed for the broad Mangyshlak peninsula on the Caspian coast, where they boarded ships for the presumably less arduous maritime voyage toward the Volga. At the time of the Islamic conquests in the seventh–eighth centuries, the lower region of the Volga was the home of the Turkic qaghanate of the Khazars, with Itil situated in the river's delta as its principal city. By the tenth century the Khazar qaghanate was in definitive decline, and some of its commercial function was being assumed by another Turkic kingdom, that of the Bulghars on the middle course of the Volga with Bulghar, not far from modern Kazan, as their capital. Whereas the Khazar elite was partly judaicized, the Bulghars eventually converted to Islam. History has fortunately preserved a vivid testimony of the inception of this process. It is an account of a mission sent in 922 by the Abbasid caliph Muqtadir (908–29) to the "King of the Bulghars" written by one of the participants, the Baghdad scholar Ibn Fadlan.

To the east of Transoxania lies Fergana (also spelled Ferghana, Fargana, and Farghana; for the sake of consistency, we shall always use the form Fergana), a large elliptical valley enclosed by the Tianshan and Pamir mountains on the north, east, and south. The valley is crossed by a river called Naryn along its upper course in Kyrgyzstan and then, after it has crossed the Uzbek border and received the Kara Darya, Syr Darya. Fergana could also be included in Transoxania, since it lies to the north of the Amu Darya. Like Sogdia, Khwarazm, and several other regions of Central Asia, Fergana is a land of an ancient agricultural civilization nourished by streams descending from the surrounding mountains with the Syr Darya and Kara Darya playing the leading role. Again, its name, still current in the sixteenth century, was for some time overshadowed by that of one of its cities when the Khanate of Khoqand (also spelled Kokand; Quqon in modern Uzbek) became the easternmost of the three kingdoms of Central Asia prior to the nineteenth-century Russian conquest, the

Emirate of Bukhara and Khanate of Khiva being the other two. The
greater part of Fergana lies today within Uzbekistan as the republic's easternmost province, except for fringes shared by Kyrgyzstan and Tajikistan;
for example the historic cities of Uzgend and Osh are on the Kyrgyz side
of the border, that of Khujand is on the Tajik side.

   To the south of Transoxania lay the aforemetioned province of
Khurasan ("[Land of] the Rising Sun" or "Orient" in Iranian), a name
which still exists today but is restricted to the original territory's south-
western segment as Iran's province of Khurasan (Ustan-i Khurasan,
with Meshed as the capital). In pre-Islamic and early Islamic times the
name covered a much larger area that also comprised central
Turkmenistan and northwestern Afghanistan and included such cities as
Nisa, Merv, Nishapur, and Herat. Ashgabad, the capital of modern
Turkmenistan, lies not far from the site of the ancient Parthian capital
Nisa (second–first centuries BC) in the foothills of Kopet Dagh, a range
that runs along the Turkmen–Iranian border. It is the streams flowing
into this northern, Turkmen part of historical Khurasan that have supported agriculture and urban life there; most originate in the Kopet
Dagh range, but two rivers, the Tejen and the Murghab, have their
sources farther southeast in Afghanistan's Kuh-i Baba (the classical
Paropamissus; it is sometimes identified with the Hindukush, or more
correctly with its western segment), and Firuzkuh ranges. The Tejen,
whose upper course is called Heri Rud (Herat river), for a short distance
forms the border between Afghanistan and Iran, and then between Iran
and Turkmenistan before it forges its way into the latter republic's Kara
Kum desert. It meets its death there, but only after its sprawling desert
delta has nourished a fertile network of agricultural settlements around
the city of Tejen. The same can be said of the Murghab some 150 kilometers to the east, where an even larger oasis complex was marked by the
famous medieval city of Merv. The Murghab, a short distance after it
has entered Turkmenistan, is reinforced by the Kushk, a river originating in Afghanistan's Safed Koh range. The town of Kushka grew up
near the border post in the period of Russian domination, and became
memorable as the southernmost point of the Tsarist and Soviet empire
and as the terminus of a railway branch extended there from Merv. The
main line ran from the Caspian port of Krasnovodsk through Merv to
Bukhara, Samarkand and Tashkent, where it linked up with lines connecting Central Asia with Russia and Siberia. The railroad's position
and function reflected both ancient and recent long-distance routes
going through Merv. In the early Middle Ages Merv lay on one of the

Silk Road's trunk routes linking Sinkiang through Samarkand with Nishapur and points farther west, as well as the routes going to Balkh and India, and those going to Khwarazm and Russia. This made the city one of the great emporia of Central Asia, a role enhanced by exports of its own products, such as textiles woven from local silk and from cotton grown in the fertile oasis. The latter benefited from a sophisticated dam built some distance upstream, later destroyed by the Mongols, and partly rebuilt not long before the nineteenth-century Russian conquest (Band-i Sultani, "The Royal Dam"). The rebuilding of the dam did not restore the city to its former importance, nor did the railroad built by the Russians; the latter did reaffirm, however, the location's strategic importance as a station on the road to India: the railroad's extension to Kushka had the purpose of a supply line in the event of a push into Afghanistan and the ensuing likelihood of a war with Britain. Merv itself is a historical name correctly applicable only to the ruins of the metropolis destroyed in 1221 by the Mongols; the modern name is Mary, a town that grew about 30 kilometers to the west of the archaeological site.

To the east of Khurasan, in present-day northern Afghanistan, is the aforementioned region known in antiquity as Bactria and called by the Arabs and Persians Tokharistan. Bactra, its capital, became the Balkh of the early Islamic centuries, and flourished until it was destroyed by the Mongols in 1221. It eventually recovered, but since the end of the fifteenth century it has had to yield primacy to a funerary sanctuary called Mazar-i Sharif located a short distance to the southeast; this shrine competes, in popular Islam, with the Iraqi town of Najaf for the distinction of allegedly being the final resting place of Ali, the prophet Muhammad's son-in-law and Shii Islam's first imam. The originally Iranian Bactria came to be known as "land of the Tokharians," in the early centuries of our era, as a result of this group's migration into its territory. Unlike their kinsmen who settled in northeastern Sinkiang and asserted their ethnolinguistic individuality there (the Tokharian-speaking inhabitants of Turfan, Karashahr, and Kucha), the Tokharians of Bactria, memorable as the people who played a leading role in the creation of the famous Kushan empire, became Iranized without leaving any trace of their original identity. The Iranian population also remained unaffected by the rule of lateral branches of Western Turks that extended there shortly before the inception of Muslim conquests. On the other hand, in more recent centuries the originally Iranian Tokharistan became infiltrated by Turkic tribes, chiefly Turkmen and Uzbek, to such an extent that it is also called Afghan Turkestan.

If we leave Tokharistan and cross the Amu Darya, we are back on the "other" side of the river, thus technically in Transoxania. The city of Tirmidh (also spelled Termez) is situated at the point where the Surkhan Darya flows into the Amu Darya, on the northern (Uzbek) side of the latter river. It was a historic crossing point on the trade and pilgrim routes between Balkh and Samarkand (such as the one passing through the aforementioned Iron Gate) or, to take a broader view, between the Indian subcontinent, Inner Asia, and Russia. Tajikistan lies a short distance to the east, and its territory here has historical as well as physical features similar to those of adjacent Uzbekistan and Afghanistan, with an ancient civilization based on irrigation from rivers originating in the Tianshan and Pamir complex to the north and east, and from rivers rising in the Hindukush, if we include the southern, Afghan tributaries of the Panj (the upper course of the Amu Darya). As we have already stated, this region was part of ancient Bactria and medieval Tokharistan.

One of the rivers flowing into the Panj is the Vakhsh, which rises in southeastern Kyrgyzstan's Alai mountains, a range located between the Tianshan and Pamir mountains near the Sinkiang border. It is called there Kyzylsu, "Red River" – a name which it also keeps in its Persian garb, Surkhab, in Tajikistan – until it is reinforced by several more streams to become the Vakhsh. The Panj originates in the eastern Pamirs near Sinkiang, and its coupling with the Vakhsh produces the Amu Darya. It is the Panj which forms the longest part of the border between Tajikistan and Afghanistan, a role then continued by the Amu Darya which separates Afghanistan from Tajikistan, Uzbekistan and Turkmenistan, before ultimately swerving northwest on its course through the latter republic toward the Aral Sea.

Dushanbe (lit. "Monday" in Persian, presumably because of a market held there on Mondays in pre-modern times; called Stalinabad between 1929 and 1961), the capital of Tajikistan, lies between the Vakhsh and the Tajik–Uzbek border on another river, the Kafarnihan. The population between the latter river and the Uzbek border includes a large Uzbek minority, whereas in the other direction all the way to the eastern Pamirs it is overwhelmingly Iranian, in contrast to the otherwise mostly Turkic Turkestan. This part of ancient Bactria and medieval Tokharistan, before receiving the official label Tajikistan from the Soviet government, was known by such regional names as Hisar, Chaghaniyan, Kubadhiyan, or Khuttalan, and, farther east, Badakhshan, which today occupies the whole eastern half of the republic. The Pamirs cover Tajik Badakhshan's entire territory, and this terrain gave it a special identity recognized, since the Soviet period, in administrative terms as the Gorno-Badakhshanskaya Avtonomnaya Oblast, "Mountain Badakhshan Autonomous Region"; its capital is Khorog, on the River Gunt near its embouchure into the Panj. Most of the inhabitants speak their own Iranian idioms; moreover, they also profess special forms of Islam, chiefly that of the Ismaili sect (one of the three main denominations of Shii Islam; they recognize the Agha Khan as their spiritual head). The territory of Badakhshan is not limited to this "Mountain Badakhshan" region, however; in fact, its most important and historically best remembered portion lies in Afghanistan on the southern, left bank of the Panj's wide bend northward, with this river's tributary Kokcha crossing it as it descends from the Hindukush mountains. The capital of the *vilayat* of Afghan Badakhshan, Fayzabad, was founded in the seventeenth century, but the city of Jurm, a short distance upstream on the Kokcha, has a history almost as ancient as the province itself. The latter's antiquity was proverbial, with reminiscences of the campaign of Alexander the Great not quite extinct: Badakhshan's rulers liked to trace their ancestry to the great conqueror, even when they had sprung from an Uzbek stock like the last local dynasty of Yarids who, having founded Fayzabad, maintained themselves there until the nineteenth century. Badakhshan was in antiquity and the Middle Ages traversed by long-distance trade routes used by such famous travelers as Marco Polo, and it gained fame for its rubies and as the only known source of lapis lazuli which was exported far and wide but especially to India.

To the east of Afghan Badakhshan and south of Tajikistan's Badakhshan Region extends the quaint Afghan "finger," which was created in 1895 to separate the Russian and British empires. It is crossed latitudinally by the Vakhan, a river considered by some geographers as the uppermost course of the Amu Darya; the Vakhan combines with the Pamir river to produce the Panj. Today the "Afghan finger" separates Tajikistan from Pakistan and Kashmir.

Delimiting Transoxania to the north poses no problem if we choose the other great river of Central Asia, Syr Darya, as its boundary on that side (and thus view it as a Central Asian Mesopotamia, a term occasionally applied to it in Russian geographical literature as *Mezhdurechie*). Called Iaxartes by the Greek geographers and Sayhun by the Arab ones, this river rises near the highest peaks of Tianshan in eastern Kyrgyzstan and, known as Naryn, flows westward through much of the republic before crossing the Uzbek border and entering Fergana, where it receives the Kara Darya near the historic city of Andijan. Known henceforth as the Syr Darya, the river crosses the whole length of that province from east to west. It then reaches the valley's only opening free of mountain barriers, an area where the western outcroppings of the Tianshan and Pamir ranges approach each other from the north and south but do not meet. The city of Khujand (also spelled Khojand and Khodzhend), on or near the site of Alexandria Eschate, "Alexandria the Furthest," founded by Alexander the Great in 328 BC, and called Leninabad between 1936 and 1991, lies near this opening. It is today the administrative center of a district protruding here from Tajikistan. Having crossed this Tajik protrusion and skirted Khujand, the Syr Darya re-enters Uzbekistan and flows by the capital, Tashkent, before exiting the republic a short distance to the north of the city; it enters Kazakh territory and starts its long course northwestward toward the Aral Sea in a direction roughly parallel to that of the Amu Darya.

Such a definition of Transoxania, however, is rather artificial, and it may be better to emphasize only the undisputable fact that Transoxania is that part of Central Asia which lies to the north of the middle course of the Amu Darya. This will enable us to view also certain segments of the area that lie on the right, northern bank of the Syr Darya as part of historic Transoxania. They include such cities as Tashkent, the capital of modern Uzbekistan and metropolis of Central Asia.

Nevertheless, once we cross the Syr Darya, we stand on the threshold of the immense Eurasian plain, and the long low range of the Kara Tau protruding from the western Tianshan into southern Kazakhstan no more changes the picture than do the occasional highlands farther north. Here loomed the realm of the Eurasian Turkic nomads when the Arabs launched the conquest of Transoxania in the first decades of the eighth century, and they appropriately called it "Bilad al-Turk," Land of the Turks or "Turkistan," in contrast to "Mawarannahr." Today, Turkestan (to follow the spelling common in Russian and other Western languages) means almost the reverse – historic Transoxania and northern (Turkmen) Khurasan – but that has resulted from a process which began some three centuries after the Arab conquest and received official sanction only after the Russians conquered Central Asia in the nineteenth century.

In our discussion of Transoxania, Khwarazm, Tokharistan, and Fergana we have emphasized the fertility of these territories as irrigated lands. The contrast presented by the vaster tracts that have not benefited from irrigation is thus especially striking: the Kyzyl Kum desert of Uzbekistan and Kara Kum desert of Turkmenistan are only the largest and most notorious examples, counterparts to the still more inhospitable Taklamakan desert of Eastern Turkestan.

Fergana, as we have said, is surrounded by the Tianshan and Pamir mountain ranges on three sides: on the north, south, and east. Both systems are also known by local names applied to their specific segments; thus Tianshan's Kungey and Terskey Alatoo, the ranges to the north and south of the Issyk Kul ("Warm Lake" in Kyrgyz) in Kyrgyzstan, for example. The elevation of this natural wall separating Western from Eastern Turkestan is breathtaking – a number of peaks over 5,000 meters high, with such giants as Zhengish Chokusu (the less well known but more appropriate Kyrgyz version of the Russian name Pik Pobedy, "Victory Peak") on the Kyrgyz–Sinkiang border (7,439 meters), Garmo in Tajikistan (7,495 meters; the highest mountain of the former Soviet Union, it was then called Pik Kommunizma, "Communism Peak"), or, still higher, Kungur in Sinkiang (7,719 meters). The Pamir ranges (nicknamed, in nineteenth-century travel literature, as the "Roof of the World") fan out through Tajikistan and Sinkiang into Afghanistan, Pakistan, Tibet, and India under such names as Kunlun, Karakoram, Hindukush, and Himalayas. Incredible though it may sound, this convergence of giant mountain chains was the crossroads, in antiquity and the Middle Ages, of the celebrated Silk Road – caravan tracks that linked Inner Asia and China with India, the Middle East, and the Mediterranean world. Man found ways to penetrate them through passes some of which lie higher than peaks considered lofty elsewhere (for example Bedel in Kyrgyzstan, 4,288 meters, or Akbaital in Tajikistan, 4,655 meters; or the track linking India with Sinkiang through Srinagar–Gilgit–Hunza–Tashkurgan–Kashgar, with Karakoram's K2 or Godwin Austen, the second highest mountain in the world – 8,611 meters high – not far to the east of there).

To the east of Fergana but separated from it by the Tianshan and Pamir ranges extends the Tarim basin, in some respects a mirror image of the Fergana valley but much vaster and starker. Sinkiang, of which it is a part, is an administrative term covering a larger area; no adequate generally accepted name exists for the region we are referring to now, but "Tarim basin" comes closest to meeting that need. It is a roughly elliptical area encompassed by three groups of mountain systems: the Tianshan on the north and northwest, the Pamirs on the southwest, and the Kunlun, Altyntagh, and Nanshan on the south and southeast. As in Transoxania, here too human settlement has depended on water brought by streams descending from the mountains. Three of these streams, the Yarkand, Aksu, and Khotan, eventually combine to produce the Tarim, a river that then doggedly pursues an easterly course through the Taklamakan desert toward the lake Lob Nor, which, however, it seldom reaches. A fourth river, the Kashgar – originating on the Kyrgyz side of the border as Kyzylsu, "Red River," near the sources of its aforementioned namesake that flows west to become the Vakhsh – after having passed by the city of Kashgar, flows toward the confluence of the other three but disappears in the sands of the Taklamakan before reaching it.

The ellipse of the basin surrounded by mountains extends farther east beyond Lob Nor, and can be viewed as closed, after having crossed the Sinkiang–Kansu border, at the town of Anshi. A glance at the map reveals a string of oasis towns along two imaginary lines that branch out, at Anshi, north and south, and, hugging the foothills of the surrounding mountains and themselves surrounding the western Gobi and Taklamakan deserts, close the ellipse as they meet again at the city of Kashgar in westernmost Sinkiang. These are the oasis towns famous for two reasons – the unique civilization that developed in some of them, and their function as way stations of the Silk Road network. Just to name the most famous ones, proceeding counterclockwise from Anshi: Hami, Turfan, Karashahr, Kucha, Aksu, Kashgar (east–west, the northern part of the ellipse); Kashgar, Yarkand, Khotan, Niya, Charkhlik, Tunhuang, and back to Anshi (west–east, its southern part).

Today, as we have implied, all these places except Anshi and Tunhuang are in Sinkiang. Sinkiang (from *hsin kiang* = new province; we follow here the customary transcription; the correct pronunciation of this Chinese name is *shin chiang*) is a name given the region in the aftermath of the 1758 conquest by China; this name was used still more emphatically after the fuller integration of Sinkiang into Chinese administrative structure in 1884. As we have pointed out, the word has a more comprehensive connotation than the Tarim basin because it also covers the large territory to the north of the Tianshan range. When they wanted to differentiate between these two parts, the Chinese used the terms Nanlu and Peilu ("Southern route" and "Northern route"). Nanlu thus corresponds to our Tarim basin. The latter term is a nineteenth-century scholarly creation, and it is not the only one; Kashgaria is another frequently used name, popular especially in French historiography (La Kachgarie) because of the importance of the region's western metropolis. The inhabitants themselves never had a truly comprehensive name for their country, with the partial exception of Altishahr and

Uighuristan; the former name means "six cities" in Turkic, the cities being Kashgar, Yarkand, Khotan, Aksu, Kucha, and Uch (or Ush) Turfan, all in the western half of the Tarim basin. Uighuristan was so named after the Turkic Uighurs who in the ninth century founded a kingdom whose capital was Qocho, now an archaeological site a short distance from Turfan in the eastern half of the Tarim basin. The two groups thus also indicate a secondary but nonetheless important division of Nanlu into a western and eastern segment, a division implied by the names "Altishahr" and "Uighuristan."

The oasis town of Turfan itself deserves attention for several reasons. One is geographical, for it lies in a depression – at 154 meters below sea level, it is the second lowest point on earth after the Dead Sea. Another is linguistic and cultural, for the inhabitants of this area used to speak Tokharian, the aforementioned non-Iranian Indo-European tongue, before they were Turkicized; and they created a remarkable Manichaean and Buddhist civilization that survived under the Uighur Turks for several more centuries until the completion of Islamization in the fifteenth century. And finally, while Turfan functioned as one of the way stations in Nanlu, it also was the starting point of a route that struck out northwest through a break in the Tianshan mountains toward Peilu and joined there the rival network of routes along the northern side of the Tianshan range. The name Turfan came into current usage only at the end of the Middle Ages, after the settlement that had existed there grew and absorbed the population of the historical Qocho, some 30 kilometers to the east. This was a reprise of an earlier shift when the town of Yar-khoto (a Turco-Mongol name; the site is also known by its Chinese name, Chiao-ho), some 10 kilometers to the west of Turfan, was abandoned in favor of Qocho in the early centuries of the Christian era. Both Yar-khoto and Qocho are precious archaeological sites today; so would probably be yet another city that pertained to the same civilization: Bishbalik or Peiting, some 100 kilometers due north of Turfan. But Bishbalik was on the other side of the Tianshan mountains, and climatic conditions are different there: the greater moisture characteristic of the northern slopes of Inner Asian mountains obliterated Bishbalik, once it was abandoned, to the point where modern archaeologists had great difficulties locating the site, at first wrongly identifying it with Urumchi, which lies some 50 kilometers to the west.

Nanlu and Peilu are terms no longer used, and Sinkiang is subdivided into a number of districts according to geographical, ethnolinguistic, and administrative criteria; nevertheless, the two names did express a lasting and emphatic contrast between southern and northern Sinkiang. Let us start, however, with a certain analogy between them: like southern Sinkiang, northern Sinkiang consists of a core that is a vast plain encompassed by several mountain chains: in this case a triangle formed by the Tianshan on the south, the Altai on the northeast, and the Tarbagatai and Jungarian Alatau on the northwest. This area is known as Jungaria (also spelled Zungaria and Dzhungaria), after the Jungars or Zungars, a Mongol people who built there a powerful state in the seventeenth century and despite the fact that they were virtually exterminated by Manchu troops in 1758–59. China had to reconquer Sinkiang in 1877 during a revolt led from Kashgar and Yarkand by a Muslim Turk named Yaqub Beg, and it was then that Urumchi (renamed Tihwa, a name that was dropped after the Communist victory in 1949) became the definitive capital of the "New Province." Before the revolt, the Chinese governor resided at Kulja (also known by its Chinese name Ining), a city in the valley of the Ili by the site of medieval Almaliq, and thus in one of the historic passageways along the southern fringe of the Eurasian steppe belt. As part of that belt, Jungaria was a land of nomads, in contrast to the Tarim basin, land of sedentaries. In historic times the nomads have been, as we have said, mainly Turks and Mongols in contrast to the Iranian and Tokharian agriculturists and urban dwellers. In the nineteenth century, however, there began a steady stream of chiefly agricultural immigrants from Nanlu to the more fertile fringes of Jungaria such as the Ili valley; these Turki-speaking settlers (basically Turkicized Iranians) came to be known as Taranchis, "agriculturalists," and they eventually played an important role in forging the sense of common identity between the main ethnic components of southern and northern parts of Sinkiang.

On the east, Sinkiang borders Mongolia and China's province of Kansu. Astride the Sino-Mongolian border lies the legendary Gobi, which occupies sizable portions of southern Mongolia and of China's Inner Mongolia. The Gobi is not a true desert like the Taklamakan or Sahara for example, but a gravelly plain with patches of sparse vegetation able to support some livestock such as camels, horses, and yaks. In the western half of Mongolia the Gobi is delimited on the north by the Altai, the aforementioned long mountain range that extends here diagonally (northwest–southeast) from southern Siberia. The somewhat smaller but still impressive Hangai range lies parallel to the Altai farther northeast, where it is followed by yet another range, the Hentei. A broad, grassy plain stretches between the Hangai and Hentei mountains, and is traversed by a number of rivers descending from them and then turning north toward Siberia. Two of these, the Orkhon and the Tula, are associated with several crucial stages of Turkic and Mongol history. It was along the Orkhon that the first Turkic empires had their political and religious centers: the Kök Turks erected here their eighth-century funerary monuments famous for commemorative inscriptions, and the Uighur Turks had their *ordubaligh* or capital, Qarabalghasun, in the same general area during the eighth and ninth centuries. When in the thirteenth century the Mongols moved to this area from the east, replacing the Turks, they founded here Qaraqorum as the charismatic center of the Genghisid empire (a decision made by Genghis Khan, but carried out only by his son Ögedey in 1235). Qaraqorum in turn dwindled with the collapse of that empire, but the site's charismatic role re-emerged in 1586 when the Mongols, converting to Lamaistic Buddhism, built there the prestigious monastery Erdeni Dzu.

The Orkhon rises in the Hangai and eventually receives the Tula, which originates in the Hentei range. It was to the valley of the Tula that the center of religious and political gravity moved in subsequent centuries; the at first peripatetic Urga, the headquarters of Bogdo Gegen, the chief lama who eventually also became the political head of the theocratic state, stabilized there by 1779. In 1924 Urga was renamed Ulan Bator ("Red Hero" in Mongolian, where it is spelled Ulaanbaatar), a name change symbolizing the transformation of Mongolia from a Buddhist monarchy to a Communist republic.

The Hentei range also gives rise to two other important rivers, the Onon and Kerulen. Although their sources lie close to those of the Tula, they flow east and eventually cross Mongolia's border, the Onon entering Siberia and the Kerulen China. It was between these two rivers that a people called Mongols emerged in the twelfth century, having moved there from their earlier habitat, believed to have been the adjacent forest zone to the north. When Temujin was acclaimed as their supreme leader and assumed the title of Genghis Khan in 1206, the ceremony took place on a sacred mountain called Burkan Kaldun somewhere among the eastern slopes of the Hentei range near the sources of the Onon.

If the territory between the Onon and the Kerulen can be viewed as the staging area of the Mongols readying themselves for the conquest of the world, the immediate neighborhood to the southeast was the home of their close relatives, the Tatars. This name and group, which appear in the Orkhon inscriptions as well as in Chinese sources, had a destiny inverse to that of the Mongols: as a people, the Tatars were partly exterminated, partly absorbed in the early stage of Genghis Khan's conquests. As a name, the word Tatar was applied by contemporary onlookers and victims – whether Chinese, European, or Muslim – to the Mongols themselves at the expense of their real ethnonym.

The Gobi straddles, as we have said, the Sino-Mongolian border. So do the Mongols themselves, for several tribes remained on the Chinese side of the Gobi after the collapse of Mongol rule in China in 1368. One of these were the Ordos, whose name still survives in that of the region within the great arc which the Hwangho (Yellow River) forms on its course from Tibet to the Pacific Ocean. The last dynasty to rule China, the Ching or Manchus (1644–1911), gained firm control of the Mongols south of the Gobi, and treated their territory as one more province of the Chinese empire. The extent of this province varied with time, and shrank commensurably with the curtailment of Mongol ethnic rights during the rule of Nationalist and then Communist Chinese regimes, before a dramatic restoration of both aspects – size and liberties – since 1979. Today, the territory of the Inner Mongolian Autonomous Region, whose regional capital is Huehot or Hu-ho-hao-t'e (a transcription that tries to express the Mongol name, Khukhe-khoto, "Blue City"; Paotou, an industrial center farther west, is larger and better known), even surpasses that of Mongolia (1,770,000 sq. km. as compared with 1,565,000 sq. km.).

By 1691 the Manchus also gained suzerainty over the Mongols in Mongolia itself, but treated their territory in a radically different manner, that is, as the dynasty's family possession (and, in administrative terms, as an autonomous protectorate) rather than as a Chinese province (a situation similar to that of Sinkiang between 1758 and 1884). Migration of Chinese settlers, mainly peasants, to Inner Mongolia was allowed and often encouraged, but forbidden to what became known in the West as Outer Mongolia. As a result, Mongols became a minority in Inner Mongolia, whereas they form the only population of the Republic of Mongolia except for a relatively small group of Kazakhs (many of whom have emigrated to Kazakhstan since its independence in 1991) in the extreme west and a still smaller one of Tuvans in the north.

On the north, Mongolia borders Siberia, more specifically four segments of the Russian Federation; proceeding from west to east, we see the Gorno-Altai Autonomous Region, the Tuvan Autonomous Republic, the Buriat Mongol Autonomous Republic, and the Chita Region. It is a large lake, Baikal, that first catches a map-viewer's eye, however. The River Orkhon joins the Selenga as the two approach the border cities of Sükhbaatar (Mongol side) and Kiakhta (Russian side), and the Selenga then heads toward Baikal, passing by Buriatia's capital, Ulan Ude, shortly before flowing into the lake. The Buriats or northern Mongols, Buddhists like their southern kinsmen, do not appear to have played any significant historical role, but their territory assumed some importance in the nineteenth century as a gateway for Russian influence reaching Mongolia usually by way of Kiakhta. The Russian presence in Siberia, a fundamental factor ever since the seventeenth century, is symbolized here by Irkutsk, which lies a short distance to the northwest of Baikal's southern tip. A little farther west is a mountain range, the Eastern Sayan, which together with the Western Sayan and a third range, the Tannu Ola on the south along the Mongol border, encompasses the greater part of the Tuva Autonomous Republic, a geographical formation somewhat resembling northern Sinkiang (Jungaria), though smaller. The great Siberian river Yenisei originates in Tuva, owing its existence to a number of mountain streams which rise in the Eastern Sayan and gradually combine as two branches, the Biy Khem and Ka Khem. These two rivers then converge at Kyzyl, the capital of Tuva, to form the Yenisei. The latter soon changes its westerly course to a northerly one as it prepares to break through the Western Sayan and embark on its course toward the Arctic Ocean. The people who inhabited the area along the upper Yenisei were in antiquity and the Middle Ages the Kyrgyz, tribes speaking a Turkic language and sharing some of the same culture that animated the Kök Turks and Uighurs of the Orkhon valley. The Tuvans of today also speak a Turkic idiom, and may be partly descended from the Kyrgyz; the latter, however, mostly migrated west and eventually constituted the principal population of modern Kyrgyzstan. The Tuvans themselves, like their Buriat neighbors to the east, underwent strong influence from the south and converted to Buddhism, the only Turkic-speaking group to do so besides the historical Uighurs. Eventually, however, Russian presence had a decisive impact both culturally and demographically, and in this sense Tuva has become, like Buriatia, an inseparable component of Russia's Siberia.

Yet another Mongol group, the Oirats or Western Mongols, used to live between the upper Yenisei and Lake Baikal, to the east of the Kyrgyz and north of the Tuvans. In the fifteenth century they embarked on a long series of migrations and conquests analogous to those of Genghis Khan's Eastern Mongols, but never as brilliant or successful.

The Gorno-Altai Autonomous Region of the Russian Federation, the capital of which is Gorno-Altaisk, is situated between Tuva and

Kazakhstan, bordering on the south the western tip of Mongolia and the northern tip of Sinkiang. It is on its territory that the Altai mountain range rises and then extends diagonally, from northwest to southeast, all the way to southern Mongolia. The Turkic-speaking inhabitants, now outnumbered by the Russians, escaped the impact of the major religions that had affected other Turks and Mongols; instead, they retained vestiges of their ancestral shamanism until its elimination by modernizing trends from Russia.

The border between Kazakhstan and Sinkiang – the northwestern side of the Jungarian triangle discussed above – presents a special interest as the historic divide between the eastern and western halves of Inner Asia. It was through its river valleys or mountain passes that most nomadic migrations and troop movements in either direction took place. The valley of the Irtysh, separating the Altai range from the Tarbagatai, was one such passageway. Another was the smaller valley of the Emil which rises in Tarbagatai and flows into Lake Alakol on the Kazakh side. Farther south is the almost legendary "Jungarian Gate," a break in the Jungarian Alatau range through which nomads and armies could pass between Jungaria and Kazakhstan. Yet another route was the valley of the Ili river, which separates the Jungarian Alatau from the Tianshan; this long and broad valley was also a favorite camping and grazing ground of many nomads, especially of the Genghisid Mongols. Roads built in recent times have followed these natural formations: the most significant case is the recently completed railway passing through the Jungarian Gate and linking Urumchi with the Kazakh capital Almaty via the station of Aktogay on the Turksib (Turkestan–Siberia railway).

The Ili flows into Lake Balkhash, whose elongated shape and surface size reminds us of the superficially similar Baikal; the similarity ends there, though, for whereas the latter is very deep (in volume of water, Baikal is the world's largest lake), the former is shallow, and while both support some fishing, the marine life of Baikal is infinitely richer and more unusual, including, for example, a herd of seals. Another difference is the fact that whereas Baikal, fed by such rivers as the Selenga, also has an outflow, the Angara, which joins the Yenisei and thus the Arctic Ocean, Balkhash is a landlocked lake. Besides the Ili, it receives several other rivers, chiefly from the Tianshan and Jungarian Alatau ranges. This may be the reason why the area between these mountains and Balkhash used to be called Jetisu, a Turkic word meaning "Seven Rivers," hence the more commonly known Russian translation Semireche (this is the form we shall use in our book). Since Semireche never was an official name, except for the half-century of the Tsarist era, it lacks precise delimitations, although Lake Balkhash and the Tianshan mountains can be assigned the role of its northern and southern brackets. The rivers Talas and Ili can assume the same role on the west and east (unless we assign this role to the expanded borders represented by the mountain range of Karatau and by Lake Alakol). Semireche is an area where sedentaries and nomads have met at various points in history – coexisting, overlapping, or competing – because it lends itself to both ways of life (as do, in fact, many other parts of the Eurasian steppe). At the time of the Arab conquest of Transoxania, Semireche's southern fringe had a flourishing agricultural and urban population chiefly composed of the same Sogdian stock, engaged in irrigated or dry farming, professing one or another of the main religions – Zoroastrianism, Buddhism, or Christianity – entertaining a lively exchange with the Turkic nomads, and acknowledging, when necessary, their suzerainty. This prosperity continued and even increased after the spread of Islam here in the tenth century, which began with the conquest of the westernmost segment of Semireche and then made giant strides with the voluntary conversion of entire Turkic tribes. In the eleventh century, Semireche became the senior province of the Qarakhanid dynasty, and shone with a florescence of Turkic–Islamic culture. This came to an end after the Mongol invasion, but not through the standard method of willful destruction accompanying the conquest; here it resulted from the fact that the Mongols preferred to live in Semireche, grazing their herds, holding there their quriltays (conventions), or fighting their internecine wars. Agricultural and urban civilization ultimately succumbed to the nomads' way of the Mongols, and reappeared only after the Russian conquest in the 1860s. A small settlement which the natives called Alma-Ata or Almaty was then developed as the administrative center of Semireche under the name Vernyi ("The Loyal [City]"), before recovering its original Turkic name (the etymology of Alma-Ata or Almaty suggests the presence of apple trees or orchards, from alma = apple). Bishkek, the capital of the future Kyrgyzstan but then a modest fort, was also included in the *oblast* of Semireche.

After the Mongols modified Semireche to suit their lifestyle, the region came to be called Moghulistan (or Mongolistan, "Land of the Mongols"; the form Moghulistan is based on its spelling in the Arabic alphabet, which tended to omit the abraded sound *n* from the word "Mongol"). The name also acquired a political connotation as the patrimony of the Chaghatayid branch of the Genghisids who ruled the area, in contrast to Transoxania and Khurasan ruled by the Timurids. The area of Moghulistan was not quite identical with that of Semireche, for it also comprised a substantial portion of the Tianshan mountains, roughly the northern part of modern Kyrgyzstan with Lake Issyk Kul as a prominent landmark. Farther east, thus in modern Sinkiang, Moghulistan bordered Uighuristan, which for some time was also under the Chaghatayids; on the south and southeast, Sinkiang's Tarim basin too was ruled by them and was thought of as part of Moghulistan. This concept was eventually replaced by other regional names; here it was Altishahr, the aforementioned area marked by oasis towns headed by Kashgar.

The name Moghulistan was thus eventually forgotten, and Semireche gained prominence as the official name of one of the principal districts of Russia's Governorate-general of Turkestan. The name Semireche in turn disappeared with the collapse of the Tsarist regime and the redrawing of internal boundaries carried out by the Soviet government. The northern part of Semireche fell to Kazakhstan, the southern to Kyrgyzstan. In the latter segment, several features deserve mention. The small town and military post of Bishkek became Kyrgyzstan's capital; it was known from 1926 to 1991 as Frunze, named after Mikhail Vasilevich Frunze, the Bolshevik general who during the consolidation of Soviet power at the center reconquered Central Asia for Russia. Bishkek lies in the valley of the Chu, a river that rises in the mountains of northern Kyrgyzstan and, after flowing east and approaching Lake Issyk Kul, turns and heads northwest toward Bishkek and the Kazakh border. Its valley, the home of Kyrgyzstan's capital and other flourishing cities, likewise had been the scene of dense settlement from the early Middle Ages down to the Mongol period, as well as one of the favorite winter grounds of western Turkic qaghans and their Qarakhanid successors; their capitals Suyab and Balasaghun both lay in this valley. Not far from the sources of the Chu are also those of the Talas, which, however, pursues a westerly course from the start. Shortly after crossing the Kazakh border it passes by the city of Jambul, so named in the Soviet period in honor of the Kazakh poet Jambul (or Shambyl) Jabaev. Earlier the city was called Auliye Ata, presumably because of a Sufi saint (*auliye*) buried in the vicinity. Nearby lie the ruins of Taraz or Talas, remembered for a historic battle fought there in 751 between the Arabs and the Chinese. Finally Lake Issyk Kul ("Warm Lake," Ysyk köl in Kyrgyz) deserves mention for its historical interest, natural beauty, and importance for modern Kyrgyzstan as a tourist resort. Its shores too were the nomads' favorite winter camping ground, and the town of Barskaun or Barskhan, on its southern shore, functioned as a place of trade and a way station on the Silk Road network.

We have already proposed the Syr Darya as the northern limit of Transoxania, a demarcation line beyond which, as we have said, lay what early Arab geographers called Turkestan (*Bilad al-Turk* or *Turkistan*), land of the Turkic nomads. A rather wide swath along the northern bank of the river, however, had the same physiognomy as Transoxania and Fergana, as we have pointed out, with irrigated agriculture, towns, trade routes, and a similar population of Sogdian stock, though with an increasing proportion of the Turkic element. This was especially true of the middle course of the Syr Darya, to the northeast and east of which loom the westernmost spurs of the Tianshan, ultimately protruding into the Kazakh steppe under the name of Karatau. Streams descending from those mountains created conditions similar to those along the Zarafshan. One of these streams is the Chirchik; an early town near its banks was Chach, which the Arabs (whose language and alphabet lack the consonant *ch*) spelled Shash or Tash, and which, with the addition of the common Sogdian suffix -*kent*, came to be known as Tashkent. Shash was also the name of the surrounding region, and it seems that a competing or earlier name for the city was Binkath before giving way to "Shash city," Shashkent or Tashkent. A number of other towns appeared in this area. Some of them succumbed to the effects of the nomadic movements and wars which frequently afflicted the area; others have survived and even risen in prominence; still others are new administrative and logistical centers developed since the Russian conquest. Tashkent is the most obvious example; from among the others, Isfijab, Otrar, Yasi, Sighnaq, and Kyzyl Orda reflect the history of this area as a transition zone. Isfijab was situated on the northern bank of the Arys, a stream flowing into the Syr Darya, on the road from Tashkent to Taraz and on to Semireche at the fringe of the steppe. In the eighth and ninth centuries it thus had the function of a borderland city facing the world of the pagan Turks, and a rallying point for the *ghazis*, holy warriors of Islam penetrating the steppe with the new message. These ghazis often preferred communal living in separate structures known as *rabats* or *ribats*, fortified cloisters or hostels situated along the *limes* of the *Dar al-Islam* or as advanced posts beyond those limits. Such were the many rabats of Isfijab, financed in part by its citizenry. The religious zeal of the Isfijabis was to earn their city an honor they could not have foreseen at the time of their conversion: for Sayram, as Isfijab increasingly came to be called with the growing proportion of its Turkic element, is the birthplace of Khwaja Ahmad Yasavi, the great Sufi shaykh of Turkestan who was born there at the turn of the eleventh century.

Otrar, an archaeological site today near the railroad juntion of Arys, was a town straddling the Syr Darya on the northern side of the estuary of the Arys; the area was known as Farab in the early Islamic period, with a town of the same name located a short distance downstream from Otrar on the Syr Darya. A settlement in the vicinity of Farab was the birthplace of al-Farabi (870–950), a Turk who, after receiving initial education at home, studied and taught in Baghdad and later in Damascus, gaining fame as one of the greatest philosophers of the Islamic world. Otrar eclipsed Farab by the thirteenth century, chiefly because of its role as a market and as a crossing of trade routes between the steppe and Sogdia. In 1218, a large merchant caravan that included envoys from Genghis Khan was detained here and then massacred, possibly on orders from the Khwarazmshah Muhammad; this incident is credited for having provoked the calamity of the Mongol invasion that descended on Central Asia two years later. Otrar itself, though it fell after a siege of several weeks, escaped destruction and continued as a way station well into the fifteenth century; it was here that Timur (Tamerlane), taken ill, died in 1405, and with him his projected campaign to conquer China.

Some 40 kilometers to the north of Otrar was another frontier town, Yasi. In the twelfth century, the aforementioned native of Sayram, Khwaja Ahmad, lived in this area and inspired, with his example and mystical poems, a wide following which after his death coalesced into a *tariqa* or Sufi "path," the Yasaviya or Yasavi order of dervishes. The founder himself was buried in Yasi, which later began to be called, after his honorific titles, Hazrat-i Turkistan or Shah-i Turkistan (the Saint of Turkestan, the Lord of Turkestan). Only the second part of these names has held ground, so that today the town is rather confusingly known as Turkestan or Turkistan. The shaykh's tomb became a place of popular pilgrimage and veneration, and the magnificent mausoleum that Tamerlane had erected over it in the 1390s is one of the architectural gems of Central Asia.

Another important town was Sighnaq, situated on the northern bank of the Syr Darya some 120 kilometers to the northwest of Yasi. Sighnaq distinguished itself as the headquarters of the steppe nomads attracted by the land south of the river, whether to invade Transoxania or to benefit from its proximity. The town itself was later abandoned and is an archaeological site today, whereas Yasi/Turkestan not only survived, but also became one of the main railroad stations on the line connecting Tashkent with Orenburg, Moscow, and St. Petersburg. This line, built in the first years of the twentieth century, follows the northern bank of the Syr Darya and, some 200 kilometers downstream from Sighnaq, passes by Kyzyl Orda, a town founded in 1820 as a fortified frontier outpost of the khanate of Khoqand at the peak of its expansion. It was then called Aq Meshit (Kazakh for "White Mosque"); its strategic position made it a prime target for Russia's incipient conquest of Central Asia, and the town fell in 1853. Its name was then changed to Perovsk in honor of General Perovskiy, the commander of the Russian troops. Kyzyl Orda means "Red Camp" in Kazakh, a name that replaced Perovsk in 1926 when the town became the capital of the Soviet republic of Kazakhstan, a distinction ceded in 1929 to Alma-Ata. One may ponder the similarity as well as the difference between the roles played by Sighnaq and Kyzyl Orda: both proved their strategic worth for invaders from the Kipchak steppe or as defense posts against them. Down to the sixteenth century, these invaders, whether Turkic or Mongol, were medieval nomads; in the nineteenth, they were the vanguard of a modern Western empire.

Another town with still more modern associations, Jasaly, grew up on the right (northern) bank of the Syr Darya half-way between Kyzyl Orda and the Aral Sea. In the final decades of the USSR it acquired the important function of a support city for the "Soviet Cape Canaveral," the space program base at Baikonur in central Kazakhstan; it was then renamed as Leninsk. In contrast to Jasaly/Leninsk, two historical cities on the lower Syr Darya are now archaeological sites. Not far downstream from where Leninsk was eventually to appear but on the bank of a now extinct branch of the Syr Darya lay Jand, near the modern town of Kazalinsk. Still farther downstream lay Yangikant, a town on the left (southern) side of the apex of the river's delta by its debouchure into the Aral Sea. Both Jand and Yangikant played a significant role in the tenth and eleventh centuries as centers of interaction between the sedentary world to the south and that of the steppe nomads to the north. The merchants and urbanites of the settlements were Muslims by then, whereas the nomads, mostly Oghuz Turks, were still pagans or on the verge of conversion.

If we draw a line due north from Yasi/Turkestan, we pass through the core of modern Kazakhstan. The republic's territory coincides with the eastern two-thirds of what Muslim authors of the Middle Ages called the Dasht-i Kipchak, the Steppe of the Kipchak Turks. The Kipchak Turks, known to contemporary Russians as Polovtsians and to medieval Europe as Cumans, succeeded there the Scythians and Sarmatians of antiquity. Their presence eventually imposed itself even on the Mongol conquerors in the thirteenth century (besides absorbing such remnants as the Germanic Goths of the Crimea), for they Turkicized the Golden Horde, a political formation initially coterminous with the geographical concept of the Dasht-i Kipchak. The longitudinal backbone of the Dasht-i Kipchak was the middle and lower course of the Volga, since the early Middle Ages the lifeline of successive Turkic and Mongol states and the location of their capitals. Itil of the pre-Islamic and partly juda-icized Turkic Khazars lay near the western arm of the river's delta estuary, as later did Astrakhan, capital of a khanate of that name. The first capital of the Golden Horde, Saray Batu, lay in the same general area but a short distance to the northeast of the estuary, whereas the Horde's second capital, New Saray, lay farther upstream near modern Volgograd but – like its predecessor – to the east of the river. Modern Kazakh territory approaches the Volga but does not quite reach it: the Russo-Kazakh border follows the river some distance upstream and then swerves east, skirting the southern outcroppings of the Ural mountains and then making a wide arc through western Siberia. This border some-what belies the demographic transformation of much of the Dasht-i Kipchak into Russian territory, a process that started in the sixteenth century with the conquests of the khanates of Kazan and Astrakhan and continued until the days of the Soviet leader Khrushchev's policy of "opening-up of virgin land," a euphemism for the last wave of Russian colonization marking the 1950s. The effect has indeed been stronger than the present-day political borders suggest. Colonization by Slavic settlers, chiefly peasants, and by dwellers of newly developed towns spilled over the borders drawn in the early Soviet period, so that today much of northern Kazakhstan is predominantly Slavic, as are the auton-omous republics of Tatarstan – which we could also view as a reincar-nation of the khanate of Kazan – and of Bashkiria (Bashqurtistan in Bashkir).

The town of Zhezkazgan lies at the geographical center of Kazakhstan. If we strike out due north from there and, crossing the northern half of the republic, enter the Russian Federation, the first dis-trict (*oblast*) that we meet is Tiumen, so named after its administrative center. The river Irtysh passes through this district, and at one point it receives the Tobol, which flows here from Kazakhstan. The city of

Tobolsk grew up at their confluence, but the site of another town slightly upstream on the Irtysh deserves special attention: Sibir, headquarters of the khanate of Sibir, conquered by the Russians in the final years of the sixteenth century. Sibir, also known as Isker, lay in an area where the Eurasian steppe belt merges with the continent's forest zone, the taiga, then sparsely populated by Finnic and paleo-Siberian peoples. The khanate's Turks, who absorbed some of these autochthones, came to be known as Siberian Tatars. The Kipchak Turkic-speaking khans of Sibir had ruled there from the thirteenth century to the sixteenth, and their realm represented the northernmost position ever occupied by an Islamic state.

ETHNOLINGUISTIC AND RELIGIOUS IDENTITY OF MODERN INNER ASIA

Ethnolinguistic Identity

(a) Turkic Languages
The principal nationalities in this group are the Kazakhs, Karakalpaks, Kyrgyz, Turkmens, Uzbeks, and Uighurs. They are called Turks because this essentially linguistic concept, despite its shortcomings, is the most practical common denominator recognized by medieval and modern scholars alike. In the past as at present, a number of Inner Asian nationalities have been felt to possess a common bond in the Turkic language of which they speak their own diverse idioms – not unlike the Russians, Czechs, Serbs, etc., who are Slavs because they speak their own versions of Slavic. The only nationality which today applies this term to itself and to its language to the exclusion of any other name, however, is that of the Turks of Turkey: the not uncommon paradox of a group that maintains certain features of its basic identity long after leaving its original or earlier habitat. For the sake of clarity, Turkish is the term used in English for the form of Turkic spoken in Turkey.

Linguists divide the Turkic languages into several groups. The most commonly accepted system speaks of the Kipchak group (Kazakh, Karakalpak), Turki group (Uzbek, Uighur), and Oghuz group (Turkmen, Azeri, Turkish), although this classification has not received unanimous recognition and scholars are at a loss where to put Kyrgyz – whether to consider it Kipchak or Turki, or to propose yet another subdivision. For our purposes, a more relevant question is how close they are to each other, and whether they are mutually intelligible. The answer is that Turkmen, Azeri, and Turkish are close enough to allow adequate communication (barring occasional lexical problems, mostly of recent date); the same could be said of Kazakh and Kyrgyz. As for Uzbek and Uighur, they are almost identical, and could easily merge into one official language if political separation did not stand in the way; this separation is graphically illustrated by the different alphabets they use: Uzbek is written in the Cyrillic script (although there is now a plan, in Uzbekistan and the other three Turkic republics of Central Asia, to switch to the Roman alphabet), Uighur in the Arabic or, less commonly, in the Roman and Cyrillic scripts. The reality of this identity is also suggested by the fact that prior to the special turns brought about by political nationalism and alien, Soviet and Chinese, rule in the 1920s, the two languages were more commonly known as Turki. A similar factor of political separation and different alphabets affects the relationship between Turkish, Azerbaijani, and Turkmen: even they, under different political circumstances, could converge into one official language. On the other hand, if a gathering of Uzbeks, Turkmens, Kazakhs, and Kyrgyz tried to use their respective languages, the participants would run into such problems that they would probably resort to a different but commonly known language – at present Russian. If the Turks of Turkey and the Uighurs of Sinkiang – neither likely to know Russian – were also present, the gathering would have to endeavor to create an improvised common Turkic with varying degrees of success and failure.

Nevertheless, the intrinsic kinship of the Turkic languages which concern us here has a powerful effect in two respects. A native speaker of any one of them, when exposed to any of the others, is likely to become used to the differences, and will up to a point be able to function in such a new milieu; and the fundamentally identical grammatical structure and lexical content of all of them make it feasible for him to learn the kindred idiom – if he makes the effort – better and faster than a member of an alien linguistic family could. This has important implications both for understanding the Turks' recent history and for assessing their future relations: once the barriers represented by political boundaries are relaxed or removed, and the imposed alien writing systems are replaced by a unified one, the sense of common identity can pass to a level of practical reality with promising potential for the future of the whole area. In Central Asia, a powerful precedent existed in the form of Chaghatay Turkic, a literary form of Turki perfected in the fifteenth century and used by subsequent generations of writers and intellectuals until its proscription by the Soviets in the 1920s.

In linguistic terms, Turkic and Mongolian are agglutinative languages, structurally related and classified as the principal components of the Altaic group. Some scholars even suspect a distant kinship with Korean and Japanese.

(b) Mongolian

Linguists speak of three groups of Mongolian languages: eastern, northern, and western. They may be genetically related to Turkic languages; this kinship, however, is so remote that mutual intelligibility is out of the question.

Eastern Mongolian is the official language of the Republic of Mongolia, and like the Turkic languages and Tajik, it is written in the Cyrillic alphabet. A combination of political and demographic factors has caused the aforementioned internal split within the area populated by the speakers of eastern Mongolian: for besides the two and a half million inhabitants of the Republic, over four million live to the south of the border, in the Mongol Autonomous Region of the People's Republic of China. Here too, political separation has caused a cultural one, the usage of different scripts being the most visible example. In the Region, Mongolian is written not in the Cyrillic alphabet but in the Mongols' own traditional script, while at the same time all educated citizens are also literate in Chinese, in contrast to the Mongolian Republic, where this is true of Russian.

Northern Mongolian is also known as Buriat, and is, together with Russian, the official language of the Buriat Autonomous Republic of the Russian Federation. Western Mongolian is also known as Kalmyk or Kalmuck, and is, again together with Russian, the official language of the Kalmyk Autonomous Republic of the Russian Federation. This republic is situated to the west of the Volga along the river's lowermost course, with a short stretch of the Caspian coast as its southeastern limit, while its capital, Elista, is farther inland.

(c) Tajik

Tajik is virtually the same as Persian, the official language of Iran; the differences are so minor that if Tajikistan and Iran were united politically, a question of two languages would not arise. As in the case of the Turkic languages, an additional artificial barrier has been different alphabets – Tajik being written in the Cyrillic, Persian in the Arabic script; removal of this barrier by a return to the Arabic alphabet would not only make their sameness obvious, but would also create a belt of three Middle Eastern countries with Persian as the official language: Tajikistan, Afghanistan (where Persian – called there Dari – is one of the two official languages, the other being Pushtu, also an Iranian tongue), and Iran. Iranian languages form an important component of the Indo-European family, and together with the Slavic languages, they form the so-called "satem" branch.

The origin and history of the ethnonym Tajik goes back to the name of an Arab tribe, the Tayy, who lived in the Iraqi confines of the last pre-Islamic Persian empire, that of the Sasanians. The Persians extended this name to Arabs in general, and the Sogdians followed their example. After the conquest of Central Asia by Muslims, not only Arabs but also increasing numbers of Persians and Sogdians professed the new religion, and all of these came to be comprised under the ethnonym "Tajik." Eventually the Persian-speaking converts outnumbered the Arabs, and the ethnonym which had once been the name of an Arab tribe ended up being reserved for Persian-speaking Muslims of Central Asia and their language.

It may be worthwhile to mention in this context yet another ethnonym, Sart, which in recent times designated the Turkic-speaking urban and agricultural population of Central Asia. It is at least as ancient as that of the Tajiks, and has an even more intriguing etymology; its ultimate fate, moreover, is a textbook case of the interaction of politics and linguistics. Sart goes back to a Sanskrit word meaning "caravan leader" (*sarthavaha*). Indians were among the earliest long-distance merchants on the Silk Road network, and the local populations ended up applying this term to such merchants in general. Eventually the Sogdians came to dominate the Silk Road trade, and the term began to be applied to them by their neighbors, the Turks and Mongols. The word thus gradually acquired a broader meaning that by the end of the Middle Ages became almost synonymous with Tajik: Persian-speaking urban and agricultural population of Central Asia, different from the nomadic or semi-nomadic Turks (known as such, Türk) of the same area. By then, however, many Turks had also settled as agriculturalists or town dwellers, and those were not thought of as Sarts, a fact clearly documented by such sources as Navai and Babur. For the time being, the difference between the ethnonyms Sart and Türk was clear; less clear-cut, though, was the relationship between Sart and Tajik; as we have said, they came close to being synonyms. Yet by the time the Russians conquered Central Asia in the nineteenth century, Sart was the name of the Turkic-speaking town dwellers and peasants of the region, in contrast to the Persian-

speaking Tajiks. A shift had thus occurred in the connotation of this ethnonym since the sixteenth century, and it was due to the last wave of
Turkic invaders, the Uzbeks of the Dasht-i Kipchak. When they irrupted
into Transoxania in 1500, they became masters of its mostly sedentary
population which spoke either Turkic (Turki in this case) or Persian
(Tajik). The Uzbeks did speak Turkic, but their own Kipchak dialect
instead of Turki. This difference, but perhaps even more the different
lifestyle, made them view the Turki-speaking sedentaries as an alien
group, which had merged in their eyes with the Persian-speaking Sarts.
The term Sart was thus transferred to Turki-speaking sedentaries of
Central Asia. They did notice, however, that many of the sedentaries
spoke Tajik, and this term, previously synonymous with Sart, began to
be applied exclusively to the Tajik-speaking community. This was the situation when Central Asia became Russian Turkestan, and the new
masters readily availed themselves of the latest terminology. Sarts were
the Turki-speaking people of such cities as Bukhara, Samarkand,
Tashkent, and of the agricultural countryside; Tajiks were their Persian-
speaking neighbors (in some cases people were bilingual, to the point of
not being *sure* whether they were Sarts or Tajiks). Meanwhile the former
masters, the Uzbeks, had retained some of their nomadic lifestyle and
continued to speak Kipchak (although when they rose to the level of high
culture, they used either the aforementioned Chaghatay or Persian).
Then came the Bolshevik Revolution of 1917 with the "national delimitation" of 1924 as one of its later stages, and the Marxists of Moscow
left their stamp even on the linguistic chart of Central Asia. Sart (both
as ethnonym and as the name of a language) was proscribed as a
demeaning term of the colonial period; Turki was shunned (no doubt
because of its troubling usefulness to proponents of pan-Turkism); and
Uzbek was proclaimed to be the name of the citizens of the new republic of Uzbekistan, and of the language they spoke. Yet it was not Uzbek
the Soviet authorities imposed as the official language, but Turki, in
other words, Sart – for that was the idiom they reached for, instead of
the Kipchak of the Uzbeks, against initial objections from some of the
indigenous leaders. One of the main differences between the two forms
of Turkic resides in the domain of the so-called "vowel harmony."
Kipchak, like most other Turkic languages including Turkish of Turkey,
requires all the vowels in a word to be either of the "front vowel" or of
the "back vowel" type. Turki does not, however, and the explanation is
sought in the Iranian substratum of the idioms spoken by the sedentaries of Central Asia. It is one of the riddles of Soviet psychology why

Moscow bothered with such trifles. Why not let the Uzbeks speak, read, and write Uzbek, rather than the strongly Iranized Turki of the cities? Perhaps because in that case the Uzbeks, Kazakhs, and Karakalpaks might have become too aware of the closeness of the Kipchak dialects they spoke (which would have worked against one of the purposes of "national delimitation," *divide et impera*), whereas Turki was spoken in an area by and large coterminous with Uzbekistan (with the qualification that this could be expanded by including Sinkiang, but that is another story). All that remained to be done was to call this Turki Uzbek, and the new nation was ready for its Soviet future.

Religious and Cultural Identity

The Turks and Tajiks are Sunni Muslims (except for the aforementioned inhabitants of Badakhshan, who are Shiites of the Ismaili denomination), and the Mongols Lamaistic Buddhists. This may sound incompatible with the official status of these polities as secular or, in the Communist period, militantly atheistic. Aside from the fact that ongoing political changes have restored to religion some of its erstwhile prestige, both Islam and Buddhism have played a powerful role in shaping the psychological, cultural, and economic climate, as well as the personal lifestyle, of these societies. Alien ideologies and political systems, and the inevitable upheavals brought about by modernization, will for a long time fail to obliterate the impact Islam and Buddhism have had on Inner Asia; above all, the two religions will always remain an indelible part of these peoples' cultural heritage.

(a) Islam

The manner in which Islam (the specific meaning of this Arabic word is "self-surrender [to the will of God]") penetrated Central Asia will be sketched in the historical segment of our book. Here a few words about its general traits as applicable to our area may be called for. Of the two main denominations, Sunni and Shii Islam, it is the former that has predominated in Central Asia. Sunni or orthodox Islam is the mainstream form of this religion, and bases its tenets on the central scripture that is the Koran, the revealed word of God as preached by His prophet Muhammad (Arabic, the literal meaning of this name being "The Most Praised One") between the beginning of his mission early in the seventh century and his death in 632 (year 11 of the Islamic era, which began with Muhammad's hijra – "emigration" – from Mecca to Medina in

622). The Koran was recorded in its definitive form under the caliph Uthman (644–56). An additional source of authority is the *sunna* or sum total of principles, precepts and examples emanating from the Prophet's life and statements and their interpretation as recorded and developed by the Muslim community during the first three centuries – hence the name of orthodox or Sunni Islam.

Islam is a religion that concerns itself not only with spiritual values, but also with the temporal aspects of life; a truly Muslim community thus has an Islamic government and Islamic laws: the caliph (from Arabic *khalifa*, [the Prophet's] successor) is the *imam* or leader of this theocratic state ("imam," however, also has a broader spectrum of connotations ranging from the prayer-leader at a mosque to the messianic *mahdi* of the Shiites), and the *sharia* or Islamic law is the foundation of all legislation. Abu Bakr (632–34) was the first caliph, and three others – Umar, Uthman, and Ali – succeeded him in Medina before a civil war rent the Muslim community asunder and gave birth to the other main denomination, the Shia. This war also led to the replacement of the non-dynastic caliphs residing in Medina by the first Sunni dynasty, that of the Umayyads (661–750), whose capital was Damascus. The cause of the schism can be traced back to the question of whether the role of the caliph should be reserved for a descendant of the prophet Muhammad. It was the Shiites (*shia* means "party," implicitly Ali's party), who opted for the latter. Since Muhammad's only surviving child was a daughter, Fatima, they championed the legitimacy of the descendants of her union with Ali, the Prophet's cousin and son-in-law. Ali, as we have said, was indeed the fourth caliph (656–61), but his political and military opponents, led by another Arab, Muawiya, outmaneuvered him until he was assassinated in the Iraqi town of Kufa by a member of yet another schismatic group, the Kharijites, in 661. By then Muawiya was installed in Damascus as the first Umayyad caliph. During this dynasty's ninety years of rule Islam achieved a prodigious expansion that spanned a good portion of the former classical world between Spain and Central Asia. Like the Umayyads, their successors, the Abbasids (751–1258), were Sunni Muslims (with the qualification that their original claim to rule was partly based on their eponym's kinship with the Prophet's family; see below), but they ruled from their newly founded capital of Baghdad.

Since its inception, Shii Islam has endeavored to assert its claim to rule with occasional success in certain parts of the Islamic world – Iran having been the area of its greatest success, starting with the sixteenth-century Safavid dynasty and culminating in the Islamic revolution led by

Ayatullah Khomeini – but it never really succeeded in Inner Asia. The two denominations were almost identical in those matters that concerned the temporal and ritualistic aspect of Islam. Even the crucial matter of legitimacy of rule caused less conflict than the Shii claim might have seemed likely to engender: for life under Sunni rulers, considered usurpers by the Shiites, was made possible by the role of the hidden imam who lives concealed among the faithful but will appear as the messianic *mahdi* or *qaim* only at the time of his choice to lead mankind to ultimate salvation. This hidden mahdi is the twelfth of the imams from Ali to Muhammad – not the Prophet but his descendant – in the "Ithna-Ashariya" or "Twelver" Shia, the largest of the three principal denominations of Shii Islam, since the sixteenth century dominant mainly in Iran. This doctrine freed the faithful from the duty of armed struggle against Sunni usurpation, and the Sunni rulers from the burden of suspecting or suppressing unceasing uprisings; by the same token, sovereigns of the Shii persuasion could rule without being accused of themselves usurping the reign from the rightful imam, because it is he who has not yet chosen to make his appearance. To be sure, bitter conflicts and bloody wars between Sunnites and Shiites did at times ravage parts of the *Dar al-Islam*, that is, the lands under Islamic rule. Moreover, another kind of cleavage between Sunni and Shii Islam could hardly be overemphasized: that of religious focus. Whereas the Sunnites expected immediate benefits and ultimate salvation from performing the basic duties prescribed by the Koran and the *sharia* (Islamic law), the Shiites, although as a rule not negating their importance, relied more on intercession by the imams, one or more members of the *Ahl al-Bayt*, the Prophet's family. This reliance could reach a degree at which the intercessors assumed a considerable portion of divinity: in other words, the imams, especially Ali and even more his grandson Husayn, rather than the majestic but distant God, became the main objects of worship and expectations. Even these towering figures with dynastic credentials gradually had to cede some of their status to other descendants of the Prophet, who were proliferating all over the Islamic world, with their tombs as so many places of worship and pilgrimage bringing comfort to the crowds of the humble believers in the intimate and immediate way that an abstract God or a universal imam could not. These descendants of the Prophet were usually known by the epithet of *sayyid* (literally, "chief"), a title that has remained a mark of distinction to this day.

Nevertheless, even the Sunni Muslims eventually began to feel the need of bridging the chasm separating them from the austere God of the

Koran, and of finding a path to His more immediate and comforting presence. Those who first took steps in this direction came to be called *Sufis* (from Arabic *suf*, wool, from which woollen robes worn by them were made – hence also the term *tasawwuf* for Islamic mysticism). The Sufis focused more on the compassionate nature of God also present in the Koran, and created an elaborate and multifaceted system of practices to approach the no longer awesome Deity as a reassuring Friend. Eventually the men – known in the eastern Islamic world as dervishes – seeking ways toward mystical union with God began to form religious orders or *tariqas* (from Arabic *tariqa*, path [toward God]). The first such orders appeared in the twelfth century and soon spread throughout the Islamic world; most were known by the names of their founders, *shaykhs* (from Arabic shaykh, old man, elder; also known by such Persian and Turkic approximations as *pir, khwaja, baba,* or *ata*) who were often *sayyids* or who claimed another illustrious lineage such as that from the first caliph Abu Bakr, and who differed from each other chiefly in the way they strove to reach their mystical goal. On the concrete level, they formed communities that lived in cloisters known in Central Asia as *khangahs* (Persian, literally "place of abode," also transliterated as *khanqah* and *khanaqah*; up to a point a synonym of the Arabic *zawiya* and *ribat*). A khangah complex could also include a mosque, accommodation for visitors and travelers, and a tomb or tombs of revered shaykhs, often sayyids; pilgrimage to such shrines, *ziyarat* (lit. "visit"), came to constitute one of the central religious rituals practiced by the masses of the Muslim faithful. The adepts themselves eventually developed a prodigiously rigorous and often sophisticated process of practices and rituals for attaining their mystical goal, but one element appears essential: that of *dhikr*, "recollection [of God]" in Arabic, which passed into Persian and Turkic as *zikr*. The method was to think of God to the exclusion of anything else, and could consist of a seemingly unending repetition of the first part of the shahada, *La Ilaha illa Llah* ("There is no god but Allah"), or of God's name in its many variants such as the pronoun *Huwa* ("He" in Arabic), meaning God. This ritual often was an elaborate process that included a special manner of breathing and affected the Sufi's physical state. The *zikr* was practiced individually or in groups or circles of dervishes, and it could be vocal (*zikr jahri, zikr jali*) or silent (*zikr khafi*).

From among the many Sufi tariqas that have spread all over the Islamic world, four are especially characteristic of Central Asia: the Qadiriya, Yasaviya, Kubraviya, and Naqshbandiya. Only one, the first, originated elsewhere – in Baghdad, where it was founded by Abd al-Qadir Gilani

(d. 1166). The other three were founded in Central Asia by Central Asians – the Yasaviya in Turkestan (which here means territories populated by Turkic tribes north of the Syr Darya) by the aforementioned Ahmad Yasavi, a Turk from Sayram (d. 1166, thus a contemporary of Abd al-Qadir Gilani), the Kubraviya in Khwarazm by Najm al-Din Kubra, a Khwarazmian from Khiva (d. 1220), and the Naqshbandiya in Bukhara by Baha al-Din Naqshband, a Tajik from the nearby village of Qasr-i Arifan (d. 1390). The tombs of these three founders of Sufi orders subsequently developed into famous shrines and objects of veneration and pilgrimage of the Muslim faithful spanning the entire spectrum of society, from rulers and those powerful and wealthy to the common folk, all bound by similar human craving for a more immediate and recognizable intercessor. This role ultimately overshadowed their identity as Sufi mystics and the importance of Sufi tariqas they had founded or inspired their followers to found. Moreover, these shrines were only the most prestigious or best known among the myriad other places of pilgrimage and worship, usually tombs of real or mythical saints whose history often reached to pre-Islamic times but who all responded to the same psychological need. The identification of these personages as "saints," common in Western perception, needs some qualification. The concept of the canonical "saint" is absent in orthodox Islam, and is only obliquely admitted by its heterodox denominations; thus none of the three core Islamic languages, Arabic, Persian, and Turkish, has a lexical counterpart to the Christian "saint" applicable to a Muslim. Furthermore, we repeatedly encounter statements in mainstream Muslim theological literature that the *sharia*, Islamic law, does not allow any veneration of holy men, and that even the men thus revered preached against it. The fact that such veneration did occur and proliferate only confirms the above-mentioned dictates of human nature, and all orthodox Islam could do was to prevent the phenomenon from being recognized on the formal and lexical level. There was no canonization process, but Muslim saints were admitted – or believed by the masses – to perform *karamat*, a concept half-way between miracle and blessing bestowed by God; and in the absence of a canonical counterpart to the Christian saint, there were words like *wali* (Arabic for *wali Allah*, "he who is close to God"), *khwaja*, *ishon*, *baba*, *ata*, or *awliya* (plural of *wali* often used in Turkic as a singular) which assumed that function. In their lifetime, these saints played often catalytic roles in spreading or affirming Islam in all directions; these roles acquired a new and special lease of life after the saints' deaths, when their tombs became the centers of shrines or *mazars*. *Mazar*, derived from the

Arabic verb *zara* = to visit, literally means "place of visitation," and in the religious context, a shrine to which the faithful perform a *ziyara* or local pilgrimage (in contrast to the *hajj*, pilgrimage to Mecca, which only a fortunate minority could ever afford). In Central Asia the "cult of saints" became especially important during the Soviet period, and we shall return to this subject in the final chapters of our book.

(b) Buddhism

At present, Buddhism is the principal religion in Mongolia. Again, this is meant in a sociological and historical sense, regardless of how many Mongols are actually believing and practicing Buddhists. We shall deal with their conversion in the historical narrative of this book; here we shall briefly sketch the origin and chief traits of the Buddhist religion.

Like Islam in Arabia, whose founder put a stamp of finality on his modification of Judaism and Christianity, Buddhism in India appeared as a development and modification of earlier religions or philosophies. Some time toward the end of the sixth century BC Buddha (a Sanskrit word, originally an epithet with the connotation of "The Awakened One"), dissatisfied with the dominant Brahmanism, kept some of its tenets but rejected others and created a new spiritual edifice. The continuity included one of Brahmanism's fundamental aspects, the doctrine of the reincarnation or transmigration of souls; the novelty introduced several concepts whose essential message was the following: this material world is one of unending suffering, whereas there also exists an ideal spiritual world whose attainment, *nirvana*, should be the goal of every human. This attainment is impeded by worldly passions that condemn a living creature's *dharmas* (constituent elements) to be trapped in a cycle of rebirths which in turn reflect the creature's earlier actions. It is through a total renunciation of passions and desires, the basic causes of evil, that a human being can hope to have his dharmas escape yet another reincarnation and attain instead the eternal bliss of nirvana.

Like virtually all the other founders of great religions, the Buddha himself left no known writings; again as elsewhere, eventually a vertiginously voluminous theological literature came into being, and Buddhism itself evolved into a number of sects. Three principal groups, however, dominate its history: two of these, Hinayana and Mahayana Buddhism, resulted from a split that occurred in India during the first century of our era; the third sect, Lamaistic Buddhism, appeared in Tibet toward the eighth century. One feature especially characteristic of Buddhism from very early on was monasticism; indeed, the very essence of the doctrine, liberation from the passions and desires of this world, fostered monastic withdrawal to a degree unequaled by any other religion. Ideally, such withdrawal should have been embraced by the entire human community, an obviously impossible goal; this in turn contributed to a paradoxical and total inversion of the originally idealistic religion in Lamaism, where extreme monasticism arrogated to itself the right to speak also for the lay segment of society, eventually assuming temporal power and establishing a theocratic state.

In Inner Asia, Buddhism – both its two principal denominations, but especially the Mahayana form – appeared in the early centuries of our era. Sinkiang became one of its avenues and intellectual strongholds, especially the city kingdom of Khotan, but soon also other centers such as Qocho (Turfan). Later on, however, several major changes occurred. In India itself, Buddhism was by the twelfth century partly extinct, partly absorbed into Hinduism, a latter-day form of Brahmanism. In Sinkiang, Islam drove out Buddhism by the end of the fifteenth century. In Mongolia, on the other hand, the formerly shamanistic Mongols converted to Lamaism toward the end of the sixteenth century, and their kinsmen the Oirats followed suit in the seventeenth.

(c) Shamanism

Shamanism held the place of religion among the hunters and herders of Inner Asia, thus also among the Turks and Mongols before Islam and Buddhism substituted themselves for it. The word "shaman" itself is believed to be of Tungusic origin – the Tungus or Tunguz being several peoples of eastern Siberia, and the languages they speak forming part of the Altaic family, as do Turkic and Mongolian. The hesitancy to consider shamanism a religion stems from the fact that it has never had an established and codified doctrine, scriptures, or "church," and that it has concerned itself little with questions of an afterlife. Its central feature is the *shaman* (*qam* in Turkic languages), a person endowed with special faculties to communicate with supernatural forces, good and evil spirits whom he or she can propitiate or manipulate for various goals. Among these goals, success in hunting held the foremost place; healing was another important function. The method used by the shaman included trance or ecstasy, a special psycho-somatic state in which he could communicate with these spirits and affect their behavior.

The fact that ensuring success in hunting was the foremost task of the shaman may explain why among the Turks and Mongols of the period we are dealing with, the system seems to have lost some of its earlier vigor, for not hunting but herding had become their principal occupation. On the one hand, the shamans had to adapt themselves to the more predictable conditions and rhythms of pastoral life, and on the other, contacts with neighboring settled regions such as China and Sogdia allowed some infiltration of religious elements from there. The appearance of *tengri* (a word found both in Mongolian and Turkic) as the supreme deity may have been inspired by the Chinese concept of *tian* or heaven. The shaman of Inner Asian pastoralists thus came to include during his trance a symbolic flight to heaven (a vertical movement, in contrast to the shaman of strictly hunting societies, whose range of movement is defined by modern anthropologists as chiefly horizontal).

Turco-Mongol shamanism thus had a somewhat contradictory effect at the moment of these peoples' conversion to Islam or Buddhism. On the one hand, the formlessness of the system facilitated its abandonment and the nomads' adoption of a new religion; on the other, the shamans' charismatic power may have resurfaced in the new garb of Islamic dervishes and Buddhist lamas.

Nomads and Sedentaries

As we have already emphasized, one of the salient features emerging from any discussion of Inner Asian anthropology is the fact that until recently, it was a world of two distinct ways of life: that of the pastoral nomad, and that of the sedentary agriculturalist or urban dweller. Moreover, a concomitant feature is the fact that the nomad has in historic times been mostly Turco-Mongol, whereas the sedentary was either an Indo-European or else the Turkicized descendant of Indo-Europeans.

A striking feature of nomadic society was its tribal structure. The tribe or a confederation of tribes, rather than nationality, territory, or state, commanded the nomad's lasting allegiance and sense of identity. The more immediate loyalty was to the extended family or clan. Nevertheless, a mostly subconscious awareness of a still broader community, remotely comparable to that of nationality, did exist among the nomads: this rested on a combination of several factors, the most important of which was linguistic. Thus the Kyrgyz, who before 1924 had never created a state of their own in their present homeland, appear to have been fully aware of their distinct identity, different from that of even such close kinsmen as Kazakhs; this identity, cemented by the common link that was the Kyrgyz form of Turkic, was so strong that it managed to absorb alien tribal elements that for a variety of reasons came to live among the Kyrgyz: only the names of some tribes such as Kalmyk, Nayman, or Kipchak point to their different origins. At the other extreme, the nucleus of Genghis Khan's transcontinental empire was conceived in 1206, when the tribes' Mongol-speaking elders elected the incipient conqueror as their leader at the *quriltay* (assembly of tribal chieftains) held near the mountain of Burkan Kaldun in the Hentei range of Mongolia. Even in cases where at first sight the common link is not language but historical circumstances, as in the case of the Uzbeks and Kazakhs, a common idiom accompanied such ethnogenesis or gradually reinforced it. The Uzbeks, steppe nomads who in 1500 swept down from the Dasht-i Kipchak to conquer Transoxania, were a mosaic of tribes speaking their own Kipchak form of Turkic, distinct from the Turki form spoken in the area; this factor as much as tribal and dynastic politics maintained the Uzbeks' awareness of their original identity. Finally, the political formation of the five republics of Central Asia – Kazakhstan, Uzbekistan, Kyrgyzstan, Turkmenistan, and Tajikistan – carried out in 1924 on orders dictated by Moscow, was based on an ethnolinguistic identification in which language played the decisive role.

Pastoralism, as we have said, was the basis of the Inner Asian nomads' economy. Horses, sheep, camels, cattle, and yaks were the main form of wealth, the emphasis shifting among these species according to the dictates of the environment and people's customs. Horses and sheep played the central role. The horse rendered a service that went beyond the usual category of mount and draught animal common among sedentary peoples, for it was also a source of food, both meat and dairy products. But it was as the means of the nomad's mobility that it played the main historical role.

Mobility was of course the very essence of nomadism, and it involved a number of characteristic features, both concrete and psychological. One was the Inner Asian nomad's universal type of dwelling, a tent which in English is called yurt (from Russian *yurta*, a borrowing from Turkic, where, however, this term means home territory; specific variants of *öy*, usually accompanied by color epithets such as *aq* = white or *boz* = grey, are the Turkic terms; significantly, in Turkish – the Turkic of Turkey – where the bulk of the population has long led a settled life, the word, in the form of *ev*, has acquired the connotation of house; the Mongol word for our "yurt" is *ger*). The yurt radically differs from other nomads' tents – Arab, Berber, those of Iran, the tepee of the American Indian – both in shape and construction material; the shape is that of a round structure covered by a hemispherical or conical roof, with a smoke hole at the top, which can be closed with a flap; the material consists of a wooden trellis frame covered with a layer of felt, ideal insulation against both winter cold and summer heat. The yurt could be larger or smaller, but a standard size of some 6 meters in diameter was predominant.

Although the nomads were by definition neither urban dwellers nor settled tillers of the soil, this did not mean that they ignored towns and agriculture. There were usually various kinds and degrees of symbiosis between these contrasting ways of life. For one thing, nomads always needed some products of sedentary economy, such as grain or artifacts, and these were acquired at strategically located market places, through trade, or, sometimes, through raids on settled areas. The peaceful method, less noticed but more common, thus involved exchange of products of the northern steppe and forest zones for those of the towns and settled country. Aside from such kinds of economic symbiosis, we also hear of cities acquired or built by nomads, even of "capitals" of nomadic empires. Again, this at first sight contradictory concept could take on a variety of forms, but one feature deserves to be emphasized: even when there were impressive cities with palaces and other amenities for the rulers – Qaraqorum, the capital of the Mongol empire, is the most famous example – the *qaghans* (*qaghan*, or its alternative form *khaqan*, or again its contracted form *khan*, was the highest title of the sovereign ruler in Turkic and Mongolian) and their retinues only occasionally stayed there; more often they lived, like their fellow tribesmen, the freer life of nomads moving about with their herds and using yurts as their shelters. It is true, though, that at certain periods a tendency toward real sedentarization did appear; the most striking pre-modern case occurred in the very same area where five centuries later Genghis Khan's son Ögedey founded Qaraqorum: this was Qarabalghasun, the capital of the eighth–ninth century Uighur empire, in whose countryside the qaghan's Turkic subjects were reported to have taken up agriculture and other trades of settled life. The experiment did not survive the collapse of that empire, however, and there occurred reverse processes in which settled and urban areas such as Semireche were turned by the nomads into pasture lands in the aftermath of the Mongol conquests.

Thus if there were varying kinds and degrees of symbiosis between Inner Asian nomads and sedentaries, the contrasts may have been even stronger and were probably affected by psychological factors. The nomads, although exposed to vagaries of climate that could wreak havoc among their herds, cherished their freedom from daily drudgery and felt superior to their peasant neighbors to the south. Aside from herding, hunting was the nomads' favorite occupation; this at times took a form that went well beyond the hunter's usual goal of acquisition of game for food, hide, and fur, or even beyond the privileged prince's favorite pastime: it could assume a paramilitary dimension, as for example among the Genghisid Mongols, where, as a unique form of battue, it became a rigorous and well orchestrated training exercise preparing the nomads for war (and was known by the technical term *nerge*). Moreover, the tribal structure of nomadic society also contained elements analogous to military organization. Mobility and a paramilitary lifestyle were thus the chief factors that gave the Turco-Mongol nomads of Inner Asia the advantage over their sedentary neighbors to the south and west in pre-modern times.

How much of the nomads' way of life, of its assets and drawbacks, still exists today? Some aspects do, but many began to disappear with the dawn of the modern era, and the rest with the uncompromising exigencies of the contemporary state, especially the authoritarian one. Herding as the main source of livelihood still exists in some areas, especially in Mongolia, but seasonal migration of tribes or families with their herds has ceased, and efforts are being made to place stock breeding on a more modern, rational basis, including winter shelters and forage supplies: these basic but previously shunned measures have begun to prevent the wholesale losses of livestock caused by a phenomenon called *jut* in Turkic (*dzut* in Mongolian), the re-freezing of the ground after the spring thaw. The yurt still functions as the most convenient shelter for those individuals or families who look after the herds. On the other hand, the military advantage of the nomads over their sedentary neighbors started to wane as early as the sixteenth century and disappeared in the eighteenth – a result of the rise of a powerful centralized Russia equipped with firearms, and of a China that likewise was beginning to use cannon and to rely on armies, which only a populous, sedentary state could maintain.

For all practical purposes, the Turks and Mongols of Inner Asia have now adapted to a sedentary way of life. Their nomadic past, however, has left such a strong imprint on human memory that most discussions of their history – and even of their society without reference to a historic period – focus on that special dimension. And for good reason: customs and cultural heritage do not change overnight, even if the present-day scene is the focus of attention. The memory of tribal affiliation and of family lineage (every Kazakh, Kyrgyz, or Turkmen – all former nomads – is still expected to know his ancestors through seven generations) lingers on, a feature studied by such anthropologists as Abramzon and Khazanov and vividly described by such novelists as Aitmatov, especially in his novel *The White Ship*, and in an article published in a volume of autobiographies written by Soviet writers. The tribes had little written literature, but a wealth of oral epics and poems, most of which portray their turbulent nomadic lifestyle and its triumphs and trials, a source of pride and inspiration for their modern descendants and a subject of research for anthropologists and literary historians who have assiduously studied and recorded this heritage.

CHAPTER ONE

The beginnings

To most contemporaries, the year 622 must have appeared fairly ordinary. No great battle or upheaval took place. The principal empires of the time – Tang China, Sasanian Iran, and Heraclian Byzantium – were busy building up their strength, recovering from recent confrontations, or preparing for new ones; and the petty princes of Transoxania were content in their prosperous though diminutive domains, while recognizing, when necessary, the suzerainty of the nomadic Turks, whose empire stretched along a long swath of Inner Asia from China's northern frontiers to the Caspian steppes. Meanwhile Sogdian and other merchants of the Silk Road trade kept criss-crossing Central Asia, as they had done since antiquity and would continue doing until the end of the Middle Ages.

China, Iran, and Byzantium were ancient empires with civilizations and records older than their ruling dynasties. The Turks, on the other hand, had established their qaghanate only recently, in the middle of the sixth century, and never raised it above the fragile and ephemeral existence characteristic of most nomadic empires. Known in modern historiography as the empire of the Kök Turks or Tu-chüeh or Türk empire, it lasted from 552 to 744. Its territory stretched along a rather narrow latitudinal steppe belt interrupted or fringed by mountain chains dominated by the Altai and Tianshan ranges. The geopolitical peculiarity of this formation may have played an additional role in the characteristic tendency of a Turkic state to split up into two branches, a senior and a junior one. The senior branch of the Ashina dynasty ruling the Kök Turks lived to the east of the Altai range, with the Orkhon valley of northwestern Mongolia as its center of gravity; this is why their group is also called Eastern Turks (or Northern Turks, a confusing concept, correct only with respect to China). The junior branch ruled in the west, with the western Tianshan and the region of Semireche as its principal home; it is thus also known as Western Turks.

In 622, too, Muhammad, an Arab of the merchant city of Mecca who had failed to convince his fellow citizens and fellow tribesmen the Quraysh that God had chosen him as His final prophet (*khatam al-anbiya*) in order to convert people to a definitive form of monotheistic faith, left that city and moved to Yathrib (eventually known as Madinat al-Rasul, "The Prophet's City," or simply Madina, our Medina), an agricultural oasis some 100 kilometers to the north. Known in Arabic as *hijra* (usually spelled hegira in English, and meaning emigration), Muhammad's move signaled a radical change in his prophetic mission; for at Medina he not only succeeded in assembling a community of believers composed of both those who had come from Mecca to join him and of local converts, but also in organizing that community along political lines – in short, in laying the foundations of a theocratic state. Islam, the religion founded by Muhammad, quickly won great victories both on the spiritual and temporal level. Not only Mecca but much of the Arabian peninsula was converted or conquered; and by the time the founder of Islam died in 632, the vigorous young state, directed from Medina by his first successor (*khalifa*, hence our caliph) Abu Bakr (632–34), was poised to launch an unprecedented series of conquests both east and west. Known as *jihad* (lit. supreme effort [in the cause of God]), Holy War, it gained under the second caliph, Umar (634–44), Syria, Egypt, Iraq, and Persia for Islam. The next major wave of conquests – the last one directed from the center – occurred during the rule of the first Islamic dynasty, that of the Umayyads (661–750), which succeeded the four caliphs (Abu Bakr, Umar, Uthman, and Ali) who had ruled from Medina. Most Umayyad caliphs resided in Damascus, and by the time their rule had run its course the Islamic empire comprised Transoxania (Mawarannahr) in the east and Spain (Andalus) in the west.

If we look again at Central Asia in that crucial year of 622, we find a multifaceted scenario that can be summarized in the following manner. Khurasan was a province of Sasanian Iran, with Merv as its chief city. Beyond the Amu Darya, Transoxania and Sinkiang were mosaics of petty principalities marked by such centers as Bukhara, Samarkand, Shash, Khujand, Kashgar, Khotan, Kucha, or Qocho (predecessor of Turfan); Khwarazm continued to be ruled by the Afrighid Khawarazmshahs residing in Kath; and the territories farther north and east, beyond the other river, the Syr Darya, belonged to the western branch of the Kök Turks, while at the same time a process of agricultural and urban colonization from the south gave them some of the characteristics of Transoxania proper. The situation was complex in many

ways: a diversity of ethnic groups, languages, religions, cultures, econo-
mies, political systems, and allegiances. The aforementioned suzerainty
of the Turks over the local dynasts of Transoxania may even have facilitated this reverse spread of the Sogdian element into the steppe fringes
of the nomadic empire. Sogdian, an Iranian tongue, was the principal
language of Transoxania. Another related language was Khwarazmian;
other languages of the same family are believed to have been spoken to
the east or southeast of there: Khotanese in the western part of
Sinkiang, Bactrian in Tokharistan for example. In contrast to Sogdian
and Khotanese, Khwarazmian and Bactrian have left virtually no
written traces; their further destinies present a curious contrast:
Khwarazm and Khotan gradually became Turkic-speaking areas,
whereas Bactria, as Tokharistan, conserved its Iranian identity but
became "Persianized," like its Sogdian neighbor to the north. There is
a double irony in this outcome; one is the adoption of the name of the
non-Iranian Tokharians for that of the region, the other the fact that at
the time of the rise of Islam, most rulers of Tokharistan were scions of
Western Turkic dynasties.

As we have said in the introductory chapter, the Iranian idioms
formed part of the eastern group of Indo-European languages called
satem, like the Slavic ones. Tokharian, the language spoken in the eastern
part of Sinkiang, was Indo-European as well, but pertained to the *kentum*
or western branch of this linguistic family (like Italo-Keltic and
Germanic); it was eventually to give way to victorious Turkic, not unlike
Khwarazmian and Khotanese. Both the Iranian and Tokharian groups
were neighbors of three other major families of languages: Turkic, Sino-
Tibetan, and Indian. Although for the time being eclipsed on the level
of cultural and religious sophistication by its neighbors, Turkic would
gradually prove the most vigorous medium of Inner Asia. In 622 and for
several centuries to come, however, it contented itself with being the
principal idiom of the steppe and mountain belt to the north of
Transoxania and Sinkiang.

Several religions coexisted in Central Asia of that time. An amalga-
mation of Zoroastrianism (and in some cases also of Hinduism) with
kindred ancient native beliefs, Manichaeism, Buddhism, Christianity,
and shamanistic cults were close neighbors without the fierce competition that would soon come with Islam. In Khurasan, Zoroastrianism, a
dualistic religion practicing fire worship and special burial customs,
occupied a dominant position – without, however, eliminating the other
cults; it had sprung into being perhaps as early as 1000 BC in that prov-

ince, and was thus the only genuinely Iranian religion among those mentioned above. Zoroastrianism's strong position in 622 may have been partly due to the support it received as the official cult of the Sasanian dynasty of Iran, which had, as we have seen, incorporated Khurasan into its empire. Significantly, beyond the Amu Darya and thus outside the direct control of Sasanian governors, Zoroastrianism had to cede primacy to other faiths, especially Manichaeism in Transoxania and Buddhism in Sinkiang. Manichaeism was another dualistic religion founded by Mani (216–77) in Iraq, then a Persian possession, but subsequently all but extirpated in territories under Persian or Byzantine rule. Mani spoke a Semitic tongue related to Syriac, a later form of Aramaic, the language spoken by Christ. Transoxania and Sinkiang became the principal home of this religion during the next few centuries, and the stamp that it left there went beyond the bounds of the spiritual: its Syriac alphabet was adapted by the Sogdians and was later passed on to the Turks – among whom it eventually ceded the place to the victorious Arabic script – and to the Mongols, who used it until 1940. Buddhism was the third, and with Zoroastrianism the earliest, of the three major creeds of Central Asia prior to the arrival of Islam. Its presence in Khurasan and Transoxania was only marginal, but in Afghanistan and Sinkiang it became the dominant religion: Balkh, Khotan, and Qocho were the foremost among Buddhist centers. The devoutness of the king of Qocho is vividly described by the Chinese pilgrim Hsüan Tsang (600–64) who passed through it in 629. Sanskrit and its derivatives and alphabets such as Brahmi, as well as another script named Kharoshti and derived, like the Sogdian one, from Syriac, came with this religion from northwestern India, but despite initial vigor these writing systems gradually gave way to the Manichaean Sogdians' Syriac script. Christianity too arrived early in Central Asia: Merv was the seat of a bishopric by the fourth century, and the religion spread in its Nestorian form throughout the area under discussion. Alongside its own sharp individuality, this denomination had certain features in common with Manichaeism: Syriac liturgical language and script in particular. Christianity never managed to gain a leading position in Inner Asia, but it later played an at times significant role among the elite of the otherwise shamanistic Turks and Mongols.

This, then, was the general situation in 622. Meanwhile the birth of Islam in distant Arabia signified more than just another religion that would soon join those existing in Inner Asia. It meant a new and uncompromising way of life, both spiritual and temporal, wherever Muslim armies or missionaries could successfully penetrate. In Khurasan, Transoxania, and Khwarazm Islam was victorious by the time the second major Islamic dynasty, that of the Abbasids, came to power in 750. Farther north and east the process took longer, and the wave never reached Mongolia. But this exception alone illustrates the phenomenal dynamism of Islam, and the seminal role it played in the history of Inner Asia.

CHAPTER TWO

The Kök Turks, the Chinese expansion, and the Arab conquest

In 622, as we have said, the steppe empire of the Kök Turks stretched from Mongolia to Kyrgyzstan and Kazakhstan, with the valleys of the Orkhon and Chu representing the cores of its eastern and western wings. At both ends the Turks had lively relations with great sedentary empires and civilizations to the south. In the east, China was the immediate neighbor; in the west, Sasanian Iran.

There was one significant diference, however: the buffer zone represented by Transoxania. Its Sogdian princes recognized the suzerainty of the Turkic qaghans ever since their earlier overlords, the Hephtalite kings of Afghanistan, were defeated by a Turko-Persian coalition in the first half of the 560s. Khurasan, also a Hephtalite possession, fell to Iran, and the two empires were thus separated only by the Amu Darya. The sedentary Sogdian inhabitants of Transoxania endeavored to foster peaceful, especially mercantile contacts with all their neighbors, and were content to recognize, as we have said, the suzerainty of the Turkic qaghans. Above all, the Persians made only rare and unsuccessful attempts to penetrate Transoxania, and never the home ground of the Turks in the steppes, in contrast to Chinese diplomacy and military campaigns. A dramatic illustration of the latter is provided by the attacks mounted by the Tang emperor Tai-tsung (600–49; ruled from 627) in 630, and by the reduction, over the next fifty years, of the Kök Turkic empire's eastern wing to the position of a Chinese vassal.

Moreover, the Chinese also carried out a successful conquest of Sinkiang, with the city of Kashgar as its western metropolis. This conquest proved more lasting and deliberate than that of the Turkic territories, possibly because it covered settled areas and was thus both more feasible and more tempting. It also made China the immediate neighbor of Transoxania and Semireche. This led to complex relationships: on the political level, some of the petty monarchs recognized nominal Chinese suzerainty, hoping to share the Middle Kingdom's prestige and

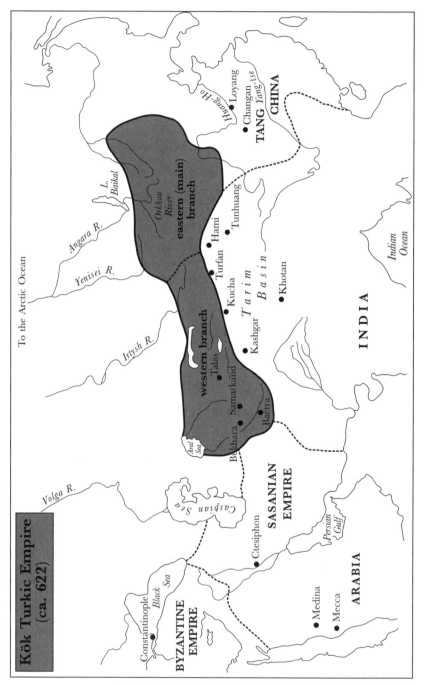

Map 2   Kök Turkic Empire, ca. 622

gain an advantage over their rivals; on the economic level, the Silk Road trade gained further from governmental participation, and no doubt contributed to the fame and quantity of Chinese luxury wares appearing in the area, and to the development of the famous breed of Fergana horses sent to China.

The new masters organized Sinkiang in a manner that left its existing structures intact and allowed it to retain its individuality, its way of life, and its local government. The area, which the Chinese called Anshi ("The Pacified West"), was divided into several (usually four or five) administrative regions, and military garrisons were posted at strategic locations; the native monarchs kept their thrones and only had to recognize the authority of the principal governor, who resided at Kucha.

With the Kök Turks of Mongolia it was a different story. Some of the nomads succumbed to the lure of China's sophisticated civilization, but others launched a liberation movement. By 680 they had regained independence and restored their empire, also bringing the western wing under their sway. Within one generation, in the early years of the eighth century, the Kök Turks undertook military campaigns still farther west and south into Transoxania and even beyond the Amu Darya into Afghanistan's Tokharistan region. Then in the 720s and 730s several members of the ruling family and the elite recorded through a series of inscriptions the story of their people's and dynasty's early history, their subsequent humiliation under Chinese rule, the dramatic liberation, and the great conquests to the east and west. The principal inscriptions were carved on funerary steles found near the River Orkhon in northwestern Mongolia, hence the name they have received in modern scholarly literature, "Orkhon inscriptions." The tombs by which the steles stood have long disappeared, but we can infer from the texts themselves that they must have been remarkable examples of funerary art, and that not only the Turks themselves but also Chinese craftsmen and artists collaborated in their creation. But it is the language of the texts, the alphabet in which they are written, and the epic, poetic beauty of the principal ones that have placed them among the great monuments of mankind's cultural heritage. The texts have been a treasure trove for philologists studying the history of the Turkic languages. The alphabet at first sight, and even on closer inspection, appears completely original and traceable to still older Turkic *tamghas* or symbols found at archaeological sites and probably having a magical or proprietary function. This is why its decipherment at first seemed all but impossible, until the Danish scholar Vilhelm Thomsen (1842–1927) broke the code and published the first translation of these inscriptions. The near-perfection with which this alphabet reproduces the Turkic phonetic structure is admirable, and it at first appeared to suggest an independent origin of this script. Eventually, however, a link was established between it and the Syriac scripts of the Near East, passed on to the Turks of Semireche and farther east by way of the trade routes and probably through the mediation of Sogdian merchants. The Turks, however, so radically modified and adapted its letters to the needs of the Turkic phonetical structure that considering this script their own original creation is not a far-fetched proposition. The best examples are the inscription of 726 by the minister Toñuquq, and those engraved on steles erected a few years later and known as the inscriptions of the qaghan Bilgä Qaghan and the prince (tegin) Kül Tegin. The interest of these inscriptions was further heightened when in the 1950s Czech archaeologists unearthed a statue that may be a portrait of Prince Kül himself.

The best-preserved inscription, authored by Bilgä Qaghan but known as the Kül Tegin Inscription, opens with a universal theme, the creation of the world, but then it immediately focuses on the Turks' past:[1]

When the blue sky above and the dark earth below were created, human beings were created between the two. My ancestors Bumin Qaghan and Istämi Qaghan rose above the sons of men. Having become their masters, they governed and established the empire and the institutions of the Turkic people. They had many enemies in the four corners of the world, but waging military campaigns, they subjugated and pacified them, making them bow their heads and bend their knees. They pushed eastward to the Forest of Qadirkhan, and westward to the Iron Gate: the realm of the Kök Turks reached this far. They were wise qaghans, they were brave qaghans; their officers were wise, brave, all their nobles as well as common people were just

The passage is referring to events shortly after the formation of the early Kök Turkic empire by the qaghans Bumin (552–53) and his son Muqan (553–72) and brother Istämi (553–75), respectively qaghans of the eastern and western wing. The above-mentioned interlude of Chinese domination of the eastern wing (630–80) came to an end with what we might call "wars of liberation" led by a member of the royal Ashina clan who then became qaghan as Iltärish (Unifier, collector [of people], 682–92); the narrative of the "Chinese interlude," of Iltärish's campaigns, and of the conquests realized by his successors is the most

---

[1] Kül Tegin stele, East 1–4; T. Tekin, *A Grammar of Orkhon Turkic* (Bloomington, 1968), pp. 232 (Turkic text), 263–64 (English translation; D. Sinor, "The Establishment and Dissolution of the Türk Empire," in *The Cambridge History of Early Inner Asia* (henceforth *CHEIA*), p. 297 (English translation).

dramatic component of the three inscriptions. Here are two examples; first, the interlude of Chinese domination:[2]

Younger brothers were unlike their elder brothers, sons were unlike their fathers, qaghans unwise and incompetent succeeded on the throne, unwise and incompetent were their officials. Because of discord between the nobles and the commoners, because of the cunning and deceitfulness of the Chinese who set younger and elder brothers, nobles and commoners against each other, the Türk people caused the disintegration of the empire that had been their own, caused the ruin of the qaghan who had been their qaghan. The sons of the nobles became slaves of the Chinese, their ladylike daughters, maidservants. The Turk nobles gave up their native offices, accepted Chinese titles and ranks, submitted to the Chinese emperor, and for fifty years they offered him their labor and their strength

The following passage tells about the liberation and subsequent conquests:[3]

My father the qaghan set out with seventeen men, and as the word spread that he had set out and was advancing, those who were in the plains went up into the mountains and those who were in the mountains came down; they gathered, and there were seventy-seven men. Because Heaven gave them strength, the army of my father was like wolves and their enemies were like sheep. Leading campaigns to the east and to the west, my father gathered the people and made them rise. And all together they numbered seven hundred men. When they were seven hundred, my father, in accordance with the institutions of our ancestors, organized those who had been deprived of a qaghan, who had become slaves and servants, who had abandoned their institutions. . . . He led forty-seven campaigns and fought in twenty battles. By the grace of Heaven he deprived of their state those who had a state, he deprived of their qaghan those who had a qaghan, he subjugated his enemies and made them bend their knees and bow their heads

The inscription thus relates, among other things, the immense rhythm and sweep of the Turks' campaigns eastward all the way to Manchuria and westward to Transoxania and Tokharistan.

Meanwhile Sinkiang and Transoxania continued to display their special individuality, with the difference that the former came under Chinese suzerainty while the latter remained a kaleidoscope of more or less independent principalities, Iranian languages, and religions, although a vague kind of Turkic suzerainty – perhaps rather an intermittent series of pragmatic political submissions – bound the local monarchs to the qaghans. Yet before long both areas would enter a process

---

[2] Kül Tegin stele, East 5–8; Tekin, *Grammar*, pp. 232–33 and 264; Sinor, "Eastablishment," p. 310.
[3] Kül Tegin stele, East 11–15; Tekin, *Grammar*, pp. 233–34 and 265–66; Sinor, "Establishment," p. 311.

that eventually transformed them into fairly monolithic societies whose principal language was to be Turkic, and principal religion, Islam. The process was complex and displayed a variety of forms and patterns of progress or quiescence, but there were two decisive and related aspects. One was the inspired dynamism of the Islamic religion that ignited the drive of Muslim armies, initially led by the Arabs, then by the Iranians, and ultimately by the Turkic converts themselves; the other was the military dynamism of the nomads, by then mostly Turks, who only needed an additional trigger to move in the opposite, southwesterly direction, and start the second part of the aforementioned process of Turkicization. Here we would point to a certain analogy between the Arab hosts inspired by their new creed, and the Turkic ones driven by their paramilitary way of life; between the inspired force of the Islamic holy book, and the poetic beauty of the Orkhon inscriptions relating the military campaigns east and west. Neither of these dimensions existed among the sedentary populations of the area. Significantly, the two giant neighbors to the southeast and northwest – China and, a millennium later, Russia – would remain unable to change the effects of the two catalytic factors – Islamization and Turkicization – despite their recurrent or eventual domination of the area.

THE ARAB CONQUEST

The Arabs entered Central Asia after their rapid conquest of Persia, whose last Sasanian ruler, Yazdgird III, fled before the advancing Muslims to Khurasan and was killed near Merv by the province's *marzban* (warden of the marches), Mahuyi, in 651. Khurasan then became for several decades the northeasternmost segment of the Islamic empire, with Merv as the governor's residence.

Compared with the conquest of the Sasanian empire of Persia (which took at most twenty years, from the battle of Qadisiya near the Euphrates in 635 to the establishment of Arab rule in Merv during the 650s), that of Transoxania proved to be a laborious and protracted affair. The Arabs needed here almost a full century to bring the province beyond the river firmly into the Islamic fold. The explanation has been sought by some in the structural difference between the Iranian polities of Persia and Central Asia. The former was a monolithic state ruled by an imperial center; once this center fell, the whole empire surrendered to the conqueror, whereas the latter, a mosaic of principalities, could not be felled by a single blow (while this argument, proposed by R. Frye in his *Heritage of Central Asia*, sounds convincing, its validity should be pro-

Zoroastrians (unified as a people under a falling empire)

jected against the fact that by the time the Arabs launched their conquests, the Sasanian empire had long passed its prime and the dynasty
had lost its erstwhile vigor; had the confrontation occurred at an earlier
time, the centralization that became the kingdom's liability could have
proved its strength and the outcome might have been different). There
were other contributing factors, such as the political, psychological, and
geostrategic ones. Khurasan was a Sasanian satrapy, and its conquest
meant the completion of the conquest of the Persian empire. At about
the same time Egypt had been conquered from the Byzantines (642),
and the caliphs, still residing in Medina, were faced with unprecedented
challenges of organizing their young empire. Finally the River Oxus,
although by no means impassable, acted both as a psychological and
strategic frontier. Significantly, the Persian empire, whether under the
Sasanians or under their predecessors, had more often extended its possessions to the east of Khurasan, thus to the territories of southern
Tokharistan, than beyond the Oxus into Transoxania proper.

The sundry sovereigns who ruled their petty principalities in
Transoxania presented a sharp contrast to the sublime kings of kings of
Persia. They sported various titles, mostly of Iranian etymology, but it
seems that they were little more than *primi inter pares*, their peers being
the landowning gentry known as *dihqans*. Moreover, being a landowner
was not the sole title to distinction. Wealthy merchants of Sogdian cities
stood only a notch below the local nobility.

For over half a century after their establishment in Khurasan, the
Arab governors undertook forays into the "territories beyond the river"
without any apparent plan to extend the frontiers of the *Dar al-Islam* in
that direction. Their recompense was booty, which has led some historians to downplay the role of Islam in the conquest of Central Asia.
Once the conquest was undertaken in earnest by Qutayba ibn Muslim,
however, implanting the new religion was an inseparable component of
the expansion.

Qutayba ibn Muslim was an Arab of the Bahila tribe, whose
members shunned the endemic internecine strife of Arab tribes in the
newly conquered territories such as Khurasan. This may have contributed to his choice, by the famous viceroy of Iraq al-Hajjaj, as governor
of Khurasan. The viceroy and his deputy were staunchly supported by
the caliph al-Walid, and for a decade, between 705 and 715, Qutayba
set about laying the foundations of an Islamic Transoxania and
Khwarazm through a series of dramatic and often heroic campaigns
retold in fascinating (and no doubt often considerably embellished)
detail by Arab historians. Bukhara, the closest major principality to

Khurasan, was Qutayba's first target. The approach from Merv leads through the desert straddling the Oxus, with the crossing point at Amul; about half-way between the river and Bukhara lay Baykand, a renowned city of merchants wealthy from the Silk Road trade with China. Qutayba captured it in 706 and withdrew to Merv; a revolt provoked his swift return and exemplary punishment of the rebels, but an attempt to take the principality's capital succeeded only in 709. The Bukharans were no strangers to dealing with the Arabs by then. The current ruler's mother, known from Islamic histories only by her title Khatun, managed to retain independence through tribute repeatedly sent to the governors in Merv. This time, however, tribute was not enough, no doubt because Qutayba had vaster plans for Transoxania. Nevertheless, he did not relinquish forthwith the method of letting a local sovereign keep his post, on the strict conditions of obedience and payment of tribute. Thus Tughshada, Khatun's son, continued as Bukhar-khudat, *khuda* or *khudat* being one of the princely titles in Iranian Central Asia. The capital of Sogdia proper, Samarkand, at first seemed to repeat the success of Bukhara's Khatun, for its king, Tarkhun, paid Qutayba off with a tribute and hostages. Eventually, however, Tarkhun paid for the peace with his life, because a faction opposing the agreement killed him and installed its leader, Ghurak, as the king of Samarkand. This led to a full-scale conquest of that city, but not immediately, for Qutayba had to mount campaigns at two other poles of Central Asia, Tokharistan and Khwarazm. The former province had already come under some degree of Arab control, but was racked by revolts and required Qutayba's personal interventions to be pacified. These events occurred in 710 or 711, and on the second occasion the Arab commander returned from Balkh via Tirmidh and the "Iron Gate" to Bukhara and Merv. By then his attention had turned toward Khwarazm, whose sovereign was inviting him to intervene on his behalf: the Khwarazmshah had indeed sent a message complaining about his younger brother Khurrazad, who despite his junior status was terrorizing him and the whole kingdom. Qutayba ibn Muslim seems to have received this message just as he was preparing for a campaign against Samarkand. He swerved with his army toward Khwarazm, and took control of the kingdom without a fight except for a punitive expedition entrusted to his brother Abd al-Rahman ibn Muslim, who apparently seized Khurrazad with 4,000 men. Qutayba, who waited in the "capital" – presumably Kath – delivered Khurrazad to the Khwarazmshah, who killed his brother, while Qutayba had the prisoners executed (possibly at the request of the Khwarazmshah). As in

Bukhara, here too the Arab viceroy allowed the local sovereign to retain his throne, under the supervision of an Arab governor. The first governor, Iyas ibn Abdallah, did not prove equal to the task, and could not prevent a revolt in which the Khwarazmians killed the vassal king. Curiously, the rebels attacked the Khwarazmshah but not the Arabs, and the action may indeed not have been meant to reject Arab suzerainty. This did not save them from a terrible retribution. After a "holding action" under another of Qutayba's brothers, Abdallah ibn Muslim, an Arab army, triumphant after the conquest of Samarkand, carried out a reconquest which included a slaughter of most of the upper classes and destruction of much cultural heritage of the province.

Samarkand's turn came on the heels of the first Khwarazmian campaign, thus still in 712. By all counts, Qutayba should have been expected to return to Merv, and he exploited this stratagem to catch the Sogdians unprepared. One of our main sources for this period of Islamic history is the great chronicler Tabari (d. 923), and it may be worthwhile to let him narrate the salient events:

Qutayba reached Sughd . . . with twenty thousand men. He reached it accompanied by Khwarazmians and Bukharans . . . and said: "When we light on a people's courtyard, how evil will be the morning of them that are warned!" He besieged them for a month. In the course of being besieged, [the Sogdians] fought [the Muslims] several times. They wrote to the king of Shash and the *ikhshad* of Fergana: "If the Arabs vanquish us, they will visit upon you the like of what they brought us!" [The latter] agreed to set out [against the Arabs] and sent [word] to [the Sogdians]: "Send [against the Arabs] those who may distract them, so that we may make a night attack on their camp!"[4]

The author then narrates how Qutayba had been apprised through his spies of the planned attack, and how the Arabs had thwarted it through a stratagem but also thanks to their fighting valor; admiration was expressed for that of the enemy as well. According to a participant,

I was present, and I have never seen people fighting more strongly or with more fortitude in adversity than the sons of those kings; only a few of them fled. We gathered their weapons, cut off their heads, and took prisoners. We asked them about those whom we had killed, and they said: "You have killed none other than a son of a king, or one of the nobles, or one of the heroes. You have killed men the equal of a hundred men." In those cases we wrote [their names] on their ears. Then we entered the camp in the morning, and there was not a single

---

[4] *Tarikh*, published as *Annales*, ed. De Goeje, series 2, vol. II, pp. 1243–53 (Arabic text); a cooperative translation project currently published as *The History of al-Tabari* (passages pertaining to this subject in vol. XXIII, pp. 191–201, by M. Hinds).

man among us who did not hang up a head known by name. We took as plunder excellent weapons, fine goods, and brisk riding beasts, and Qutaybah let us have all that as personal booty.

The victory broke the Sogdians' capability of facing the Arabs in the open field, and the rest of the campaign consisted of the siege of the city. Qutayba was unstintingly assisted and advised by Bukharan and Khwarazmian auxiliaries, which provoked a taunt from Ghurak that touched the Arab commander's raw nerve:

Ghurak sent [word] to [Qutayba]: "You are fighting me with my brothers and family from [among] the non-Arabs. Send Arabs out to me!" Qutayba became angry, summoned al-Jadali, and said: "Review the [army] and pick out the bravest people!" [al-Jadali did so, and] Qutayba took them forward and fought [the enemy] with them, [using both] cavalry and infantrymen. He bombarded the city with mangonels, and made a breach which [the defenders] blocked with sacks of millet. There emerged a man who stood on top of the rampart [lit. breach] and shouted abuse at Qutaybah. The latter said to the archers who were with him: "Choose two of your number!" and they did so. Qutayba said: "Whichever of the two of you will shoot at this man, if he hits him, he will receive ten thousand [dirhams], but if he misses, his hand will be cut off." One of the two held back, but the other came forward and shot [the man on the rampart], right in the eye. Qutayba ordered that he be given ten thousand dirhams.

Tabari then relates how the Arabs pressed on, expanding the breach, and finally the infidels sued for peace. Qutayba made peace with them the next day, on the condition of delivery of the following assets: (1) a sum of 2,200,000 dirhams; (2) 30,000 slaves free of defect and including neither young boys nor old men; (3) they would clear the city for Qutayba, and would not have in it any fighting men; and (4) a mosque would be built in Samarkand for Qutayba, for him to enter and pray, and a pulpit (*minbar*) would be set up there, from which he might preach a sermon. The peace treaty was implicitly made with Ghurak, who even kept an undefined role in the resulting arrangement. The transformation of the idolatrous Sogdian city into an Islamic stronghold was, however, emphatic. This is how Tabari narrates it:

[Qutayba] was brought the idols, which were despoiled and then placed before him; amassed, they were like an enormous edifice. He ordered that they be burned, and the non-Arabs said to him: "Among them are idols the burner of which will be destroyed!" Qutayba said: "I shall burn them with my own hand!" Ghurak came, knelt before him, and said: "Devotion to you is a duty incumbent upon me. Do not harm these idols!" Qutayba called for fire, took a brand in his hand, stepped forward, proclaimed "God is great!," set fire to them, and they burned fiercely. In the remains of the gold and silver nails that had been in them, they found fifty thousand *mithqals*.

Qutayba finally returned to Merv, and here is what Tabari tells us about the final measures he took before leaving Samarkand:

Then Qutayba set off, returning to Merv. He deputed [his brother] Abdallah ibn Muslim over Samarkand, and left with him massive [numbers of] troops and much war matériel, saying to him: "Do not let a [non-resident] polytheist (*mushrik*) enter any of Samarkand's gates without having a seal on his hand. If the clay has dried before he goes out, kill him! If you find on him a piece of iron, or a knife, or anything else, kill him! If you close the gate at night and find any one of them inside, kill him!"

Qutayba ibn Muslim can thus rightly be considered the founder or consolidator of Arab and Islamic power in three crucial segments of Central Asia: Tokharistan, Sogdia, and Khwarazm. He was in his early fifties at the time of the abovementioned campaigns, thus still in the active phase of his life, and seemed ready to undertake new ones into Turkestan of that time, the territories beyond the Syr Darya toward Shash (Tashkent). All that was thwarted by events which took place in the Arab homeland, first in Iraq and then at the center of the empire in Damascus. Qutayba's powerful sponsor, the governor of Iraq (in fact, the viceroy of the entire Islamic east) Hajjaj, died in Kufa, and then the caliph Walid died in Damascus. The throne passed to Walid's brother Sulayman (715–17), who was hostile to Qutayba (because the latter had supported the candidacy of another member of the Umayyad family for the caliphate), and promptly dismissed him from the governorship of Khurasan. Qutayba tried to challenge the new caliph's authority and carry on independently, but found no support among the Muslim troops and was killed, still in 715, in Fergana.

Qutayba's campaigns coincided with the last and most impressive stage of Kök Turkic power in Inner Asia. The expeditionary forces of the qaghan invaded Sogdia several times between 689 and 712. In one of the versions of the war between the Arabs and the Sogdians, Tabari states that Ghurak also wrote the "Turkish khaqan" requesting help. It seems that the Eastern Turks were chiefly eager to bring under control their junior partners the Western Turks, but the mention on the Kül Tegin inscription that "Together with my uncle, the qaghan, we went on campaigns . . . westward as far as the Iron Gate"[5] – a campaign that

---

[5] Kül Tegin stele, E18; Tekin, *Grammar*, pp. 234 (Turkic text) and 266 (English translation).

would have skirted Samarkand – may indeed have been connected with such appeals.

Qutayba's death put a halt to the Muslim expansion in Central Asia. When the *jihad* was resumed over a century later, its leaders were no longer the Arabs but the Ajam (a term often translated as "non-Arabs" but which really meant Iranians, both before and after their conversion), and its chief target was the lands beyond the other river, the Syr Darya. The halt coincided with growing tensions in the senior province of Khurasan, whose accounts may however also obscure the daunting challenge of consolidating Islamic rule in Transoxania. The tensions stemmed from a variety of factors, such as inter-tribal Arab rivalry (often pitting the tribes of the Arabian south, lumped together under the name of Kalb, against those of the north, called Qays), rebellions of local commanders, and frequent apostasies of those Central Asian chieftains who had converted to Islam when the turbulence seemed to offer them a chance to promote their own interests. The last-named feature was a symptom of a ferment on the popular level which caused a number of uprisings, mostly cloaked in sectarian religious garb but which often had deeper socio-economic as well as spiritual roots.

Toward the middle of the eighth century, Khurasan became the staging area for a movement that eventually toppled the Umayyad dynasty and replaced it with the Abbasids, who then founded a new capital, Baghdad. The ostensible justification for the "Abbasid revolution" was a desire of the *umma*, the Muslim community, to be ruled by caliphs who belonged to the Prophet's family, the concomitant assumption being that they would more assiduously carry out the precepts of Islam. This of course became the main theme of the Shii movements, but it appears that in the early period direct descent through Ali and Fatima was not absolutely indispensable. Other affiliations were staking out their claims, and one of these was that of the Hashimiya. This party's dynastic candidates traced their eponym to al-Abbas, an uncle of the Prophet, whose fourth generation descendants al-Saffah and al-Mansur were the first Abbasid caliphs. The epithet of Hashimis had two interpretations. One was the name of Hashim ibn Abd al-Manaf, the father of Abd al-Muttalib and grandfather of al-Abbas; his name could thus serve as proof of membership in the Prophet's family, for Abd al-Muttalib was Muhammad's grandfather. In this case, however, the common ancestry could be brought one generation closer to the Prophet, and the question could be asked why not Abd al-Muttalib but Hashim became the party's eponym. The explanation can be found in

the name of another Hashim, Abu Hashim Abdallah. This Hashim was
a grandson of the Prophet's son-in law and cousin Ali; his father
Muhammad's mother, however, was not the Prophet's daughter Fatima
(in contrast to Hasan and Husayn), but another woman called al-
Hanafiya, hence the standard form by which he is known, Muhammad
ibn al-Hanafiya. This line ended with Abu Hashim Abdallah, who died
childless in 716. In the proliferation of Shii groups opposing the
Umayyad dynasty, the one propounding the candidacy of Muhammad
ibn al-Hanafiya had become especially active, and by the time the latter's
son came to the fore as the possible imam, a special theory had been
elaborated – that of the transferability of the imamate to the person of
the existing imam's choice. As he lay on his deathbed, Abu Hashim is
said to have bequeathed the imamate to Muhammad ibn Ali, a great-
grandson of al-Abbas. The bequest, *wasiya*, was said to have occurred
near Humayma (a town in southern Jordan between Maan and Petra),
the residence of the Abbasid family. From then on the Shii party of the
Abbasids methodically organized political propaganda aimed at sub-
verting Umayyad rule and preparing the ground for an eventual takeover. Humayma remained for a time its brain center, but soon the
garrison town of Kufa in Iraq became the headquarters, and eventually
Khurasan the staging area, for armed uprising and military operations.
The critical years were 742–49, when the campaign was directed by the
Abbasid Ibrahim, although still from Humayma. It was he who in 745
invested his *mawla* (freedman) Abu Muslim with the mission to organize
a campaign in Khurasan. The choice of both Abu Muslim and
Khurasan was significant. The Muslim community of this frontier province included many *mawali*, freedmen of mostly Persian origin (such as
Abu Muslim himself), ready to join dissident movements that promised
greater equality preached by egalitarian Islam. A great source of dis-
satisfaction was the fact that the Umayyad authorities as a rule continued to impose the *jizya*, poll tax applicable according to Islamic law only
to non-Muslim subjects of the caliph, also on those who had converted
and thus should have been exempted from it. At the same time, Arab
garrisons and settlers, irked by certain policies pursued by Umayyad
governors and racked by internal rivalries between such groups as
Kalbites (Yemenites) and Qaysites, were ready to support the dynasty's
overthrow. Abu Muslim thus found ample response in Khurasan, and by
747 the heretofore secret campaign openly challenged the Umayyads.
Abu Muslim displayed a true genius at organizing the political side of
the uprising, while Ibrahim again demonstrated good judgment by

appointing the Arab Qahtaba as leader of the military operations. The last Umayyad governor, Nasr ibn al-Sayyar, was by 748 ousted from Merv where Abu Muslim appointed the Yemenite Ali ibn al-Karmani as the first Abbasid governor of Khurasan. In contrast to the effectiveness of the Abbasid movement, the Umayyad caliphs in Damascus acted late and ineffectually. It was only after Qahtaba had started his march from Khurasan toward Iraq in 749, that Marwan II had Ibrahim arrested in Humayma and brought to Syria, where the latter died in August, either killed or victim of plague. Meanwhile the Abbasid troops stormed Kufa and resumed their march toward Syria. In November 749 Ibrahim's brother Abu al-Abbas al-Saffah was proclaimed caliph in the great mosque of Kufa.

Abu Muslim did not accompany the victorious Abbasid troops to Iraq but stayed in Merv, eventually as the new dynasty's governor of Khurasan. His presence was certainly needed to keep an eye on its restless population, for soon even those who had furthered the revolution began to challenge the new masters on the grounds that the promises of pious rule had not been kept. There flared up a series of revolts, some in the name of the Alids, others inspired by charismatic leaders who claimed their own definitive versions of prophethood, but most of which had roots in an amalgam of earlier messianic cults with the craving of the masses for greater social justice. Two of these phenomena stand out as especially characteristic. In Nishapur there appeared a man named Bih-Afarid, who claimed to have a divine mandate to found a new cult which contained elements of Zoroastrianism mixed with his own accretions. He did not challenge Abu Muslim or the Muslim community, but rather the Zoroastrian priesthood which had preserved their role of leaders of the local religious community enjoying the status of *dhimmis* or protected minorities. These *mubadhs* (official clergy) complained to Abu Muslim about the matter, drawing his attention to the fact that the trouble-maker represented a danger both for them and for him. The governor thus suppressed the movement, just as he did a simultaneous turbulence in Transoxania led by the Alid partisan Sharik ibn Shaykh al-Mahri. Sharik gained to his side even some segments of the Arab establishment in Bukhara and Khwarazm, as well as the urban population of Bukhara, whereas the local nobility, led by the Bukhar Khudat Qutayba (this Sogdian nobleman was no relation to Qutayba ibn Muslim but a son of the aforementioned Bukhar Khudat Tughshada; the latter, a convert to Islam, named his son Qutayba in honor of the Arab commander), stayed on the side of the new masters. Abu Muslim did not intervene personally, but sent troops under Ziyad ibn Salih who speedily and ruthlessly crushed the insurgents: first in Bukhara, then in Samarkand. Ziyad stayed on in Samarkand as governor, and soon was to fight and win a battle whose historical importance (which no doubt escaped him) will be mentioned below.

One of Abu Muslim's partisans was a certain Hashim ibn Hakim (his exact name is a matter of debate), a native of Balkh who early moved to the vicinity of Merv. He took part in the Abbasid *dawa* (religious and political propaganda), and after the murder of Abu Muslim in 755 joined other groups of Shii extremists often characterized by the epithet *ghulat*, "those who exaggerate." These dissidents often claimed to possess an understanding of the inner meaning (*batin*; hence their collective name *Batiniya*) of the Koran and thus felt free to give it the interpretation of their choice, in contrast to the more orthodox believers who followed its outer meaning (*zahir*). Some of the Batiniya went so far as to attribute prophethood or even divinity to the founders or leaders of their sects. A striking example is that of a sect founded by Hashim ibn Hakim when he emerged, sometime in 759 or soon thereafter, with claims of being a prophet and an incarnation of divinity. He also began to appear only with his face hidden under a *qina* or veil (either of green silk or a mask of gold), and thus came to be known in Arabic as *al-Muqanna*, "The Veiled One." The reason for this comportment received two explanations: according to his adherents, he wanted to shield the mortals from the impact of his divine radiance, or, according to his detractors, he wished to hide the deformities of his face. Al-Muqanna gained a devoted following in Khurasan, but not enough to openly challenge Abbasid authority there. His *dais* or missionaries, however, met with remarkable success in Transoxania, so that he himself eventually joined them and launched an open uprising that came close to overthrowing Abbasid rule in Central Asia. The struggle lasted for some fourteen years, until after several reverses the caliph al-Mahdi's troops managed to surround the rebels' mountain stronghold Sanam, to the east of the Sogdian city of Kesh, and storm it in 783. Al-Muqanna perished in the assault, and historical sources offer conflicting versions of his death. One states that he had thrown himself into a fire, wishing to be consumed by it to the point of annihilation which would make his followers believe that he had risen to heaven. The subsequent destinies of his movement bear out, if not the letter, then the spirit of this version. It existed as an underground sect for perhaps two centuries, outwardly professing Islam but secretly expecting al-Muqanna's triumphant return. The initial strength of the movement and its subsequent tenacity has been attributed by some historians to its socio-religious message: al-Muqanna, it seems, preached freedom from the strictures of Islamic ritual, as well as communal ownership of not only the means of production but even of women. The name of the sect, *al-Mubayyida* in Arabic and *Safid-jamagan* in Persian ("wearers of white raiments"), usually understood as a symbol of resistance to the Abbasids, whose color symbol was black (and thus were also called *al-Musawwida*), might also be explained through the white garments worn by the masses that constituted the bulk of al-Muqanna's followers, the peasants of Transoxania. A curious feature of the movement, however, was the success it seems to have had among the Turks of the adjacent steppes; at least the sources state that he had written the "khaqan of the Turks," and that some of the latter had joined the Mubayyida. They may of course have been attracted by the initially successful raids on the settled areas under Abbasid control. The "socialist" (or even "communist") features of the sect have been linked by some historians with the proto-communist movement founded by Mazdak in Sasanian Iran during the reign of Kavad (488–531), and suppressed by the latter's successor Chosroes I Anushirvan. It is this social message preached by al-Muqanna that secured him favorable comments and considerable interest in Soviet historiography.

THE UIGHUR QAGHANATE

With Transoxania firmly in their grasp, the Arabs began to probe the territories beyond the other river, the Syr Darya. This land was Semireche, the region under the control of the western wing of the Turkic qaghanate. By the middle of the eighth century, when the Arab thrust into Semireche had begun to gain momentum, the senior, eastern wing of the Kök Turk empire in Mongolia had collapsed and had been succeeded by another Turkic group, the aforementioned Uighurs, whose empire lasted from 744 to 840. The change may have been more a displacement of the leading dynasties, clans or tribes than a truly ethnic or linguistic one, and it probably involved even less intrinsic transformation than the almost contemporary switch, within the Islamic empire, from the Umayyad to the Abbasid caliphate. The Uighur language and alphabet, and the location of the qaghans' political center, were barely distinguishable from those of the Kök Turks. The main initial difference may have been the fact that the ruling clan remained contented with its possessions in Mongolia and eastern Sinkiang and did not undertake major campaigns east and west. Furthermore, the Uighurs had lively, mostly friendly relations with China, including trade and family alliances with the Tang dynasty. There were other differences between them and the Kök Turks. The new dynasty had a distinct capital city, called Qarabalghasun or Ordubaligh; some segments of the population began to settle and practice agriculture; and Manichaeism became the state religion when Tengri Qaghan (759–79), on a visit to the other Chinese capital, Loyang (one of the two capitals of Tang China, the better-known one being Changan, the present-day Xian), was converted by missionaries who came there with the Sogdian trading colony. The conversion effected a psychological switch in the mentality of the elite, a change quite palpable in the contrast between the tenor of the inscriptions on steles erected by the Uighur qaghans at Qarabalghasun and that of the earlier ones of the Kök Turks. The martial pride of the pagan dynasty was replaced by the compassionate ethic of the new converts, a mutation not unlike that effected many centuries later by the conversion of the Eastern Mongols to Buddhism. Here is an excerpt from an inscription in Qarabalghasun:

Let the people accept the Religion of Light. Let the country with barbarous customs and reeking blood change into one where the people abstain from eating meat. Let the state where men kill be transformed into a kingdom where good works are done.

The Uighurs did, however, retain for the time being one remarkable feature of the Kök Turkic civilization – their rune-like script.

THE BATTLE OF 751

Meanwhile, in the territories formerly identifiable as the western wing of the Kök Turkic empire, an evolution not unlike that in the east took place, when tribes commonly labeled as Türgesh gained ascendancy and developed a symbiotic relationship with the settled fringes of their domains and with Transoxania. In addition to Suyab, a city in the valley of the Chu, we should also mention Talas (also spelled Taraz, near modern Jambul), another such town farther west near the Talas river, as counterparts to the Qarabalghasun of the Uighurs. Moreover, the still shamanistic Turks of Semireche soon experienced the approach of the Muslims, and eventually were converted to Islam. This process was first triggered by a relatively minor incident which would, however, have historic consequences.

Sinkiang had by this time – the middle of the eighth century – been for almost a century under the domination of Tang China, its petty monarchs being beholden to the authority of the governor residing at Kucha. The tentacles of Chinese power now began to probe the territory to the west as well, and the rulers of Tashkent and Fergana appear to have been among the vassals of the Tang. The former carried the Turkic title *chabish*, the latter the Iranian title *ikhshid*, possibly a reflection of their ethnolinguistic background. Like them, the nomadic Türgesh too recognized Tang suzerainty. In 750 there erupted a quarrel between the chabish and the ikhshid, with the Türgesh taking part as the allies of the chabish. The ikhshid requested help from the Chinese. The emperor instructed Kao Hsien-chih, the governor of Sinkiang, to intervene, and despite the fact that the king of Tashkent had submitted, the city was sacked and the chabish – together with the qaghan of the Türgesh – led away as prisoner. Eventually he was executed in Changan, while Kao Hsien-chih was rewarded. Meanwhile, however, the chabish's son had fled to Samarkand and appealed to Ziyad ibn Salih, the aforementioned governor, for help. Ziyad asked Abu Muslim for reinforcements, and by next summer, 751, was ready to take on the Chinese. Kao Hsien-chih marched in with his troops and Qarluq auxiliaries as well as a contingent from Fergana. As the two adversaries met in battle at the end of July near Taraz, the Qarluq switched sides. The Chinese were crushed, and Kao Hsien-chih barely escaped.

The Arabs' victory had more lasting and far-reaching consequences than this relatively obscure battle seemed to promise, for China never again ventured to claim mastery over territories beyond Sinkiang – with minor exceptions during the rule of the last dynasty to rule China, that of the Ching (Manchus), as we shall relate in due course. The effect of the Arab victory was heightened by the opportune time at which it occurred. The Islamic empire had just emerged from a civil war that brought to power the Abbasid dynasty, whereas China was on the threshold of an upheaval that would come close to destroying the Tang dynasty. Moreover, not only were the Abbasids at the peak of their youthful vigor, but their outlook had a more eastern orientation than that of the Umayyads. Besides the obvious factor of the location of their capital, Baghdad, this meant that a greater role was played by non-Arab Muslim converts from the eastern marches of the empire, both at its center and in the provinces, especially the Central Asian ones. These converts were chiefly Iranians (Persians, Sogdians, Khwarazmians, Tokharistanians) and Turks. Thus after the brief Arab interlude, the main actors in the history of Central Asia would soon again be members of its native populations – albeit through the new prism of Muslim civilization, in which the Arabic language and script retained a permanent and important place.

The Arab victory of 751 had yet another consequence: the victors captured a certain number of Chinese, some of whom were expert at manufacturing paper, an art practiced in China but unknown in the West. The Arabs were quick to learn from their captives, and paper manufacture spread throughout the Islamic world from where it also reached Christian Europe. The innovation replaced the much less flexible and more costly papyrus and parchment, with far-reaching economic and cultural consequences.

CHAPTER THREE

The Samanids

The Arab victory at Talas in 751 was barely noticed by contemporary chroniclers, Muslim or Chinese, but the modern observer, with the advantage of hindsight, assigns to this event the exceptional historical importance it deserves. We see here what an effect a combination of geopolitical realities with an inspired militant religion can have. Distance compounded by the mighty barrier of the Tianshan and Pamir mountains made the territories to the west and northwest of Sinkiang remote and difficult of access for China, but the main cause of Muslim success and Chinese failure lay in the fact that the Celestial Empire was not fired by any comparable proselytizing zeal. In contrast, the Arabs were driven by the ideal of the *jihad* or Holy War, and the fact that the fruits of victory also brought the conquerors great material rewards does not diminish the catalytic role of the primary motivation. The Arabs subsequently transmitted this zeal to the converts of newly conquered Central Asian territories, so that when the caliphate began to lose its youthful vigor, the jihad was no longer led by them but by a new Iranian dynasty of Transoxania, the Samanids. Islam's penetration of these eastern marches was then consummated by the wholesale conversion of a Turkic dynasty, the Qarakhanids, with its territories and tribes joining the *Dar al-Islam*.

The Samanids were of Iranian stock; this underscores the fact that henceforward not Arab governors but native, at first Iranian, and later mostly Turkic, but always Muslim dynasts would rule Islamic Central Asia – except for a few special periods, the latest of which ended, for Western Turkestan, in 1991. Not that the caliphs would have lost all authority there. The pious Samanids never ceased to acknowledge them as their suzerains, or to send regular tribute to Baghdad; and even later, when the Turks gained ascendancy, investiture from the caliph remained a coveted if only ceremonial distinction.

Tokharistan was the original home of the Samanids. The family's

70

eponym was remembered as Saman-khuda, and the name suggests that he was the local landord (*khuda*) of a place named Saman in the vicinity of Balkh. He entered the service of the Arab governor of Khurasan and converted to Islam, but the family's political fortunes really began with his four grandsons, whom the Abbasid caliph al-Mamun (813–33) rewarded for their services by having them appointed to as many regional governorships: Samarkand, Fergana, Shash (Tashkent), and Herat. Gradually, rule came to be concentrated in the hands of a single *amir* (or emir; commander, prince – an Arabic title preferred by this first indigenous Islamic dynasty of Central Asia; it was also used by the last one, the Manghit emirs, whose rule ended in 1920 when Bolshevik troops stormed Bukhara), and Bukhara became the Samanids' chief residence. Not only Transoxania but also Khurasan and at times other neighboring regions came under their rule, and the Khwarazmshahs recognized their suzerainty.

It was under the able and felicitous reign of the Samanids that Islamic Central Asia came of age, acquiring the major features of a mature Islamic civilization. One of these was its firm adherence to the new religion. This manifested itself not only through overall loyalty to Islam, but also through the activities of its religious scholars such as Bukhari (810–69), born in the vicinity of Samarkand but active chiefly in Bukhara. The *Sahih*, a compendium of *hadith* or sayings attributed to the Prophet, compiled in Arabic by Bukhari, eventually became one of the most revered books throughout the Islamic world. Another feature was the substitution of the Persian linguistic identity for the Sogdian and Khwarazmian identities within the Iranian framework of Central Asia. This may at first sight seem surprising, in view of the role that Arabic and Turkic came to play there. Arabic of course at first enjoyed the prestige of being the master's idiom, and drew additional vigor from the fact that whole tribal segments moved in as part of the conquering hosts and subsequently settled there – especially in Khurasan, less so in Transoxania and hardly at all in Khwarazm. A more lasting title to glory for Arabic, however, was assured by its role as the sacred language of the Koran, and hence of most of the religious literature that would soon proliferate there, as the case of the *Sahih* shows, for example. Furthermore, Arabic also became the medium of the exact sciences and medicine that began to flourish in Central Asia.

The true rise of Turkic would occur only after the Samanids; for the moment it was the Turks themselves who began to make their presence felt: the Iranian dynasty gradually built up troops composed of mostly

Turkic *ghulams*, military slaves who were preferred by the rulers not only for their prowess but also for their loyalty, which was unadulterated by other allegiances. The ghulams were acquired through the slave trade that flourished along the frontiers of the *Dar al-Islam*. Samarkand functioned in the ninth and tenth centuries as an important slave market, and Turkic slaves were the choicest part of the tribute which the governors of Transoxania and later the Samanids regularly sent to Baghdad. Both the Samanids and the caliphs themselves used these Turks in the same manner: as praetorian guards at the center of the empire, and, increasingly, as governors in the provinces. This process, also characteristic of other parts of the Islamic world and of other periods, and drawing on other ethnic groups, may seem contradictory or paradoxical to us; in Islam, however, it played an at times crucial role, even to the point where these slave soldiers seized power and formed their own ruling dynasties. During the period under consideration, Turks and Slavs – the latter mainly western Slavs acquired by the Umayyads of Spain and Fatimids of Tunisia – were the two main sources of military slaves.

Nevertheless, at the cultural and linguistic level, Samanid rule in Khurasan and Transoxania played a catalytic role in the rise of a new Iranian identity, which was Islamic. A new language, Persian, came into being and replaced the kindred Sogdian and Khwarazmian idioms as the language of statecraft (besides Arabic) and literature. Its roots went back to the official language of the last pre-Islamic dynasty, that of the Sasanians, who in turn were heirs to predecessors of whom the earliest historical dynasty, that of the Achaemenids, had its ceremonial capital in Fars, a province in southern Iran. The prestige of this city and province, known to the Greeks as Persepolis and Persis, throughout Iran's pre-Islamic past, reasserted itself after the Arab conquest less there than in Central Asia; for through a special process of cultural shift, the now Muslim Iranians from Fars joined the Arab conquerors to rule Khurasan and Transoxania, and were in turn joined by those local Iranians who proved to be fervent converts not only from Zoroastrianism to Islam but also from Sogdian or other Central Asian idioms to Farsi, as the Persians now call their language. Furthermore, the impact of the new religion with its powerful Arabic text, the Koran, of the voluminous theological literature in Arabic, and of the status Arabic had as the original ruling elite's language, effected a rapid transformation of Middle Persian into New Persian, a lexically hybrid language molded through a fusion with the conqueror's speech not unlike the way English was molded through a fusion of Anglo-Saxon with Latin and French after 1066. In the early stage of this process contemporary Islamic authors called this new language Dari (a name retained or resurrected in modern Afghanistan), probably because they associated it with the royal court (*dar*) of the Sasanians. It was in the final decades of Samanid rule that the process reached its definitive consecration with the appearance of major poets writing in this language, above all Rudaki (d. ca. 941) and Firdawsi (d. ca. 1020). Rudaki was born near Samarkand and spent much of his life as a court poet in Bukhara. Firdawsi ("the paradisiac one," a pen-name derived from *firdaws*, "paradise," adaptation of an ancient Iranian word which also entered Greek and thence other European languages with this connotation) hailed from the Kurasanian city of Tus, near modern Meshed. He composed his great epic, the *Shahname*, probably by 999, and subsequently spent some time at the court of Mahmud of Ghazna in Afghanistan before returning to his hometown. We cannot but be bemused by history's unpredictable whims: the first great flowering of Islamic Iranian culture occurred in Central Asia, a region whose major segment would soon embark on a process that would turn it into Turkestan; only after this process had run its normative course in Central Asia and the Caucasus, did this new Persian return to its erstwhile home province, where the city of Shiraz, near the ruins of Persepolis, attained deserved fame with such poets as Sadi (1210–91) and Hafiz (1327–90).

The Samanid dynasty's power and glory peaked under the reign of three great amirs: Ismail (892–907), Ahmad (907–13), and Nasr (913–43). It was during their rule that Transoxania emancipated itself from the role of being Khurasan's subordinate province and moved to the forefront of Islamic Central Asia. At the same time, however, the Samanids, content with the relatively modest title of *amirs*, never ceased acknowledging the Abbasid caliphs as their suzerains in the *khutba* (Friday sermon) and *sikka* (minting process in which the legends struck on coins included the names of the amirs' suzerains). They continued to send regular tribute to the caliphs, and to suppress any Shii and Khariji attempts to challenge Sunni Islam and thus the caliph's authority. Prosperity based on agriculture, handicrafts, and trade made their realm the envy of visitors from other parts of the Islamic world, as we can infer from reports by visitors like the aforementioned diplomatic envoy Ibn Fadlan and the geographer Ibn Hawqal, a native of Nusaybin in what is today southeastern Turkey. Ibn Hawqal came to the Samanid domains in 969 after having visited much of the Islamic world in the course of journeys that began in 943 and first took him all the way to Spain and the Sahara. Here are a few excerpts from his *Kitab Surat al-ard* ("Book of Geography"):

Bukhara is the seat of the government of the entire Khurasan; the province lies on the road that leads to the districts of Transoxania. Adjacent regions also enter under its jurisdiction. The name of the city is Numijkat. It lies in a plain. Houses built with lattice arranged in a trellis manner crowd the place. [However], the city has [also] palaces, orchards, paved roads, and neighborhoods which extend over twelve parasangs lengthwise and crosswise. This whole complex – the palaces, buildings, neighborhoods and inner city – is surrounded by a wall. None of this space is deserted or dilapidated or uncultivated, and the city is a real home, summer and winter, for its citizens. There is in the interior another wall, a strong rampart which encompasses [the inner] city with a diameter of one parasang; the citadel stands outside this rampart but next to it, so that this part has the appearance of a small town provided with a fortress. The Samanid lords of Khurasan live in this citadel. There is an extensive suburb; the Friday mosque rises in the [inner] city by the gate of the citadel. The prison is inside the citadel, whereas the bazars are in the suburb. No city of Khurasan and Transoxania is more densely populated than Bukhara. The suburb and the bazars are traversed by the Sughd River, which reaches here its terminus; it drives the water mills, waters the domains and cultivated land, and the surplus devolves into a basin near Baykand.

Ibn Hawqal thus describes here the classical Central Asian city of the early Islamic period. It consisted of three basic segments: the citadel (*ark, quhandiz, qala*), inner city or city proper (*shahristan, madina*), and outer city or suburb (*rabad*). He then gives a detailed description of Bukhara's topography, especially of its gates and of the irrigation canals into which the Zarafshan River ramifies as it enters the area, and he continues:

The fruits of Bukhara are the best and tastiest of all Transoxania. A remarkable proof of the soil's fertility is that the yield of a single *jarib* can provide enough sustenance for a man with his family and servants. Nevertheless, the density of Bukhara's population is so high and the living expenses so great that the food produced there covers only one half of the need, so that they have to acquire the rest from other parts of Transoxania.

After having described the surroundings of Bukhara, Ibn Hawqal describes the city's inhabitants:

The language of Bukhara is Sogdian (lisan al-Sughd), with some minor peculiarities, but the people also speak Dari (la-hum lisan bi 'l-dariya; i.e. Farsi, Persian). The inhabitants surpass all other Khurasanians in their culture, their knowledge of religion and their legal expertise, their religious spirit, their loyalty, their good manners and perfect social relationships, their absence of bad instincts, their zeal for good works, their excellent intentions and the purity of their sentiments... Their basic coin is the dirham, whereas the dinar serves only as the theoretical monetary unit. . . .

. . . They say that the population of Bukhara was in remote antiquity composed of immigrants from Istakhr [a city in Fars]. The Samanids chose Bukhara as their capital because it was the closest Transoxanian city to Khurasan: whoever possesses this city has Khurasan before him and Transoxania behind him . . . The territory of Bukhara borders Sogdia on the east; some people, however, consider Bukhara, Kesh and Nasaf to be part of Sogdia. . . . The chief city of Sogdia is Samarkand.

Spiritual, intellectual and artistic life in the Samanid domains thrived, although it is impossible to isolate it from similar florescence in several other parts of the Islamic world, beginning with the neighboring Khwarazm. Ceramics, metalwork, and wall painting are all attested by archeological finds or through literature. Buildings erected by the Samanids have not survived, except for a mausoleum in Bukhara attributed to the aforementioned Ismail: famous as the "Samanid mausoleum," it is a gem rightly cherished as one of the most appealing and original examples of Islamic architecture.

The Samanids are also remembered, however, for the *jihad* that they waged on the northeastern frontier of their territories, in the *Bilad al-Turk*, the Turkestan of that period. One significant date is 893, when Ismail crossed the Syr Darya, took Talas (which we have mentioned as the scene of the memorable battle between the Arabs and Chinese in 751; although they won, the Arabs withdrew after the event) and turned the local Nestorian church into a mosque. This incident reminds us of the symbiotic relationship that had existed between the heathen Turks and the Christian, Buddhist, and other sedentaries – whether Sogdian or Turkic – in these fringes of the Inner Asian steppe belt. Most Turkic nomads were still pagan despite the inroads made by Christianity and Buddhism among them, and it was the Samanid campaigns that set in motion their massive conversion to Islam. *Jihad* was only an initial and relatively minor stage in the process, however. Two other forms of conversion were characteristic of this area and period, that is, Semireche and westernmost Sinkiang in the second half of the tenth century and first half of the eleventh: namely, the proselytic one practiced by inspired *dais* or missionary dervishes who on their own ventured into the steppes and, often living in the aforementioned *ribats*, preached to the nomads, and a pragmatic or political one by which Turkic chieftains chose to adopt the new religion and effect wholesale conversions of their tribes. Modern historiography has labeled these chieftains as Qarakhanids or

Ilig (also spelled Ilek) Khans, a family dynasty whose origins are sought among the tribes of Qarluq, Yaghma, and Chigil toward the end of the ninth century. The Qarakhanids thus made their appearance as slightly later contemporaries of the Samanids and their immediate neighbors. Their story will come in a later chapter, but a certain paradox should be mentioned without delay. Once they entered the community of the *Dar al-Islam* as Muslims, these Turks reversed the trend of actual conquest and themselves conquered Transoxania. Turning against the Samanids, by 999 – or by 1005, if a final attempt of the losing party is included – they extinguished the last non-Turkic rule there and established themselves in Samarkand and Bukhara. But even more crucial was the fact that this Qarakhanid victory set in motion the eventually victorious process of the Turkicization of Transoxania, and of the transformation of the entire region into Turkestan – with the qualification that this victory was never complete, for Islamic Persian culture remained firmly entrenched in the entire area, and New Persian was the idiom of that culture. On the other hand, the Turkicizing wave – represented there by Oghuz Turkic tribes moving southward – eventually also crossed the Amu Darya and engulfed the territory between it and the Persian border to such an extent that this region, today's Turkmenistan, is barely remembered as once being a part of Khurasan but is felt to be inseparable from Turkestan.

The turn of the millennium thus heralded a marked increase in the presence of Turks in Central Asia, as well as their political and military ascendancy over its Iranian populations. Some parts of this process started as early as the beginning of the ninth century, but it was during the second half of the tenth century that it quickened and finally burst into the open.

CHAPTER FOUR

The Uighur kingdom of Qocho

The ninth century was marked in Transoxania, as we have said, by a *de facto* reaffirmation of Central Asian identity at the expense of the Arab conquerors. For the time being, this identity, while Islamic religiously and culturally, was chiefly Iranian, despite the strengthening of Turkic elements. In Sinkiang, on the other hand, there occurred the first of the events that opened the gate toward the eventual Turkicization of the greater part of Inner Asia. It was triggered by another event in Mongolia whose importance lay mainly in setting this process in motion.

The Uighur qaghanate of Mongolia was in 840 overthrown by the Kyrgyz, a Turkic people who at that time lived in southern Siberia along the upper Yenisei and in what is today the republic of Tuva, where the Yenisei has its sources. Most of the Uighurs then moved west, chiefly to two areas: to the Chinese province of Kansu, where they became known as Yellow Uighurs but otherwise did not leave much trace; and to eastern Sinkiang, where they founded the Uighur kingdom of Qocho, which would last for four centuries (850–1250).

As we have said in the introductory chapter, Qocho is today an archeological site, situated about 30 kilometers to the east of Turfan; Turfan, in turn, is flanked on the west by another ruin, a still older city known by its Chinese name of Chiao-Ho ("City [between] two rivers") and, later, by its Turco-Mongol name Yar-khoto ("Cliff city"). The three sites symbolize the cultural chronology of the area: (1) Chiao-Ho of antiquity and the early Middle Ages, the center of a kingdom whose people spoke an Indo-European tongue labeled by modern scholars as Tokharian. These city dwellers and agriculturists developed toward the end of their kingdom's existence a remarkable civilization, chiefly Buddhist and Manichaean; (2) Qocho of the Uighurs, who Turkicized the area linguistically but absorbed its Buddhist and Manichaean culture; (3) and Turfan, which grew toward the end of the Middle Ages at the expense of the other two as an increasingly Islamic city with a Turki-speaking population.

The Uighurs who established their kingdom in Qocho by 850 did not move to an unfamiliar territory. The qaghans already had some control over these western reaches from their erstwhile capital of Qarabalghasun in Mongolia. What is more, they did not come as cultural strangers: we have mentioned their prior conversion to Manichaeism. It does appear, however, that their elite had retained to some degree the nomadic lifestyle once common among most Turks of Inner Asia; and that in this respect the fusion of the newcomers with the indigenous population proceeded only gradually. The Uighur kings resided in Qocho, a depression to the south of the Tianshan mountains, only in winter; summers were spent on the cooler, northern side of the Tianshan. That was the site of a secondary capital, Bishbalik ("Pentapolis"), also known by its Chinese name, Peiting ("Northern residence"). Located some 100 kilometers almost due north of Turfan, Bishbalik eventually disappeared even as a ruin, so that modern scholars were at first tempted to identify it with today's capital of Sinkiang, Urumchi, until the site was proved to lie some 50 kilometers east of the latter city.

The contrast between the lifestyle of the still partly nomadic Turks and that of the settled natives was many-faceted, but perhaps the most striking example is how the two groups faced the summer heat of the Turfan depression. The natives stayed home and took refuge in the underground structures of their houses, whereas the Uighurs moved to the cooler northern slopes of the Tianshan, where yurts rather than houses were their shelters. There were of course other differences: irrigated agriculture as the main occupation of the natives in contrast to livestock rearing as that of the Turks; consumption of agricultural products and duck by the sedentaries versus horse meat and kumys eaten and drunk by the newcomers; and indigenous pastimes based on the home scene as compared with the paramilitary pursuits of the nomads, namely, horseback riding and hunting. This atmosphere was captured in an account written by Wang Yang-ti, an envoy from the Sung emperor of China to the Uighur king of Qocho, who visited the kingdom in 982:

In this country it neither rains nor snows, and the heat is extreme. Every year, when summer is at its hottest, the inhabitants move underground. . . . Houses are covered with white clay. . . . There is a river which flows from a mountain defile called Ching-ling: it has been regulated in such a way that its waters pass around the capital, irrigate its fields and gardens, and move its mills. The country produces the five principal types of cereals. . . . The nobility eat horse-flesh, while the rest of the population eat mutton, ducks, and geese. In music, they play a sort of mandoline and a five-chord guitar. The men enjoy horseback riding and archery. . . . Their calendar is the Chinese one published in the seventh year of the kai-huang period (= 587). . . . Those who like to take long walks never forget to bring along a musical instrument. There are some fifty Buddhist monasteries, and their names are written on their gates: these names were given to them by the Tang emperors. In one of the monasteries there is a large number of Buddhist books, the Chinese dictionaries Tang-yun and Yu-pien, and the Ching-in. There are in Kaochang (= Qocho) several collections of [Chinese] imperial decrees; in a locked box they keep a decree written per-sonally by the emperor Tai-tsung [627–50]. There is a Manichaean temple called Ma-ni-se or the Temple of the Pearl; the priests are from Persia, they strictly observe their own rites and qualify the Buddhist books as *wai-tao* ("alien doctrine"). There are no destitute people in the kingdom: those who cannot provide for themselves are cared for by public welfare. Many people reach advanced age.[1]

In other respects, however, a fairly rapid process of symbiosis and fusion did take place. The Indo-European "Tokharian," deprived of its official status, faded into oblivion as the population adopted the new-comers' language. On the other hand, if the Uighurs were victorious on the linguistic level, they mostly succumbed, as we have said, to the natives on the religious and cultural level: they converted to Buddhism, and gave up their rune-like alphabet for the local one, which eventually and rather incongruously became known as the Uighur script. Their kingdom adapted and further developed the Buddhist civilization that they found there, with its hallmarks of tolerance, propensity for sacred figural art and painting, and a literature which was chiefly religious but which also included some belles-lettres and legal documents. Manichaeism and Nestorian Christianity were allowed to exist beside the dominant Buddhist faith, and both – especially the former – have also left valuable examples of texts and art. The heyday of the Uighur kingdom of Qocho coincided with the final stage of the florescence of Buddhism in China, and the Silk Road functioned as one of the two principal avenues between that religion's holy places in India and the Celestial Empire, with pilgrims and scholars frequently passing through way stations like Qocho. The result was a strong impact of Chinese Buddhist culture, and a lively translation activity of Sanskrit texts into Uighur Turkic through their Chinese versions. We may also add a third

[1] S. Julien, "Relation d'un voyage officiel dans le pays des Ouigours (de 981 à 983) par Wang-yen-te," *Journal Asiatique* 4 (1847): 50–66.

factor here, the frequenting of Qocho by Sogdian merchants: for the city was one of the most important hubs of the Silk Road trade and concomitant travel – an aspect that intensified its physiognomy as a gallery of cultures and religions.

Some of this art and literature has survived, mostly stored in temples at Qocho or other sites, such as the cave monasteries of nearby Bezeklik or the more distant Kyzyl and Tunhuang; since the beginning of the twentieth century these cultural depositories have been the goal of archeological expeditions from several European countries as well as Japan and now China itself. The finds brought back have become a treasure-trove for philologists and cultural historians, and their study and publication still continues. We have already mentioned the interest which texts in "Tokharian" hold for the study of this unique Indo-European tongue; here we need to stress the role played by the much larger collections of texts in Uighur Turkic, dating from between the tenth and fourteenth centuries: they are invaluable documents for Turcologists, but also for historians of Manichaeism, a religion persecuted to extinction and even to the destruction of all trace of it in the areas of its origin and subsequent spread, whether in Iraq, Egypt, or France. In a previous chapter we have mentioned the transformation wrought by conversion to Manichaeism among the Uighurs during their imperial period in Mongolia (744–840). The process resumed in this second and much longer incarnation of Uighur statehood, and the psychological effect is palpable in the mass of Manichaean and Buddhist literature written in Uighur.

As we have said, the philological interest of this literature is at least as great, for it documents the rapid process of Turkicization of the area. A characteristic case is the aforementioned biography of Hsüan-tsang. In addition to the Chinese original, there is also an Uighur translation made in 932 by a certain Singqu Sali of Bishbalik. By then Buddhism had peaked in China, and the flow of Buddhist missionary and cultural activity, which had been reaching Sinkiang from India, now began to reverse itself and stream in from China. Thus many Uighur texts, originally Sanskrit, were actually translated through their Chinese intermediary. In the case of Hsüan-tsang's biography the Chinese version was of course the original. It may be worthwhile to quote one of the two colophons of the Uighur translation in order to illustrate the linguistic climate as it was perceived by its contemporaries:

Now in the blessed great land of China the disciple Hui-li, who has fully penetrated the Doctrine of the Three Treasuries, became inspired and created [this book] in the Chinese language; a master scholar by the name of Yen-tsung expanded it; the district military governor Singqu Sali of Bishbaliq in turn translated it from the Chinese language into the Turkic language (*Türk tilintä*).

The Uighur kingdom of Qocho thus became an amalgam of an indigenous people and civilization, originally Indo-European, practicing agriculture of the irrigated oasis type, and professing one or other of the three religions (Buddhism, Manichaeism, and Christianity) and cultures brought along the Silk Road, with a ruling layer of originally nomadic Uighurs who Turkicized it linguistically but merged with it culturally. Their Buddhist rulers no longer called themselves *khan* or *qaghan*, the most common titles of Turkic monarchs, but rather preferred *idiqut*, a word composed of two elements, *iduq* plus *qut*, both with a connotation of spiritual auspiciousness. The relative stability and longevity of this peaceful kingdom was remarkable, for it even survived the first decades of Mongol expansion under Genghis Khan and his immediate successors as a loyal vassal: the idiqut Barchuq had the foresight to send envoys with a declaration of allegiance, and then himself appeared before the formidable conqueror at his court (1210). Survival of the kingdom was not the only reward; the people of Qocho and other cities of Sinkiang were spared the horrors of Mongol conquest, and the new empire's bureaucratic class was in large part composed of Uighur learned bureaucrats, *bakhshis* who brought with them the writing system that then became the classical Mongolian script.

Let us briefly return to Mongolia as it was four centuries before the rise of Genghis Khan, when the Kyrgyz destroyed the Uighur qaghanate on the Orkhon in 840 and extended their rule over parts of the country. The Kyrgyz were, as we have said, Turks like the Uighurs. Epigraphic monuments, chiefly funerary, show that they used, like the Kök Turks and Uighurs, the angular script of the Orkhon inscriptions; indirect sources, chiefly Chinese, suggest that while they shared with other Turks the semi-nomadic way of life, they also practiced some degree of agriculture and trade, mainly in Siberian products such as furs and mammoth and walrus ivory. Unlike their Kök Turk and Uighur predecessors, however, the Kyrgyz qaghans never moved their political center to Mongolia proper, but contented themselves with marginal control of the country. Their rule of some eighty years thus left little trace other than that they had triggered the Uighur emigration, and they themselves were not much affected when in 925 a people known in the sources as Khitan or Qitan, and believed to have been linguistic kinsmen of the Mongols, moved in from the northeast and substituted their rule for that of the Kyrgyz. The Khitan too showed only marginal interest in Mongolia, although they maintained some degree of sovereignty over the area even after they had conquered northern China by 965 and established their own rule there under the dynastic name of Liao. That sovereignty ended with the destruction of Liao rule by new invaders from the northeast, the Jürchen of Manchuria, in 1124 and the establishment of their own rule in northern China under the dynastic name of Chin. Unlike the Liao, the Chin paid no attention to Mongolia, and from then on until the rise of Genghis Khan toward the end of the twelfth century, there was a shifting mosaic of tribal movements, alliances, and conflicts. The people still consisted of various Turkic tribes – whose presence, after the emigration of the Uighurs and the withdrawal of the Kyrgyz, indicates the fluidity of nomadic habitat in the Inner Asia of the period – but also to an increasing degree of Mongols. The two groups – Turks and Mongols – shared the common lifestyle of pastoral nomads; the literary and religious culture of the Kök Turks and Uighurs was forgotten, and shamanism dominated their successors' spiritual outlook, despite minor though tenacious inroads of Nestorian Christianity and Buddhism.

CHAPTER FIVE

The Qarakhanids

The turn of the millennium, as we have said, coincided in Central Asia with the collapse of the Samanids and their replacement by the Qarakhanids. To their contemporaries, this change was probably less revealing than to a historian pondering its impact. The Qarakhanids were by then Muslims like the Samanids, and the fervor of some khans seems to have surpassed that of their predecessors. Religion continued to be based on the Holy Book in Arabic, and the linguistic and cultural physiognomy of Samarkand, Bukhara, and other cities and towns as well as of the agricultural population of the countryside remained Iranian, though with an increasing shift from the Sogdian and Khwarazmian variants to Persian.

The Qarakhanids were Turks, however, and their arrival signaled a definitive shift from Iranian to Turkic predominance in Central Asia. The rule of the Turks over Transoxania was not unprecedented: we have seen that in its periods of strength, the steppe empire of the Kök Turks claimed suzerainty over the petty rulers of Central Asia. That relationship was, however, marginal and intermittent, for those Turks were nomads whose lifestyle and psychological orientation had remained immersed in the steppes of Inner Asia. The Islamization of their descendants or kinsmen changed this orientation. The Qarakhanids, who replaced the Samanids at the turn of the millennium, looked up to the caliph in Baghdad and the holy cities of Mecca and Medina as their ultimate spiritual authority, and Transoxania became part of their permanent home.

"Qarakhanid" is a name devised by European Orientalists in the nineteenth century and applied both to the dynasty and to the Turks ruled by it. Arabic Muslim sources called this dynasty *al-Khaqaniya*, "That of the [Turkic] Khaqans," while Persian sources often preferred the name *Al-i Afrasiyab*, "The Family of Afrasiyab," on the basis of the legendary kings of pre-Islamic Transoxania. The Qarakhanids ruled a confederation of tribes living in Semireche, westernmost Tianshan (roughly identical with much of present-day Kyrgyzstan), and western Sinkiang (Kashgaria). The aforementioned tribes of Qarluq, Yaghma, and Chighil are believed to have been the core of this confederation. When it was formed some time in the ninth century, this qaghanate probably differed little from its predecessor, that of the Türgesh, and from the latter's predecessors, the western Kök Turks, or again from their own contemporaries to the east, the Uighurs. All these groups shared a common language, social structure and the lifestyle of pastoral nomads, practicing a lively exchange with the neighboring settled populations and acquiring a taste for the products of agricultural and urban civilizations. Initially they differed from their neighbors to the southwest, the Samanids, in three fundamental aspects: religion, language, and way of life. Toward the middle of the tenth century, however, the first of the three aspects underwent a radical change when a Qarakhanid khaqan, Satuq Bughra Khan, converted to Islam and brought about a wholesale conversion of his people. This time the crucial step occurred at the Turks' own volition – albeit in response to inspired dervishes – in contrast to the events of half a century earlier when the Samanid amir Ismail applied the more standard method of *jihad* in gaining Talas for the *Dar al-Islam*. These dervishes in fact displayed some of the characteristics of Turkic shamans, and certain aspects of popular Islam among the Turks are believed to go back to this fusion of Islamic and pagan elements.

Whether by coincidence or through the effect of a heightened awareness of the Islamic emirate to the southwest, the Qarakhanids, once they became Muslims, turned their main attention toward that quarter, and by 1005 the last member of the Samanid dynasty gave up the struggle. From then on and until well into the twelfth century, the new Turkic dynasty ruled Transoxania in addition to its original domains farther north and east. Following the time-honored custom of Turkic and Mongol nomads, the Qarakhanids practiced family or clan rule rather than that of a single monarch. The territory was divided up into two, four or more appanages, and individual members sometimes moved up according to an order of seniority and corresponding status of the area (a kind of "musical chairs" succession). At the same time, Semireche and Kashgaria appear to have conserved the prestige of the dynasty's original domains, and their qaghans retained an implicit, though often only theoretical, seniority over those members who ruled in Transoxania and Fergana. This relationship no doubt reflected the Turks' attachment to their older and more congenial homeland astride the western Tianshan mountains, and especially to Semireche, along the plains fringing the northern slopes of that range and the river valleys descending from there. The Qarakhanid appanages are associated with four principal urban centers: Balasaghun in Semireche, Kashgar in Sinkiang, Uzgend in Fergana, and Samarkand in Transoxania.

Although we have emphasized the "Turkicness" of the Qarakhanids and what this meant for the destinies of Central Asia, we have also pointed out their fervor as new converts. Islam and its civilization flourished under this dynasty, a fact attested by the devoutness of the rulers, their deference to men of religion, the endowments they made to pious foundations, and the monuments of religious as well as utilitarian architecture with which they embellished their realms. Of the earliest examples of *madrasas* (Islamic theological seminaries) and hospitals, two were founded in Samarkand by Ibrahim I ibn Nasr Tamghach Khan (1053–68). Some other Qarakhanid structures are still standing, however: the most famous are a minaret built by the side of the main mosque of Bukhara in 1127, and three mausolea in Uzgend. The latter are not as intact as the above-mentioned Samanid mausoleum in Bukhara – only the frontal parts are preserved – but two inscriptions have survived on the northern mausoleum dated 1152; one is in Arabic, the other in Persian.[1] The former, in the Kufic script of the Arabic alphabet, reads: "The just, the very great khaqan Jalal al-dunya wa 'l-din Alp Kilich Tonga Bilgä Türk Toghrul Qara Khaqan al-Husayn ibn al-Hasan ibn Ali, God's elect, helper of al-Nasir, Commander of the Faithful, the King." The other inscription, in the decorative *naskh* script of the Arabic alphabet, reads: "The construction of [this] mausoleum began on Wednesday 4 Rabi II of the year 547 of the hijra of Mustafa Muhammad the Prophet, God's greetings be upon Him and upon His family and all His companions. The [ultimate] kingdom is God's."

On the cultural level, the Iranian citizens of Central Asia still continued to play a dominant role (although Arabic and Persian must have ceded primacy to Turkic as the language spoken by the new ruling elite). This is exemplified, at the turn of the millennium and in the first decades of the eleventh century, by the appearance of three towering figures in the three principal areas of Central Asia: Ibn Sina (980–1037) in Transoxania, Biruni (973–1050) in Khwarazm, and the already men-

---

[1] A. Yu. Yakubovskiy, "Dve nadpisi na severnom mavzolee 1152 g. v Uzgende," *Epigrafika Vostoka* 1 (1947): 27–32.

tioned Firdawsi (ca. 934–1020) in Khurasan. They all eventually left their hometowns and went to serve other societies and rulers: Ibn Sina the Buwayhids in Persia, Biruni and Firdawsi the Ghaznavids in Afghanistan and India. Ibn Sina wrote in Arabic, Biruni in Arabic and Persian, Firdawsi in Persian; in this respect they were typical of the Islamic civilization flourishing in Central Asia of their time.

Ibn Sina,[2] born near Bukhara and educated in the Samanid capital, was a philosopher and physician whose magnum opus, *al-Qanun fi al-tibb*, became one of the most widely used medical textbooks of the Middle Ages in Islam and Christendom; to Europeans the author became known as Avicenna, and his work was translated as *Canon* into Latin by Gerard of Cremona (1114–87). Even more significantly, it went through fifteen printed editions during the half-century after the invention of printing in 1453. This in turn led to a new translation by Andrea Alpago in 1527, and it was still part of the curriculum at medical schools for at least another century, besides attracting the attention of the first stirrings of Orientalist scholarship which resulted in a printed edition of the Arabic original at Rome in 1593.

Ibn Sina's life falls into two distinct phases: his formative years in Bukhara, where he lived until the age of nineteen; and the years of professional and public service, mainly in Isfahan and Hamadan. He eventually began to write an autobiography which was then completed by his disciple Abu Ubayd al-Juzjani. Excerpts from the early part convey the human and cultural atmosphere in this core of Central Asia on the eve of the substitution of Turkic for Persian rule:

My father was originally from Balkh. He moved from there to Bukhara in the days of the amir Nuh ibn Mansur [976–97] and held civil service posts during the latter's reign in a town of the Bukhara district called Kharmayshan. In a nearby village called Afshana my father married my mother, settled there and had children: I was born first, then five years later my brother. Subsequently we moved to Bukhara.[3]

Ibn Sina then tells about the schooling he received from men whom his father had hired for that purpose, with a recurring and intensifying theme: the pupil quickly surpassed his masters and increasingly became an autodidact, avidly reading most worthwhile books he could lay hands on. The following episode is characteristic:

---

[2] W. E. Gohlman, *The Life of Ibn Sina* (Albany, 1974; a critical edition and annotated translation of Avicenna's autobiography).   [3] *Ibid.*, pp. 16 ff.

I read the book of *Metaphysics* [by Aristotle] but did not understand its content . . . One day at the time of the afternoon prayer I happened to be in the [street of] the booksellers, and there appeared a broker with a tome in his hand searching for a buyer. He accosted me, but I impatiently brushed him off. He said: "Buy it, for its owner needs money and it is cheap. You can have it for three dirhams." So I bought it, and it turned out to be Abu Nasr al-Farabi's commentary on the *Metaphysics*. I returned home and read it forthwith, and the meaning of [Aristotle's] book opened itself up to me, for I had memorized it by heart.

Ibn Sina's curiosity was all-embracing, as we can see from the following passage:

I read books – originals as well as commentaries – in the fields of natural sciences and theology, and the gates of knowledge kept opening before me. Then I became interested in medicine, and read books on that subject. Medicine is not one of the difficult sciences, so that I quickly excelled in it to the point where expert doctors began to consult with me. I examined the sick, and discovered countless types of treatment on the basis of experience . . . I was then sixteen years old . . . At that point the reigning sultan in Bukhara, Nuh ibn Mansur, was struck by an illness which baffled the physicians. The renown of my name had spread among them by then, and they asked him to summon me before his presence. I came and joined them in treating him, and became distinguished in his service.

Significantly, the greatest reward for treating the ruler was not money but permission to use the royal library:

One day I asked him to grant me access to their library [*dar kutubihim*] and inspect it and read what it contained. He did, and I was ushered into a building with many rooms, each of which had boxes with stacks of books. One room had books on the Arabic language and poetry, another books on jurisprudence, and so forth, each room being reserved for a specific category. I consulted the catalog of the classics (*fihrist kutub al-awa'il*) and requested what I needed. Some of the books, by authors whose names were known to few people, I had not seen before and never would see again. I read these books and benefited from them. By the time I reached the age of eighteen, I had finished [studying] all these sciences.

The takeover by a Turkic elite represented by the Qarakhanids did not change the essentially Iranian character of Central Asian culture, but aside from setting in motion an inexorable demographic and ethnolinguistic shift, it meant that some of the new rulers were sophisticated men fully aware of their separate identity and became ready to formulate this awareness in scholarly or literary terms. One proof of this is the *Diwan lughat al-Turk*, or *Dictionary of Languages [spoken by] Turks*, written between 1072 and 1077 by Mahmud ibn al-Husayn ibn Muhammad, better known as Mahmud Kashgari, probably a member of the Qarakhanid dynasty.[4] Mahmud Kashgari hailed originally from Barskhan or Barskoon, the aforementioned Silk Road way station near the southeastern shore of Issyk-kul (thus from what is today the core area of Kyrgyzstan), and he may have lived some time in Kashgar at the Qarakhanid court. His work suggests that he drew on personal experience from his original homeland through extensive travels, thereby acquiring a thorough knowledge of other Turkic dialects and of the folk customs of Inner Asia. At the same time, the fact that the rich repertoire of Turkic words, phrases, and samples from folk poetry is discussed in Arabic – hence also the Arabic title of the dictionary – suggests that the author had received a solid Islamic education, which invariably started with the Koran. Today, the *Divanu lugat it-Türk* is a priceless document for the linguistic and anthropological study of Inner Asia's Turkic populations in Qarakhanid times. In certain respects it can be compared to the *Shahname*, composed by Firdawsi two generations earlier. Both are masterpieces and testimonies of the dedication of two great minds, a scholar and a poet, to their respective cultures, Turkic and Iranian, emerging from civilizations hitherto dominated by their inspired Arab element. The parallel, however, ends here, and the differences between the two works also deserve attention. Aside from the obvious contrast in subject matter (one is a lexical and philological treatise, the other an epic poem), the *Diwan* was little noticed by the Turks – let alone by the Persians or Arabs – and has survived in a unique manuscript. The *Shahname*, on the other hand, went through countless copies and redactions, many illustrated, and pervaded the thoughts and even actions of virtually all Persians. In fact, over the centuries it even became a part of the cultural patrimony of educated Turks. What conclusion can we draw from these parallels and contrasts? The *Diwan* is a testimony to the natural vigor of the Turkic element in Inner Asia, while the *Shahname* also attests the fact that on the level of high literary culture the Turks for a long time acknowledged the dominant position of the Persians. Central Asia would over the centuries become to a considerable degree Turkicized, but culturally the Turks came close to becoming Persianized

---

[4] The dictionary has been published by B. Atalay as *Divanu lugat-it-Türk* (Ankara, 1939–57), 6 vols., followed by a modern Turkish translation: *Divanu lugat-it-Türk tercümesi* (Ankara, 1985–86), 4 vols. An English translation of the Arabic part with a transliteration and translation of the Turkic segments, with a thorough introduction and analysis, by R. Dankoff and J. Kelly has appeared *as Compendium of the Turkic Dialects* (Cambridge, Mass., 1982–85), 3 vols. vol. 1, parts 1–3 (1982–85).

or, in certain respects, Arabicized: it was Arab lexicographers and philologists who served Mahmud Kashgari as inspiration and model.

The *Diwan* is primarily what it claims to be: a Turkic–Arabic dictionary, with the Arabic part often expanded into a lengthy excursus. Besides the fact that it is a treasure-trove of Turkic lexicography and ethnography, the circumstances of its composition are also significant. The author wrote the *Diwan* in Baghdad during the last three years of the reign of the Abbasid caliph al-Qaim (1031–75) and the first two years of that of al-Muqtadi (1075–94), dedicating it to the latter. In 1055, the Seljukid sultan Tughril I had entered Baghdad and "freed" the Abbasid caliph from the tutelage of the Shii and Persian Buwayhids; the grateful caliph gave the Turk his daughter in marriage and bestowed upon him the title *Malik al-Mashriq wa-al-Maghrib*, "King of the East and West," thus officially delegating temporal power to him. This act consecrated a historic transformation in the Islamic Middle East, passage of effective power from the Arabo-Persian elites and armies to those of the Turks. The dynasty of the Seljukids, which was the trailblazer of this transformation, will be discussed below; here we wish to point out that it belonged to the ethnolinguistic group of Turkic tribes known as Oghuz, whereas the Qarakhanids belonged to a less comprehensively defined group whose most prominent tribes were the Qarluq, Tukhsi, Chigil, and Yaghma. The official or court language at Kashgar and other Qarakhanid centers, which Mahmud al-Kashgari often calls *Khaqani*, "Royal," was partly based on the dialects spoken by these tribes, while also possessing the qualities of linear descent from Kök and Uighur Turkic; the "Türk" script displayed in the introductory part of the *Diwan*, for example, is that of the contemporary Uighur kingdom of Qocho. The term *Türk*, as used by Mahmud Kashgari, thus appears to have had two partly overlapping meanings. Türk, we have seen, was the name of the core group that created the empire of the Kök Turks. This suggests that the prestige of that empire had a lasting effect by spreading the name of the chief constituent group throughout the world of its ethnolinguistic kinsmen – as exemplified by the dictionary's title. At the same time, the author also uses it as an implicit eastern counterpart to the western dialects, those of the Oghuz and Kipchak groups; in other words, as a term that included the Qarakhanid "Khaqani" or court language and the eastern dialects on which it was based.

It is not known why Mahmud Kashgari moved to Baghdad, thus leaving his Turkic homeland and a kingdom ruled by his relatives, for an alien land ruled by a Turkic but foreign dynasty. We may infer, however, that the new, essentially Arab milieu made him that much more keenly aware of the importance of the role Turks had begun to play in the Islamic world. The Sunni caliph now depended on protection provided by the Sunni Turks, and in 1071 – just two years before the lexicographer began work on his dictionary – the Seljukid sultan Alp Arslan had defeated the Byzantine emperor Romanos Diogenes at Manzikert in eastern Anatolia. Mahmud Kashgari also knew the rich philological literature devoted to the Arabic language produced by Arabs and non-Arabs alike, including Farabi's *Diwan al-adab fi bayan lughat al-Arab,* "Literary dictionary explaining the language of the Arabs." In contrast, there was little or nothing on Turkic, and we can thus visualize how the sophisticated and perhaps somewhat homesick Qarakhanid scholar-aristocrat decided to compose his priceless work. The introduction is revealing:[5]

The slave,[6] Mahmud ibn al-Husayn ibn Muhammad, states: When I saw that God Most High had caused the Sun of Fortune to rise in the Zodiac of the Turks, and set their Kingdom among the spheres of Heaven; that he called them "Türk," and gave them rule; making them Kings of the Age, and placing in their hands the reins of temporal authority; appointing them over all mankind, and directing them to righteousness; that He strengthened those who are affiliated to them, and those who endeavor on their behalf; so that they attain from them the utmost of their desire, and are delivered from the ignominy of the slavish rabble; – [then I saw that] every man of reason must attach himself to them, or else expose himself to their falling arrows. And there is no better way to approach them than by speaking their own tongue, thereby bending their ear, and inclining their heart. And when one of their foes comes over to their side, they keep him secure from fear of them; then others may take refuge with him, and all fear of harm be gone!... I heard from one of the trustworthy informants among the Imams of Bukhara, and from another Imam of the people of Nishapur; both of them reported the following tradition (*hadith*), and both had a chain of transmissions going back to the Messenger of God, may God bless him and grant him peace. When he was speaking about the signs of the Hour and the trials of the end of Time, and he mentioned the emergence of the Oghuz Turks, he said: "Learn the tongue of the Turks, for their reign will be long!" Now if this *hadith* is sound – and the burden of proof is on those two [transmitters] – then learning [this language] is a religious duty; and if it [i.e. the *hadith*] is not sound, still wisdom demands it.

  I have travelled through their cities and steppes, and have learned their dialects and their rhymes: those of the Turks, the Turkman-Oghuz, the Chigil, the Yaghma, and the Kyrgyz. Also, I am one of the most elegant among them in language, and the most eloquent in speech; one of the best educated, the

  [5] Dankoff and Kelly, *Compendium,* vol. I, pp. 70–1.   [6] The meaning is "the slave of God."

most deep-rooted in lineage, and the most penetrating in throwing the lance. Thus I have acquired perfectly the dialect of each one of their groups; and I have set it down in an encompassing book, in a well-ordered system. I wrote this, my book, asking the assistance of God Most High; and I have named it *Diwan lughat al-Turk*, in order that it be an everlasting memorial, and an eternal treasure; and I have dedicated it to His Excellence, of the Hallowed and Prophetic, Imami, Hashimi, Abbasid line: our Master and Patron, Abu l-Qasim Abdallah ibn Muhammad al-Muqtadi bi-Amrillah, Amir of the Believers and Deputy of the Lord of Worlds.

Another example is the term "Türk" itself. After offering one of the conventional definitions based on the Koranic version of the Bible (*"Türk*: the name of a son of Noah; this name was subsequently passed on to Noah's son Türk's progeny"), Mahmud Kashgari discusses various aspects of this name, and one of the passages is in the form of a *hadith*, the classical statement attributed to the Prophet Muhammad:

We have said that the Lord Himself bestowed the name *Türk* [on these people], for [this can be deduced from] a statement traced back to the Noble Prophet [Muhammad] . . . who said: "The Lord says: I have a host whom I have called Turks and whom I have set in the East; whenever I become wroth at a people, I make [the Turks] masters over them." This reveals that Turks are superior to all other beings. For the Lord took it upon Himself to give them a name. He placed them in the loftiest location in the world, in regions with the purest air and has called them "My own army." Moreover, one can observe among them such praiseworthy qualities as beauty, friendliness, good taste, good manners, filial piety, loyalty, simplicity, modesty, dignity, bravery.[7]

Contemporaneously with the political and linguistic Turkicization of Central Asia that began under the Qarakhanids, a related process began about the same time farther south and southwest, thus closer to the Islamic heartland. As we have said, by 1055 that heartland was under the dominance of the Seljukids; we shall discuss this process below, but here we want to emphasize the Persian culture, political as well as literary, of the Seljukid dynasty. A remarkable illustration of this Turco-Persian symbiosis is the *Siyasetname*, a book on the art of government written in Persian by Nizam al-Mulk. As the principal minister of the Seljukid sultan Malikshah (1072–92), the Persian Nizam al-Mulk was active chiefly in Baghdad; this city retained its prestige as the seat of the Abbasid caliph, who continued to rule as the spiritual head of the Muslim community, though under the authority of the Turkic sultan.

---

[7] Dankoff and Kelly, *Compendium*, vol. I, p. 274. The Arabic version of this remarkable *hadith* is as follows: *"Yaqulu Allah jalla wa-azza: Inna li jundan sammaytuhum al-Turk, wa-askantuhum al-mashriqa; fa-idha ghadibtu ala qawmin sallattuhum alayhim."*

Significantly, an analogous work appeared among the Qarakhanids: the *Qutadghu Bilig* ("The Wisdom of Felicity"), a didactic poem written in Turkic by Yusuf of Balasaghun, the "Khass Hajib" or personal secretary of the Qarakhanid ruler. Dated to 1069, it is a near-contemporary of Mahmud Kashgari's dictionary, and predates by a few years Nizam al-Mulk's work. We can discern several characteristic strains in the *Qutadghu Bilig*: one is an Islamic religious veneer, for the author opens with the customary formulas of praise of God and Muhammad; another is a politico-philosophical substance, drawing on two different but mutually complementary systems: Iranian traditions of kingship and relationship between the sovereign, his ministers, and the people (it is in the sovereign's interest to rule justly), and Turkic principles of the ruler's duty to rule justly (because the heavenly mandate that makes his rule legitimate also makes him accountable for his actions and responsible for the people's welfare); and a third veneer, local color, expressed above all in the poem's Turkic language, but also in the delightful portrayals of the author's and his Turkic compatriots' homeland: the awakening of nature in the springtime, the boisterous joy of living creatures, the passing of a Silk Road caravan on its way from China. Like Mahmud of Kashgar, Yusuf of Balasaghun eloquently asserted his ethnic identity by giving his work a Turkic form and setting. We have already mentioned the efforts of some Qarakhanid rulers to rule justly, which are evident from their pious foundations and behavior; the *Qutadghu Bilig* is another illustration of the political and cultural climate characteristic of this first Turkic dynasty to rule Islamic Central Asia.

The *Qutadghu Bilig* has survived in three undated manuscripts. Arabic script was used for two of these, but the third is in the Uighur alphabet. Internal evidence suggests that it was copied in the Timurid period (fifteenth century), when that script received new currency thanks to the ubiquity of Uighur *bakhshis* in the nomadic monarchs' chanceries, or even to a certain Turkic pride among the elite. Today this didactic poem ranks among the priceless monuments of Turkic antiquity, cherished by linguists as well as by cultural and social historians.

CHAPTER SIX

Seljukids and Ghaznavids

The turn of the millennium inaugurated in the originally Iranian part of Central Asia, as we have said, the rule of dynasties that issued from among Inner Asian nomads, primarily Turkic but soon also Mongol. A similar process began farther southwest and southeast, thus in the central lands of Islam and on the Indian subcontinent, where Seljukid and Ghaznavid dynasties came to power. Whereas, however, in Central Asia this process led to a permanent change and large-scale Turkicization of the populations, this did not happen elsewhere – with a few exceptions, the most notable being Turkey itself. In Iraq, Iran, and Afghanistan, to name just the core lands affected by this change, native dynasties or governments soon or eventually reassumed power, and the process of Turkicization, if at all noticeable, gave ground to a reaffirmation of Iranian or Arab demographic, cultural, and political realities.

The subject is relevant to our topic for several reasons. Both the dynasties mentioned originated in Central Asia, and their scions spoke Turkic; the staging area for their push into the heartlands of Islam and India was the province of Khurasan; and they had protracted and complex relations with the Qarakhanids. The Seljukids never relinquished Khurasan: they won it by 1040 in the historic battle of Dandanqan with the Ghaznavids; and the last monarch of its senior branch, Sanjar, who ruled from 1118 to 1157, chose it a century later as his home province, with Merv as his capital and final resting place.

Like the Qarakhanids, the Seljukids appeared in Central Asia during the tenth century, but farther west on the lower course of the Syr Darya, near the Aral Sea, and as members of a different group of Turkic tribes called Oghuz. The Oghuz moved westward into the steppes of western Eurasia after the collapse of the Kök Turkic qaghanate, and became the dominant nomadic element there. Unlike other Turks who had at times created great though ephemeral empires and impressive civilizations,

93

they seem to have stayed below that level prior to their entry into the *Dar al-Islam*. Their ruler did not style himself qaghan but *yabghu*, a lesser title in the complex hierarchy of Turkic royal titulature. Toward the turn of the first millennium, the Oghuz yabghu used the aforementioned town of Yangikant near the estuary of the Syr Darya as his winter quarters. The Turco-Sogdian name Yangikant appears in Arabic sources as Qarya haditha,[1] and in Persian ones as Dih-i naw, all three meaning "new town." Jand farther upstream was another town paying taxes to the yabghu, and there were other settlements; they were peopled mainly by Muslims from across the river to the south, but some scholars view this symbiosis as a hint that the Turks themselves had shown some inclination toward settled and urban life. Like most other Turks of the time, the Oghuz were pagans, but *qams* or shamans and the idea of a principal deity, *tengri*, do seem to have played a role in their spiritual orbit. By 1003, however, the yabghu had converted to Islam, boasting the thoroughly Muslim name Abu l-Fawaris Shah Malik ibn Ali; the last component ("son of Ali") suggests that he may even have been born a Muslim. Concurrently with the yabghu's family, however, another clan was adopting Islam: that of their *subashi* or military commander Seljuk, who gained the upper hand in Jand and freed its population from taxes paid to the yabghu.

Seljuk's three sons who reached maturity had the names Israil, Mikail, and Musa, probably an effect of the prestige the memory of the Khazar kingdom still had among the steppe nomads rather than an indication that they too had converted to Judaism. Their conversion to Islam proved more effective than that of the yabghu's clan, a circumstance that must have contributed to the increased hostility between the two groups and gradual drift of the Seljuk clan southward into Muslim territories, at first into those of the Qarakhanids and Ghaznavids. There were other factors causing this important demographic, political, and socio-economic revolution, such as possible overpopulation in the steppes, vagaries of the climate, the concomitant tribal disturbances. Attraction of settled territories with rumored riches to plunder, and opportunities armed bands could find by hiring out their services to the strongest bidder must also have played a role. The group led by Seljuk's three sons was among such *condottieri*, and their modest beginnings could hardly have presaged the glorious destiny decreed for their descendants as the

---

[1] I hope to be forgiven for mentioning an irrelevant but interesting detail: this Semitic form of "Newtown" can also be discerned in the name of Carthage.

main political force in the Islamic Middle East for the next two centuries.

The Seljukid clan, we have said, belonged to the Oghuz group of Turkic tribes. Before the great migration southward started, these tribes formed the majority of nomads in the steppes of what is today central and western Kazakhstan, in other words, in the eastern part of what subsequently came to be known as the Kipchak steppe. The Kipchak Turks were then occupying the western portions of this steppe, and only after the emigration of the Oghuz did they extend their presence into the latter's territory. The Oghuz, also known in Islamic sources as Ghuzz, then became the permanent Turkic element in the Middle East, starting with Turkmenistan and ending with Turkey. It was also during this period of Oghuz migration and Islamization that the ethnonym Turkmen (more exactly Türkmän) began to gain currency. The implied nuance may thus have meant those Oghuz who had become Muslims. Gradually the name Turkmen (or Turcoman in European usage) prevailed and Oghuz has receded into the parlance of modern Turcology.

The rise of Seljukid power was prodigious: from Khurasan they extended their rule over much of Iran, and over Iraq, Syria, and southern Caucasus; as we have pointed out while discussing Mahmud Kashgari, by 1055 – just fifteen years after the battle of Dandanqan – they had entered Baghdad, where, as we have said, the caliph had no choice but to name their leader, Tughril Beg, "Amir (or Malik) al-Sharq wa-al-Gharb" ("Commander of the East and West"), to give him his daughter in marriage, and to accept his tutelage, in return for the right to continue as the nominal head of the Muslim community. Another decade and a half later, in 1071, the Seljukid sultan Alp Arslan won the aforementioned historic battle against the Byzantine emperor Romanos Diogenes at Manzikert in eastern Anatolia – an event that opened the gate to Turkic penetration into Asia Minor and its eventual Turkicization and Islamization. The new empire was soon divided into several regional segments ruled by various members of the dynasty; this may have been an echo of the Inner Asian nomads' concepts of family rather than individual rule, but geopolitical as well as psychological factors probably played a more decisive role here. Despite his brilliant victory against the Byzantines, Alp Arslan left further conquests in the west to junior members of the family and resolved to extend his realm in the opposite direction at the expense of the Qarakhanids. This cost him his life, for in 1072 he died during a campaign in Transoxania. His son and successor Malikshah (1072–92) fared better, for on his first campaign he reduced the Qarakhanid ruler of Transoxania to vassal-age, and on his second expedition he even pushed into Sinkiang, where the Qarakhanids of Kashgar briefly acknowledged his suzerainty. That the latter success was so short-lived can again be ascribed to geopolitical factors. One might of course wonder why the Seljukids endeavored to impose their suzerainty on the Qarakhanids, fellow-Muslims and Turks like themselves, and who moreover never appeared to pose a major threat despite occasional claims to Khurasan. The expansiveness of a basically nomadic people might be one of the reasons; the proximity of Transoxania, a sister region to Khurasan, might be another; its economic prosperity under the just and successful administration of the Qarakhanids, yet another; and perhaps also rivalry with the Ghaznavids, the Seljuks' neighbors to the east.

It was thus these northeastern reaches of the *Dar al-Islam*, especially Khurasan, which the Great Seljuks – as the family's senior branch is called by modern historians – considered the core of their possessions and place of residence. Of the junior branches, the Seljuks of Rum – Rum being the Islamic name for Anatolia – stand out for having outlived all the others and set in motion the process of Islamicizing and Turkicizing that country, thus of transforming it into Turkey. Meanwhile in Khurasan, Merv, the center of a flourishing agricultural region but also situated on one of the trunk lines of the Silk Road network, rose to the preeminent position of a capital and flourished more than ever as a center of culture, industry, and trade. Sultan Sanjar, the last Great Seljukid, chose it as his residence and built there a grandiose mausoleum for himself. His realm was thus powerful and prosperous: junior Seljukid branches ruled farther south and west; the once dangerous Ghaznavids had definitively oriented themselves toward India; and the Qarakhanids were vassals whose loyalty was further cemented by family ties. Yet Sanjar was to end his days a broken man, and his dynasty would founder soon after him. The causes of this dramatic collapse were complex, but a catalytic role may have been played by a defeat that Sanjar suffered in 1141. We shall return to this event below, but first a few words about the Ghaznavids.

Like the Qarakhanids and Seljukids, the Ghaznavids were Turks, with their roots among the nomads of Inner Asia, and they had recently converted to Islam. These parallels were accompanied, however, by differences symptomatic of the variables marking the period's Islamic political structures. Whereas the first two dynasties established their authority as free families or clans by means of a successful regimentation of tribes, the Ghaznavids came to power through a completely different channel: as slave soldiers of the Samanids. We have already mentioned the importance of *ghulams*, praetorian guards owned by Islamic rulers such as the Samanids and the Abbasid caliphs themselves; we have pointed out that in Islam's eastern and central areas, these ghulams were mostly Turks, and that they gradually gained power to the point of controlling their masters or making themselves independent in the provinces that they were sent to govern. Such was the origin of the Ghaznavid Sebüktegin, a slave general who from 977 till his death twenty years later governed a growing array of territories in Afghanistan and Khurasan for the Samanids. The collapse of this dynasty a few years after Sebüktegin's death enabled his son Mahmud (998–1030) not only to shed any acknowledgement of vassaldom but also to share the spoils with the Qarakhanids, Khurasan being the main prize.

Mahmud of Ghazna and his first sucessors, Muhammad and Masud (1030–41), had lively relations with both the Qarakhanids and the Seljukids. Conflicts between the Ghaznavids and Qarakhanids were overshadowed by friendly contacts that sometimes included stately meetings between monarchs – such as between Mahmud of Ghazna and Qadir Khan of Kashgar in 1025 near Samarkand – and family alliances. Here is an excerpt from an account of the encounter, written in Persian by the Ghaznavid historian Gardizi:[2]

When Qadir Khan, who was the Chief of all Turkestan and its Great Khan, received the report that Yamin al-Dawla [i.e. Mahmud of Ghazna] had crossed the Jayhun, he set out from Kashgar in order to meet with him and conclude a new pact [*ahd-i taza*]. He came to Samarkand and proceeded from there, with intentions of peace and friendship, until he was within a *farsakh* of the Amir Mahmud's army. There he halted, ordered that tents be pitched, and sent envoys to inform Mahmud about his arrival and desire to see him. The Amir Mahmud responded positively and proposed a specific place where they would meet. Subsequently Amir Mahmud and Qadir Khan, each with a small cavalry retinue, arrived at that place. When they came within sight of each another, they dismounted; the Amir Mahmud gave a precious stone wrapped in a cloth to the treasurer and instructed him to deliver it into the hands of Qadir Khan. The latter had also come with a precious stone, but was so overawed that he forgot [to reciprocate]; only after the meeting had ended did he recall the stone, and had it hand-delivered by one of his attendants with expressions of apology. The next day the Amir Mahmud ordered a large tent of embroidered satin [*khayma-i buzurg az diba-yi mansuj*] to be pitched, and everything to be prepared

[2] *Zayn al-akhbar*, ed. Habibi (Tehran, 1347/1968), pp. 406–10; Barthold, *Turkestan*, English translation on pp. 282–4.

for an entertainment; he then sent a messenger to Qadir Khan inviting him to be his guest. When Qadir Khan arrived, Mahmud ordered the banquet to be arranged as magnificently as possible; the two then ate together at the same table. After the meal they went to the hall of gaiety [*majlis-i tarab*]; it was splendidly adorned with rare flowers, delicate fruits, precious stones, gold-embroidered fabrics, crystal, beautiful mirrors and [other] rare objects, so that Qadir Khan could not regain his composure. They remained seated for some time. Qadir Khan drank no wine, as it is not customary for the kings of Transoxania, especially the Turkic kings, to do so. They listened to music for a while, then [Qadir Khan] rose. Thereupon the Amir Mahmud ordered presents to be brought, namely, gold and silver goblets, precious stones, rarities from Baghdad, fine fabrics, costly weapons, valuable horses with gold bridles and sticks studded with precious stones, ten she-elephants with gold ornaments and goads studded with jewels; mules from Bardhaa with gold trappings, litters for journeys by camel with girths, gold and silver sticks and bells, also litters of embroidered satin; valuable fabrics and carpets, of Armenian work, as well as *uwaysi* and parti-colored carpets; embroidered headbands; rose-colored stamped stuffs from Tabaristan; Indian swords, Qamari aloes, Maqasiri sandal wood, grey amber, she-asses, skins of Barbary panthers, hunting dogs, falcons and eagles trained to hunt cranes, antelopes and other game. He saw Qadir Khan off with great ceremony, showing him many favors and apologizing [for the inadequacy of his entertainment and presents]. On returning to his camp and examining all these precious things, jewels, arms and riches, Qadir Khan was filled with astonishment and did not know how to requite him for them. Then he ordered the treasurer to open the door of the treasury, took thence much money and sent it to Mahmud, together with the products of Turkestan, namely fine horses with gold trappings, Turkic slaves with gold belts and quivers, falcons and gerfalcons, sable, miniver, ermine and fox furs, vessels of the skins of two sheep with horns of the *khutuw*, Chinese satin and so forth. Both sovereigns parted entirely satisfied, in peace and amity.

With the Seljukids, on the other hand, the rivalry knew no compromise, and the Ghaznavids were the losers; it was their aforementioned defeat at Dandanqan (a site in Turkmenistan, some 70 km southwest of Merv), in 1040 that definitively deflected their efforts away from Central Asia toward India.

By the time Sultan Sanjar came to power in 1118, then, the Seljukid empire seemed firmly established and, if the lateral branches of the family as well as the vassal states are included, it was the most extensive realm that Islam had known since the heyday of the Umayyad and Abbasid caliphates: from Transoxania in the northeast to Iran, Iraq, part of Syria, and a good deal of Anatolia. In 1141, however, the sultan suffered a defeat whose consequences may not at first sight have seemed too disastrous, for all that it cost him was Transoxania. Its delayed effect was, however, more serious; and with the benefit of hindsight, we can add that it portended a terrible calamity.

The conquerors who invaded Transoxania and defeated Sanjar were the Qarakhitay, descendants of the aforementioneed Khitan who had two centuries earlier invaded northern China and, adopting the dynastic name of Liao, founded their own state there. By 1125, however, that scenario was replayed when another invader from the northeast, the Tungus Jürchen, drove out the Khitan and ruled northern China under the dynastic name of Chin. A substantial number of the Khitan migrated westward, approximately following the northern Silk Road, and gained strength to the point of defeating an eastern Qarakhanid khan in Sinkiang a mere three years after their ouster from China. It was then the turn of the western Qarakhanids and of their suzerain, Sanjar. The sultan and his vassals met them on the Qatvan steppe, a short distance to the northeast of Samarkand, in 1141. The Khitan soundly beat them, and Sanjar barely escaped.

To Islamic historians, these western Khitan (who probably spoke a Mongol language) came to be known as Qarakhitay, and they were as much a puzzle to them as they are to modern historians. The Qarakhitay allowed some of the Qarakhanids to continue their rule as vassals, and themselves lived in Semireche with their headquarters, remembered by the Turco-Mongol name of Ordubaliq, near Balasaghun. The Uighur idiqut of Turfan too acknowledged their suzerainty, as did the Qarluq rulers of Almaliq and Qayaliq. The Khitan were partially Sinicized by the time the Jürchen drove them out of China, and they retained that veneer throughout their second incarnation: the sources mention only the Chinese form of their names, and their coins have Chinese legends; and despite their relatively long rule of eighty years in a mostly Muslim territory, they never converted to Islam. Living under infidel rule is anathema to Muslims, yet Muslim historians grudgingly concede that the Qarakhitay were surprisingly fair-minded and tolerant rulers.

With the benefit of hindsight, however, we can say that there was something sinister about the manner in which the Qarakhitay defeated Sanjar and his allies in 1141. The newcomers had despite their Chinese veneer remained essentially steppe nomads, and they overcame the larger host of a Turkic monarch who had in contrast become more acculturated to the ways of Near Eastern sedentaries and their manner of fighting. Greater mobility, together with superior maneuvering of cavalry and archers, carried the day for the Qarakhitay. The same assets, increased many times over through superb planning, discipline, and concentration of troops at critical points, would a century later make the Mongols of Genghis Khan and his successors the greatest conquerors in history.

The Qarakhitay contented themselves, however, with the aforementioned arrangement after their victory, and that enabled the last two generations of Qarakhanids to outlast their erstwhile Seljuk overlords and carry on almost down to the Mongol invasion. Almost, but not quite: for Sanjar's defeat and the collapse of the Great Seljuks gave a freer rein to the perennial Khwarazmshahs, who in their delta oasis kingdom found new energy for expansion into former Seljuk territories. At first, however, they had to free themselves from Qarakhitay domination, for they too had been compelled to submit and pay regular tribute. The Khwarazmshah Ala al-Din Muhammad (1200–20) did so in two stages: he eliminated the Qarakhitay's Qarakhanid vassal of Samarkand, and he then defeated the Qarakhitay themselves, who had set out to counter the upstart. This happened in 1210, and from then on Muhammad turned his main attention westward toward the heartland of the *Dar al-Islam*, driven by ambition to upstage the Seljuks and in his turn become the "protector" of the caliph in Baghdad (or, according to some sources, to rid Islam of the Sunni caliph and install himself as the champion of the legitimacy of the *Ahl al-Bayt*, the Prophet's descendants symbolized by the hidden *mahdi*, the Khwarazmshah having espoused the Shii cause for that purpose). Ala al-Din Muhammad almost succeeded, for much of Iran fell to him, and he was on the verge of the final push into Iraq when alarming news from Central Asia demanded his immediate return.

By then, in 1218, both the Qarakhanids and their overlords the Qarakhitay – who despite their failure against the Khwarazmshah Muhammad had maintained themselves in Semireche – had been overthrown by Küchlüg. The son of the defeated chief of the Nayman tribe, Küchlüg had fled with its remnants from Genghis Khan's Mongols, and gained strength to the point of substituting his rule for that of the Qarakhitay. Converting to Buddhism through the influence of his Qarakhitay wife, Küchlüg began to terrorize the by then devoutly Muslim inhabitants of western Sinkiang. He eventually also attacked and killed the Qarluq ruler of the city of Almaliq, however, and this proved to be his doom, for the victim's son appealed to the Mongols for help. Küchlüg fled before an advance party led by the general (*noyon*) Jebe, but was overtaken and killed while seeking refuge in the Pamir mountains. His case is significant chiefly because it more quickly attracted Genghis Khan's attention to Inner Asia's western marches. This event brings us to the cataclysmic turning point of Inner Asian history, the rise of the Mongol empire of Genghis Khan.

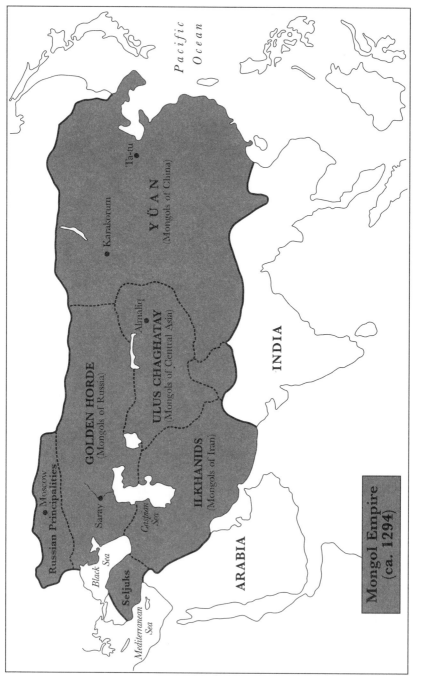

Map 3   Mongol Empire, ca. 1294

CHAPTER SEVEN

The conquering Mongols

Few historical events can illustrate the unpredictability of the future as vividly as the sudden rise of Genghis Khan's Mongol empire in the second and third decades of the thirteenth century. The energy and genius of the relatively small number of people who were at the core of this enterprise have baffled all historians trying to explain the phenomenon, just as the effects, ranging from horrifying massacres and devastations to periods of admirable cross-cultural exchange and stimulation, have never ceased repelling and attracting them.

The effects of the Mongol invasion and rule were complex and, as we have implied, of varying type and degree across the vast swath of Eurasia they covered. Three areas and civilizations, however, can be singled out as having been affected far more radically than the rest: China, Central Asia, and Russia. In all three, history can be broken down into two periods, pre-Mongol and post-Mongol.

The first enigma of the Mongol phenomenon is the relative insignificance of the tribes and territories where Genghis Khan had arisen. We have dwelt on Mongolia during its "Turkic" period, the sixth through tenth centuries; a contemporary observer could with some legitimacy have characterized Mongolia as the real and original Turkestan, land of the Turks, whether Kök Turks, Uighurs, Kyrgyz, or an amorphous conglomerate of contending tribes. Once the Kyrgyz had lost interest in Mongolia and withdrawn to their homeland in southern Siberia, and the Khitan lost theirs thanks to their transformation into a Chinese dynasty – both of which developments took place in the tenth century – Mongolia became a country of nomads, mainly Turkic, grouped into tribes but lacking any larger political cohesion or cultural dynamism. The script of the Orkhon valley was forgotten, the Manichaeism of the Uighurs was gone, and the incipient cities and agriculture had receded. Nevertheless, the very fluidity of the situation exposed the tribes living there to external influences. Trade was not absent, and the geo-economic position of Inner Asia meant that some of it was long-distance trade passing through Mongolia. Manichaeism may have disappeared, but Christianity made some headway among such Turkic tribes as the Kereit, Merkit and Öngüt. The fact that it was the Nestorian denomination rather than, say, the Roman Catholic or even Orthodox or Jacobite ones was no accident: there had been a Nestorian bishopric in Merv, and Nestorianism too could spread from there along the special avenue that was the Silk Road network.

Such was the situation until the second half of the twelfth century and the appearance of Temujin, the future Genghis Khan. The country was still more Turkic than Mongol, especially its central and western part, with the Tula and Orkhon rivers as the delimiters. East of there, along the Onon and Kerulen rivers all the way to the longitudinal Khingan mountains that separate Mongolia from Manchuria, lived tribes speaking Mongolian languages: the Tatars and those among whom we find some calling themselves Mongols. Both groups, along with many Turkic ones, are mentioned in Chinese sources as factors in the border politics of northern China; there, the Liao dynasty of the Khitan had succumbed to another invader from the northeast: the aforementioned Tungus Jürchen, who by 1125 had established their own Chinese dynasty, the Chin ("Golden"), with Beijing as the capital (or more exactly, a city whose successor began to be called Beijing, "Northern capital," only after 1368 in the Ming period, in contrast to this dynasty's southern capital, Nanjing).

Temujin was born probably in 1167. After a youth of extreme hardship and struggle just to survive, he emerged as the leader of a growing coalition of clans and tribes – first Mongol, then increasingly also Turkic. By 1206 he was acclaimed at the *quriltay*, a diet of tribal leaders convened along the upper course of the Onon, as Genghis Khan, their undisputed ruler. The title "Genghis" is still a matter of debate among scholars, although most seem to agree that it probably had the connotation of "oceanic" and thus "world-embracing."

Almost at once Genghis Khan launched campaigns aimed at lands beyond Mongolia: northward into Kyrgyz and Oirat country on the upper Yenisei, southwestward against the Tangut kingdom of Hsi-Hsia, and southeastward against the Chin, the aforementioned Jürchen dynasty ruling northern China. The Hsi-Hsia kingdom, occupying the "Kansu corridor" and the Ordos region of China, was formed in 1038 by the Tanguts, a people of Tibeto-Burman extraction. It flourished especially in the twelfth century, partly thanks to the Silk Road trade that passed through its territory. Like the Uighur *idiqut* of Turfan, the Hsia king submitted (though more reluctantly) to Genghis Khan in 1209, but later the Hsi-Hsia court reneged on the promise and the kingdom paid for this mistake with its extinction in 1227.

Despite occasional reverses, the Mongol chieftain was successful in all his undertakings. He displayed the flexibility and pragmatism characteristic also of some of his successors: a peaceful surrender or, better still, an anticipatory declaration of allegiance could enable a ruler to keep his throne and a population to escape a massacre; resistance almost invariably meant decimation or extermination. In 1209 the aforementioned Uighur *idiqut* of Turfan had the foresight to submit in time, and when summoned, to come in 1211 to pay homage to the incipient conqueror at his headquarters. By doing this he saved his kingdom, but also did the Mongols a favor whose value probably few realized at the time: for educated Uighurs entered Mongol service as bureaucrats and provided the rapidly growing empire with the kind of expertise that the initially illiterate nomads lacked.

By 1215 Beijing had fallen to the Mongols. Instead of pursuing the retreating Chin, however, Genghis Khan turned his main attention westward, possibly stimulated by an embassy from the Kwarazmshah Ala al-Din Muhammad which he received soon after his sack of Beijing. The Khwarazmshah was proposing peaceful relations and commercial cooperation.

Nevertheless, Genghis Khan's hosts soon resumed the east–west trend of Inner Asian nomadic movements. There was an important difference here, however. Whereas other such phenomena – earlier as well as later – resulted from a variety of natural or human stimuli such as climatic vicissitudes or political infighting forcing the losing party to move elsewhere, Genghis Khan and his immediate successors – basically three generations – undertook their gigantic conquests only after careful and comprehensive preparations, by means of an organization that surpassed any other such undertaking, and with a universalist vision which some historians ascribe to an ideology claiming a mandate from Heaven to rule the world. The genius that three generations of Mongol leaders displayed in all these respects, and the dimensions of the empire which they created, is a unique historical phenomenon, and it alone may justify the subsequent charisma which descent from the House of Genghis Khan retained among the Turco-Mongols of Asia for centuries to come, even after the myriad scions themselves had lost any merit or real power.

In Central Asia, as we have seen, a sudden expansion of Khwarazm eliminated both Qarakhanid authority and that of the latter's suzerains, the Qarakhitay. We have already remarked that if the Khwarazmshah Ala al-Din Muhammad did not push all the way to Semireche and finish off the Qarakhanids and Qarakhitay, it was probably because he was eyeing more prestigious conquests in the west – ultimately that of Iraq, with the promise of suzerainty over the caliph. It was the Nayman adventurer Küchlüg, as we have seen, who put an end to Qarakhitay domination in Semireche and western Sinkiang, and then briefly tormented their populations before a Mongol advance detachment under Jebe Noyon – looking in this instance more like a rescue party – redressed the situation. By 1218 Central Asia was thus divided into two main political spheres: Khurasan, Transoxania, and Fergana pertained to the Khwarazmian empire, Sinkiang and Semireche had local rulers beholden to Genghis Khan.

The Khwarazmshah perhaps wished to let his Mongol neighbor rule the Orient, but he failed to perceive how mighty an opponent had appeared on his eastern frontiers. This alone may explain the seemingly inexplicable: why in 1218 he issued the improvident order – or condoned the act of his governor claiming that spies were among the merchants – of massacring a caravan that had arrived from the Mongol conqueror's domains at the border post of Otrar on the Syr Darya. An additional, psychologically plausible trigger is mentioned by the foremost authority on these events, the Ilkhanid historian Juvayni. Inalchuq, the governor of Otrar and uncle of the Khwarazmshah, assumed the name Ghayir Khan when appointed to that post. One of the Muslim merchants detained at Otrar was his acquaintance and addressed him as Inalchuq ("little Inal") instead of as Ghayir Khan. The governor, feeling insulted, placed the embassy under arrest, and sent a messenger to the sultan campaigning in Iraq proposing the massacre. On the other hand, the opinion of some modern scholars that both the governor and the Khwarazmshah rightly suspected that there were spies among the merchants is plausible as well. The two aspects are not mutually exclusive: wounded pride of the already suspicious governor may have affected the tenor of his report to the equally suspicious shah.

One year later Genghis Khan was poised on the Syr Darya with his army, ready for the conquest of the Khwarazmshah's realm. Mongol power had by then matured into the military and organizational wonder that in the course of the next several decades so amazed the world. Ala al-din Muhammad, who had mustered troops numerically superior to Genghis Khan's, was nonetheless defeated and some months later per-

ished, as a fugitive, on an island in the Caspian. The main military operations consisted of sieges of cities or acceptance of their surrender, and
of the pursuit of the Khwarazmshah's son and successor, Jalal al-Din
Mangubirti. By 1223, all of Central Asia, including Khwarazm and
Khurasan, was under Mongol control, and Genghis Khan returned to
Mongolia. In contrast to Ala al-Din Muhammad, Jalal al-Din
Mangubirti proved to be a tough opponent whose valor and resilience
elicited the Mongols' admiration. He retreated through Afghanistan to
the Indus, which he crossed swimming to escape capture after a hard-
fought battle; it was at that point that Genghis Khan reportedly said to
his sons: "Such sons should a father beget! Having escaped the two
whirlpools of water and fire and reached the shore of safety, he will be
the author of countless exploits and troubles without number. How can
a wise man fail to take him into account?"

The conqueror had four sons by his principal wife: Juchi, Chaghatay,
Ögedey, and Toluy. They all assisted him in the main campaigns, often
receiving fairly independent and important assignments: the earliest
such example was Juchi's two campaigns against the Kyrgyz in 1210 and
1218. In Central Asia, Chaghatay and Ögedey (to be eventually joined
by Juchi) were sent to conquer the Khwarazmian capital Urgench, and
Toluy was left to carry out the conquest of Merv. The manner in which
Genghis Khan organized his empire and prepared the succession bore
traces of the frequently mentioned nomadic concept of authority: succession need not follow the principle of primogeniture, nor even be
linear. Such a system of course contains an inherent weakness: a steppe
empire was created by a single strong leader, but its preservation was
jeopardized by the absence of a regular and undisputed system of succession. This is why few nomadic empires outlasted their founders. The
Mongol empire did not escape this logic either, but for at least two more
generations a sufficient degree of discipline and cohesion assured its
continuation and further expansion. Here too this success may have
owed much to Genghis Khan's lucidity, for the choice of Ögedey,
according to some historians, was an excellent one. At the same time,
luck too was on the Mongols' side. Genghis Khan apparently expressed
his intention to name Ögedey as his successor already in 1219. The conqueror's eldest son, Juchi, taking umbrage at his father's decision, displayed a growing tendency toward insubordination while campaigning
in the Kipchak steppe. A military clash between the two may have been
averted only by Juchi's untimely death a few months before that of
Genghis Khan. Had he survived his father, a civil war might have put an

end to the Mongol empire – or at least to its expansion – before the conquest of the Russian principalities, Iran, and Sung China.

The patrimony was divided up as fiefdoms called *ulus* (whose original meaning was not territorial but military-logistical: a group of tribesmen, with their families, assigned to a leader) among Genghis Khan's sons and grandsons. The youngest, Toluy, received the home territory of Mongolia as *otchigin*, "prince of the hearth." This did not mean that Toluy inherited the title of *qaghan* or Great Khan, however: Genghis Khan, as we have seen, had designated Ögedey as his successor. Ögedey was also loyally backed by Chaghatay, the eldest surviving son, who had thus honored his father's wishes. Besides receiving the supreme title, Ögedey was given *his* ulus: central Siberia and eastern Sinkiang; his favorite area was the valleys of the Emil and upper Irtysh. The complexity (and in another sense unity) of the Mongol empire, however, is illustrated by the fact that as *qaghan*, Ögedey still used Toluy's fiefdom – the hearth of the royal house – for ceremonial purposes: it was he rather than his younger brother who carried out their father's command to found an imperial city at Qaraqorum. Chaghatay himself received Central Asia, a decision of greater importance than may have seemed at the time. Juchi, the eldest, was dead, so it was his sons who acceded to his fiefdom: Orda, the eldest, received western Siberia roughly from the River Irtysh to the River Ural; Batu, the second, was given the territories west of there. Besides these principal uluses, there also briefly existed two smaller ones apportioned to Genghis Khan's brothers Juchi Qasar and Temüge-Otchigin; they were located at the northeastern fringes of the empire, in what would today be northern Manchuria, northern Korea and the Maritime Province of the Russian Republic. Juchi Qasar's ulus partly corresponded to what was the original Mongol territory before the expansion launched by Genghis Khan.

It took two years before Ögedey was enthroned as qaghan in a ceremony that again took place on "native grounds" between the Onon and Kerulen. Benefiting from the loyalty and cohesion his brothers and nephews displayed, he set in motion two grandiose waves of conquests: the first (1230–33) put an end to what was left of the Chin kingdom in central China, the second (1236–40) engulfed the Russian principalities. The latter conquest also created the appanage promised to Batu by Genghis Khan.

The fact that the territories given to Batu still remained to be conquered reveals the supreme confidence of the Mongols that he and his generals and troops would prove equal to the task, and they did. The territories in question, geographically corresponding to western Kazakhstan, southern Russia, and southern Ukraine, had already been reconnoitered by the Mongols in 1223 at the end of the Central Asian campaign, when a detachment rounded the southern rim of the Caspian and entered that area through the Caucasus, incidentally defeating a coalition of Kipchak and Russian princes on the Kalka river near the Azov Sea. They did not stay, however, and it was not until 1238 through 1240 that the real conquest was carried out by Batu, valiantly supported by such commanders as Sübedey. Sübedey, probably the most brilliant of Mongol generals, here too masterminded the military operations (his son Uriyangkhaday later distinguished himself in the conquest of southern China and northern Vietnam). On the dynastic level, the campaign's significance was marked by the presence of representative scions of the four branches – Juchi's son Batu, Chaghatay's son (or grandson) Büri, Ögedey's son Güyük, and Toluy's son Möngke (*Secret History*, #270). The Mongol victory meant the end of Kievan Russia (more correctly, Rus') and indirectly led to the eventual rise of Moscow.

The conquest of these westernmost marches – western Kazakhstan, southern Russia, and Ukraine – represented the second major stage of Mongol expansion. It was carried out, as we have said, under the auspices of Genghis Khan's son and successor, Ögedey. Ögedey's death in 1241, almost immmediately followed by that of Chaghatay, cut short a further push into central Europe and gave rise to decade-long tensions over the succession that came close to civil war. The deceased khan's widow, Töregene, acted as regent until in 1246 her son Güyük was acclaimed qaghan. Güyük had been on bad terms with Batu ever since the Russian campaign, during which both he and Büri refused to acknowledge Batu's authority as the senior member of the group and insulted him at a victory celebration (for a dramatic rendering of the clash, see *Secret History*, #275), whereas Möngke remained unflinchingly loyal. These incidents presaged the eventual dynastic struggle and victory of the Toluyids, supported by the Batuids. That happened only in 1251, however, and for the time being the Ögedeyids seemed able to prevail. In 1248 Güyük set out for what looked like a planned attack on his cousin. Once again fate intervened to save the empire's cohesion, for Güyük died in Semireche as he was approaching Batu (who had been forewarned by Toluy's widow Sorqaqtani, and thus came with his own troops ready for war). Güyük's widow Oghul Qaymish acted as regent, but less successfully than Töregene, and in the end paid for her failure with her life, for the victors executed her together with several other members of the Ögedeyid family. In the succession struggle, the Toluyids joined forces with the Juchids (or more accurately Batuids, since this line's effective founder was Juchi's second son Batu), and by 1251 managed to have Toluy's son Möngke acclaimed as qaghan. As in the case of Juchi, Chaghatay, and Ögedey, the empire was saved by a coincidence of luck and unity between the most effective partners, the cousins Batu and Möngke. One of the results was the third and final wave of grandiose conquests.

The final phase of Mongol expansion thus occurred under the third generation Genghisids – Genghis Khan's grandsons and Toluy's sons Möngke, Qubilay, and Hülegü. Sung China and Korea on the one hand, and southern Iran and Iraq on the other, were the countries brought under Mongol rule by these three brothers. In both cases the conquest had been started by Genghis Khan himself, but only the northern regions of these areas were overrun; the greater part had to wait until the Mongols could launch the campaigns whose success must again be sought in their characteristically methodical and grandiose preparation – this time by Möngke, the Great Khan (1251–59).

The conquest of Iran and Iraq was delegated to Hülegü, and its two highlights were the destruction of the Assassins ensconced in central Iran (1256), and of the Abbasid caliphate in Baghdad (1258). It was followed by the conquest of Syria and might have included that of Egypt, but in 1259 fate intervened once more and in a manner reminiscent of 1241: the Great Khan Möngke died, and Hülegü, wary of the imminent succession contest in the Mongol empire, refrained with the greater part of his troops from participating in the march through Syria toward Egypt. Thus it happened that a smaller contingent under General Ket-Buqa was defeated in 1260 by the Mamluk General Baybars at the Syrian site of Ayn Jalut ("Goliath's Spring"), and the civil war that broke out between Hülegü's brothers Qubilay and Arigh Böke prevented the Mongols from doing what they routinely did after any setback – trying harder and succeeding the next time. The outside world, especially the Islamic one, of course knew little of this background, and the Mamluk victory had an immense psychological effect, for it broke the myth of Mongol invincibility. The conquest of Iran and Iraq, however, had been accomplished, and Hülegü, the head of the new Mongol domain, assumed the title of *ilkhan* – a khan subordinate *(il)* to the qaghan at the empire's center.

The conquest of China was launched in 1258, and was not completed until 1279 – a testimony to the vastness and difficulty of the terrain (even though only the southern half had remained to be conquered) but also to the tenacity of the Sung dynasty and their subjects. Moreover, both the Great Khan himself and his brother Qubilay took part in the military operations against the Sung. The campaign cost Möngke his life, for he died in the province of Szechwan, probably from a wound sustained during a siege, in 1259. Qubilay hurried home where he knew his brother Arigh Böke would claim the title of Great Khan. Qubilay had his troops acclaim him as *qaghan* even before they reached the ancestral grounds in Mongolia, while his brother assumed that title at Qaraqorum. Thus began the first full-fledged civil war in the Mongol empire, and although by 1264 Qubilay had emerged victorious, he soon had to wage war against other relatives who were laying similar claims; the foremost among these was Qaydu (d. 1303), a son of Ögedey's fifth son Qashi and one of the few members of the Ögedeyid branch who had survived the purges of 1251–52.

The contest with Qaydu proved to be an even more protracted affair than the conquest of China, and it presents another significant contrast. Much as Qubilay cherished the title of Great Khan and demanded submission from his relatives farther west, his main focus was on China. He no longer considered Qaraqorum as his headquarters, but moved to a site where in 1215 his grandfather Genghis Khan had destroyed the capital of the Chin dynasty. Qubilay built there his own city which became known by the Chinese name Ta-tu ("The Great City") and by the Mongol name Khanbaliq ("The Khan's City", Marco Polo's Cumbalic; the eventual Beijing). More than one-half of his long reign was devoted, as we have seen, to the completion of the conquest of China (1260–79). The remaining years – 1279 to 1294 – were spent mainly in Beijing, where Qubilay assumed the posture of a Chinese emperor and an urbanite. He took a keen interest in Buddhism, and had enough sense to let mostly able and honest officials administer the country which became a far greater source of wealth for him than any *ulus* in Inner Asia could have been. He identified with his vastly expanded new realm also in the manner characteristic of other conquerors from the north: in 1271 he adopted for his ruling house a Chinese dynastic name: Yüan ("Origin").

Meanwhile his rival Qaydu remained a steppe nomad to the hilt. The center of the originally Ögedeyid *ulus* lay between the rivers Emil and Black (Upper) Irtysh and the Tarbagatai mountains, thus in one of the geographical cores of Eurasia. From there, he could operate both east and west to enforce his claim. He met with partial or intermittent success in the west, where some princes and territories of the Chaghatayid ulus deferred to his authority. He even managed to convene a quriltay, probably in 1269 on the Talas, where the princes and chieftains of both the Chaghatayid and Ögedeyid branches acclaimed him as qaghan. He fared less well in the east, however, although his expeditions several times reached Mongolia; the fact that this had little effect on Qubilay's and his grandson and successor Temür Öljeytü's (1294–1307) solid rule in China reveals how wide the chasm between the nomadic warrior chieftain and the first two Mongol qaghans who were now also emperors of China had become. The latter now had the formidable resources of their populous realm at their disposal, while they still possessed much of the Mongol military prowess and knowhow. Qaydu's yet another attempt to seize Qaraqorum ended in defeat, and he died while retreating, probably in 1303.

With Qaydu's death, the *ulus* of the Ögedeyids definitively disappeared, its components having been absorbed by the Chaghatayids, Juchids, and Toluyids (the Yüan). This was ironical, considering the Ögedeyids' promising beginnings with their eponym as the first Great Khan and successor of Genghis Khan. The event also signified the final apportionment and stabilization of the Mongol empire. It now consisted of four basic units ruled by descendants of three Genghisid branches: (1) the Toluyid Yüan empire of China, which also comprised the ancestral lands of Mongolia, but with Beijing instead of Qaraqorum as the capital; (2) the domain of the Chaghatayids, which consisted of Transoxania, Semireche, and Sinkiang; its khans still clung to their nomadic ways and mostly lived in the valley of the Ili, while holding their annual quriltays in the vicinity of the city of Almaliq; (3) the domain of the Juchids, known to Muslim historians as the Khanate of Kipchak; it consisted of two principal uluses: that of the Batuids (later known to Europeans as the Golden Horde), and that of the Ordayids, besides some smaller appanages such as that of the Shibanids and that of the Toqay-Timurids; and (4) the Toluyid Ilkhanid realm of Persia, Iraq, and eastern Anatolia.

Chaghatay died in 1242, and was succeeded by his grandson Qara Hülegü (1241–47 and, briefly, 1252). Thus began a new stage in Central Asia's history, that of the Chaghatayid dynasty. Its duration and effect are too complex for an adequate account here, but certain salient features can be brought out. Khwarazm did not form part of "Ulus Chaghatay," but fell to "Ulus Juchi," Batu's and his successors' fiefdom in the Dasht-i Kipchak. Neither did Khurasan, which for the most part remained in the orbit of Ilkhanid Persia. Transoxania proper, Fergana, Semireche, and western Sinkiang represented Chaghatayid territories, each of which would gradually assert its own individuality and distinctive evolution. For over a century, Chaghatay's descendants lived mainly in the aforementioned steppes of Semireche and the Ili valley; most retained their nomadic lifestyle and remained pagan; the political and moral norm they respected was the *yasa*, the traditional Mongol code of behavior as formulated under Genghis Khan or, more probably, shortly after his death. Both their nomadism and yasa presented a striking contrast to the sedentarism and the *sharia*, Islamic law, of the ulus's mostly Muslim townspeople and agriculturalists. The Mongols, following the characteristic religious tolerance (or indifference) of Eurasian nomads, did not interfere with their subjects' Islam (except in those instances where Islamic rituals clashed with the Mongol *yasa* strictly upheld by Chaghatay; this applied especially to Mongol strictures against ablution in running water and against the Muslim way of ritually slaughtering animals) – nor, for that matter, with other religions such as Christianity (their rule even gave a brief opportunity for Roman Catholic proselytism), and on the whole they let the settled areas be administered by Muslim governors (monitored by usually Mongol or Turkic residents called *darughachis*). The Mongol term *darughachi*, the Turkic term *basqaq* (both apparently deriving from the verb to "press," meaning "to impress a seal"), and the Arabic term *shahna* seem to have been used synonymously by Muslim historians. There may have been shifting nuances of meaning between them, but it does appear that the term was often applied to types of functionaries translatable as "governor," "resident," or "tax collector."

A remarkable illustration of the last-named feature is the career of Mahmud Yalavach, originally a Khwarazmian merchant who was appointed governor of the settled segments – urban as well as agricultural – of Transoxania in 1225 and was then succeeded by his son Masudbek (1239–89). These Muslim governors were under the jurisdiction of the Great Khan rather than under that of the Chaghatayid ruler of the *ulus*; this gave the cities and areas under cultivation considerable autonomy, relative peace, growing prosperity, and a special cultural dimension under what some modern historians are fond of calling the *pax mongolica*: for the fact that Ulus Chaghatay was a component of the Mongol empire, and eventually lay at the geographical core of this unprecedented formation with China at the eastern end and southern Russia and Iraq at the western, reinforced Central Asia's role as the crossroads of trade and civilizations. True, this structure had begun to break down by the time Qubilay and his kinsmen came to power in the second half of the thirteenth century; moreover, their internecine struggles for both supreme and local power were compounded by the first appearance of religious "defections" – the Islamization of the Ilkhanids under Ghazan Khan (1295–1304), and of the Batuids (the Golden Horde) under Uzbek Khan (1312–41).

What then was the effect that the Mongols had on Central Asia? The picture presents a kaleidoscope of contradictions. Let us consider the cities and urban civilization. Taken as a whole, the effect was initially disastrous; most cities suffered plunder and decimation of their populations. But there were two kinds of final outcome: those that sooner or later recovered, as Samarkand, Bukhara and Urgench for example; and those that never really did, as Merv for example. Moreover, this statement applies mainly to Transoxania proper and Khurasan; the outcome was different in Semireche, where not only cities but settled life disappeared altogether. The explanation lies in a variety of factors. One is the magnitude of the original blow. Merv appears to have been fully and deliberately obliterated, for the complete massacre of its population – with the exception of some 400 craftsmen deported to Mongolia – deprived it of the labor force necessary to maintain the irrigation of its oasis and protect it from the surrounding desert. The disappearance of this Khurasanian metropolis is lamented in almost Biblical terms by a contemporary witness, the renowned Arab geographer Yaqut:

I stayed there three years, and if it had not been for the destruction that befell the country with the Tatar invasion, I would not have left Merv to the end of my days: this because of the supportiveness [of the people], gentle climate, good company, and multitude of excellent scholarly books there. When I left it, there were ten endowed libraries [in Merv] whose like I have not seen anywhere else in the world in terms of size and excellence. There were for example two collections in the main mosque; one of these was called Aziziya, because it had been endowed by a certain Aziz al-Din Abu Bakr Atiq al-Zanjani; he used to be Sultan Sanjar's *faqqa'i*, [and before that] he had been selling fruit and aromatic plants at the market of Merv, then he became the sultan's maker of drinks. He enjoyed his esteem; the library [he had endowed] contained about twelve thousand volumes. The other collection [in the mosque] was called Kamaliya, [but] I do not know [which Kamal] it was attributed to. Then there was the library of Sharaf al-Mulk al-Mustawfi ibn Sad Muhammad ibn

Mansur, located in his madrasa; he was of the Hanafite madhhab, and died in the year 494 [1101]. Then there was the library of Nizam al-Mulk al-Hasan ibn Ishaq, [again] in his madrasa; two libraries [endowed] by the Samani family; another library was in the Amidiya madrasa; [then there was] the library of Majd al-Mulk, one of the recent viziers; the queen's library (khatuniya) located in her madrasa, and the Damiriya library in one of the dervish lodges (khangah) there. The use of these collections was so convenient that at any given moment I had at home two hundred volumes or [even] more, without having to leave a deposit, [even though] their value amounted to as many dinars. I gorged myself with these collections and benefited from them, and they made me forget [my own] people and family. The qualities of this book and of whatever else I have compiled derive from the collections I have described. As I was leaving Merv, I kept turning my loving glance back toward it, and began to hum a Bedouin's composition: "The nights when we were together in Marw al-Shahijan".

Indeed, it seems that the depopulation of Merv may have originally been part of a plan that the Mongols had of converting the Murghab and other valleys of northern Khurasan – modern Turkmenistan – into one of their nomadic "habitats." They were dissuaded from doing so by advisers suggesting that taxing settled populations brings more profit than replacing them with herds of livestock; a similar case occurred in northern China where the Mongols' aforementioned Khitan adviser Ye-lü Ch'u-ts'ai saved the situation. If Transoxania escaped this fate, Semireche was less lucky: there, the conversion of a territory with a thriving urban and agricultural civilization into a nomads' steppeland did take place, although this time not as the result of a deliberate plan but through the sheer suitability – in contrast to the half-desert, half-oasis tracts of Transoxania and Khurasan – of this area for the nomads' lifestyle. It was Semireche and territories farther east where for a long time the Mongols of Ulus Chaghatay chose to live, with the aforementioned result. This transformation is vividly described by several contemporary and native observers. Here is what the Syrian geographer Shihab al-Din al-Umari (d. 1349) writes:

A person who has travelled in the provinces of Turkestan and passed through its villages told me that only scattered traces and collapsed ruins have remained; the traveller sees from afar what appears like a village with solid buildings and green surroundings, and he looks forward to finding friendly inhabitants, but upon reaching it, he finds the buildings still standing but devoid of humans except for some nomads and herders, without any agriculture, for what is green there consists of grass as the Creator has let it grow, with steppe vegetation which nobody has sown or planted.

Some two centuries later two native authors mention the consummation of this change. Babur (1483–1530) writes in his *Memoirs* (the *Baburname*):

On the north [of Fergana], though in former times there must have been towns such as Almaliq, Almatu, and Yangi, which in books they write Taraz, at the present time all is desolate, no settled population whatever remaining, because of the Mongols and the Uzbeks.

Babur's cousin and slightly younger contemporary, Muhammad Mirza Haydar, sketches in his book *Tarikh-i Rashidi* the following picture:

Some of the towns of Moghulistan are mentioned by name and described in standard works. Among them is Balasaghun. In books of repute and histories, Balasaghun is said to have been one of the cities built by Afrasiyab, and [the authors] have praised it very highly. The author of the *Surat al-lughat* gives the names of eminent men of every town. In Samarkand, he reckons fewer than ten, but in Balasaghun he mentions the names of a great number of learned and notable persons, and quotes traditions concerning some of them. The mind is incapable of conceiving how there could have been, at one time and in one city, so many men of eminence, and that now neither name nor trace is to be found of Balasaghun. Another town mentioned in books is Taraz. It is said that the Moghuls call Taraz "Yangi". Now in those steppes which they called Yangi, there are remains of many cities, in the form of domes, minarets, and traces of schools and monasteries; but it is not evident which of these ruined cities was Yangi, or what were the names of others.

Finally yet another possible effect of the Mongol invasions deserves mention. The steppes of Eurasia are the home not only of nomads but also of other creatures, marmots among them. These rodents tend to be infested with fleas, which in turn harbor the virus that can cause bubonic plague among humans. It seems that the disease was indeed affecting the Mongols but stayed at a low endemic level among them. Once it reached outsiders, however, it broke out in the catastrophic epidemic of the Black Death that by the end of the fourteenth century wiped out a good third of Europe's population. The gate of entry was, some historians suspect, the Crimean port of Caffa, and the year was 1347. Caffa was a Genoese colony at the time, and a disagreement with Janibeg, the Khan of the Golden Horde (1341–57), led to a siege of the city by the Mongols. The besiegers apparently tossed the bodies of people who had died of plague into the city, and the disease, catching on and traveling in Genoese ships, spread like brushfire – first in Egypt and then on the European side of the Mediterranean.

CHAPTER EIGHT

The Chaghatayids

About a century after the Mongol invasion, some Chaghatayid khans began to convert to Islam. This tended to happen when they chose to live not in Semireche but in Transoxania, thus among staunchly Muslim populations. True, many of their subjects there were Turks, who had entered that territory since Kök Turkic and Qarakhanid times, and some of whom nevertheless remained nomads and lived in a style not unlike that of the Mongols themselves; but the area's settled population, whether Iranian or Turkic, and whether urban or agricultural, had survived and conserved or recovered the florescence of its Islamic civilization – in contrast, as we have seen, to Semireche.

Islam played a fundamental role in the resilience of native identity and renaissance during these years of Mongol rule, and an especially seminal part was assumed by its Sufi dimension (just as it was to do centuries later during the years of Soviet rule). In the thirteenth and fourteenth centuries, the dominant orders in Mongol Central Asia were the Kubravi and Yasavi tariqas. The Kubravi Shaykh Sayf al-Din Bakharzi of Bukhara can serve as an example.

Shaykh Sayf al-Din Bakharzi had been a disciple of Najm al-Din Kubra in Urgench, the founder of the Kubraviya order of dervishes, who at a critical moment sent him with a proselytizing mission to Bukhara. While Kubra perished during the storming of Urgench by the Mongols, Bakharzi not only survived their seizure of Bukhara but subsequently attained such prestige that the aforementioned Berke (Khan of the Golden Horde, 1257–67), a convert to Islam, came to Bukhara to visit the shaykh. Moreover, Sorqaqtani, the widow of Toluy and mother of the Great Khans Möngke and Qubilay, herself a Christian, is said to have donated the considerable sum of 1,000 *balish*[1] of silver for a

---

[1] *Balish*, Persian for "cushion," was the standard thirteenth-century Mongolian monetary unit (interestingly, it rather than its Turkic synonym *yastuq* seems to have been the term used by the Mongols). See B. Spuler, "Balish," *EI*, vol. I, p. 996.

madrasa to be built and maintained in Bukhara, and gave instructions that Sayf al-Din Bakharzi become the *mudabbir* (principal) of the school and *mutavalli* (administrator) of the *waqf* endowment. Both the shaykh himself and the shrine complex that subsequently developed around his tomb in the Bukharan suburb of Fathabad illustrate the aforementioned role played by the religious establishment, especially that of the Sufi type, in the rehabilitation of Central Asia as prosperous Islamic society recovering from the devastations wrought by the Mongol invasion and its aftershocks.

Sayf al-Din Bakharzi also may have had influence on temporal Muslim power serving the Mongols. Thus when Qutb al-Din Habash Amid served as vizier under Chaghatay, the shaykh sent him what might be called an "open letter" in the form of a poem reminding him of his accountability before God for the way he treated Muslims. "Since you have been appointed to make the [divine] truth prevail in this realm, if you do not do that, what will you offer as excuse on Doomsday?..." There is of course a pardonable inaccuracy in the shaykh's address: Chaghatay certainly did not appoint Habash to "make the divine, i.e. Islamic, truth prevail," unless the assumption is that the Mongol unwittingly acted on God's command. At any rate, this exchange must have happened before 1242, the year of Chaghatay's death, thus also before the abovementioned visit by Berke and donation by Sorqaqtani. Those events suggest that the shaykh's authority kept increasing especially in the final years of his life. Little is known about the order's role under his son and first *khalifa*, Abu al-Muzaffar Ahmad, but one can infer that the internecine wars among the Mongols, characteristic of the empire after the death of Möngke and so crippling for the regions affected, could not but adversely affect the Kubravi lodge. Things had begun to improve by the time of the third generation, when in 712/1312–13 Sayf al-Din's grandson Abu al-Mafakhir Shaykh Yahya (d. 736/1335–36) acceded to the stewardship of the Bukharan branch. There was a general economic upturn, and the shaykh was able to increase the resources of the lodge whose spiritual as well as organizational center was his grandfather's mausoleum, by turning a portion of his personal wealth into a *waqf* or endowment destined for the benefit of the shrine. He purchased eleven agricultural villages, and the result was a considerable expansion of the shrine complex and of its principal function, spiritual pursuits of the community and provision of material means for doing so. Shaykh Yahya's endowment is vividly documented by three copies of the original *waqf-name* or endowment deed preserved in Uzbek libraries and published in a critical edition with a Russian translation by Olga Chekhovich.[2] In certain basic respects this document resembles most other waqfiyas throughout the Islamic world: after the praise of God, the prophet Muhammad, and the angels, the donor identifies himself and states the reasons for the donation;[3] then follows a detailed description of the property or goods constituting the endowment, and specifications of how the income from their yield should be used for the pious purpose; this in turn is followed by stipulations about the administration and activities of the endowment. The final part consists of a long list of witnesses certifying the genuineness of the document. The date of the deed is 1 Ramadan 726/1 August 1326, the first year of the Chaghatayid Tarmashirin's reign.

The Fathabad shrine was visited by Ibn Battuta a few years after the establishment of the endowment, and the famous Moroccan traveler was one of its first foreign guests. His account vividly conveys the atmosphere at the khangah:

We alighted in a suburb (*rabad*) of Bukhara known as Fathabad, where there is the tomb (*qabr*) of the learned, devout, ascetic shaykh Sayf al-Din Bakharzi, one of the great saints (*awliya*). This lodge (*zawiya*)[4] is connected with the shaykh; it is immense, and has vast endowments from which travellers are fed. Its superior, Yahya al-Bakharzi, is one of his descendants. He entertained me in his home, and invited the prominent men of the city [of Bukhara] for the occasion. The Koran-readers recited with beautiful modulations, the preacher delivered a sermon, and they sang melodiously in Turki and Persian (*ghannaw bi l-turki wa-l-farsi*). We passed there a wonderful night. I met on this occasion the Sadr al-Sharia, an excellent learned jurist (*faqih*) who had come from Herat."[5]

As for the Mongols, conversion to Islam proved at first to be risky for some of the khans. A poignant example is that of the aforementioned Ala al-din Tarmashirin (1326–34), who was deposed at the ulus's annual *quriltay* in Almaliq, and subsequently perished in flight, probably at Nakhshab near Samarkand.[6] His offence, the Mongol elders charged, was that he did not observe the *yasa* as the supreme code of the state. The fact that most of the time he disdained their company and followed

---

[2] O. D. Chekhovich, *Bukharskie dokumenty XIV veka* (Tashkent, 1965).
[3] The principal reason was of course a wish to please God and reap rewards in the next world. A secondary but important reason was the preservation of property as a source of the endower's and his descendants' income by reserving the right of often lucrative trusteeship for them.
[4] Ibn Battuta thus translates the Persian word *khangah* into Arabic as *zawiya*.
[5] *Voyages*, vol. III, pp. 27–28; *Travels*, vol. III, p. 554.
[6] *Voyages*, vol. III, pp. 41–43; *Travels*, vol. III, pp. 560–62.

a still alien religion with *sharia* instead of *yasa* as the supreme code must have further irritated them. Tarmashirin's fervor as a new convert, force-fully portrayed by Ibn Battuta, may indeed have blinded him to the mood of his peers:

> Here is an illustration of the virtues of this king [i.e. Tarmashirin]: One day I was present at the afternoon prayer, but the sultan had not yet come; instead, one of his pages came with a prayer-rug and, placing it in front of the mihrab where he usually prayed, said to the imam Husam al-Din al-Yaghi: "My master wants you to wait with the prayer while he is performing his ablutions." The imam stood up and said [in Persian]: "Namaz (which means 'prayer') birayi Khuda aw birayi Tarmashirin?" or, "Is the prayer for God or for Tarmashirin?" Then he ordered the muezzin to proceed with the prayer. The sultan came after the first two prostrations had already been performed, and he joined the prayer with the last two [prostrations] behind the assembly by the door of the mosque where people leave their shoes; he then peformed what he had missed [by himself], stood up and, smiling, walked to the imam in order to take his hand, and sat down in front of the mihrab with the shaykh imam beside him and me beside the imam. He said to me: "When you return to your country, tell [your countrymen] that this is how the lowest of Persians treats the sultan of the Turks."[7] This shaykh preached every Friday, ordering the sultan to do what is right and to refrain from doing what is forbidden and from injustice; he used the harshest language, and the sultan listened to him and wept[8]

One also wonders how the Chaghatayid elite's probably still domi-nant Mongol language and consciousness meshed with what seems to have been an increasingly Muslim Turkic identity of the convert, as the quoted passage shows. Moreover, the characterization of the imam as a Persian ascetic confirms the force of the Iranian element, whether of local origin or from Persia itself.

Tarmashirin was succeeded by several pagan khans, but his tragic end illustrates a cleavage that went deeper than the unorthodoxy – from a heathen nomad's standpoint – of a renegade khan. Semireche and the adjacent territories, from the Talas river all the way to the upper course of the Ili, together with present-day northern Kyrgyzstan, had devel-oped a special identity, that of a Mongol homeland, to the extent of acquiring a new name, Moghulistan – in other words, Mongolia. We

---

[7] Tarmashirin was a Mongol and a descendant of Genghis Khan. His reference to himself as "sultan of the Turks" suggests that he had not only converted to Islam but also became more attuned to the principal component of his subjects, the Turks, whose language he probably spoke as well as Mongolian or better; in addition, he also seems to have known Persian (the sermon that brought the sultan to tears was delivered in that language) and, obviously, Arabic in its religious dimension (the Koran). [8] *Voyages*, vol. III, pp. 36–38; *Travels*, vol. III, p. 559.

have discussed the transformation of that area from a partly settled urban and agricultural country into the grazing grounds of nomadic tribes: the new name was symbolic of the change. This development presented a sharp contrast to Transoxania and Khurasan, where no or little such change took place. It was thus no accident that this cleavage eventually took on a political form: by 1370 a Muslim Turk, Timur, had seized effective power in Transoxania and had founded a dynasty that brought an end to Chaghatayid rule there; in Moghulistan and Sinkiang, on the other hand, Chaghatayid khans ruled until the seventeenth century. Timur's emergence in 1370 can thus be considered another watershed in the history of Central Asia, a formal end to Mongol hegemony that had begun a century and a half earlier with the conquest led by Genghis Khan. During the fourteenth century, this hegemony collapsed or began to falter all over the once unified Mongol empire. In China the last khan of the Yüan dynasty, Toghon Temür (1333–70), was driven out by a national resurgence spearheaded by Chu Yüan-chang, a peasant who then became, as Hong-wu, the first emperor of the native Ming dynasty (1368–1644). In the Golden Horde, the rule of Janibeg (1341–57) was followed by years of turmoil and infighting that in 1380 enabled the Russians to win their first great victory over the Mongols: this was the "Battle on the Kulikovo field," or also "on the Don river," hence the epithet "Donskoy" by which Prince Dimitriy of Moscow, the victor over the Mongol khan Mamay, has been known in chronicles and popular memory. In Iran, the Ilkhanid dynasty had collapsed even earlier when Abu Said's death in 1335 led to convulsions that by 1353 extinguished Mongol rule there. Gradually areas ruled by people who claimed Genghisid ancestry, spoke Mongolian, and had not become Muslims shrank back to Mongolia proper and, up to a point, Moghulistan; even there, however, Islam demonstrated its resilient dynamism by eventually reasserting itself and resuming its spread farther east and over the rest of Sinkiang: for with Tughluq Timur (1347–63), the conversion of the Chaghatayid khans became definitive. Some of them, such as Mansur (1502–43) took up the *jihad*, aimed chiefly at eastern Sinkiang, as the major mission of their reign; it was during this period that formerly Buddhist places like Turfan definitively entered the *Dar al-Islam*. By then, however, even these Mongol tribes of Moghulistan and Sinkiang had probably become Turkicized linguistically; in this they followed the example of most of the other remaining dynasties claiming Genghisid ancestry except for those in Mongolia. In Transoxania, the

Chaghatayids' effective rule came to an end by 1370 with the emergence of the above-mentioned Timur, our Tamerlane (not to be confused with Tughluq Timur; *timur*, "iron" in Turkic – and its variants such as *temür* and *demir* – was a favorite name among the Turks and Mongols, present even in the original name of Genghis Khan, Temujin).

CHAPTER NINE

Timur and the Timurids

If the Mongol interlude (1220–1370) was a traumatic experience in the history of Central Asia, the Timurid period (1370–1507) can be a viewed as ultimately its most glorious one. It is true that the founder of this dynasty, Timur (ruled 1370–1405), was a ruthless conqueror not unlike Genghis Khan, and spent much of his life engaged in military campaigns that wrought similar massacres and destruction. These, however, befell other areas (Iran, the Golden Horde), while sparing Central Asia itself. At any rate, Timur's successors showed less aptitude for large-scale conquest than for enjoying the good life at home; and despite frequent infighting for the possession of this or that portion of the inheritance, many of them also encouraged culture and the arts. Timur himself had endeavored to embellish his capital, Samarkand, with grandiose architectural monuments some of which still constitute the pride of modern Uzbekistan: his own mausoleum, the Gur-i Emir ("The Sovereign's Tomb"), is the most famous example. Timur's quaint European appellation, Tamerlane, is a deformation of Timur-i lang, "The lame Timur," a Turco-Persian name as it appears in certain Persian sources because of a leg maimed by a wound he sustained early in his life.

Timur was born around 1336 in Transoxania near Kesh – later known as Shahrisabz – in the Kashka Darya region of what is today the Republic of Uzbekistan. He was a Turk of the Barlas tribe; this tribe, like many others, boasted a Mongol name and ancestry, but for all practical purposes it was Turkic. Turki was thus Timur's mother tongue, although he may have known some Persian from the cultural milieu in which he lived; he almost certainly knew no Mongolian, though Mongol terminology had not quite disappeared from administrative documents and coins.

The process by which Timur seized power, and then exercised it, was similar to Genghis Khan's; namely, through personal and tribal alliances

123

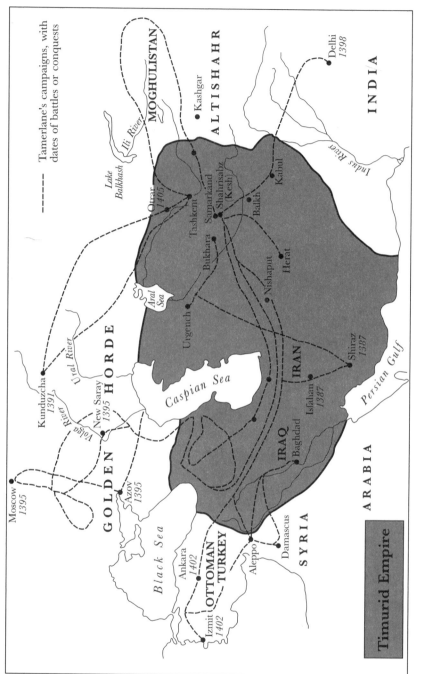

Map 4 Timurid Empire

in which he showed a mastery and endurance quite comparable to Genghis Khan's. In one respect, however, he never could match his model's stature: that of the legitimacy of rule. While Genghis Khan was unencumbered by the overpowering prestige of any rival regal figure or dynasty during his arduous beginning and ultimate hegemony, Timur's rise and hold on power was in this sense more difficult: by his time, the charisma of Genghisid descent was so great that virtually no nomadic ruler in Inner Asia, from those of the Golden Horde all the way to those of Sinkiang and Mongolia, felt legitimate unless he possessed it or could state that he was ruling in a Genghisid's name. There were various ways to do the latter: alliance through marriage or setting a puppet scion of the house of Genghis Khan on the throne and ruling in his name were the most frequent ones, and Timur had recourse to both. He thus never assumed the supreme title of khan but only that of *amir* and *gurgan*, more correctly *küregen*, a Mongol term meaning son-in-law – by virtue of his marriage to a princess of the Genghisid line. A symptom of the purely formal value of the second stratagem, that of setting up puppet khans of Genghisid descent, and of the latter's function as tools in Timur's hands, is the fact that the specific line he chose in 1370 was Ögedeyid rather than Chaghatayid. On the other hand, unlike Genghis Khan, Timur could claim the right to rule in virtue of being an Islamic monarch whose success reflected God's will. It seems, however, that this posture played a rather marginal role in Timur's case, and that the main thrust of his confidence and authority was generated by his political and military genius.

Timur's military exploits were spectacular. His campaigns spanned Eurasia from eastern Sinkiang to southern Russia – Moscow escaped sack by sheer luck – to India, Syria, and Anatolia. Sacked or conquered cities such as Delhi, Isfahan, Baghdad, Damascus, Saray, and Izmir reveal their range. He won signal victories over such adversaries as Tokhtamish, khan of the Golden Horde, in 1395, Nasir al-din Mahmudshah, the sultan of Delhi, in 1398, and Bayezid I, the Ottoman sultan, in 1402. Nevertheless, the empire he founded was in no way comparable to that established by Genghis Khan, either in size or structure; and his sons and grandsons themselves lacked the conquering verve of the successors of Genghis Khan. In this may lie one secret of "Genghisid charisma," derived from an altogether unprecedented, and subsequently unequaled, imperial edifice.

Timur died in 1405 at Otrar – a curious coincidence, for that was the locality where the incident of 1218 provoked Genghis Khan's invasion of Transoxania – as he was poised to launch his planned "conquest of China." A brief feud for succession ensued, and ended with the victory of his son Shahrukh (1409–47).

THE TIMURIDS

The realm which Shahrukh inherited included Transoxania, Khwarazm, Fergana, Khurasan, and Iran – an extensive territory by most standards, but not by those of the empire bequeathed by Genghis Khan to his sons; above all, its subsequent evolution was one of shrinkage, not continuing expansion as in the case of the second and third generation Genghisids.

Shahrukh's capital was not Samarkand but the Khurasanian city of Herat. All his principal successors resided there (except for the brief interlude of Ulugh Beg in Samarkand from 1447 to 1449), and that was where the political center of the Timurid empire had moved. Transoxania, with Samarkand as its capital, came to play a secondary but still important role. The Timurids after Timur, as we have pointed out, stood out not as conquerors but as patrons of the arts and science to a degree that makes the century of their rule, the fifteenth, the pride of Islamic civilization and of the peoples of Central Asia. At the same time we notice two distinct stages in this flowering: that of the first half of the century in Samarkand, and that of the second half in Herat. Another binary feature here is the coexistence of two strains of high culture, the established Persian one and the new Turkic one.

With Shahrukh, the Timurids of Khurasan and Iran also began to emancipate themselves from the Genghisid charisma that had still seemed to hypnotize Timur himself: for the ruler in Herat no longer felt any need for a Genghisid puppet sovereign in whose name he would reign. Instead, Shahrukh ruled fully in his own right under the more standard Islamic title of sultan, and it was with him that the remarkable symbiosis of Perso-Islamic administrative and cultural traditions with the customs and methods of the still largely tribal and nomadic Turco-Mongols came to full fruition. One of the Turco-Mongol methods of government was family rule, the division of the kingdom into appanages to be governed by various members of the royal family. The empire which Genghis Khan bequeathed as so many *uluses* to his sons is the most striking if rather special example, and the successors of Timur present a somewhat similar though more fragmented and less successful picture: for although the conqueror divided his empire among his sons and

grandsons in a manner reminiscent of Genghis Khan's, the resulting
structure lacked the initially genuine solidity, sophistication, and discipline of the Mongol edifice. Each such act of bestowal, known in the
Timurid period by the Turkic term of *soyurghal*, transferred too much
administrative, fiscal, and hereditary independence to the grantee,
without integrating his appanage into an overall structure such as had
proved its worth under Genghis Khan's sons Chaghatay, Ögedey, and
Toluy. The practice of soyurghal, although reminiscent of the *iqta*
system of central Islamic lands on the one hand and of European feu-
dalism on the other, retained its own physiognomy of excessive autonomy and military independence that contributed to the recurring wars
among the numerous recipients, who coveted their relatives' possessions
or tried to substitute their own rule for that of the ruling monarch.
Shahrukh expended much energy on efforts aimed at subduing rebellious nephews in Iran.

One fortunate exception was his own son Ulugh Beg (1394–1449) in
Samarkand; this prince, while never disloyal, ruled as the virtual
monarch of Transoxania. That is the lesser reason for which he deserves
our attention, however. It is his career and achievements as a mathematician and astronomer and as a patron of other scientists that make him
stand out not only among his Muslim contemporaries, but also among
his learned peers elsewhere, including those of Europe.

Ulugh Beg was born at Sultaniya, a town in northwestern Iran near
the road from Tehran to Tabriz. Sultaniya is noteworthy for the splendid mausoleum built there for the Ilkhanid Öljeytü by 1313. This at first
sight surprising birthplace was characteristic of the prince's childhood,
during which he usually participated in Timur's far-flung military campaigns. The great conqueror was also a doting grandfather, and he saw
to it that expert preceptors gave the child an excellent classical Islamic
education, with the standard solid grounding in Arabic and Persian. By
the time the boy was ten, Timur had given him as *soyurghal* the northeastern portion of his empire, including the city of Tashkent and extending into Moghulistan – the latter area later to be reclaimed by its
Chaghatayid rulers. The next year Timur died, however, and it was
Ulugh Beg's luck that his own father, Shahrukh, emerged victorious from
the struggle for succession in 1409. The youth was still too inexperienced
to withstand envious relatives by himself, and it took Shahrukh's intervention in 1411 to install him definitively as the subordinate but soon for
all practical purposes independent ruler of Transoxania, with
Samarkand as its capital.

Ulugh Beg soon revealed where his main interests lay when by 1420 he built a remarkable madrasa in Samarkand. It was one of three such schools erected by him: of the other two the first was in Bukhara (built in 1417), the second in Gijduvan (also spelled Ghijduvan, Ghijduwan, Gizhdavan, etc.; for the sake of consistency, we shall always use the form Gijduvan), a locality to the northeast of Bukhara (built in 1433). Madrasas, as we have said, were the highest institutions of learning in the Islamic world, a counterpart to Europe's universities, but their main mission was to train theologians and legal experts; the exact sciences were either absent or had a minor place in their curricula. Ulugh Beg's madrasa in Samarkand, however, became a famous center of mathematics and astronomy. Like some of our modern institutions, it had a real astronomical observatory, which was built by the Timurid prince on the outskirts of the city in 1428 at a place called Kuhak ("Hill") – in Tajik and Chopanata in Uzbek.

Before giving full vent to his temperament as a scholar and patron of scholars, however, Ulugh Beg tried his hand at military campaigns against his neighbors: a quite devastating one against the Chaghatayid Shir Muhammad, Khan of Moghulistan in 1424, and another against the Juchid Baraq, Khan of the Golden Horde, in the Dasht-i Kipchak in 1427. The latter war turned out to be a disaster, and Ulugh Beg barely escaped alive. This defeat was a blessing in disguise, for the prince henceforth gave up war and politics, for which he had inherited none of his grandfather's genius, and took up science, to his own benefit and that of the world of learning.

The main importance of the Samarkand madrasa lay in the scholarly activities taking place there, but it was remarkable also as a building. Its general structure is that of most madrasas: a rectangular complex of buildings enclosing a courtyard, with cells for students, one or more lecture halls, and a mosque as the essential components. Ulugh Beg's madrasa is distinguished for its spacious ground plan (81m by 56m), its location on the Rigistan or main square of Samarkand, and the complexity and wealth of its specific features and decorations. It faces the square with an imposing *pishtak* or entrance facade; the visitor passes through a front hall into one of the four lecture rooms located on each of the four sides of the school; if he proceeds farther, he enters the square courtyard (30m on each side), which he can cross in order to reach the lecture room at the end of the structure and, behind it, the mosque; the latter is an elongated prayer room (22m by 8m). The courtyard is lined by two floors of fifty units of living quarters for students and faculty, for this madrasa, like most others, also functioned as a boarding school. Each unit, apparently housing two students, consisted of a closet, a bedroom, and a living room. At each of the four corners of the entire complex stood a minaret. The walls are decorated with several types of tiles and bricks of exquisite design and workmanship. The school also had a *hammam* (bath) noted for its beautiful mosaics. Finally the inscriptions adorning the building, some bearing Ulugh Beg's name, others making such statements as "The search for knowledge is every Muslim's duty," deserve attention.

The school's main interest of course rests on the accomplishments of the scholars whom Ulugh Beg gathered there. It included such mathematicians and astronomers as Kadizade Rumi, a Turk from Bursa, Ghiyath al-din Kashi, a Persian from Kashan, and Ali Qushchi, a Central Asian Turk and thus the prince's compatriot. Both the origins and eventual destinies of these people are revealing for the cosmopolitan intellectual climate then prevailing in the *Dar al-Islam*. The community could achieve brilliant results in the exact sciences that still matched those of contemporary Europe, if it was stimulated by an inspired sponsor like Ulugh Beg. Without such support, however, scientists had little institutional framework within which to develop and flourish. Moreover, in Central Asia they had to compete not only with conventional learning represented by the madrasa as a theological seminary, but also with a rising tide of religious fervor that found its growing institutional framework in the form of a new Sufi order, the Naqshbandi *tariqa* of dervishes. After Ulugh Beg's time, it was the latter – about whom more will be said below – who set the intellectual tone in their society. This is also reflected by the example of Ali Qushchi: the noted mathematician left Samarkand for Tabriz and ultimately was invited to Istanbul by another enlightened sponsor, the Ottoman sultan Mehmet the Conqueror.

The achievements of the Samarkand group are intimately linked with the aforementioned observatory, about which a few words should be said as well. First of all, it must be emphasized that we are dealing with the period before the invention of the telescope (Galileo was the first to use this instrument in 1609). Secondly, the Samarkand observatory had by the nineteenth century so completely disappeared that only archeological excavations undertaken in 1908 managed to identify its location and unearth its extant portion. Subsequent study has led to the partial reconstruction of a giant quadrant whose segment measured 40.2 meters; it was aligned along the meridian with its southern segment consisting of an underground gallery; its presumed northern segment would have risen to a height of 30 meters above the ground. A circular structure, three storeys high (30.4m), is believed to have surrounded it, and to have housed a number of other astronomomical instruments. Observations carried on here by Ulugh Beg together with his colleagues eventually produced the famous *Zïj-i Gurgani* (also called *Zïj-i Jadid-i Sultani*) a book consisting of two parts: a theoretical introduction written in Persian, and a catalog of 1,018 fixed stars together with tables of the planets, of calendar calculations, and of trigonometry. The whole work – in particular the catalog – was based on Islamic and classical astronomy whose ultimate authorities were Hipparchos and Ptolemy, but it corrected or updated them. This was its value, which Europe's scientists came to appreciate and exploit for their own rapidly improving work. I. Greave published the first Latin translation of the *Zïj-i Gurgani* as *Binae tabulae geographicae, una Nassir-Eddini Persae, altera Ulug-Beigi Tartari* (London, 1652), and T. Hyde followed with his version, *Tabulae longitudinis et latitudinis stellarum fixarum ex observatione Ulug-beigi* (Oxford, 1665); the Polish astronomer Jan Hevelius (1611–87) included substantial parts from it in his *Atlas firmamenti stellarum*; and even after all these stages were superseded by newer data, Ulugh Beg continued to receive recognition as one of the trailblazers in man's discovery of nature. Ulugh Beg and his school also made remarkable discoveries in mathematics and trigonometry, such as the solution of the third-degree algebraic equation.

Along with these activities, Ulugh Beg displayed a breadth of vision that encompassed other, more traditional fields of Islamic learning and art. He paid attention to religious sciences, apparently memorizing the Koran in all the seven established textual traditions; and like virtually every educated Muslim of his milieu, he appreciated and wrote poetry and – a less common feature – composed music. His activity as a composer reveals that the Timurid prince's life was not all science and religion but included times of relaxation and perhaps even revelry, in which wine was no stranger. Finally Ulugh Beg also fostered the study and writing of history; in this he rivaled several other Timurid rulers, beginning with Timur himself, but he was less lucky: the *Ulus-i arbaa-i Jingizi* (The Four Genghisid Fiefdoms), written in Turki, may have been a valuable complement to Rashid al-Din's and Juvayni's famous works, but it has survived only in a few abridged manuscripts.

Ulugh Beg should have ascended his father's throne at Herat when Shahrukh died in 1447, and he did indeed make a briefly successful attempt to do so; but here again this grandson of Timur showed that he had inherited none of his ancestor's political and psychological acumen. For although he won the ensuing struggle militarily in a battle fought near Herat in the spring of 1448 against his nephew Ala al-Dawla, he failed to give adequate credit to his elder son Abd al-Latif for the victory. Instead, he showed undisguised preference for his younger son Abd al-Aziz. This was followed by another injustice and a fatal blunder: the injustice was to deprive Abd al-Latif of the treasury which he had gathered in Herat; the blunder was to return with Abd al-Aziz to Samarkand while leaving Abd al-Latif as governor in Herat. Ulugh Beg thus provoked an intense hatred on the part of his elder son while leaving him in a position to take revenge. The inevitable clash occurred a year later, when Abd al-Latif marched on Samarkand with an army and defeated his father in September 1449. Ulugh Beg returned to the city as a virtual fugitive and eventual prisoner of his irate son; worse still, the religious authorities, never fond of the prince-scientist, issued a *fatwa* (legal ruling) mandating his deposition and execution. Ulugh Beg, in a manner not uncommon in similar situations, had meanwhile set out on a pilgrimage to Mecca. He was arrested a short distance from Samarkand and beheaded on 27 October 1449. He was accorded the proper burial, however, in Timur's own mausoleum, the Gur-i Emir, where he thus joined his illustrious grandfather and other principal members of the family: his cousin Muhammad Sultan, his uncle Miranshah, and his father Shahrukh. He lay there undisturbed until 1941, when a team of Soviet archeologists led by the Uzbek scholar T. N. Kari-Niyazov opened his sarcophagus. They found the skeleton as the historical sources had led them to expect, with the head severed by what must have been a blow with a sword. Following a technique devised by Soviet anthropologists, A. V. Oshanin studied the physiognomy of the skull, and his colleague M. M. Gerasimov then sculpted a reconstruction of Ulugh Beg's face.

While Ulugh Beg was launching his and his team's scientific work in Samarkand, in Herat his younger brother Baysunghur (1397–1433), who seemed to be the favorite of their parents, Shahrukh and Gawhar Shad, also displayed a genius for culture and the arts. Both brothers revived and brought to new heights several branches of learning and art. Ulugh Beg created an ambience that made it possible for Islamic astronomy to reach back to its earlier achievements and raise it to a still higher level. Baysunghur focused on the classical epic of Iran, Firdawsi's *Shahname*, and in 1426 sponsored the compilation of what we might call a critical edition, providing it with an introduction that included the poet's biography, and had his calligraphers and painters produce splendid copies of the work; this meant a rebirth of Persia's national heritage after the traumatic centuries of destruction wrought by Genghis Khan and, ironically, Timur. The prince himself appears to have been an accomplished calligrapher, besides gathering other such artists around him; it is said that for the blue decorations in *thuluth* and *kufi* scripts on the mosaics of the great mosque his mother had built in Meshed, the architect Kivam al-din Tayyan used a pattern drawn by the prince. Baysunghur died at the early age of 37, apparently felled by the excesses of a boisterous life that included inordinate drinking, a widespread penchant among the Turco-Mongols.

We have already pointed to the relative tranquillity of the Timurid empire under Shahrukh, especially striking when we compare it to Timur's far-flung campaigns or to the grandiose conquests realized by Genghis Khan's sons and grandsons. This static state or even shrinkage, as we have implied, was more than offset by the cultural flowering, reconstruction, and well-being of the population. A fusion, complementary evolution, or sheer coexistence of a complex and multifaceted society with recognizable or even salient strains of Arab, Persian, and Turkic elements, this was a renaissance of Central Asia after the cataclysm of the Mongol invasion. One of the aspects of this peace and prosperity was further flourishing of long-distance trade on the Silk Road, which at this time seems to have involved even diplomatic and cultural contacts between the Timurids and the Ming dynasty of China. It was in this context that Shahrukh sent an embassy to Emperor Yung-lo (ruled 1403–24) in 1420; personal envoys both from Ulugh Beg and Baysunghur joined the mission, and one of the latter, Khwaja Ghiyath al-Din Naqqash, left a vivid account of the journey, which followed the age-old route through the string of oases of Sinkiang on the way to Kansu and on to Nanjing, the Ming capital. Sinkiang, along with Moghulistan, was the other remaining part of the possessions of the incumbent Chaghatayid dynasty, which by then, as we have said, had also converted to Islam; the conversion facilitated the already natural trend of this religion to spread eastward, and by the time of the Timurid mission it had reached the ancient Uighur Buddhist bastion of Turfan, which was also the easternmost city in Chaghatayid possession; farther east, the oasis of Hami, although ruled by a local prince, had the Ming emperor as its suzerain.

Abd al-Latif was himself executed shortly after Ulugh Beg's murder, and by all counts the Timurid dynasty should have fallen prey to the rapidly rising power of the nomadic Uzbeks of the Dasht-i Kipchak then and there. The Uzbek khan, Abulkhayr (ruled 1428–68), however, contented himself with helping another Timurid, Abu Said (ruled 1451–69), gain the throne in Samarkand, thus deferring a takeover that would be carried out half a century later by his grandson Muhammad Shaybani.

Shahrukh's death in 1447 and Ulugh Beg's murder two years later thus did not, as they might have done, sound the deathknell of the dynasty; quite to the contrary, the second stage of the Timurid florescence was yet to come. In political terms, it is associated with the rule of Timur's great-great-grandson Sultan Husayn Bayqara (ruled 1470–1506) and, in a special and indirect manner, with that of a still later descendant, Zahir al-Din Babur (1483–1530), who succeeded to his father Umar Shaykh's *soyurghal* of Fergana in 1494 but later, in 1526, founded the empire of the Great Mughals in India.

If we can safely say that despite Baysunghur, the most remarkable manifestation of the first stage of Timurid cultural florescence occurred in Transoxania thanks to Ulugh Beg's and his circle's scientific achievements, we must acknowledge that its second and final stage gravitated toward Herat and the province of Khurasan – excepting the special case of Babur, which will be treated in due course. The difference was not only one of geography or period; it was also thematic and linguistic. Interest in the exact sciences declined after Ulugh Beg, but literature, poetry, and the arts reached unprecedented excellence. This time the patrons and their elite went beyond celebrating the heritage of past centuries such as the *Shahname*. They created original works of their own; and both classical and new works were embellished by an ever more accomplished school of calligraphers, painters, and artists of the book. Moreover, although much of this culture continued to be Persian in both theme and language, there also appeared a remarkable blossoming of literature and poetry in Turkic. Modern scholars call this language and culture Chaghatay, thus allowing themselves a latitude defensible on the grounds that this florescence occurred among people once pertaining to Ulus Chaghatay, the aforementioned Chaghatayid portion of the Mongol empire; its creators and contemporaries, however, called the language Turki, and used various terms for themselves according to their local origin or tribal affiliation.

One of the noteworthy aspects of this stage of Timurid florescence was its bilingual nature: both Persian and Turki were common currency at the court of Herat. The most remarkable personage there was a wealthy native of that city, the poet Mir Ali Shir (1441–1501), better

known by his pen name Navai ("The Melodious One"). This lifetime
friend and informal adviser of Sultan Husayn Bayqara was a Chaghatay
Turk like the sovereign, although he did not belong to the Turco-Mongol
tribal aristocracy but was descended from the Uighur *bakhshi* (scribal)
class. He wrote in both Turki and Persian, using the pen-name Fani
("One who has reached the state of *fana* or separate existence in God,"
a Sufi concept) in the latter case; but especially his poetry in Turki
became a source of delight and inspiration throughout the Turkic world.
Its importance, however, was not confined to enjoyment and aesthetics;
for it played a catalytic role in the crystallization of Turki as a major literary language, and in fact as proof that Turkic high culture too had
come of age and could safely take its place beside Persian.

The poet himself may have consciously pursued this goal, and indeed
indirectly admitted as much by writing a prose treatise in Turki to which
he gave the Arabic title *Muhakamat al-lughatayn* ("Arbitration between the
two languages"). The two languages are Turki and Farsi (Persian), and
Mir Ali Shir endeavors to demonstrate that Turki has an edge over its
senior partner in expressiveness and in wealth of vocabulary. From
among his works of poetry, two stand out: the *Khamsa*, and the *Khazain
al-maani*. The *Khamsa* (an Arabic word based on the number five, translatable as "Quintet") is a cycle of five lyrico-epic poems modeled on the
work of the Persian poet Nizami (1141–1203). Choosing famous models
and reworking them in a new fashion was customary, and the challenge
lay in the originality and mastery displayed in the reworking; Navai,
according to both contemporary and modern critics, more than met that
challenge. The *Khazain al-maani* (again an Arabic title, as was customary:
"Treasure-troves of meanings"), on the other hand, has a less obvious
model; for it consists of four *divans* or collections of lyrico-philosophical
poems composed at various periods but organized in this fashion, by
Navai himself, toward the end of his life; their Arabic titles hint at the
contents: *Gharaib al-sighar* ("Oddities of childhood"), *Navadir al-shabab*
("Curiosities of adolescence"), *Badai al-vasat* ("Splendors of adulthood"),
and *Favaid al-kibar* ("Benefices of maturity").

Navai's importance, however, lay not only in his own compositions but
also in the role he played as the dean of the literary and artistic circle
gathered around Sultan Husayn Bayqara; its intellectual splendor shone
far beyond the confines of the Timurid realm, and especially the poetry
and art of the book that were flourishing in Herat inspired appreciation
and emulation throughout the Turco-Persian Islamic world, from India
to Ottoman Turkey and Mamluk Egypt. Finally, mention should also be

made of Navai the citizen; for he used his wealth to finance and endow extensive public works and religious as well as utilitarian buildings. The respect and popularity he enjoyed both at court and among the people surpassed that of any other contemporary, and the grandiose funeral organized by the sultan, whom he predeceased by five years, is vividly described by a participant, the historian Khwandamir.

We have emphasized the "Turkicness" both of Navai and of the Turco-Mongol, originally tribal aristocracy that ruled the Timurid realm, with the sultan at the top. This should not obscure the fact, however, that its high culture remained essentially Arabo-Persian, with the Persian dimension dominant. The corpus of Navai's poetry is mainly Turki in language, but the form is Persian; elements of Turkic folk poetry and lore play a secondary role, and endeavors to discern specifically Turkic concepts in works like the poet's *Khamsa* have yielded inconclusive results. Moreover, many personalities of the Timurid florescence were exclusively Persian in language and form; although again their sponsors and audience were of the characteristic Turco-Persian type that dominated the core of the eastern Islamic world at this time. The poet Jami (1414–92) and the painter Bihzad (d. 1537) can serve here as examples.

Jami, a native of Khargird near Herat, moved to the Timurid capital when his father became a professor at one of the madrasas there. He himself attended this school and eventually entered the same profession, but not before he had proved to possess a vaster vision and intellect. He first went to Samarkand to study the exact sciences, especially mathematics, at the famous madrasa of Ulugh Beg. Later, in his middle age, Jami again left for Transoxania, primarily to seek out the company of the Naqshbandi shaykh Khwaja Ubaydallah Ahrar (1404–90; see below). This happened while the two core provinces of the Timurid realm, Transoxania and Khurasan, were ruled by the same sovereign for the last time; for after Abu Said's death (1469) his son Ahmad succeeded him in Samarkand, whereas Herat fell to Husayn Bayqara. Jami did not return forthwith to his hometown but accompanied Khwaja Ahrar to Tashkent and Farab. He did so because of the attraction that this Sufi dervish and his tariqa exercised on him. Sultan Husayn not only did not hold this absence against him, but honored him even more profusely after his return to Herat, for by then Jami had gained renown as the other great poet of his time.

The manuscripts of some of Jami's works were copied and illustrated by the foremost calligraphers and miniaturists of the time. One of the latter may have been Bihzad (b. after 1450, d. 1537), whose fame rose to almost legendary proportions. His professional life falls into two halves: the years of apprenticeship and prime florescence in Herat (from the 1480s to 1510), and those of later maturity and old age in Tabriz (1510–1537). Otherwise little is known of his personal life; even his ethnic identity is uncertain, for the customary assumption that Bihzad was an Iranian – perhaps fostered by what must have been a pseudonym, "The Well-born One" – is not necessarily correct, and he may have had Turkic ancestry. It is significant that to his contemporaries, whether Timurid, Safavid, Ottoman or other, this did not matter; matters of ethnic pride had a different ring then, and the special case of Navai's and Babur's predilection for Turki should not mislead us. Bihzad was a painter cherished by the elite and courted by rulers of any linguistic or even denominational persuasion, from the Timurids to their rivals the Shaybanids to the latter's arch-enemies the Safavids. Like other Muslim painters of his time, Bihzad concentrated chiefly on book illustration, but separate scenes and even portraits on loose sheets and medallions have also survived: thanks to him we thus have pictures of such personalities as Sultan Husayn Bayqara and the Uzbek ruler Muhammad Shaybani, and what may have been a self-portrait. In general, however, most of his work consisted of illustrating such classics of Persian literature as Nizami's *Khamsa* or Sadi's *Bustan*. Bihzad is praised for a mastery both of attention to details such as facial expression and of superb composition depicting dramatic battle scenes and tender romances, besides a tasteful combination of color with a special role assigned to blue. The Timurid painter's almost proverbial fame served as a symbol for the excellence of the book arts of his time, and for the legacy he left through his disciples and influence, especially in sixteenth- and seventeenth-century Bukhara and Tabriz.

Our discussion of the highlights of Timurid civilization could logically conclude with Zahir al-Din Babur (1483–1530) and his great autobiography, the *Baburname*. Let us first glance at the political and social evolution of Transoxania and the rest of Inner Asia in the course of the fifteenth century.

We have already mentioned Abu Said, a nephew of Ulugh Beg and thus Timur's great-great-grandson (1424–69), who by 1451 emerged as the victor in the contest for Ulugh Beg's succession in Transoxania, partly thanks to the help he had received from the Uzbek khan Abulkhayr. Quite naturally Abu Said wished to inherit the totality of the Timurid realm, besides coveting Herat as the most prestigious city. He lost the prize to his cousin Abu l-Qasim Babur, but he resumed the struggle after the latter's death in 1457 and finally succeeded; this meant that from 1458 to 1469, the core of the former Timurid empire was again and for the last time united under the same sovereign, and Abu Said had reasons for satisfaction; for despite recurrent rebellions and invasions from restless relatives and nomadic Uzbeks, Moghuls – the Turco-Mongols of Moghulistan – and Kalmyks, there was relative peace and prosperity in Khurasan and Transoxania. This reflected, for example, the praiseworthy interest that Abu Said took in measures designed to improve agriculture, both through more humane taxation of peasants and through irrigation projects carried out by an able minister. The sultan further consolidated his position on the home front by courting a religious brotherhood that was fast becoming a formidable political and economic force: the Naqshbandi order of dervishes, in particular its superior, the aforementioned Khwaja Ubaydallah Ahrar. A few words about the origin and subsequent role of the Naqshbandi order up to the end of the Timurid dynasty may thus be called for.

The eponym of the order, Khwaja Baha al-Din Naqshband (1318–89), was born in Qasr-i Hinduvan, a village situated a short distance to the northeast of Bukhara, and spent the greater part of his life in his birthplace where he was ultimately buried. The shrine that developed around the saint's sepulcher became – and is now again after the Soviet interlude – a famous place of pilgrimage, and led to a change of the site's name from "Qasr-i Hinduvan" ("Castle of Indians") to "Qasr-i Arifan" ("Castle of Gnostics," i.e. Sufis). Like most sedentary inhabitants of the area, Baha al-Din Naqshband was a Tajik, in other words, a person of Persian language and culture. His early years – in the 1320s and 1330s – coincided with the aforementioned expansion of the Kubravi shrine at Fathabad, and no one could have foreseen that the youth from the nearby village was going to inspire a Sufi order that would in due course completely eclipse or absorb the senior *tariqa*. Yet he did, and the process shows both features common to those of most other orders and unique ones. Unlike Najm al-Din Kubra for example, Baha al-Din Naqshband never traveled to the central Islamic lands in quest of learning, but received his formation in his hometown of Bukhara or nearby; and his training, poorly documented, seems to have had a mystical slant from very early on. He received guidance from several shaykhs; a crucial role was played by Khwaja Muhmmad Baba Sammasi, who apparently divined the kernel of sainthood in Baha al-Din soon after his birth, adopted him, and in due time turned over the youth's education to his *murid* and *khalifa* Khwaja Amir Kulal.

Sammasi was the fifth *khalifa* (successor) of Khwaja Yusuf Hamadani, a Sufi from Merv (d. 1147) active mainly in Bukhara. Yusuf Hamadani's honorific title, *khwaja*, subsequently became the hallmark of most of the shaykhs of the two great Sufi orders, the Naqshbandis and Yasavis, that were formed by his khalifas (the title, in fact, became an alternative name for the Naqshbandis as *Tariqa-i Khwajagan*, "Order of the Khwajas").

We shall return to the Yasavi order below. Here we want to resume the story of the Naqshbandis. Khwaja Yusuf Hamadani's immediate khalifas – those formed by him personally – had not yet quite coalesced into a full-fledged tariqa: that role was reserved for Baha al-Din Naqshband, although even in his case it was more *his* khalifas, starting with Khwaja Muhammad Parsa (d. 1419), who gave the movement the palpable structure of a Sufi order. Baha al-Din Naqshband's chief merit may be sought in the form of the Sufi path he devised for guiding an adept toward mystical experience, and in the personal example he gave as the role model on this path. An original feature of his spiritual development apparently was its relative independence, or at least little dependence on living preceptors. The already familiar poet Jami tells us in his biography of saints *Nafahat al-uns* that Baha al-Din Naqshband was an "*uwaysi*," a Sufi who could be guided by a master who was absent, whether in terms of space or time. The master here was Khwaja Abd al-Khaliq Gijduvani (d. 1220), the fourth *khalifa* of Khwaja Yusuf Hamadani. Unlike many other Sufi shaykhs – including successive Naqshbandis – who wrote voluminous treatises, Baha al-Din Naqshband left little written record either about himself or expounding his path, but Jami was able to base accounts attributed to him on the memories recorded or passed on by the shaykh's disciples.

Jami narrates a number of short question and answer excerpts in which Baha al-Din, in response to questions, expounds the methods of his Sufi path. Its main elements were "reclusion in the community" (*khalvat dar anjuman*), "externally amongst people" (*bi-zahir ba khalq*), "internally with God" (*bi-batin ba Haqq*). These seemingly somewhat contradictory principles are based on the idea that a dervish need not leave the world in order to attain or retain his retreat conducive to closeness to God, but that in fact he can live a life externally identical with that of other people, while his internal life can very well be that of a devout ascetic committed to God. An important concomitant was the practice of silent zikr (*zikr-i khafi*). As we have said in the introductory chapter, *zikr*, "remembrance [of God by repeating – sometimes for extended periods – the words *La ilaha illa Allah*, 'There is no divinity but

Allah']," is an essential element in Sufi religious practice and thus in the practice of virtually every *tariqa*. Most orders do this by means of vocal litanies (*zikr-i jahri*) performed in unison by groups of dervishes, but Baha al-Din Naqshband came to prefer the above-mentioned silent zikr, *zikr-i khafi*, a practice an individual can engage in mentally, with no participation or interference from the external world – and thus do it under practically any circumstances.

These radical and hitherto atypical principles or methods were to have far-reaching consequences for the evolution of sufism in Central Asia. Baha al-Din Naqshband himself seems to have led a life of modesty if not seclusion in his home village, except for two pilgrimages to Mecca and a visit to Herat. He could hardly have foreseen what effects his charismatic personality and bold innovations (*pace* Khwaja Abd al-Khaliq Gijduvani's admonition to avoid *bida*, [impious] innovation) would have. The latter could be rationalized into a system that allowed subsequent generations of Naqshbandi dervishes to claim a hefty share in the economic and political life of their society, to form virtual dynasties of wealthy landowners, businessmen, political advisers or even, on occasion, rulers. In an inverted or paradoxical sense, it may also have served them well during the Soviet interlude, when external display of sufism was in their case not needed for a continuation of their *tariqa*.

Baha al-Din, in fact, may not have been fully aware that he was founding a Naqshbandi order. This was not atypical of the founders of other orders or even of religions, nor was the fact that during the first years after his death the community of his disciples and the path he had preached was all but smothered in Bukhara by the mainstream religious establishment of the *ulama*, clerics of the secular type. Baha al-Din Naqshband's aforementioned khalifa Khwaja Muhammad Parsa (d. 1419) found a more congenial atmosphere in Herat, where Shahrukh looked with favor on him, and eventually supported his victorious return to Bukhara. Nevertheless, fifteenth-century Herat overshadowed Bukhara as a center of Naqshbandi power, chiefly because of the support received from the Timurid elite of that city. The order also scored tremendous success in Samarkand, again thanks to the bonds it forged with the Timurid rulers of Transoxania. Only in the sixteenth century did the order's birthplace begin to surpass the other centers, no doubt because the founder's shrine reasserted its prestige, but perhaps even more because the most important Shaybanid rulers resided in Bukhara; while spiritually spellbound by the shaykhs, they also found it politically opportune to support them there.

The abovementioned Khwaja Muhammad Parsa is also credited with having anchored the Naqshbandi tariqa in a firm doctrinal base through his numerous writings. Of a different but equal importance was Mawlana Yaqub Charkhi, originally from the Afghan city of Ghazni, for he was the *murshid* of the most striking personality among Baha al-Din Naqshband's khalifas, the aforementioned Khwaja Ubaydallah Ahrar (1404–90).

Khwaja Ahrar was born into a well-to-do family of landowning and mercantile shaykhs from the village of Baghistan near Tashkent, but he did his formal studies in Samarkand at a *maktab* and a *madrasa*. Attraction to Sufi ways made him drop the latter school and leave Samarkand for Herat, the reputed center of Naqshbandi *pirs*. It was there or, according to another report, in the nearby province of Chaghaniyan that he linked up with Mawlana Charkhi. The *murid* eventually returned to his hometown, presumably released by his *murshid* as a mature *khalifa* and *murshid*, and his subsequent trajectory amply corroborated those expectations. He again left Tashkent, this time definitively for Samarkand, in whose suburb of Kafshir (now called Kamangaran) he founded a khangah as the kernel of the Ahrari lodge.

Khwaja Ubaydallah Ahrar's charismatic personality gained enormous prestige, political role and wealth both for him and for his family as well as for the Naqshbandi *tariqa*. The shaykh's intervention may have contributed to the victory of the Timurid Abu Said in the contest for the throne in Samarkand in 1451, and his subsequent influence on the ruler was only matched by that he exercised on Abu Said's son and successor, Sultan Ahmad (1469–94). His prestige and activities were far-flung and included Herat. At both centers he acted as a moral mentor, protector of the Muslim community, and shrewd businessman, exhorting the sultans to abolish unlawful taxes and be generous to the Sufis. The wealth of the order, through waqf endowments, and of his family through successful business ventures (the two are not always easy to distinguish) grew exponentially under Khwaja Ahrar's tutelage, and not only in Samarkand but in other parts of Central Asia as well. Like the order's founder Baha al-Din Naqshband, Khwaja Ubaydallah Ahrar was a strong upholder of the *sharia* and Sunni Islam, and the moral force the tariqa possessed served the next dynasty, that of the Shaybanids, well in their life-and-death struggle with the Shii Safavids.

The Ahrari branch of the Naqshbandi tariqa will come up again in our discussion of the next dynasty to rule Central Asia, the Shaybanids. Here a few words about the decline and demise of the Timurids in

Central Asia, and about their special reincarnation in India, are needed. Abu Said's foreign policy, to use a modern term, brought him a victory on his most important frontier, for in terms of legitimacy of rule, the Timurids' chief rivals were the Chaghatayids of Moghulistan, who could at any time lay claim to Transoxania as their heirloom; and this is exactly what Esen Buqa (1434–61) attempted to do. Abu Said stood his ground on the battlefield, but he also had recourse to a political stratagem by giving the Moghul khan's elder brother Yunus, since his childhood exiled to Shiraz, the means with which to drive Esen Buqa back and recover the western part of Moghulistan. An alliance ensued between Abu Said and Yunus Khan (1461–86) that was not only political and military but also personal, for two of the Timurid's three sons – Ahmad and Umar Shaykh – married two of the Chaghatayid's three daughters, Mihr Nigar Khanim and Qutlugh Nigar Khanim (the third daughter, Khub Nigar Khanim, was married to a member of the prestigious Dughlat clan). The alliance even helped Abu Said to more effectively block the recurrent raids of the nomadic Uzbeks from the north across the Syr Darya into Transoxania. The Timurid sultan, however, took a step – apparently encouraged by Khwaja Ahrar – that was to be his undoing: he intervened in a war between the two Turcoman dynasties of northwestern Iran and eastern Anatolia, the Aqqoyunlu and Qaraqoyunlu, and in 1469 lost both the campaign and his life.

If Abu Said's nemesis was the Aqqoyunlu chieftain Uzun Hasan, the Timurid dynasty succumbed a generation later to another Turkic conqueror, the Uzbek khan Muhammad Shaybani. Despite his illustrious Genghisid ancestry, this khan was linguistically a Kipchak Turk and culturally a devout Muslim. He had spent a part of his youth in Bukhara as a student of Islamic science and culture, at a time when the Naqshbandi order of dervishes was in the ascendant throughout the Timurid realm. Muhammad Shaybani, however, retained his attachment to another Sufi order, that of the aforementioned Yasaviya.

The Yasaviya could be considered a sister order of the Naqshbandiya for two reasons: both originated in Central Asia, and both traced their roots back to the same Sufi master, the aforementioned Khwaja Yusuf Hamadani. Khwaja Yusuf was a Persian, and, as his *nisba* suggests, came from Hamadan. His early training took him to Baghdad, where he studied the standard Islamic sciences, especially *fiqh* (jurisprudence) under the renowned Shafii jurist Abu Ishaq al-Shirazi. He rose in stature to the point of becoming a teacher himself, but then he abandoned these formal sciences and chose the Sufi path instead. Rather than attaching himself to a prominent *living* master, he came under the spell of a long-deceased one, Bayezid Bistami (d. 874; in this sense he could be considered an *uwaysi*, like his spiritual descendant Baha al-Din Naqshband), whose mystical utterances had inspired successive generations of Sufis before the actual formation of tariqas. Yusuf Hamadani's own charismatic personality gained him a following of disciples and invitations from other centers of Islamic culture, especially Merv, Herat, and Bukhara. He lived in what was politically the empire of the Great Seljuks, and his final years coincided with the reign of Sultan Sanjar and of his vassals the Qarakhanids – two Turkic dynasties ruling the chiefly Iranian part of the *Dar al-Islam*. It was in Bukhara that the shaykh formed four of his principal *khalifas*: after the death of the first two, Ahmad Yasavi was honored with that role in 1160, but did not stay long there; turning over that function in this still essentially Iranian city to Abd al-Khaliq Gijduvani, he returned to his hometown of Yasi, presumably to spread his master's path among his fellow Turks. The Tariqa-i Khwajagan, the Path of the Khwajas thus named after its initiators' title (that is, after Khwaja Yusuf Hamadani), found its characteristically Central Asian expression through two branches, the Iranian one starting with Khwaja Abd al-Khaliq Gijduvani in Bukhara, the Turkic one with Khwaja Ahmad Yasavi in Yasi. The Iranian branch, as we have seen, coalesced into a full-fledged tariqa only two centuries later with Khwaja Baha al-Din Naqshband and then assumed this founder's name as the Naqshbandiya; the Turkic branch, on the other hand, flourished from the beginning as the Yasaviya, and became the great Sufi order of Central Asian Turks.

Khwaja Ahmad Yasavi did not live long after his return to Turkestan, for he died in 1166 or 1167 (the Hijra year 562). Those six or seven years among his countrymen sufficed, however, for the khwaja to gain a great following of steppe Turks, and he passed the torch to khalifas who insured the preservation of his memory and of the type of Sufi poetry he devised for the benefit of unsophisticated but enthusiastic recent converts. The didactic poems he composed became known as *hikmats* ("wisdoms," a loanword from Arabic), and gained tremendous vogue among Central Asian Turks, and, through imitators, even among those of Turkey. In its present form, the *Divan-i Hikmat* could hardly have been penned by him or written down by others directly from his utterances. The earliest extant copies can be dated to the seventeenth century, and their language is demonstrably not the Turkic of the twelfth century. It certainly harbors the spirit which inspired the Khwaja and with which he inspired his followers and imitators, however.

As an organized *tariqa*, the Yasaviya eventually succumbed to the Naqshbandiya (or, more exactly, was absorbed by it), but less completely than the third of the Central Asian tariqas, the Kubraviya. As we might expect, it retained some of its identity among the Turks of the Kipchak steppe despite the inroads of the Naqshbandiya. Moreover, Khwaja Ahmad Yasavi's enduring example and tomb continued to play their role as powerful anchors of Islam among the nomads of the Kipchak steppe or, if we shift the chronological angle, among the Muslim masses of Kazakhstan and the other Central Asian republics. As in the case of other Muslim saints, his tomb became the goal of pilgrimage of the common people as well as the object of veneration and generosity of the mighty. We have already mentioned the magnificent mausoleum erected over his tomb by Tamerlane in 1395. A century later Khwaja Ahmad Yasavi's example served as inspiration to another conqueror, this time an Uzbek Turk from the Kipchak steppe – the aforementioned Muhammad Shaybani. The khan was not only a man of the sword but also of the pen, the author of politico-religious poetry and treatises written in Turki. One of this monarch's ghazals expresses his veneration for Ahmad Yasavi, and the process that transformed the town of Yasi into the great place of pilgrimage of Turkestan:

> Avliyalar sarvari ol Shah-i Türkistan emish * Yär yüzini nuri tutqan
> Mah-i Türkistan emish…
> Dedilär: "Qayda barur sen, köp Samarqandda vali!" * Bu Shabani
> arzusi Dargah-i Türkistan emish.

(The chief of saints is this Lord of Turkestan * He is the Moon of Turkestan shining over the face of the earth … People said: "Where are you going? There are many saints in Samarkand!" * I, Shabani, had one desire: the Court of Turkestan [i.e., the shrine of Ahmad Yasavi].)[1]

---

[1] A. J. E. Bodrogligeti, "Yasavi ideology in Muhammad Shaybani Khan's vision of an Uzbek Islamic Empire," *Harvard Journal of Turkish Studies* 18 (1994): 41–56.

CHAPTER TEN

The last Timurids and the first Uzbeks

Abu Said was succeeded by two of his sons, the aforementioned Ahmad (ruled 1469–94) and Mahmud (ruled 1494–95), and by the latter's son Ali (ruled 1495–1500), pale personalities whose long years of rule may have been helped – or may have received a special reprieve – by a contrasting set of circumstances south and north of Transoxania. To the south of the Amu Darya ruled their pacific relative Sultan Husayn Bayqara; to the north of the Syr Darya the nomadic Uzbeks, Kazakhs, Moghuls, and Kalmyks were still too busy fighting each other or consolidating their newly formed positions to challenge the Timurids beyond frequent but transitory raids.

We have already mentioned the Uzbek khan Abulkhayr (1412–68; khan from 1428), who in 1451 helped Abu Said gain the throne in Samarkand. Abulkhayr had a Genghisid genealogy going back to the conqueror's eldest son Juchi, as did most other Genghisids of the Dasht-i Kipchak. He traced his descent, however, not through Batu of the Golden Horde or Orda of the White Horde, but through a younger brother of theirs, Juchi's fifth son Shiban. Shiban too had received an *ulus*, but farther north, near the southern outcroppings of the Ural Mountains. His descendants benefited from events which had set the khans of the White and Golden Hordes – the Ordaids and Batuids – against each other and which had also provoked Timur's devastating intervention in the last years of the fourteenth century, for the Shaybanids managed to penetrate into what we might call a power vacuum in the territories of the White Horde all the way to the Syr Darya. By then the dynasty of the Shaybanids was an extended family whose various scions were vying for power, with little effect on their neighbors; but this changed when in 1428 the sixteen-year-old Abulkhayr was proclaimed khan.

Abulkhayr, despite his illustrious Genghisid ancestry, was a Muslim and, linguistically and culturally, a Turk, like most Turco-Mongol

144

nomads of the Dasht-i Kipchak; by then this transformation may have taken hold even among the Moghuls, the Chaghatayids of Moghulistan. The tribes under his leadership, most of which spoke the Kipchak form of Turkic, had their own lineages and appellations, but they were also known by the general name of Uzbek, a word whose origin is a matter of debate; it may indeed derive from Uzbek (or, more correctly, Özbeg), khan of the Golden Horde who ruled from 1312 to 1341. Abulkhayr spent the early years of his reign still deep in the steppe as khan of Tura and Sibir, rivers and sites just east of the southern Urals; but in 1431 he swept down beyond the Syr Darya all the way to Khwarazm, where he seized the city of Urgench. This was a rather eccentric expedition without lasting results, except as a precedent and proof of what the vigorous nomads of the steppe were still capable of doing. The aforementioned intervention of 1451 that enabled Abu Said to win the Timurid succession in Samarkand was another demonstration of that vigor, and a preview of a still bolder step that Abulkhayr's grandson Muhammad would take half a century later. Abulkhayr, however, perhaps still under the spell of Timurid prestige, contented himself with moving the political center of his fiefdom to the right bank of the Syr Darya, where he secured several key fortified towns and chose one of them, Sighnaq, as his headquarters. The Uzbek khan's move made him the immediate neighbor of Timurid Transoxania and put him almost as close to Chaghatayid Moghulistan. The implications or potentials of this situation were, however, suddenly thrown into confusion by the irruption of the Kalmyks.

This was the first of the three major invasions of these nomads from the east. The second took place a century later, and the third in the seventeenth and eighteenth centuries. The Kalmyks were Mongols, but of a group that differed from those of Genghis Khan in the dialects they spoke and in the territories they ultimately inhabited; hence also the designation "Western Mongols," which the Kalmyks and related tribes have received in linguistic literature. Once again, the application of their several ethnonyms is rather confusing and abitrary; Oirats, Ölöts, Jungars are genuinely Mongol names, whereas Kalmyk has Turkic etymology; we prefer it here for several reasons. First of all, only those Western Mongols who penetrated into Central Asia and southern Russia are normally associated with this name (those who stayed farther east and had contacts, both peaceful and bellicose, with Eastern Mongols and China are usually called Oirats or Jungars); it is also for this reason that Kalmyk is the term most often found in Muslim sources, where it usually appears, however, as Qalmaq; Kalmyk is the form prevalent in Russian, while in English the spelling has also appeared as Kalmuck.

The Kalmyk khans began to play a political role in Mongolia soon after the return of the Genghisid Yüan Mongol dynasty, driven out of China by the Ming in 1368. They only briefly and marginally rose to positions of supremacy there, but greater fortunes awaited them farther west, in Sinkiang and the Kipchak steppe, and even at times in Tibet and Khwarazm. Their case of course immediately suggests an analogy with the Genghisid Mongols. It did have similarities, but there were more fundamental differences: the essential one being the fact that Kalmyk invasions were of the elemental, common type resulting chiefly from migrations of whole tribes, not a repetition of the boldly conceived, carefully planned, yet grandiose conquests that made the events of the thirteenth century a historically unique phenomenon. The victories, conquests, and empires realized by the Kalmyks were only a pale shadow of those achieved by their eastern cousins. In two respects, however, both groups ultimately experienced a similar fate: abandoning their ancestral shamanism, they converted to Buddhism; and they ended up paying a heavy price, demographically, to the demands of their far-flung campaigns and migrations and of their new religion. Moreover, the third stage of Kalmyk expansion, directed toward China and Russia, collapsed in part because radical transformations had begun to tilt the military balance away from the mobile steppe nomads toward modern armies of sedentary states equipped with artillery.

In 1456, however, the Kalmyk khan Amasanji, irrupting with his mounted troops into Moghulistan and the Kipchak steppe, defeated the similarly armed horsemen, first those of Yunus Khan and then those of Abulkhayr. The Uzbek chieftain fled to Sighnaq and withstood the Kalmyk siege, but the defeat meant a fatal blow to his prestige, and he ceased to play the role that had held such promise for him. An additional and specific effect of this disaster was the withdrawal of many Uzbek tribesmen from Abulkhayr's authority; these nomads joined the followers of two other Genghisids, Janibeg and Girey, who had recently established the nucleus of a new khanate farther to the northeast, deeper within the territory of the former White Horde in what is now central Kazakhstan. These rebel Uzbeks came to be known as Kazakhs, a word believed by some to have the same etymology as the Russian "kazak" and the English "Cossack." Later, when contacts between Russians and Kazakhs intensified in the eighteenth and early nineteenth centuries, "Qazaq" sounded to the Russians too much like "Kazak," and by the time the territory was annexed to their empire, the conquerors changed the name of its inhabitants to Kirghiz (Kirgizy) in order to distinguish it from that of the Cossacks. The real Kyrgyz (to use the latest official – and indeed correct – spelling) themselves were then called Karakirgizy ("Black Kyrgyz") or Dikokamennye Kirgizy (a somewhat unflattering appellation, approximately meaning "Wild rock Kyrgyz," possibly a reference to their mountainous habitat), in distinction from the "Kirghiz," that is, Kazakhs. This curious reshuffling of ethnonyms caused endless confusion in Western travel and even scholarly literature. The restoration of correct terminology based on the native ethnonyms was one of the better measures taken by the Soviets at the conclusion of National Delimitation in 1925.

Luckily for the Timurids, the Kalmyk khan made no serious attempt to push south of the Syr Darya, and the new threat further diminished with Amasanji's death in 1470. Abulkhayr predeceased Abu Said by one year, in 1468, and for the rest of the century the Uzbeks, Kazakhs, Moghuls, and Kalmyks were too busy elsewhere, as we have said, to bother the Timurids. Of Abu Said's other sons, one, the aforementioned Umar Shaykh, received as *soyurghal* Fergana, where he ruled until his death in 1494. The fiefdom was not the only lot that fell to him; for like his brother Ahmad, he married a daughter of Yunus Khan (the aforementioned Qutlugh Nigar Khanim) and thus secured a distaff (cognatic) Genghisid ancestry for his progeny. As a result, his son Zahir al-Din Babur, born in 1483, was a Timurid on the sword (agnatic) side and a Genghisid on the distaff (cognatic) side. By the time Babur died in 1530, the world had changed beyond recognition, but it is doubtful whether this ruler himself was aware of these transformations, except for those upheavals of which he was the unfortunate victim, the reluctant catalyst, or the inspired creator. His early dream was the Timurid throne in Samarkand, but both he and the dynasty succumbed in that contest to the khan of the Uzbeks, Muhammad Shaybani. It was almost as a refugee that Babur crossed the Hindukush to Kabul with his troops, and his epic conquest of India, which was consummated with the battle of Panipat in 1526, never became more than a consolation for him. Babur defeated the sultan of Delhi, Ibrahim Lodi, and the Great Moghul Empire of Hindustan was born. He died a mere four years later in Agra, probably unaware or unconcerned that in the course of his relatively short life the Europeans had crossed the oceans and had reached India by rounding Africa, had discovered America, and had circumnavigated the globe. Nor would he have known that in Europe itself a new world of another kind was making its first stirrings, a world in which man would discover his potential for understanding and mastering nature to a degree undreamt of before. For Babur's life coincided with a time of ferment in Europe which we have labeled the Renaissance, a somewhat inaccurate term because the rebirth of classical or past values was only the initial aspect of this revolution.

CHAPTER ELEVEN

The Shaybanids

rise
description
Decline
movements

Muhammad (ruled 1500–10), the Uzbek khan who dashed Babur's lifetime dream, accomplished more than that, for he put an end to the Timurid dynasty and replaced it with his own, that of the Shaybanids (1500–99) and thus carried out a restoration of Genghisid rule in Central Asia. He was a grandson of Abulkhayr, whose Genghisid lineage, as we have seen, went back to Genghis Khan's grandson Shiban. The *nisba* derived from the Mongol name was vocalized as Shaybani by Muslim historians who preferred its unrelated Arabic approximation. By 1501 Muhammad Shaybani had crossed the Syr Darya, seized Samarkand from Babur's cousin Ali, and fought off all attempts by Babur and other contenders to recover their Timurid heirloom; seven years later, in 1507, he made a successful lunge for the other Timurid prize, Herat, so that the greater part of Central Asia now passed under the control of the nomadic Uzbeks from the Kipchak steppe. Up to a point the change was only one of degree. The Shaybanids were Turks like the Timurids, although they spoke a different dialect, Kipchak, in contrast to the local Turki; both led a partly nomadic way of life and had a tribal social structure, although again this must have been more pronounced among the newcomers; both were Sunni Muslims, like the bulk of the sedentary population of the area; and the Uzbeks had been sufficiently exposed to Arabo-Persian Islamic culture to ensure a fundamental continuity. The subsequent behavior of the Shaybanids does indeed reveal more continuity than change, and it may be that our infatuation with the intellectual brilliance of Timurid Herat and Samarkand, and our fascination with such figures as Ulugh beg, Husayn Bayqara, Mir Ali Shir Navai, Bihzad, or Babur, has tended to obscure this continuity.

In other respects, however, changes *were* taking place. We have already referred to the most dramatic and radical changes that were gathering momentum elsewhere in the world. Although geographically remote, they would eventually have an impact on Central and indeed on much of Inner Asia. To begin with, the transcontinental Silk Road, whose principal lines passed through Sinkiang and Transoxania, now had a European rival in the long-distance maritime route. At its most extreme, the effect of this change could be viewed as one that transformed a once busy crossroads of world trade into a landlocked backwater. How much and how soon this new competition began to affect the economic and cultural climate of Inner Asia is a matter of debate, and the tradition-ally held view that it was responsible for the decline of this part of the world may have to be modified. The decline did happen, but unevenly, gradually, or later, and it was a protracted process caused by complex factors among which the enhanced importance of maritime trading routes may have played only a marginal role. On the economic level, six-teenth- and even seventeenth-century Central Asia in fact seems to have experienced a period of prosperity and growth, due to the internal dyna-mism of its agricultural and mercantile population, to the policies of such rulers as the Shaybanid khan Abdallah II, and to the rise of such trading partners as Mughal India and imperial Russia. Nevertheless, some of the seeds of the eventual transformation were sown in the six-teenth century, but they may be better understood if we substitute the concept of a decline of the East with that of a rise of the West. On the one hand, Europe, including Russia, began to undergo a technological and economic revolution – to be later followed by an industrial and mil-itary revolution – that would dramatically increase its strength but that was completely missed by the rest of the world; and on the other, a newly created ideological antagonism between Central Asia and Persia would gradually contribute to the landlocked region's cultural provincialism or atrophy, again a phenomenon that under the Shaybanids was camouflaged by the influx of luminaries fleeing Safavid persecution.

In 1501, the same year in which Muhammad Shaybani had van-quished the Timurids and become the sovereign of Transoxania, Shah Ismail, having overcome the Aqqoyunlu Turcomans in western Iran, founded a new dynasty, that of the Safavids; their first capital was the city of Tabriz. Both Muhammad Shaybani and Shah Ismail were Turks, at least on the linguistic level; and Ismail, like most rulers of Iran since the Seljukids, based his military strength on Turkic tribal elites and man-power. Both men claimed Iran as their legitimate prize for a variety of reasons, one of which was a sense of mission: the Safavids were Shii Muslims, whereas the Shaybanids were staunchly Sunni, and both sides claimed to be fighting for a sacred cause.

The inevitable clash occurred by the end of the decade near Merv; the Uzbeks lost, and their khan fell on the battlefield. Over the next few years the shah of Persia tried to press the newly gained advantage against Muhammad's successor Köchkunju (ruled 1512–31), but without avail. The confrontation ended in a lasting stalemate, pitting schismatic Iran against orthodox Central Asia for 300 years, right down to the latter's conquest by Russia in the nineteenth century. Besides having intrinsically harmful effects (especially on the cultural plane), this antagonism – although mitigated by periods of peaceful contacts and even pragmatic cooperation – isolated Central Asia from Turkey and the Arab lands of the Near East: for hostile and powerful Iran, unified by the dynamic ideology of Shii Islam, to a considerable degree blocked direct communications of merchants, pilgrims, and scholars between the eastern and western parts of the Muslim world.

Shah Ismail was less lucky in the war against his other Sunni adversary, the Ottoman sultan Selim I, who in 1514 defeated him at Chaldiran, a locality in eastern Anatolia. The Turkish victory owed much to powerful artillery, a new weapon that was revolutionizing warfare in Europe at a time when most Muslim rulers still ignored or shunned this innovation.

Besides Selim, another exception was Babur, but only after he had left Central Asia and launched his conquest of India; there, thanks to his qualities as a leader and to the devotion of his troops, but also to occasional use of artillery, he defeated larger armies of rajas and sultans supported by elephants. There are indications that the Timurid – or Mughal – conqueror acquired this innovation through master armorers who came from the Ottoman empire. Nevertheless, much as we may find Babur's conquest of Hindustan captivating and important, that alone would not secure him the special place which he occupies among history's great figures. He stands out because of the *Baburname,* an autobiography compiled partly on the basis of a diary he had kept. Written in his mother tongue, Turki, it is one of the most original and engaging prose works of pre-modern Muslim literature, for Babur vividly and faithfully portrays life as he saw and experienced it, his own and that of the world around him, whether human or natural. And since it was a rich life in many ways, the *Baburname* is also a priceless document for our study of the period's society: its natural setting, social customs, political events, noteworthy personalities, literary and artistic pursuits, not counting Babur's own military campaigns and the adventures he encountered in the process. He himself emerges as a vigorous but compassionate leader, family man, and friend, and as a perceptive literary critic and observer of nature. After Babur, the history of the dynasty he founded at Agra only indirectly and marginally touches upon our theme. His descendants considered themselves and indeed were Timurids, as well as Genghisid Mongols, as we have seen; the name "Great Moghuls" popularized in the days of British rule would have startled them. Turki must have been spoken among them for at least two more generations. Bayram Khan (d. 1561), a minister who served Babur's son Humayun and grandson Akbar, wrote poetry in both that language and Persian. Gradually, however, as the emperors began to marry Indian women, and the dynasty adjusted itself to the new milieu, the Persian veneer of India's Muslim culture reasserted itself. Thus in 1590 Akbar instructed the *khan-i khanan* (prime minister) Abd al-Rahim Mirza, Bayram Khan's son and successor, to translate the *Baburname* into Persian.

The endearingly personal and unusual character of the book is conveyed right from the start. Babur dispenses with the lengthy conventional preface so customary in his period, and defines an important date – the year 1494 – and the milieu in which he spent the first part of his life:

In Ramadan 899, in the province of Fergana, I became king (*padishah boldum*). Fergana is one of the provinces of the Fifth Climate. It lies at the edge of the inhabited world. On the east is Kashgar; on the west, Samarkand; on the south, the mountains that delimit Badakhshan; on the north, although there used to be cities like Almaliq and Almaty and Yangi (whose name is recorded in books as Otrar), [settlements] have been ruined by Mongols and Uzbeks, and none remain.

It is a small province, abounding in grains and fruits. It is surrounded by mountains except on the west, where there are Samarkand and Khujand. No enemy can invade it in winter except from that direction.

The river Sayhun [Syr Darya], known as Khujand River, comes from the northeast and traverses this province westward.

Babur then describes the provinces, towns, and qualities in charming detail, and this is what he says about the speech of the people of his hometown, Andijan:

The people are Turks (*Eli Türktür*). There is no one who wouldn't know Turki, whether among the townspeople or at the bazaar. Their speech is identical with the written idiom, for the literary compositions of Mir Ali Shir Navai, although he was born and bred in Herat, are in this language

Both the *Baburname* and Navai's works are written in the aforementioned special kind of Turkic which eventually came to be called

Chaghatay, especially by modern Turcologists. As we can see from the quoted passage, Turki was the more common term still in Babur's time, and only gradually did it become reserved for the everyday spoken language, whereas Chaghatay was reserved for the literary idiom. A century after Babur, another Central Asian prince, Abulghazi Bahadur Khan, incisively commented on the difference (see below, p. 185–86). Babur's remark that Navai wrote in Turki, "although he was born and bred in Herat," is also significant. This Khurasanian city lay in a Persian-speaking area, but in Navai's time it was the capital of the Timurids, whose court language was primarily that of the Turco-Mongol elite of the time – Turki. Babur eventually passes to what we could call a "prosopography" of the Turco-Mongol elite of his time. He appropriately starts with his father:

[Umar Shaykh Mirza] was born in 860 [1456] at Samarkand. He was Sultan Abu Said Mirza's fourth son . . . He was a Hanafite, a devout believer, and would not skip any of the five daily prayers, and throughout his life he made up those he had missed. He frequently recited the Koran, and was devoted to His Eminence the Khwaja Ubaydallah [Ahrar]. He felt greatly honored by engaging in discussions with him, and his Eminence the Khwaja in turn addressed him as "[My] son." He was fully literate, used to read the two *Khamsas*[1] and the *Masnavi*,[2] [but] most of all the *Shahname*.[3] He had poetic talent, but no ambition to compose poetry. His sense of justice reached such a degree that [once] when he received a report that a snowstorm in the foothills to the east of Andijan had decimated a one-thousand-tents strong caravan coming from China with only two individuals surviving, he sent tax collectors to record all the assets of the caravan; although there were no heirs present, he of necessity kept [these goods] for a year or two, after which he invited them to come and reclaim their property.

Nevertheless, the sixteenth century was in Central Asia a Shaybanid century, despite Babur's valiant efforts to stem the tide. We have suggested that continuity with the Timurid fifteenth century was stronger than the innovations introduced by the change of dynasties and by a renewed influx of nomadic Turkic tribes. After the vain hopes that Muhammad Shaybani had cherished to found an empire still more legit-

---

[1] The first *Khamsa*, in Persian, was by the poet Nizami (1141–1209); the second was the aforementioned Turki version by Navai.

[2] *Masnavi-i Manavi*, a long Sufi poem in Persian composed by Mevlana Jalal al-Din Rumi (1207–73). Nizami was born and spent his whole life in Azerbaijan; Rumi, although born in Balkh, lived mainly in Anatolia (Rum), then ruled by a local branch of the aforementioned Seljukid dynasty.

[3] Firdawsi's *magnum opus*. Babur's remarks illustrate the by then refined, chiefly Persian culture of the Turco-Mongol elite.

imate than that of the Timurids and to reinstall Sunni rule in Iran, the khans spent their efforts on reaffirming their hold on Transoxania, Fergana, and eastern Khurasan. Samarkand and Bukhara took turns or combined as the ruling family's capitals, while Balkh became the heir presumptive's seat, and Tashkent the center of the fourth major appanage. Most khans endeavored to stimulate agriculture through new irrigation works and dams, to encourage the crafts and trade by building more caravanserais and bridges, and to please God and the religious class by building more mosques, madrasas, and khangahs, showing munificence to both the secular clergy and the powerful Naqshbandi *tariqa*. They also proved to be respectable patrons of the book arts, in both the artifactual and literary sense; Tabriz may have been the principal beneficiary from the collapse of Timurid Herat, with Bihzad and other craftsmen joining the ateliers of the Safavid rulers, but Shaybanid Bukhara and Samarkand also received their share.

From among the khans of the dynasty, three may be singled out as especially prominent: the realm's founder Muhammad Shaybani or Shaybak Khan (1500–10), his nephew Ubaydallah Khan (1533–39; effective ruler since 1512), and Abdallah Khan (Abdallah II, 1583–98; effective ruler since 1557).

The founder, as we have said, competed with Shah Ismail for the Timurids' Iranian heritage and lost both the contest and his life in this struggle. His successors contented themselves with periodic raids into Persian Khurasan, although in 1528 the contest just missed a reprise of 1510 when Shah Tahmasp (1524–76) defeated Ubaydallah Khan, this time partly thanks to the cannon which the Persians learned to appreciate since the disastrous battle of Chaldiran. Ubaydallah was nevertheless less reckless, and by the time he added the official title to his effective exercise of power, he was paying more attention to the conditions in his own territories. He acquired the reputation of a just and pious ruler, and his favorite city Bukhara flourished to the point where Shaybanid civilization came close to a revival of the achievements of the Timurid age. One example is the splendid Mir Arab madrasa, built in 1535 under the khan's auspices but through the direct sponsorship of the *shaykhulislam* (chief justice) Mir Arab. This madrasa also served as the final resting place for both the khan and his cleric; and it was one of the two Islamic seminaries in Uzbekistan (the other was the Barak Khan madrasa in Tashkent) which were allowed to function throughout the Soviet period. Here is what Ubaydallah Khan's younger contemporary Haydar Mirza

(1499–1551), the author of the *Tarikh-i Rashidi*, says about the khan and Bukhara under his rule: [4]

It is my view that in the course of these last hundred years, in the whole world where there have been sovereigns, none like him has been heard of or seen. First of all he was a *Muslim* ruler, devout, pious, abstinent. He scrupulously applied the tenets of the Holy Law to all matters of religion, confession, common-wealth, state, the army, and the populace, and would not suffer a deviation from this law by a hair's breadth. In the thicket of valor he was [like] a charging lion, in the sea of generosity his palm was [like] a pearl-bearing shell – an individual adorned with an array of good qualities. He wrote the seven styles of calligraphy, the *naskh* best of all. He copied several exemplars of God's Word [i.e. the Koran] and sent them to the two noble cities [i.e. Mecca and Medina]. He also wrote *nastaliq* well, and had a divan of poetry in Turki, Arabic, and Farsi [Persian] to his credit. He was versed in the art of music, and his compositions are [still] sung by musicians. [In short,] he was a sovereign [endowed] with every kind of laudable quality. In his time, there was such a gathering of learned men and such a large population in Bukhara, which was his capital, that one was reminded of Herat in the days of Sultan Husayn Mirza.

Abdallah Khan at first ruled in the name of his father Iskander, whose succession he secured only after tough competition with several relatives of the extended dynastic family; for the principle of family rule, characteristic of Turco-Mongol nomads, still lingered on, and other princes supported by their parties of Uzbek emirs were ready only too often to throw off allegiance to the khan or to start claiming the throne for themselves. Even after the consolidation of his rule and during his official tenure of office, Abdallah had to wage campaigns to reaffirm his authority. Beyond the limits of Transoxania to the south, Khurasan remained the chronic battleground with the Safavids, but just east of there, northern Afghanistan – the ancient Tokharistan – became a prized Shaybanid territory. The importance of Balkh, its capital, turned partly on the role this city came to play as a communications and commercial link between Central Asia and Timurid or Mughal ("Great Moghul") India, where Babur's antagonism to the Shaybanids gave way, by the time of his grandson Akbar (1542–1605; ruled from 1556), to friendly relations which, besides trade, included diplomatic and cultural contacts. A good-neighbor policy and even alliance and personal contacts also developed

[4] Mirza Haydar Dughlat, *Tarikh-i-Rashidi: a History of the Moghuls of Central Asia*, tr. E. Denison Ross, London 1898, p. 283; and ed. and tr. W. M. Thackston, Harvard University Department of Near Eastern Languages and Civilizations, 1996, vol. 1 (Persian text) pp. 233–34; vol. 2 (English translation), p. 182.

between the Shaybanids and the Chaghatayids; the latter continued to rule Moghulistan and the Tarim basin throughout the sixteenth century and were to do so, although with diminishing authority, even into the seventeenth.

The Shaybanid century also witnessed a steady growth of Naqshbandi sufism in Central Asia, with intimate relations between this order and the khanly families matching or even surpassing those under the Timurids. The beginnings seemed inauspicious, however. Shaykh Muhammad Yahya, the son and *khalifa* of Khwaja Ubaydallah Ahrar, may have sided with the opponents of Muhammad Shaybani at the time of the Uzbek conquest, and the khan, although outwardly deferential to the shaykh, did not forgive him. Feeling threatened, the dervish resolved to perform the *hajj* and set out for Mecca, but did not get far: a party of soldiers sent by hostile Uzbek emirs overtook him in Khurasan and killed him, together with his companions including three of his sons. The khan, although not openly involved in the murder, was suspected of at least condoning it.

The Ahrari lodge soon recovered from this tragedy. Shaykh Ubaydallah Ahrar's prestige among the Uzbeks had even preceded their conquest of Transoxania, a fact exemplified by the name of Muhammad Shaybani Khan's nephew and eventual successor Ubaydallah Khan, apparently named after the shaykh. The Khwaja's tomb generated the growth of the Ahrari shrine, which in turn functioned as the headquarters of the Naqshbandi tariqa. The Ahraris became a virtual dynasty of Sufi saints, religious authorities, owners of agricultural and manufacturing properties not just around the eponymous shaykh's shrine but in many other parts of Central Asia. They drew their wealth from their role as trustees (*mutavallis*) of the continually growing *waqf* endowments serving the shrine and its components, from personal property (*milk*) which they were able to accumulate thanks to the largesse of royal as well as other devout well-wishers, and through the economic activities of investment, manufacture, and trade they and their agents engaged in. Uzbek archives contain a number of *waqfnames* certifying numerous endowments, as well as other documents revealing the Ahraris' economic strength and the respect shown them by the khans.

One such document was issued in 1543 by Abd al-Latif Khan (1540–52; Ubaydallah Khan's successor), certifying the ownership and tax-exempt status of several properties of Shaykh Muhammad Yahya. This individual was a grandson of Khwaja Ubaydallah Ahrar and son and namesake of the founder's murdered successor. The document can also serve as an indicator of the Turkic dimension of this otherwise so Arabo-Persian cultural atmosphere, for unlike the Qarakhanid *waqfname* from the eleventh century written in Arabic, and that from the fourteenth century written in Persian, this order (*nishan* or *yarliq*) is in Turki (although peppered with Arabo-Persian technical terms). Here are a few excerpts:[5]

We recognize that it befits our lofty discernment to treat with affection, munificence, respect, consideration, and veneration the great descendants and noble progeny of His Holiness Khwaja Ubaydallah...[A report] has reached our august presence that since several years a certain person (*bir kishi*) has taken and, contrary to the pure *sharia*, has held as usufruct (*mutasarrif bulghan irmish*) the properties and buildings (*amlak va havilar*) listed on the back of this document, – [properties belonging to] Khwaja Muhammad Yahya, may his elevated status last, who is a grandson of the above-mentioned Holiness . . . Since our generous thought is favorable in the highest degree to the above-mentioned well-born person, having examined and understood [the situation] . . . we seize and give [this grantee] as *soyurghal* (*musallam tutub soyurghab birdik*) the properties and objects, orchards, store, and houses with yards . . . so that the representatives of this high person annually receive the tithe (*dahyak*) and double tithe (*dahdu*) of the revenue, and expend it on their sustenance . . . [Moreover, tax collectors] must not levy taxes (*mal*) [of any kind on these properties] – such as the double tithe (*mal-i dah-du*), the extraordinary expenditure tax (*kharj-i kharajat-i avariz*), *bikar* (unemployment tax?), [impose] corvée (*hashar*), homestead tax (*dudi*), tithe (*dahyazdah*), gift (*savari*), wedding tax (*madad-i toyana*), victory tax (*fathana*), or any [other] tax imposed on this province . . . [The properties in question] should be known as free and exempt . . . And if there is a general levy (*Agar harz-i kull bulsa*), the perceptor and scribe (*harraz va bitikchi*) must not enter [these properties] in order to [include them in the] collection . . . [These officials] must not act contrary to [our] order (*yarlighin khilaf itmesinlär*), and must not request [every] year a new order and regulation (*nishan va parvancha*) . . . [This] order (*nishan*) was issued (lit. written, *bitildi*) on the third [day] of the month of Shawwal, the year of the hare (*tavushqan yil*), the date being 950 [of the Hijra; 30 December 1543].

Another illustration of the status, vitality and adaptability of Ahrari shaykhs is the fact that they retained the benefits of royal favors throughout the vicissitudes of Central Asian politics, when power passed from one branch of the Shaybanids to another, and, at the turn of the century, from the Shaybanids to the Toqay-Timurids. Their authority even invaded the hitherto unchallenged preserve of the secular clergy, for in

---

[5] Published, together with a Russian translation and commentary, by Olga D. Chekhovich, *Samarkandskie dokumenty XV-XVI vv.: O vladeniyakh Khodzhi Akhrara v Sredney Azii i Afghanistane* (Moscow, 1974), doc. 16 on pp. 311–15.

1580 Khan Abdallah II transferred the office of *shaykhulislam* of Samarkand to them. This office, somewhat comparable to that of our Supreme Court, was then occupied by the Ahraris on a hereditary basis at least until the end of the seventeenth century.

The Ahraris, however, did not retain a monopoly on dynastic prominence and wealth among the Naqshbandis. First of all, the shrine that developed around the tomb of Baha al-Din Naqshband near Bukhara possessed an implicit primacy over the Ahrari shrine near Samarkand, a fact illustrated by the choice of the more important Shaybanid khans to be buried at Qasr-i Arifan near the "Great Khwaja's" sepulcher. Secondly, at least two other dynasties of Naqshbandi shaykhs arose in the course of the sixteenth century and came to play significant roles. The founder of one of these dynasties was Ahmad Khwajagi Kasani, also known as "Makhdum-i Azam" ("The Great Master"; 1461–1542). As his *nisba* suggests, he hailed from Kasan, a town in northern Fergana near present-day Chust. He left it for Tashkent, presumably in order to become a *murid* of Muhammad Qazi Burhan al-Din (d. 1515), one of Khwaja Ubaydallah Ahrar's *khalifas*. Becoming a *pir* and *murshid* himself, he gradually gained fame as a saintly person and author of many learned treatises. His renown reached Ubaydallah Khan, who showered favors and gifts on him, enabling him to build a khangah in Bukhara near his residence. The khwaja subsequently became a *murshid* of both Tajiks and Uzbeks – of such people as Muhammad Sultan Juybari (1481–1563) and Jani Beg Sultan for example. The former is important as the founder of the dynasty of Juybari shaykhs, Naqshbandi custodians of the shrine of Imam Abu Bakr Ahmad ibn Sad in the village of Sumitan just west of Bukhara; the latter as an Abulkhayrid Shaybanid whose branch, the Janibegids, gained primacy in the mid-sixteenth century and held it until the end of the Shaybanid period. As for Imam Abu Bakr, he was a tenth-century theologian described in a sixteenth-century document as the person whose tomb was provided for by a *waqf* endowed by himself; the document also states that the waqf was established for the benefit of the imam's male descendants, and implies that Khwaja Sad Juybari is at the moment in that position. Khwaja Sad (d. 1589) was Muhammad Sultan Juybari's son and successor, and with him began the prodigious growth of the Juybari shrine at Sumitan on the western outskirts of Bukhara. He enjoyed the gratitude and favors from the khan Abdallah II, a grandson of Jani Beg Sultan, who did not forget that his dynastic branch owed much to the Juybari shaykhs for its victory. The shrine, which came to be known as Char Bakr, grew into a complex that included a khangah, a mosque, a madrasa, and the endowments supporting it dramatically increased after the Janibegid victory in 1557. The Juybaris too increased their wealth by becoming involved in commerce, manufacturing, and agriculture, and sent their agents as far as Moscow on trade missions. On the third side of this special triangle, these Naqshbandi *pirs* and wealthy entrepreneurs came to occupy the post of *shaykhulislam* in Bukhara, an honor and function also attained, as we have seen, by the Ahrari *pirs* in Samarkand. What is more, this post, which in Central Asia tended to be hereditary, was held by the Juybaris through the nineteenth century.

To return to Khwaja Kasani (Makhdum-i Azam), he spent the greater part of his life in the village of Dahpid or Dahbid just north of Samarkand, where his tomb became the nucleus of a shrine. His main importance lies in the Naqshbandi lodge and dynasty which this shaykh founded in Kashgar, however, although he himself never seems to have visited that region. Invited there by the Chaghatayid khan Abd al-Rashid Khan, Makhdum-i Azam sent instead two of his sons as deputies, a step that was the first act in the remarkable expansion of Naqshbandi presence in Sinkiang and China herself. That story will come up in our account of Sinkiang at this and subsequent periods.

The Chaghatayid khans were by the sixteenth century solidly Muslim, as were their tribesmen themselves; they now had, however, to fight or absorb new arrivals, chiefly the Kalmyk and Kyrgyz nomads. We have already mentioned the Kalmyks' first wave, which during the second half of the fifteenth century engulfed an area roughly corresponding to Moghulistan. It seems that about the same time, and possibly as allies, the Kyrgyz also made their appearance in this area. Unlike the Mongol Kalmyks, the Kyrgyz were Turks. We have described them as residents of southern Siberia around the upper Yenisei river who in the ninth century swept down into central Mongolia and destroyed the Uighur kingdom; most of the Kyrgyz stayed in their ancestral area, however, and that was where the Genghisid Mongols found them and incorporated them into their growing empire. There is little specific information as to how the Kyrgyz functioned subsequently, but it does seem that they participated both in the original expansion westward and in the campaigns waged by Genghis Khan's successors, especially those of his great-grandson Qaydu (c. 1262–1303). Many probably stayed in the mountainous part of western Moghulistan – modern Kyrgyzstan – from then on, although some may have temporarily moved back closer to their old homeland, fleeing from Timur during his campaigns of the

1380s. Other Kyrgyz, however, had remained in their ancestral territories, and Kyrgyz chieftains played a role in the attempts of the Oirats to wrest Mongolia from the Genghisids in the first years of the fifteenth century. The Oirats, as we have seen, did not succeed there, and the thrust of their energies again swerved in the opposite, western direction; during the fifteenth and sixteenth centuries the Kyrgyz became their frequent targets. The majority of the Kalmyks, however, did not stay in western Moghulistan but changed their abode through a series of tribal and political movements that stretched from western Mongolia to southern Russia; meanwhile the Kyrgyz became receptive, in their new and definitive homeland, to the inspired proselytism of dervishes from Transoxania or to the forcible methods of the Chaghatayid khans themselves, and became Muslims, whereas the Kalmyks converted to Buddhism.

The Chaghatayid khans, despite the dynasty's charismatic lineage, saw their authority circumscribed by certain factors. One was the usual concept of family rule, perhaps overshadowed in their case by simple rivalries among the various scions; the geopolitical contrast between Moghulistan proper, Kashgaria (Altishahr), and Uighuristan (the area of Turfan) may also have had an effect. Another factor was the influence of some tribal leaders, especially those of the Dughlat clan, whose power at times surpassed that of the khans themselves. A third factor was the penetration of the Naqshbandi order of dervishes. Encouraged by the hospitality of Chaghatayid rulers, a number of them moved from Transoxania to Kashgaria; one of them, Khwaja Muhammad Yusuf, so impressed the pious Said Khan (1514–32) that the latter contemplated becoming a dervish himself; the Khwaja dissuaded him from doing so on the grounds that a temporal ruler should not abandon his duty of championing Islam with temporal means. The main impetus, however, came with the aforementioned Ahmad Khwajagi Kasani (Makhdum-i Azam), who indirectly set an example of this principle himself, for both the khangah which his emissaries founded at Kashgar and the sons whom he engendered by two wives became the foundation of two memorable dynasties in Kashgaria: those of the White Mountain (Aqtaghliq) and of the Black Mountain (Qarataghliq) Khwajas. These dervish aristocrats vied for an ever greater share of temporal power with the Chaghatayids, and in 1678 replaced them altogether as the rulers of the Altishahr portion of Sinkiang until their suppression by the Chinese in 1759.

From among the noteworthy Chaghatayid khans, the aforementioned

Yunus Khan (ruled 1461–86), his grandson Mansur Khan (ruled 1502 or 3–1543), the latter's brother Said Khan (ruled 1514–32), and Said's son Abd al-Rashid Khan (ruled 1532–70) stand out. The fact that the last three monarchs' reigns overlap illustrates the concept of family rule, for Mansur Khan's domain was Moghulistan proper and northern Altishahr with Aksu as the capital, whereas Said Khan ruled from Yarkand in the south. The most interesting personality in this society, however, is not a prince of the dynasty but a member of the Dughlat clan, Mir Haydar or Muhammad Haydar Mirza (1499–1551), who wrote the already quoted *Tarikh-i Rashidi*, a memorable account of the dynasty's history and of the country under their rule. Mir Haydar was a younger contemporary and a cousin of Babur (his mother, the afore-mentioned Khub Nigar Khanim, was a younger sister of Babur's mother Qutluq Nigar Khanim), and the analogy between their works immediately springs to one's eyes. In contrast to the *Baburname* written in Turki, however, the *Tarikh-i Rashidi* was written in Persian.

One of the bonds between the Shaybanids and the Chaghatayids was wariness of their immediate neighbors to the north, the Kazakhs of the eastern Dasht-i Kipchak. These were the territories of what is now central and southern Kazakhstan, where the formation of a distinct Kazakh nationality, triggered by the aforementioned and almost anec-dotal defection of Janibeg and Girey, really took shape during the six-teenth century. Political structure in the Dasht-i Kipchak had become much looser than that bequeathed by the Mongol empire, and the most constant feature was the unceasing ebb and flow of alliances, conflicts and nomadic movements. The Genghisid ancestry of the Shaybanid line continued to play a role, but it failed to produce personalities strong enough to create a realm and nation that could play a major role. A new destiny for Inner Asia had indeed begun to dawn by the middle of the sixteenth century, and by the turn of the seventeenth its course was firmly set.

CHAPTER TWELVE

The rise of Russia, the fall of the Golden Horde, and the resilient Chaghatayids

The rule of Husayn Bayqara (1469–1506) coincided for the most part with that of Ivan III (1462–1505), the *knyaz* or prince of Moscow (or Muscovy, to use the contemporary English name of the principality). If the Timurid's reign shone with the sophistication of cultural life in Herat, the Muscovite's stood out for different reasons: definitive emancipation from the "Tatar yoke" in 1480, and rapid unification of other principalities under that of Moscow. By the time Ivan III's grandson, Ivan IV "the Terrible" (1530–84), ascended the throne in 1547, Muscovy had become Russia, a nascent empire ruled by an ever more powerful tsar.

The rise of a unified Russia was mirrored, in reverse fashion, by the decline of her erstwhile Mongol suzerain. The Khanate of Kipchak, the "Golden Horde" of the Russians, had already been dealt a heavy blow when Timur devastated its capital city Saray and other economic centers in 1395, and it was in due course rent asunder by mutual rivalries that by 1466 produced four separate khanates: the "Great Horde," a paltry remnant of the once mighty khanate, located to the west of the lower Volga; and the Khanates of Kazan, Astrakhan and the Crimea. In 1502 the ruler of the last-named khanate, Mengli Girey, did Russia's work at her adversary's expense, for he destroyed what was left of the "Great Horde," thus removing the one unit that might have attempted a reconstitution of the Golden Horde.

The Mongol rulers and people of the three remaining khanates had by then adopted Islam and become Turkicized, and were carrying on lively relations with other Islamic countries, especially with Central Asia and the Ottoman empire. The Ottoman Turks in 1475 seized the southern fringe of the Crimea and subsequently extended their suzerainty over that khanate; and in the sixteenth century they made attempts to establish a cooperation, a kind of "common front," with the Shaybanid Uzbeks. The new alliance was directed primarily against Shii Iran, but for a brief period, under Sokollu Mehmet Pasha – grand vizier from 1565 to 1579 – its target was also Russia. This far-sighted Ottoman statesman was rightly concerned: Ivan IV had in two vigorous campaigns destroyed the khanates of Kazan (1552) and Astrakhan (1556) and annexed their territories, an unprecedented reverse at a time when no obstacles to constant expansion of the *Dar al-Islam* led by the mighty Ottoman empire appeared possible; worse still, the conquests created almost overnight a new and powerful neighbor for the Ottoman and Central Asian Turks. Sokollu conceived the bold plan of digging a navigable canal from the Don to the Volga rivers and thus making it possible for Ottoman ships to reach the Caspian Sea. The project was attempted in 1569 in cooperation with the Crimean Tatars, but lack of enthusiasm both at the empire's center and at the khan's court stymied the work until it was abandoned with the approach of winter. Had it succeeded, the Turks might have been able to liberate Astrakhan; and had they subsequently adopted an expansive policy in competition with Muscovy for the still Turkic and sparsely populated Kipchak steppe instead of engaging in interminable and ruinous wars against the Habsburgs in the Balkans or Venice in the Mediterranean, their empire might have ultimately fared better. If Sokollu Mehmet feared Russia, however, few of his co-religionists shared his apprehension, and for some time to come her behavior seemed to prove them right. The Russians appeared contented with having reached the Volga estuary and the shores of the Caspian, but otherwise did not press their advantage farther south toward Ottoman or Shaybanid possessions; instead, their expansion took an eastward tack, beyond the Ural mountains into the vast expanse of Siberia. The only serious resistance, that of the Khanate of Sibir, which the Russians attacked for the first time in 1582, collapsed by 1600 with the death of its khan Küchüm. By 1649, the Russians reached the Pacific and anchored their presence there by constructing the fortification of Okhotsk; and a mere three years later they staked out their ownership of Siberia against possible Mongol or Chinese claims by erecting, in the continent's geographical center, the fortress of Irkutsk. It was the most grandiose growth of a continental empire ever – with the notable exception of Genghis Khan's; but fundamental structural differences separated the two, for the Mongol empire was little more than a frail artificial edifice, whereas the Russian empire was to become solid as a rock.

Closer to home, Russia waited for another age before annexing the Crimea in 1783 and conquering Central Asia between 1865 and 1884;

the latter conquest, however, began in the eighteenth century, if we include northern Kazakhstan in this area. Each step had its special characteristics and internal as well as external ramifications. The Siberian expansion appears at first sight to have been almost elemental, undertaken by the spontaneous dynamism of Cossacks and merchants. It was methodically propped up by strategic or logistical settlements, however; above all, Moscow just as relentlessly extended firm government control over the freshly acquired possessions, thus becoming a permanent neighbor of much of Inner Asia as conceived of in this study.

Until directly attacked by Russia, however, the people of Inner Asia remained absorbed in their more immediate goals and conflicts. The Kazakh khans, despite witnessing the expansion of the infidel giant to the north and his absorption of the khanate of Sibir, had their sights turned chiefly southward toward the Syr Darya and Ili and the territories beyond these two rivers. Their khan Qasim (1511–23) was the first personality under whom the recently formed nationality acquired the more discernible structure of a khanate. From then on and for the rest of the sixteenth century, his successors would usually hold on to the northern bank of the Syr Darya and to such cities as Tashkent and Sayram, except for periods when the campaigns of the Shaybanid Abdallah II made them withdraw deeper into the Kazakh steppe. Haqq Nazar (1538–80), on the other hand, made significant inroads into Moghulistan, especially into the Issyk Kul area, where he and his Kazakhs struck up friendly relations with Muhammad, leader of the Kyrgyz. Qasim and Haqq Nazar could with some legitimacy claim to speak for all Kazakhs. From the seventeenth century until the Russian conquest in the nineteenth, however, these nomads only seldom and for brief periods recognized the authority of a single khan; usually they formed three separate tribal confederations or "Hordes," thus called by the Russians ("Orda") but known as "Jüz" ("Hundred") in Kazakh: the Lesser Horde in western Kazakhstan, the Middle Horde in central Kazakhstan, and the Greater Horde in southeastern Kazakhstan (more or less coterminous with Semireche). This fragmentation could not but undermine their power to resist subsequent incursions by the Kalmyks and eventual conquest by the Russians.

The Shaybanids had mostly peaceful relations with the Chaghatayids of Moghulistan and Kashgaria, but only after the latter had given up their ambitions in Fergana, an area claimed by most rulers of Transoxania; this rivalry caused an initial conflict between the two dynasties, which ended in 1508 with the capture and execution of Mahmud, the khan of Altishahr (Kashgaria), by Muhammad Shaybani. Mahmud's elder brother, Ahmad, the khan of Moghulistan, had meanwhile died in 1503, and it was his two sons, the aforementioned Mansur and Said, who would propel the dynasty to a relatively successful reign in Sinkiang for several more generations. Mansur Khan (1503–43), a devout Muslim, spent his chief efforts on a *jihad* eastward into the grey zone of lingering Buddhism and Mongol and Chinese claims, as for example were the oasis towns of Hami (Qomul) and Tunhuang. He also endeavored, on the home front, to quicken the conversion of those of his subjects who still remained alien to Islam, chiefly the Kyrgyz. Said Khan (1514–32) meanwhile directed his efforts southward toward Ladakh; he was assisted in this by Muhammad Haydar Mirza, the aforementioned Dughlat emir and historian who subsequently also served Said's successor Abd al-Rashid (1532–70). A break soon occurred between the latter two, however, and resulted in Haydar Mirza's retreat to India in 1541, where he entered the service of Babur's son Humayun and was given the task of governing the province of Kashmir.

Abd al-Rashid became preoccupied with events in northwestern Moghulistan, the area of the Tianshan mountains around lake Issyk Kul and the lower Ili region. It was thither that the Kazakh khan Haqq Nazar, as we have mentioned, directed the thrust of his campaigns. Haqq Nazar was unopposed by Mansur Khan's successor Shah Khan (1545–70), who was too preoccupied with his brother Muhammad's rebellion farther east. The latter complication illustrates the weakness of this diminished resurrection of the Chaghatayid principality, its break-up among family members who seldom displayed a concord of the kind that had produced a minor "Chaghatayid renaissance" under Mansur Khan and Said Khan. Moreover, their successors gradually lost control of northern Moghulistan, an area increasingly overrun by Kazakhs and Kalmyks, so that only Sinkiang proper – Kasgharia and Uighuristan – remained their principal possession. There their rule tended to split up into three segments whose urban centers were usually: (1) Aksu, the northwestern fringe of the area and, although reckoned as one of the cities of Altishahr, also viewed as part of Moghulistan; (2) Kashgar or Yarqand (Altishahr); and (3) Turfan (Uighuristan). Kashgar, which like Turfan enjoyed a special status for a variety of reasons – as an ancient intersection on the Silk Road and gateway to Transoxania, as a time-honored capital of regional kingdoms, and as the residence of venerated religious personalites with their tombs nearby – was an ancient city with a recurrent political role. It was thither that in the 1530s the aforementioned Makhdum-i Azam sent from Bukhara his emissaries who founded a dervish lodge and a dynasty of religious leaders who would in due course usurp temporal power from the Chaghatayids themselves.

CHAPTER THIRTEEN

The Buddhist Mongols

Toghon Temür, the last Yüan emperor of China and a Genghisid of the Toluy-Qubilay line, fled in 1368 to Mongolia after the dynasty's defeat and replacement by the national Ming Dynasty. From then on, his descendants and those of other Genghisid lineages would claim the right to rule the Mongols, but without achieving the re-establishment of even a unified Mongolia, to say nothing of a resurrection of the Genghisid empire. The challenge of reconquering the northern and western portions of Mongolia itself, with the historic region of Qaraqorum, from their linguistic cousins the Oirats proved an arduous and protracted task. The able and energetic Dayan Khan (enthroned in 1470, ruled from 1481) failed to do so despite the campaigns he waged from 1492 on, and success was granted only to his equally remarkable grandson Altan Khan (1543–83) and the latter's great-nephew Khutukhtai Sechen Khungtaiji, chief of the Ordos tribes (1540–86). Their victory over the Oirats in 1552 was to benefit especially the Khalkha component of the Eastern Mongols, who occupied these central and northwestern segments of the country that eventually became the core of modern Mongolia. For the time being, however, the center of political power among Eastern Mongols was in territories corresponding to what is now Inner Mongolia, more specifically areas inhabited by the tribes of Tümet and Ordos. Meanwhile the Oirats retreated west after their defeat to join their kinsmen in the Eurasian steppes, a move that would contribute to the creation of the Jungar khanate in Sinkiang and the Kalmyk khanate in southern Russia.

While ruling China as the Yüan Dynasty, Qubilay and his successors began to abandon their people's ancestral shamanism, which was marked by religious indifference or tolerance, and to display a growing interest in Buddhism. They – especially Qubilay – seemed to favor this religion over others. The massive conversion of the Mongols to Buddhism happened only after the dynasty's return to Mongolia, however. The conversion of Altan Khan set in motion a rapid adoption of Buddhism by most Eastern Mongols; moreover, in the following century Buddhism gained a similar success among the Oirats, and eventually also among the Buriats of southern Siberia. In all three cases the form adopted was the Tibetan denomination of the Yellow Hat, better known as Lamaism – and more correctly, in scholarly terminology, given its Tibetan name Gelugpa. It was famous for its extreme monasticism, theocracy eventually symbolized by the person of the Dalai Lama reigning from Lhassa, and a complex system of reincarnations. This also meant a lasting and mutually supportive relationship between the Mongol and Tibetan churches, which began in 1578 when Sonam-Gyatso (or bSod-nams rgya-mts'o, if we follow the generally accepted scholarly transliteration), chief of the Tibetan church, came to Mongolia to organize the new junior branch. It was at that point that the title *Dalai Lama* appeared for the first time – a Mongolian–Tibetan hybrid with the connotation of "Universal Lama" – apparently bestowed upon the Tibetan prelate by Altan Khan and from then on assumed by the spiritual and temporal chief of the Tibetan church. Sonam-Gyatso then returned to Tibet, but not without leaving in Mongolia a substitute of sorts, a "Living Buddha" who then resided at the aforementioend Köke-khoto or Huehot, a city in Inner Mongolia near the northeastern bend of the Yellow River and now the capital of China's Inner Mongolian Autonomous Region.

The effect of this conversion, especially on the Eastern Mongols, was profound, pervasive, and persistent, lasting until the establishment of Communist rule in 1921. It affected the Mongols' political, social, and economic structure, cultural life, and demography. Demographically, it ended up draining some 40 percent of the male population into the country's numerous lamaseries, with a nearly suicidal effect on the population. It is indeed an irony of Mongol history: a nation that paid a heavy demographic price for its dazzling military empire in the Middle Ages, and then again for its total abandonment to a quietist religion in the modern era.

The social structure of the Mongols meant that their conversion proceeded along tribal lines, the Tümet and Ordos of the southern territories – what is now Inner Mongolia – under Altan Khan preceding those of the north by a few years. The conversion of Tümen-Sasakhtu (1557–93), another descendant of Dayan Khan and chief of the Chakhar tribes, deserves attention for the fact that it was this khan who initiated the promulgation of a new Mongol law code based on

Buddhism. Most important in the long run, however, was the conversion of the Khalkha in 1588, for it was among them that the incarnation of the new Dalai Lama was identified among the descendants of Dayan Khan; the newborn child stayed at Urga, the nomads' initially peripatetic headquarters, until the age of thirteen; then the youth was solemnly installed in Lhassa as the fourth Dalai Lama. Meanwhile another "Living Buddha," Maidari Khutukhtu, was installed at Urga as the Jebtsun-damba-khutukhtu, head of the sect among the Khalkha. His spiritual descendants eventually also became temporal rulers, like their senior peers the Dalai Lamas, and their authority embraced all of Mongolia until the replacement of the theocracy by the republic in 1924 (not 1921; the apparent contradiction will be explained below).

Conversion to Buddhism also occurred, as we have said, among the Oirats, but not until the seventeenth century, after the major part of their tribes had migrated to Jungaria and points farther west. Curiously, embracing this quietist religion did not immediately produce a radical transformation of their society to the degree that it did among the Eastern Mongols. Quite to the contrary: the expansiveness of the vigorous Jungar state in Sinkiang, and the campaigns of the Kalmyks through the Dasht-i Kipchak, occurred concurrently with or just after their conversion to Buddhism early in the seventeenth century.

We have already mentioned the first wave of Oirat (Kalmyk) expansion westward into the Dasht-i Kipchak, more specifically the area of southernmost Kazakhstan, in the second half of the fifteenth century. The Oirats then withdrew to territories closer to their original homeland in southern Siberia, and in the process occupied western Mongolia until they were thrown back, as we have said, by Altan Khan in 1552. This repulsion incited some of the turbulent tribes to undertake the second wave of raids into the aforementioned parts of Kazakhstan, but without attempting any real conquests; instead, the majority concentrated in Jungaria.

The most prominent tribes among them were the Choro, Dörböt, Torghut, and Khoshot, but it was the epithet "Jungar" (also spelled Dzungar or Zungar) by which they and their new territory, Jungaria, became known. This special ethnonym (the literal meaning of *zungar* is "left hand," as opposed to *barungar*, "right hand"; it appeared at an ill-defined moment when they were identified with their position within a larger tribal confederation) has survived the people themselves in the name of Jungaria. It was there that the Oirats embraced Buddhism, about a generation after their cousins the Eastern Mongols had done so.

The process, consummated by 1620, was similar: tribal leaders such as Boibeghus-baatur of the Khoshot, Khara-kulla of the Choros, Dalai-taiji of the Dörböt, and Khu-Urluq of the Torghut converted, and their tribes followed suit. The conversion was followed, whether coincidentally or through a causal relationship, by several developments of historical importance and ultimately tragic consequences.

Those Oirats who stayed in Jungaria, led by the Choros under their khan Baatur-Khongtaiji (1634–53), consolidated their hold on the area, symbolizing this by stabilizing their headquarters in the form of a city which became the modern Chuguchak (Tacheng). Baatur-Khongtaiji also sent one of his sons, Galdan, to Lhassa as a novice in a lamasery. Galdan, however, eventually received a dispensation to break his vows and return to Jungaria in order to join the succession struggle that had flared up among his brothers after their father's death. By 1676 he emerged as the victor, inaugurating his own reign (1676–97). It was he who transformed the small khanate into the relatively short-lived but memorable Jungar empire of Sinkiang, which lasted until its destruction by the Chinese in 1758. He founded it in two stages: the first was the unification of all the Oirat tribes of Jungaria under his rule; and the second was the extension of his suzerainty over the entire Sinkiang. The fact that Galdan subsequently directed his main and ultimately unsuccessful efforts toward Mongolia and China underscores the almost accidental and anomalous nature of the second step; for it was provoked by the aforementioned quarrel between a descendant of Genghis Khan and a descendant of the Prophet Muhammad: the Chaghatayid Ismail made an effort to recover some of the power which the Khwajas, in particular Hazrat Apak of Kashgar, had usurped in Altishahr from the Genghisids. The Khwaja fled to Tibet where he found refuge with the Dalai Lama, who instructed Galdan Khan to restore the dervish to his former position. The Oirat khan occupied Kashgar, sent Ismail a prisoner to Kulja, and in 1678 re-established Hazrat Apak in his former position but as his vassal. The irony of these events is striking: the Dalai Lama, a Buddhist incarnation, is asked by a descendant of the Prophet of Islam to restore him to his position of prestige and power, and the latter is reinstalled by an infidel khan.

Galdan Khan's main ambition lay, however, farther east. After consolidating his hold on Sinkiang by taking Turfan and Hami in 1681, he repulsed in 1688 an attack by Tsaghun-Dorji, one of the five Khalkha chieftains of Mongolia, and then himself invaded their territory. The Khalkha retreated to Tümet territory in Inner Mongolia, requesting

Chinese protection. The emperor Kang-hsi (r. 1661–1722) set out to counter Galdan's advance, and in 1690 the two armies clashed between Urga and Kalgan, some 300 kilometers north of Beijing. The Chinese won, partly thanks to the cannon made for them by Jesuit missionaries. Galdan withdrew from Mongolia and the Khalkha princes returned to their dominions. The next year, 1691, at Dolon Nor – a town some 250 kilometers north of Beijing in the southeastern corner of Inner Mongolia – the Manchu emperor received their homage as his vassals. This act officially established Manchu suzerainty over the eastern Mongols living in Mongolia proper.

The tribes living in what would evolve into Inner Mongolia had been annexed since the rise of the Manchus as early as 1644. For Inner Mongolia, incorporation in the Chinese empire proved a permanent arrangement, on both the political and demographic levels: politically, it outlasted the Manchu Dynasty beyond its demise in 1911 and exists today as the Inner Mongolian Autonomous Region of the People's Republic of China; demographically, the Mongol population has been swamped by Chinese settlers. In Outer Mongolia too, Chinese suzerainty lasted until the twentieth century – until 1911 or later dates depending on interpretation, the latest *terminus* being 1945 – but without the demographic transformation that befell Inner Mongolia.

Galdan Khan, after a second and equally unsuccessful attempt against China in 1696, withdrew his forces and died a year later. This time the Manchu emperor pursued the Oirats all the way to Hami, which he occupied as a foretaste of the offensive that half a century later would lead to the fall of the Jungar empire and the establishment of Sinkiang as a Chinese possession. Galdan was succeeded by his nephew Tsevang Rabdan (1697–1727); like his predecessor, the new khan clashed several times with Kang-hsi, but there was a significant difference: it was the Manchu emperor who took the offensive and attacked the Mongol. The first important conflict that had long-lasting effects was their fight over the control of Tibet, where internal convulsions led to the installment of a Chinese-supported Dalai Lama in 1710. This provoked Oirat intervention. The troops sent by Tsevang Rabdan occupied Lhassa in 1717 and achieved an initial success against a Chinese army, but were then defeated by a second Manchu expeditionary force, which in 1720 enthroned a new Dalai Lama and set up Tibet as China's protectorate with two imperial residents to supervise the Buddhist theocrat's rule. This event came close to being paralleled in Sinkiang itself, where another confrontation between the Oirats and the Manchus was taking place. It was provoked by Tsevang Rabdan's attempt of 1715 to reoccupy Hami, and led to the arrival of a Chinese expeditionary force that by 1720 penetrated into the heart of Jungaria and defeated the Oirats near Urumchi. The death of emperor Kang-hsi and accession of the relatively pacific Yung-cheng (1722–35), who granted the Oirat khan a peace treaty in 1724, contributed to the postponement of the impending annexation.

Unlike Galdan Khan, Tsevang Rabdan does not appear to have entertained hopes of building an empire at the expense of China, and his conflicts with Kang-hsi were chiefly defensive. On the other hand, he pursued an expansive policy westward into what had once been Moghulistan and the Dasht-i Kipchak, but was changing into what is now Kyrgyzstan and Kazakhstan. The Kyrgyz, whom the Oirats called Buruts, came under their rule; they had by then become Muslims, although their conversion may still have been quite superficial and replete with shamanistic beliefs. On the Kazakh front, Kalmyk incursions produced confrontations such as the defeat of Tauke (1680–1718), khan of the Middle Horde, in 1698, and of his successor Pulad (1718–30), in 1723. The latter defeat especially caused untold misery among the Kazakh masses and was remembered as *Aqtaban shubyryndy*, "The Great Calamity."

In 1727, when Tsevang Rabdan died and his son Galdan Tsereng (1727–45) ascended the throne, the relations between the Jungars, the Khalkha, and the Chinese appeared to have stabilized. The Chinese held easternmost Sinkiang or parts of historic Uighuristan as far as Turfan; the Khalkha were firmly established in central and eastern Mongolia with Urga as their headquarters; and the Jungars controlled, besides most of Sinkiang, westernmost Mongolia with such places as Kobdo and Uliassutai. Galdan Tsereng, however, provoked a conflict with both the Manchu emperor and his vassals the Khalkha. The Chinese and their clients began to gain an edge in the seesaw struggle, but in 1735 Yung-cheng granted Galdan Tsereng a peace treaty that was confirmed by his successor, emperor Chien-lung (1735–95), in 1740. It was the lack of internal stability that ultimately doomed the Jungars. Troubles began with Galdan's son and successor Tsevang-dorji-namgyal (1745–50), and intensified after his fall with the ensuing struggle for succession. One of the contenders, Amursana, failing to overcome his rivals, fled to China, where in 1755 he declared his readiness to accept Manchu suzerainty. A Chinese army under General Pan-ti defeated Davaji, the reigning khan, and occupied Kulja with the intention of carrying out the proposed reorganization of Jungaria with Amursana as a Manchu vassal. When the latter tried to renege on his commitment, Pan-ti seized him and sent him to Beijing, but the Oirat chieftain escaped and managed to organize an uprising against the Chinese force. Pan-ti committed suicide, but Amursana's triumph was short-lived: the Manchu general Chao-hui came with another army and by 1757 crushed all resistance. Amursana fled to Siberia, where he died soon afterwards. Meanwhile Chao-hui with his Manchu troops had decimated the Oirat tribes living in Jungaria to the point where the area, annexed as a crown possession of the Manchu dynasty (1758) but almost depopulated, needed recolonization. The Manchus proceeded to repopulate the province with various elements, but excluding the ethnic Chinese; eventually these elements included also those Torghut Kalmyks who had left their khanate on the lower Volga in 1771.

While Jungaria was being agitated by the upheavals that led to the extermination of its Oirat population, Kashgaria continued to be ruled by four sons of the Qarataghliq Khwaja Daniyal: Yusuf at Kashgar, Jagan at Yarkand, Ayyub at Aksu, and Abdallah at Khotan. Led by the energetic Yusuf, they exploited the disorders agitating their infidel suzerains by declaring full independence in 1753. Two years later Amursana, who had just returned with Chinese troops to Jungaria, arranged for a small force of Chinese to expel the rebellious Qarataghliq Khwajas and install, as vassals in their stead, their rivals the Aqtaghliq Khwajas Burhan al-din (the Great Khwaja) and his brother Khwaja Jan (the Little Khwaja), who had since 1720 languished in semi-captivity at Kulja. The project succeeded, but as soon as Amursana and the Chinese began to quarrel, the two Aqtaghliq Khwajas proclaimed themselves independent and even defeated the small force sent against them by the Chinese in 1757. The next year, however, more troops came and besieged Burhan al-Din at Kashgar and Khwaja Jan at Yarkand. The cities were taken in 1759, and both Khwajas fled to Badakhshan, where the local Muslim ruler yielded to Chinese pressure and had them executed. Kashgaria, like Jungaria, became a Manchu possession as part of the crown's Sinkiang province.

Among the Oirats of Jungaria it was the Khoshot, as we have said, who dominated the scene since their khan Khara-khula (d. 1634) and his son Baatur-Khongtaiji (1634–53) had consolidated Oirat control of the area. The first expansion of the Jungars was directed against their neighbors to the west, the Kazakhs of the Greater Horde. In two memorable campaigns, Baatur defeated the khan Ishim in 1635, and then his son

Jahangir in 1643. Subsequently the aforementioned Galdan Khan became too involved with Sinkiang, Tibet, Mongolia, and China to repeat Baatur's exploits against the Kazakhs, but this was made up for by Galdan's successor Tsevang Rabdan, whose reign coincided with that of the Kazakh khan Tauke. The latter stands out in Kazakh history as a powerful leader and one of the few khans whose rule extended over the three hordes; in 1694 he received a Russian embassy, and Oirat envoys came to him four years later. Tauke, however, had the latter executed, an act that provoked Tsevang's swift retaliation, for he attacked and defeated him in the same year.

The main Oirat blow, however, fell on Tauke's successor Pulat Khan (1718–30) in 1723 (the aforementioned *Aqtaban shubyryndy*). The Oirats raided Kazakh territory all the way to the right bank of the Syr Darya, sacking the cities of Sayram, Tashkent, and Turkestan. This raid displays an eerie resemblance to those of the fifteenth and sixteenth centuries, in which the Oirats – better remembered in that context as Kalmyks – sacked the same area, and at first sight there is even another kind of parallel: the earliest raid sapped the might and prestige of the Uzbeks, especially of Abulkhayr Khan; the later ones did the same to the Kazakhs. There was one important difference, however. Whereas earlier, once the Oirats had pulled back, the Uzbeks and Kazakhs regained their strength, the defeat in the eighteenth century happened at the very time when the Russian empire, having absorbed all of Siberia, was beginning its relentless push southward into Kazakhstan and Central Asia. The calamities caused by this third and last wave of western Mongol invasions should have ended with the destruction of the Jungars by the Manchus, but by then the Kazakhs had become too dislocated and weakened to attempt effective unified resistance to the incipient Russian expansion.

The Kazakhs of the Greater and Middle Hordes were not the only ones afflicted by the Oirat invasions. There was too much rivalry between the Khoshot and Torghut tribes for both to share Jungaria; so in 1616, at about the time the Khoshot were consolidating their Jungar realm, the Torghut under Khu-Urluq abandoned that area and migrated farther west to the territories of the Lesser Horde, thus roughly between the rivers Emba and Volga. In 1643 the khan of the Torghut established his headquarters near the Volga estuary, and the Kalmyks – as these Oirats became known not only to the Muslim Turks but also to the Russians – straddling that river's lower course and nomadizing in the steppes from the lower Volga all the way to the estuary of the Emba along the northern rim of the Caspian, became the principal nomadic power in the area. They remained so until 1771, when a substantial part of them carried out the same migration but in reverse, back to the Ili basin and Jungaria. The story of this Kalmyk khanate is an unusual and poignant historical episode. Its formation created a special cultural dichotomy and a religious trichotomy: in an area populated chiefly by Nogays who were Muslim Turkic nomads, a new Buddhist Mongol nomadic element made its tempestuous entry and quickly dominated them, but had to find a *modus vivendi* with Orthodox Russia, which was emphatically displaying its power through the presence of the tsar's governor at Astrakhan. The Kalmyks, like their Jungar cousins, remained a turbulent element engaged in predatory campaigns throughout much of their khanate's existence, but the targets of these raids were chiefly their Turkic neighbors to the southeast, in particular the Turkmens of Mangishlak and the Khanate of Khiva. In contrast, their relations with Russia not only remained amicable, but the khans did not shrink from acknowledging themselves as the tsar's vassals. This relationship was especially striking during the long reign of the khan Ayuka (1670–1724), who in 1673 came to pay his homage to the governor at Astrakhan, and whom half a century later, in 1722, Peter the Great received with great pomp at Saratov. In the following decades, however, Russia's suzerainty became increasingly onerous, until in January 1771 over 11,000 tents or 150,000 people – about two-thirds of the total Kalmyk population of the khanate – set out on a return migration to Jungaria. By the time they reached the recently established Chinese possession in the fall of that year, the Kalmyks had suffered horrendous losses – perhaps as many as two-thirds again had perished – caused by severe weather conditions and attacks by hostile Kazakhs as well as by Russian troops. Jungaria had just been conquered by Manchu troops who then decimated its Jungar population, so that the Chinese government welcomed the arrival of the latter's Kalmyk relatives in the depopulated province. The empress Catherine the Great, who considered the Kalmyks her subjects, in vain pressured the Ching (Manchu) government to return them to Russian territory.

The Kalmyks who participated in this reverse migration had all lived to the east of the Volga. Those who at that point lived to the west of the river stayed, and became the nucleus of the Kalmyk nation that after the formation of the Soviet Union received the status of an Autonomous Republic within the Russian Federation.

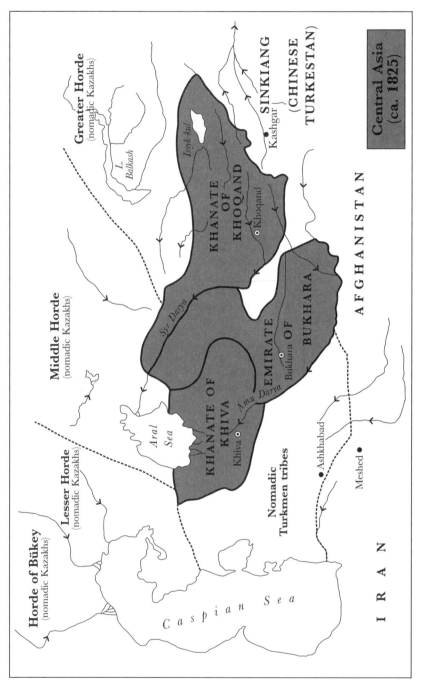

Map 5   Central Asia, ca. 1825

CHAPTER FOURTEEN

Bukhara, Khiva, and Khoqand in the seventeenth to nineteenth centuries

Differences / similarities

BUKHARA

When Abdallah II died in 1598, his son and successor Abdalmumin, who had spent a number of years as governor of Balkh, managed to stay on the throne only a few months before he was ousted and killed in the disorders that followed his father's death. No other adult male son of Abdallah II had survived to take over – a curious feature in a system where a plethora of sons and grandsons born of a ruler's several wives was often the problem; it seems that in this case Abdallah II, perhaps inspired by the example of his allies the Ottomans but applying his own modified version, had suppressed all the male contenders for succession except Abdalmumin.

What Abdallah did not do, however, was to eliminate his brother-in-law Jani Muhammad, whose father Yar Muhammad had taken refuge with the Shaybanids of Bukhara after the conquest of the khanate of Astrakhan by the Russians in 1556. Jani Muhammad married the Uzbek khan's sister, and he acceded to the vacated throne in Bukhara as the first ruler of a dynasty called Janid or Ashtarkhanid; the Janids too were Juchids, but not through Shiban but through Tuqay Timur, one of Juchi's other sons (in fact, his thirteenth son), so that some historians prefer the name "Tuqay-Timurids" to the genealogically less revealing appellations Janids or Ashtarkhanids. Under their rule the city and khanate crystallized into an almost classical pattern of a Muslim polity of its time, cherishing and even enhancing traditional values while ignoring or rejecting the vertiginous changes initiated by the Europeans but now reaching other parts of the world. Most khans, especially the virtuous Abdalaziz (ruled 1645–81), were devout Muslims who favored the religious establishment and adorned Bukhara with still more mosques and madrasas. Samarkand was not neglected either, but the center of political and religious activities had definitively shifted to

177

Similarity
Struggle for control

Bukhara, so much so that the outside world came to think of Central
Asia as Bukhara; to the Russians, Central Asian merchants who began
to frequent their empire were known as "Bukharans," and even Sinkiang
received the nickname of "Little Bukhara." On the religious level, its
madrasas – the Mir-i Arab madrasa being the most famous one – gave
the city the reputation of one of Islam's foremost centers of learning and
orthodoxy, while its Sufi shaykhs and dervishes – here the aforementioned shrines of Baha al-Din Naqshband in Qasr-i Arifan and of Abu
Bakr in Sumitan led the roster – added their dimension of wide appeal
and participation by the masses. The Janid capital thus became famous
as Bukhara-i Sharif, the Noble Bukhara, both as a center of learning of
Sunni Islam and as a place where dervishes inspired the populace with
their kind of worship and their way of life.

We have seen that the cultural florescence characteristic of Timurid
Herat and Samarkand continued in Shaybanid Bukhara, Samarkand,
and Balkh to such a degree that we can speak of a silver age of the same
cultural tradition. A similar statement can be made with respect to seventeenth-century Janid Bukhara, and, in a special sense, also to Khiva.
Architecture, literary culture, and the book arts continued, although at
a lower level of refinement than those of the preceding centuries and
dynasties. One example is a history which Mahmud ibn Vali, a member
of the Uzbek aristocracy, began to write in 1634 and which he called
Bahr al-Asrar fi Manaqib al-Akhyar ("Ocean of Secrets about the Legends
of the Best Ones"); it was commissioned at Balkh by the future khan
Nadhr Muhammad (1641–45). This compendium is in line with the
historiographic school that began with Rashid al-Din in Mongol Iran
and flowered under the Timurids with such works as Hafiz Abru's
Zafername and Sharaf al-Din Yazdi's book of the same title, or again with
several biographies of Shaybanid khans such as the aforementioned
Sharafname-i Shahi, a history of the rule of Abdallah II by Hafiz Tanish
Bukhari. Belletristic and musical culture is documented by *tezkere* books
(biographical dictionaries) compiled by Qadi Badi-i Samarqandi and
Mir Muhammad Amin-i Bukhari. Of architectural monuments, the
most remarkable ones were erected in Samarkand due to the patronage
of the governor Alchin Yalantush Bek, who ordered the construction of
two beautiful madrasas on that city's *rigistan* or main square; the first,
completed in 1618, is called Shirdar ("With Lions," so named after two
zodiacal lions painted on the spandrels of the main portal), and was built
by a famous architect, Abdaljabbar Naqqash. The other, the Tilakar

madrasa ("Madrasa with gold facing"), completed in 1630, is also situated on the rigistan; the three buildings – Ulugh Beg and Shirdar facing each other, Tilakar delimiting the third side of the square – form an exquisite composition and one of the justly famous examples of Central Asian architecture and urban planning.

Abdalaziz Khan is also remembered for valiant efforts to bring Balkh, traditionally the heir presumptive's appanage, under closer control, and for favoring the religious and scholarly class; both the *khwajas* of the Naqshbandi and other dervish orders, and the *alims*, secular Islamic scholars, benefited from his patronage. Nevertheless, he could not prevent frequent raids by the Khivans which reached their climax under Anusha Khan; the raid of 1681, which resulted in a temporary seizure of Bukhara, broke the aging monarch's spirit and made him abdicate the throne.

Abdalaziz Khan was in 1681 succeeded by his brother Subhanquli Khan (1681–1702), and the latter by his (Subhanquli's) sons Ubaydallah Khan (1702–11; not to be confused with his Shaybanid namesake) and Abulfayz Khan (1711–47). The crisis that had led to the abdication of Abdalaziz reinforced the growing independence of Uzbek tribal leaders and precipitated the decline of the Janids, which was consummated with the murder of Abulfayz Khan in 1747 by the Manghit emir Muhammad Rahim Bi, the *ataliq* or major-domo of the dynasty. The decline manifested itself in the *de facto* rule of this family of tribal emirs, initially as ataliqs, and from 1785 officially as the last dynasty to rule Bukhara (1785–1920). The first Manghit ataliq was Khudayar Bi, who occupied this position from 1714 until he died in 1722. His son Muhammad Hakim Bi succeeded him in this post and reinforced his authority despite a traumatic spell of disorders visited upon Bukhara, which included a seven-year-long series of raids by nomadic Kazakhs, themselves refugees from the aforementioned invasions of the Dasht-i Kipchak by the Oirats of Jungaria. A mere decade after the withdrawal of the Kazakhs, Transoxania was invaded by the Persians: in 1740 Nadir Shah, the new ruler of Iran, crossed the Amu Darya and, accepting the submission of Muhammad Hakim Bi which was then formalized by the acquiescence of Abulfayz Khan himself, proceeded to attack Khiva. When rebellions broke out in 1743 upon the death of Muhammad Hakim, the shah dispatched the ataliq's son Muhammad Rahim Bi, who had accompanied him to Iran, to quell them. This led to Muhammad Rahim's establishment as the next ataliq, a position which he strengthened upon Nadir

Shah's death in 1747 by having the still officially reigning Abulfayz murdered and ridding himself of the khan's twelve-year-old son Abdalmumin in the same manner. Between that year and 1785, the Manghit ataliqs still maintained the fiction of legitimate Genghisid reign by allowing puppet khans to occupy the throne, but effective rule was in their hands at least since the second phase of Muhammad Rahim's tenure of office (1753–58). Nevertheless, it is customary to associate the beginning of the Manghit Dynasty with the accession of Muhammad Rahim's cousin Shah Murad (1785–1800).

The Manghits were the first non-Genghisid dynasty to rule Transoxania since the Timurids (besides being the last native monarchy). A similar evolution was taking place in Khiva and Khoqand, where khans of Uzbek tribal origins no longer felt any need to legitimize their rule through a Genghisid genealogy (although in Khoqand, it seems, the Ming rulers did make an attempt to link themselves to Babur and thus to gain a Genghisid genealogy on the cognatic side). The new tack taken by the Manghits in Bukhara was emphasized by the switch of the ruler's title from khan to emir, which in this case meant a shift from tribal Turco-Mongol to Islamic legitimation: for emir stood here for Amir (al-Muminin), "Commander of the Believers," the once prestigious Arabic title of the Caliph (although according to some scholars Manghit rulers called themselves "emirs" simply because that was their original identity, emirs or begs, members of the Turco-Mongol tribal and military elite of non-Genghisid ancestry).

The Manghits succeeded better than their Genghisid predecessors in the efforts to achieve centralized rule by reducing the power of Uzbek tribal chieftains and relying on a small, partly non-Uzbek standing army and on a Persian-speaking bureaucratic class often recruited from the emir's Persian slaves; assuming the image of devout Islamic rulers and sponsoring the religious class, both secular and that of the Sufi orders, was another means of the emirs to consolidate their authority. This produced greater internal stability, population growth and a certain economic revival, which in turn benefited from increasing trade with Russia. At the same time, however, the despotic and conservative nature of the regime made it incapable of grasping the dramatic changes going on elsewhere, especially where it would matter the most, in Russia. This had two major consequences: one was conquest by Russia in 1868, the other the continuation of an almost medieval social structure of the emirate as an informal Russian protectorate until 1920.

KHIVA

After the establishment of the Abulkhayrid Shaybanids in Transoxania proper (1501), another group of nomadic Uzbeks from the Dasht-i Kipchak, the Yadigarid Shaybanids, installed themselves as the khans of Khwarazm by 1515. This event suggests that the passing of the whole of Central Asia proper under Uzbek rule was not an accident but resulted from the inability of the native population to replace the declining local power with a new alternative of its own. The Turco-Mongols to the north, by virtue of their nomadic lifestyle predisposed to military mobility, conquest, and rule, seldom failed to seize an opportunity to attempt incursions and conquest, and both Transoxania and Khwarazm proved perfect targets at this period. Yadigarid conquest and rule also demonstrated the force of geopolitics, for despite periodic attempts of the Abulkhayrid Shaybanids and their successors the Tuqay-Timurids to seize this territory, Khwarazm retained its own identity and independence throughout the long rule of this dynasty. It did so also under their successors the Inakids until the Russian conquest 1873, and even until 1919 as a Russian protectorate. As in Transoxania, in Khwarazm too the dichotomy between the rulers and the ruled, the nomads and the sedentary urban or agricultural population, persisted or even grew: under the still charismatic Genghisid authority of the khans, political and military power remained in the hands of the Turkic tribal oligarchy, while the town dwellers and peasants, called Sarts, were excluded from it. A good number of these sedentaries were descended from the original Iranian population of the area, but unlike those of Transoxania they were by now almost totally Turkicized.

Khwarazm under the Yadigarids suffered a general decline caused by a variety of factors. One was the turbulence of the political process referred to above. There was too much tribal movement and insubordination to let the khans impose the necessary law and order. The ensuing insecurity further aggravated the dwindling of long-distance trade that had been practiced by Khwarazm or that used to pass through it, linking the Silk Road network with the Pontic steppes and Russia. Gradually, the khanate's center of gravity stabilized in an area on the left (southern) bank of the Amu Darya near the apex of the river's delta, with Khiva, New Urgench, and New Kath as the foremost urban agglomerations. The right bank with the historical Kath was virtually abandoned to the encroaching Kyzyl Kum desert. Farther northwest the original Urgench, by then given the epithet Kunya ("Old"), became a ruined site. Its destruction had been started by Timur in 1381, but as we have remarked in the introductory chapter, the area was not abandoned until 1576, when the Uzboy, the northwesternmost branch of the delta, swerved its course back to the Aral Sea instead of to the Caspian and thus left the city waterless.

Immediately to the south of Yadigarid Khwarazm was the Kara Kum desert, extending all the way to the oases along the Murghab and Tejen rivers and those along the fringes of the Kopet Dagh and Balkhan mountains. In Sasanian and early Islamic times this region had been considered part of Khurasan, but now it was Turkmen territory, even more turbulent than the Uzbek territory of Khwarazm and Transoxania or the Kazakh territory of the Dasht-i Kipchak, for the Turkmen tribes never united to form a khanate of their own on a par with their neighbors to the north. They consisted of a number of tribes such as Tekke, Yomud, Ersary, Chavdur, Saryq, Salar, and Göklen; the first three were the most prominent, with the Tekke dominating the territory's center, the Yomud the west (including the Caspian littoral), and the Ersary the east. Raiding Persian territories to the south had religious merit (since people there were of the heretical Shii denomination) and brought material rewards in the form of captives for the slave markets of Khiva and Bukhara.

The Yadigarids were at times strong enough to encompass Turkmen territory within their realm; on such occasions, they conceived of their realm as consisting of two parts or sides, that of the "river" (*su tarapy* or *su boyu*, meaning the Amu Darya), and that of the "mountains" (*dagh tarapy* or *dagh boyu*). The northernmost part of the Amu Darya delta, called Aral, often remained outside the Yadigarids' control and formed a khanate of its own, consisting of other Kipchak-speaking nomadic tribes whose range extended from the lower Syr Darya along the eastern shore of the Aral Sea all the way to the Amu Darya estuary.

Another special area was the territory between the Aral and Caspian seas, whose two most important portions were known as Ust Yürt ("Plateau") and Mangyshlak, the large broad peninsula stretching along the northeastern Caspian. Formerly pertaining, with Khwarazm, to the Golden Horde, this area owed its importance to its position on the trade routes between Transoxania and the Dasht-i Kipchak. It now lay outside the reach of any recognizable authority, and was inhabited by a changing mosaic of Turkmen and Kazakh tribes, serving as a corridor of movement for these tribes between the Dasht-i Kipchak and the south.

In the seventeenth century, it was also the avenue of the aforementioned raids by the Kalmyks, who at one point forced two Turkmen tribes of the Mangyshlak peninsula to move to the northern Caucasus.

It was the Yadigarid khan Arab Muhammad I (ruled 1603–23) who in 1619 chose Khiva as the headquarters of his rule. The city's past went back to pre-Islamic times (as Khivak), but this was the first time it functioned as the capital of a realm; eventually, the khanate itself came to be known as that of Khiva, a case of psychological oscillation between capitals named after a country ("madinat Khwarazm" for Urgench in Ibn Battuta's account) and, more frequently, countries named after a city (Bukhara, for example). Khiva came to play a minor but significant role in the history of Central Asian civilization, displaying an individuality that might be explained by both its geopolitical situation and its historical roots. An especially felicitous aspect of this individuality was a florescence of historiography in the seventeenth and nineteenth centuries. In the seventeenth, two khans, Abulghazi Bahadur Khan (1643–63) and his son and successor Anusha (1663–85), were the historians. Abulghazi Bahadur was a man of the pen no less than of the sword; as in the case of Zahir al-Din Babur a century and a half earlier, both his writings and his life are valuable documents on the state of Central Asian society and politics of the period.

Abulghazi was born in 1603, shortly after his father Arab Muhammad I, himself newly enthroned, had repelled a raid by the "Yayik" Cossacks, that is, Cossacks of the River Ural. This dramatic episode symbolized the turbulent life awaiting the boy, though the Russian danger receded for at least another century. For the time being, the political infighting, alliances, and internecine, intertribal, and even up to a point interethnic and religious wars were reserved chiefly for the Inner Asian nomads themselves: the participants were Uzbeks, Turkmens, Kazakhs, Persians, and Kalmyks; and the leaders were the tribal chieftains, the Uzbek khans of Bukhara, the Kazakh khans of Turkestan and Tashkent, the Kalmyk khans of the lower Volga, and the shahs of Safavid Iran.

Abulghazi was precipitated into this whirlwind at the age of twenty with the murder of his father by the latter's two other sons, until personal skill and luck brought him to the throne after his brother Isfandiyar's death in 1642. During the two intervening decades the young man visited as a refugee, ally, guest, or prisoner the Uzbek khan of Bukhara, the Kazakh khans of Turkestan – that is, the town of Turkestan – and of Tashkent, the Kalmyk khan of the lower Volga, and the Safavid shah of Iran at Hamadan, besides experiencing a spate of briefer sojourns which included Khiva. Abulghazi's longest visit occurred, paradoxically but significantly, at Hamadan (1630–40), where the Uzbek prince, a Sunni Muslim, was an almost pampered prisoner of the Shii shah. There, Abulghazi could refine his understanding of Arabo-Persian culture, while at the same time he seized with enthusiasm the opportunity of studying manuscripts dealing with the history of the Turks and Mongols. Thus in addition to providing him with invaluable personal experience and knowledge of his Central Asian countrymen, these adventurous years gave Abulghazi the possibility to pursue his interest in history and to gather materials from written and oral sources, for what would eventually become two major histories, the *Shajara-i terakime*, and the *Shajara-i turk*.

It was the death of his elder brother Isfandiyar in 1642 that enabled Abulghazi, after a final year of maneuvering, to gain the throne. Once installed, he proceeded, somewhat like the Roman Emperor Claudius, to write history, while imposing his own will on its contemporary course. Abulghazi had to remain active as a warrior khan if he wanted to stay in power: he had gained the throne partly thanks to the support of the Uzbek party – chieftains of the Uzbek tribes of Khwarazm, in contrast to the Turkmen card played by his predecessor; so throughout much of his reign Abulghazi had to mount successful expeditions in order to reward his Uzbek supporters and hold the turbulent Turkmen tribes of the Kara Kum and Mangyshlak areas in check.

Unlike most Central Asian historians of the time, Abulghazi wrote his books not in Persian but in his native Turki. This is one of several parallels between him and Babur. His works are thus linguistic documents apart from their primary value as historical sources. The first of the two, the *Shajara-i terakime*, was completed in 1659; it narrates the history of the Turco-Mongols, in particular of those of the Genghisid dynasty, as the author could piece it together from such written sources as Rashid al-Din's *Jami al-tavarikh*, Sharaf al-din Yazdi's *Zafername*, but more interestingly also from other now lost sources such as seventeen *Genghisnames* or histories of the Genghisids, besides oral epics and legends. Even more valuable is the second work, *Shajara-i turk*,[1] which was still being written at the time of Abulghazi's death; his son and successor Anusha com-

---

[1] Edition and French translation by P. Desmaisons, *Histoire des Mongols et des Tatares par Abou-l-Gazi Behadour Khan* (St. Petersburg, 1871–74), 2 vols.

pleted the manuscript. It at first overlaps with the earlier book, but then it focuses on the history of the author's own family and dynasty until 1663. An excerpt from Abulghazi's preface to the latter work conveys its spirit:

Reasons for writing this book: The son of Arab Muhammad-Khan, Abulghazi Bahadur Khan, the Genghisid, the Kwarazmian, says: "Historians have written, both in Turki and Persian (*Turki ve Farsi tili birlen*), the history of the ancestors and descendants of Genghis Khan who had reigned in different countries . . . Gradually, ten, twenty or thirty such histories were written on behalf of these sovereigns. I myself now have before me eighteen tomes on the history of the descendants of Genghis Khan who have reigned either in Iran or in Turan. However, both because of negligence on the part of our ancestors and of the ignorance of the people of Khwarazm, no one has written a history of the rulers of our family . . . I had at first planned to charge someone with the task of writing this history, but I found nobody capable of doing so. This is why I have decided to do it myself . . . Now do not think that while writing this history, I have been guided by any feeling of partiality, or altered the truth, or praised myself without justification. God has been generous to me, and in particular He has granted me knowledge of three things: (1) Knowledge of the art of war, of its principles and rules; (2) Knowledge of diverse types of poetry, such as mesnevi, qasida, ghazal, muqatta, rubai, as well as knowledge of Arabic, Persian, and Turki; and (3) Exact knowledge of names, of the life and deeds of all the rulers who have reigned since Adam until our own day in Arabia as well as in Iran, Turan, and Mongolia."[2]

Abulghazi subsequently mentions one of his principal sources, the *Jami al-Tavarikh* ("Compendium of Histories") compiled in Persian by Rashid al-Din. This principal vizier of the Ikhanid ruler Ghazan Khan (1295–1304) was commissioned to do so by his sovereign, who had issued the order with the following justification: his people were forgetting both their language and their past. Unless the dynasty's and the Mongols' history were written while there were still several old-timers left who remembered some of the lore and could read texts in Mongolian, the memory would be irretrievably lost. Ghazan Khan placed these Mongols at the service of Rashid al-Din, and the monumental work that resulted from the cooperation came to enjoy great vogue among the Mongol and Turkic elites of Central Asia. When Abulghazi decided to write his book, he was faced with up to thirty manuscripts of the *Jami al-Tavarikh*, besides a number of other histories. This was a mixed blessing for the following reason:

---

[2] *Ibid.*, vol. I, pp. 1–2 (Turki text) and vol. II, pp. 1–3 (French trans.).

For 372 years that ignorant scribblers have kept copying this book [the *Jami al-Tavarikh*], twenty or even thirty manuscripts have been produced. With each redaction, errors have crept into some words, to the point where a whole third or even half are incorrect. The names of mountains, rivers, places, persons are Mongol or Turki. Both authors and copyists were Persians or Tajiks, and knew neither Mongol nor Turki. If you try to teach a Tajik [a Turkic or Mongol word], his tongue will not learn it, so how could he write it [correctly]? [Meanwhile] God the Sublime has bestowed upon this poor slave [i.e. me] the knowledge of the Turki and Persian languages, words, terms more than [He has bestowed upon] any Turk or Tajik; what is more, for a certain reason I spent one year among the Kalmyks, and familiarized myself with the Mongol language, terminology, and customs. I have written this history, its good and bad [events], in the Turki language. Now the Turki I have used is such that a five-year-old boy will understand it. In order to make [the meaning] clear, I have refrained from adding Chaghatay, Persian, or Arabic words[3]

Abulghazi has demonstrated in these preliminary pages his remarkable lucidity and good taste. Like Babur, he rises above the period's norms which required that an author display literary erudition and verbal virtuosity. His remark about Chaghatay looks at first sight puzzling. In terms of modern Turcology, it was indeed Chaghatay in which he wrote his works, just as Babur did his. In this instance, however, Abulghazi differentiates between Chaghatay and Turki, the way one could differentiate between Ottoman Turkish and modern Turkish. He speaks here somewhat like Kemal Atatürk who championed a "purification" of Turkey's Turkish by replacing words of Arabic and Persian origin with genuinely Turkic ones. While in Turkey this process was later – after Atatürk – exaggerated, for nationalistic reasons, to the point of sometimes defeating the main purpose, that of intelligibility, for Abulghazi the latter was the guide: one proof is the very word he used for "clear, intelligible": *rawshan*, which is Persian but which by his time had become completely naturalized in Turki.

Shir Ghazi (1715–28) was the last effective Yadigarid khan. The reign of this patron of learning and literature began auspiciously when in 1717–18 he withstood what may have been the first official onslaught of colonialism: for Peter the Great sent to Khiva a 750-men-strong expedition, led by a Circassian named Bekovich (Bekovich Cherkasskiy), but Shir Ghazi destroyed it. In 1728, however, internecine tribal struggle between the Kongrat and Manghit tribes led to the khan's murder and to the enthronement of candidates put forward by the rival factions;

---

[3] *Ibid.*, vol. I, pp. 36–37 (Turki text) and vol. II, pp. 35–36 (French trans.).

some of these phantom khans were Yadigarids, usually sponsored by the Kongrat tribe; others were procured from among the inexhaustible pool of other Juchids proliferating among the Kazakhs and sponsored by the Manghits. Nominally, however, the Yadigarids ruled until 1804, when the last khan of the line, Abulghazi III, was removed from the throne by Iltüzer, an Uzbek beg of Kongrat affiliation and the grandson of a line of chieftains who had begun to assert their own power as early as 1762; in that year Temir Ghazi Khan appointed Mehmet Emin as *inak* or prime minister; the next year the latter killed the khan and a number of Manghit tribal chieftains who were his supporters, and ruled Khiva while parading eleven more khans on the throne; some of these were Yadigarids, others of different but always Genghisid ancestry.

With the Inakids a new and final chapter began in the history of the khanate of Khiva. One innovation was the fact that as in Bukhara, for the first time a non-Genghisid dynasty acquired not only effective but also titular power; another was the tendency of the Inakids to place more power in the hands of Sarts, members of the non-tribal urban or other sedentary classes, with the implicit goal of shaking off the power of the tribal aristocracy of whom they themselves were a product; yet another was its very finality: the Inakids presided over a khanate that would try to cope with the challenges of the nineteenth century, the foremost of which was the onslaught of European colonialism represented here by Russia, before collapsing in the upheavals brought about by the Bolshevik Revolution.

KHOQAND

The valley of Fergana has been, as we have seen, a special part of Central Asia since antiquity, not unlike Khwarazm in its individuality and geopolitical situation. One could visualize the two as the wings of an area whose central body was Transoxania proper or Sogdia, with Khwarazm on the left and Fergana on the right as one faces north. The two regions were delimited differently but equally distinctively: Khwarazm by the surrounding deserts and the Aral Sea, Fergana by the Tianshan and Pamir mountains. Both regions owed their fertility to irrigation made possible by the two great rivers of Central Asia, the Amu Darya with its ramified delta in the case of Khwarazm, the Syr Darya with its mesh of tributaries in the case of Fergana. And both regions, lying within the network of Silk Road arteries, had commercial and political links with distant but important countries: to the east, China; to the west, Russia and the Mediterranean world; to the south, Iran and India; and to the north, the nomads of the Eurasian steppe and the dwellers of the taiga. Nevertheless, unlike Khwarazm, Fergana never rose to form a distinct political unit of its own beyond the existence of a scattering of local landlords – that is, before the eighteenth century, or, to put it in another way, before the eve of the Russian colonial conquest. This development was foreshadowed, however, by the status of *soyurghal* which it acquired toward the end of the Timurid period, and then again by its role as a theocratic state ruled by *khwajas* analogous to those in Sinkiang and Tashkent. We have seen that the Timurid Abu Said had allotted Fergana to his son Umar Shaykh. Following the khan's death in 1469, his son Ahmad succeeded him in Samarkand, while the latter's brother Umar Shaykh was able to consolidate his position and to rule from the city of Andijan until he died in 1494 and was succeeded by his son Babur. Andijan, located in the east of the province near the Tianshan mountains, had by then gained some prominence among the region's agglomerations, and it figures among the seven cities enumerated by its illustrious native in the *Baburname*. After the Uzbek conquest of Transoxania and Babur's withdrawal to Afghanistan and India, however, the city lost its status as capital, and the province lost its relative independence, apart from the inordinate power of local tribal chieftains endemic in the khanate of Bukhara.

Curiously but significantly, the first new step toward fuller independence was successfully accomplished not by one of the beys or tribal leaders but by a khwaja of Chadak, a locality in northern Fergana between Chust and Namangan. This was the expression of a movement toward theocratic rule whose earlier forms had appeared already with the *sadrs* of Bukhara several centuries back; but whereas there the protagonists were members of the official religious establishment, the emphasis gradually shifted toward the Sufi shaykhs and dervishes, whose charismatic power over the masses enabled them to vie with the tribal leaders and dynasties in their quest for temporal rule. The Kashgarian part of Sinkiang, as we have seen, developed as the most salient example of this evolution. By the seventeenth century the trend toward theocratic rule occurred also in Fergana, and a little later Tashkent too came under the rule of a khwaja regime. In the long run, none of these theocratic states managed to survive the determined action of tribal dynasties and chieftains, and even less that of the Manchu empire of China; but their occasional rule was perhaps less important than the influence they retained at the popular level.

We have seen how in Kashgaria the khwajas competed for power with the last remnants of the Chaghatayids, and then lobbied for it at the courts of the Dalai Lamas and Jungars before succumbing to the Manchu conquerors of Sinkiang. In Fergana, they had to yield, by 1710, to Shahrukh Biy, a chieftain of the Ming, one of the Uzbek tribes drifting into Transoxania and adjacent areas from the Kipchak steppe. The rise of the Ming Dynasty – thus called after the tribe, and of course totally unrelated to the Ming Dynasty of China – from the position of tribal leaders to that of rulers of an expanding khanate filled much of the eighteenth century. It was associated with the growth of the city of Khoqand from a site where the new rulers built a fortified palace. Khoqand, situated in the western part of Fergana some distance to the south of the Syr Darya, may have been chosen instead of an existing capital like Andijan partly because it was farther from the Tianshan mountains and thus less exposed to raids by the Kyrgyz and Kalmyks. On the other hand, the new capital was closer to the possessions of the emirs of Bukhara, and subsequently suffered in the wars between the two khanates; but again, this could and did turn into an asset when the Khoqandis were strong enough to become conquerors themselves in their favorite direction, that is, southern Kazakhstan and the eastern confines of the emirate of Bukhara.

The title that the Ming applied to themselves throughout the eighteenth century was the relatively modest *biy* (local form of the pan-Turkic title *beg*), but their possessions acquired the definite structure of a principality under Irdana Biy (1740–69). With most of Fergana under his control, Irdana Biy saw himself both forced and tempted to engage in international politics and alliances. His reign coincided with upheavals in both Bukhara and Sinkiang, a circumstance that may have facilitated the evolution of Fergana into what would soon become the khanate of Khoqand. Irdana Biy's recognition of Manchu suzerainty, quoted by scholars on the basis of Chinese sources, may have been more a clever expression of respect for a mighty neighbor than an actual state of vassaldom, and it harkened back to pre-Islamic times, when local rulers in Fergana had had a similar relationship with Tang China. At the same time, Irdana Biy formed a curious alliance with Ahmed Shah Durrani of Afghanistan (1747–73), possibly against the troublesome Kyrgyz tribes of the Tianshan rather than against China herself; in any case, the Afghan connection was a short-lived episode overshadowed by Khoqand's lasting relations with its neighbors to the east, west, and north. The consolidation continued under Narbuta Biy (1769–88), and

Khoqand began to assume urban proportions when a madrasa, the Madrasa-i Mir, was built there. Chinese "suzerainty" continued, but its ceremonial nature was illustrated by the fact that Beijing addressed the rulers of Khoqand as "khans," according to a Russian visitor. At any rate, it was Narbuta's son and successor Alim who some time around 1800 officially asumed the title of khan.

It was indeed under Narbuta Biy's sons Alim (1788–10) and Umar (1810–1822), and grandson Muhammad Ali or Madali (1822–42), that Khoqand came into its own as a vigorous and expanding khanate. Expansion was undertaken especially in the north and northwest, where between 1803 and 1809 the cities of Tashkent, Chimkent, and Sayram were conquered and Akmeshit (Kazakh pronunciation of Aq masjid, "White mosque"; Perovsk of Tsarist Russia and Kyzyl Orda of the Soviet period) was founded in 1820, and northeast into Kyrgyz territory, where a stronghold was built at Bishkek. These acquisitions and fortifications, garrisoned by Khoqandi troops, served a military purpose, but some also had considerable economic importance: at Akmeshit for example trade routes between Central Asia and Russia converged and intersected.

Khoqand now competed with Bukhara for primacy in Central Asia, and the khans had the temerity to claim parts of the emirate's eastern territory, including the towns of Jizakh and Ura-tepe. During the rule of Madali Khan the khanate reached its greatest extent and power. Its territories stretched from the Kipchak steppe with Akmeshit, Turkistan, Tashkent, the valleys of the Chu and of the lower Ili – thus from what is now southern Kazakhstan and northern Uzbekistan, to the Pamir regions of Karatekin, Darvaz, Shughnan, Rushan, and Gulab – thus comprising much of what is now Tajikistan, and they included most of modern Kyrgyzstan. Moreover, as a paradoxical and bizarre encroachment on Chinese sovereignty in Sinkiang, the rulers of Khoqand in 1826 extracted the right to send tax collectors among the Muslim population of Altishahr (Aksu, Ush Turfan, Kashgar, Yangishahr, Yarkand, and Khotan), after the collapse of Khwaja Jihangir's rebellion in Kashgar, which they themselves had supported. Meanwhile they had their first official contacts with Russia: in 1812 a Khoqandi embassy visited Orenburg, and the following year the Tsar's envoys came to Khoqand.

Most remarkable, however, were the activity and energy characteristic of this khanate, which produced a minor renaissance in art and literature, and an upswing in agricultural production through the construction of impressive irrigation canals. It is hard to decide how much of it was due to the khans themselves, and how much was generated by an internal dynamism in the area and its population that simply coincided with Ming rule, or how much was due to the influx of refugees from turbulent Bukhara, or again what the growing trade with Russia had to do with it. The first major canal, the Shahr-i Khan Say ("The Stream of the Khan's City," so named after the new town whose foundation accompanied the project), was dug under the rule of Umar Khan to the west of Andijan; 120 kilometers long, it irrigated an area of about 77,700 hectares. Similar projects appeared elsewhere, and not only in Fergana but also in the annexed fringes of the Greater and Middle Hordes, which were administered by governors from Tashkent; in the area of Tashkent itself the Khan Ariq ("Royal Canal") was dug in 1835; canal-building reached its height under the *beglerbegi* (governor) Mirza Ahmad (1853–58), thus on the very eve of the Russian conquest, and covered an area from the city of Turkestan to the valley of the Chu; and even after the conquest had already begun and the khan had acknowledged the Tsar's suzerainty, the largest canal in Fergana, the Ulugh Nahr ("Large River"), was dug under the sponsorship of the last Ming khan, Khudayar (his third rule, 1865–75). Silk and cotton, the cultivation of which was an ancient tradition in Fergana, continued to supply a local textile industry; cotton, moreover, had by then become an increasingly important cash crop grown for export to Russia, partly due to the effects of the Civil War on American exports.

Urban architecture, both civic and religious, benefited from the new prosperity. The great mosque of Khoqand, called Madrasa-i Jami because of its double function as a school and a mosque, was built by Umar Khan. Also remarkable were the madrasas Hakim Ayin and Sultan Murad Bey, and the royal palace called Urda; the last-named building, completed by Khudayar Khan in 1871 and thus on the eve of the Russian conquest, is remarkable for its facade decorated in a characteristic local style and the painted wooden ceiling of the main reception hall. Under Umar Khan and Madali Khan there sprang up a florescence of literature, above all poetry, remarkable especially for its Turki language, and for the appearance of women among the poets. One of these luminaries was Nadira (1790–1842), the wife of Umar Khan and mother of Madali Khan. A native of Babur's birthplace Andijan, she gained fame as a dominant figure in Khoqand for several reasons – her beauty, her art, and her power as the khan's wife and his successor's mother. Nadira's poems, in Turki and Persian, have been collected in two divans. The theme of one of her poems is the reunion of the faithful every evening during the month of Ramadan, after having fasted all day; it is an occasion not only to enjoy the meal but also the company of friends, until the wee hours of the morning if the means are there and the companions congenial. Such was Umar Khan's circle, but women were excluded: here the strictures of Islamic morals prevailed over the lingering nomadic customs which gave women greater freedom, and over the unconventional intellectual atmosphere at the khan's court which appreciated brilliance, even if it was displayed by women. The religious establishment, however, eventually had its revenge: Nadira's behavior, deemed an impermissible innovation (*bida*) from the Islamic point of view, was to play a role in her condemnation and execution along with her son Madali and her grandson Ali in 1842.

Umar Khan cultivated the friendship of the religious establishment partly for political reasons, for he strove to enhance his own power by breaking that of his tribal peers, the Uzbek chieftains. Moreover, he created a mercenary army composed not of Uzbeks or even other tribesmen but of the mostly Iranian highlanders from the Pamirs. Under his successors, strains also appeared more generally between the settled population and the nomadic elements. Of the settled citizens, those who spoke Turki were here called Sarts, those who spoke Persian were called Tajiks; the ranks of the sedentaries were also swelling with the rapidly sedentarizing Uzbek tribes like the Ming. The still nomadic elements included the Kipchak tribe (this is what the word Kipchak means here, a connotation different from the ethnolinguistic term applied by modern linguists to those Turks who spoke or speak the Kipchak form of Turkic), who had recently moved into Fergana from the Kazakh steppe (following in this other tribes such as the Ming who had arrived a century earlier), and the Kyrgyz nomads of the khanate's mountainous periphery fringing the Fergana valley to the east and south. These tensions, perhaps more than the routinely mentioned dissolute character of Madali Khan and of his successors, and the readiness of the emirs of Bukhara to intervene and exploit the situation, caused the decline and collapse of the khanate's political structure between 1840 and 1876. In 1840 rebels asked the emir Nasr Allah for help. The latter came with his troops and defeated Madali, who had to declare himself a vassal of Bukhara; two years later another rebellion overthrew Madali, however, he was killed while trying to flee, and Khoqand was occupied by the troops of Nasr Allah, who this time annexed the territory outright. His governor was almost instantly driven out, and Madali's uncle Shir Ali Khan (ruled 1842–45) assumed power. The emir again appeared before

Khoqand in 1843 and besieged it for forty days, but an attack on Bukhara by the khan of Khiva Allahqulikhan forced Nasr Allah to hurry home and saved the city and the khan, who also recovered Khujand and Tashkent.

The depravity of some khans, wars with Bukhara, and the unresolved tension between the khans' authority, tribal factions, and the settled population, together with the resulting civil wars, eventually deprived the khanate of what there was left of political stability, and in the end the Russians were virtually forced to impose their own solution. This instability is illustrated by the career of the last ruler, Khudayar (1845–75): he was removed from the throne in 1858 when another member of the dynasty, Malla Khan, replaced him (1858–62); in 1862 he regained his throne, but lost it to yet another relative (1863–65); finally in 1865 Khudayar ascended the throne for the third and last time, thanks to the support he had received from the emir of Bukhara Muzaffar. The squabbles among the Central Asians were characteristic of the incomprehension they had of the historic events that were changing their world. The Russians captured Tashkent in that same year of 1865; in 1868 they defeated the emir of Bukhara and, drastically reducing his territory, made him their *de facto* vassal. In the same year, without even having to resort to military action, they imposed a treaty on Khudayar Khan that had a similar form, and after having annexed all of the khanate's northwestern and northern territories. The new arrangement, however, did not suffice to save the khan or the khanate, in contrast to Bukhara. In 1873 a series of rebellions, led by Ishaq Hasan and Abdurahman Awtobashi, broke out and by July 1875 forced Khudayar Khan to seek refuge at the Russian mission. The Russians helped him leave the khanate and find safety in Tashkent, which by then was the administrative center of the newly established *guberniya* or imperial province of Turkestan. Khudayar's son Nasriddin was placed on the throne at Khoqand, but in October of the same year he was overthrown by a usurper named Pulat Khan and had to seek asylum in Russian-held Khujand. The disorders in the khanate continued, until in February 1876 the Russians occupied the entire territory and annexed it, as the *oblast* (region) of Fergana, to the province of Turkestan.

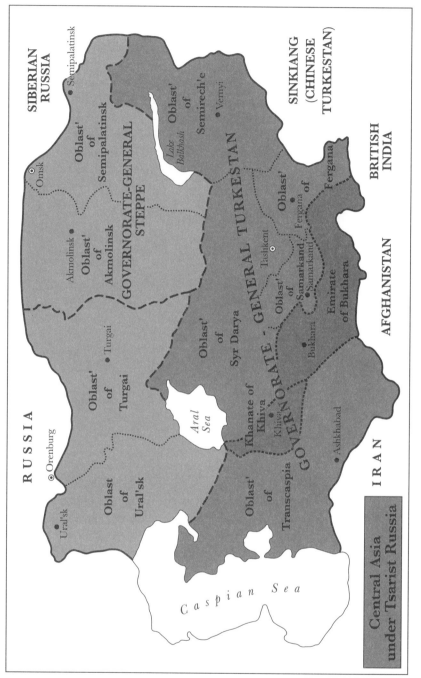

Map 6   Central Asia under Tsarist Russia

CHAPTER FIFTEEN

The Russian conquest and rule of Central Asia

The time, manner, and purpose of this conquest can be divided into two stages: in the first, Russia acquired the greater part of Kazakhstan except its Semireche and Syr Darya – thus southernmost – segments; in the second, the latter two and all the rest, thus territories of present-day Uzbekistan, Kyrgyzstan, Tajikistan, and Turkmenistan. The earlier stage was longer and more gradual (1730–1848), and at certain points structurally resembled the preceding acquisition of Siberia (which in turn could be viewed as an analogy to the "winning of the West" by the United States); the later stage was relatively brief – lasting from 1864 to 1884, the decisive move, however, being compressed into several campaigns between 1865 and 1868 – and stood squarely in the psychological context of Europe's contemporary "scramble for the colonies."

By 1730 the Kazakhs, as we have seen, had asserted themselves as a distinct group of nomadic tribes living in the eastern part of the Dasht-i Kipchak, speaking a distinctive Kipchak Turkic idiom, but lacking overall political unity. As a somewhat peculiar substitute for the latter, though, the tribes had coalesced into three confederations, the aforementioned Greater, Middle, and Lesser Hordes. Geography as much as tribal politics no doubt played a role in their formation: the Greater Horde occupied a territory roughly coterminous with Semireche, the Middle Horde that of central Kazakhstan, and the Lesser Horde that of western Kazakhstan. Although the Russian "orda" and English "horde" are originally Turkic words, the more common Kazakh name for their hordes was "jüz," meaning "hundred" (thus Ulu Jüz, Orta Jüz, Kishi Jüz). Except for brief periods early in their history, the Kazakhs never managed to forge a unified khanate that would in turn become a steppe empire, in the manner of their medieval Turkic and Mongol predecessors. One of the reasons for this may have been the proliferation of sultans – in this instance steppe aristocrats claiming Genghisid descent who alone were entitled to become khans – still holding positions of prestige and some authority, but stifling the rise of a truly charismatic new leader able to repeat the exploits of his great ancestor. On the other hand, the prestige enjoyed by the steppe aristocracy of Genghisid ancestry may have been a factor in the peculiar vertical division of Qazaq society into two layers, the so-called "White Bone" and "Black Bone" (*Aq Süyek, Qara Süyek*). Certain other credentials, such as descent from eminent Muslim ancestors, could also entitle some individuals, often called *qojas* (Kazakh form of *khwaja*) to claim "White Bone" status. The social and political structure of Kazakh society received a definitive codification, known as *jeti jarghy* ("seven verdicts"), during the reign of the khan Tauke (1680–1718) somewhat in the manner of the Mongol *yasa*, but took much longer to be written down – in fact only after the annexation of Kazakhstan to the Russian empire.

The rise of Russia as a modern power, which began under the aforementioned Ivan IV ("The Terrible"; ruled 1547–84) and was quickened by Peter the Great (ruled 1682–1725), made Russia overwhelmingly stronger than any of her Asian neighbors. In view of this new and growing disparity, the Russian penetration of the Kazakh steppe was only a matter of time and determination. The initially slow pace and oscillating success may have been due to the fact that the occupation of Siberia presented enough challenge and reward for the time being. The Russians at first contented themselves with accepting offers of vassaldom from various Kazakh leaders, without actually acquiring military or administrative control over their territory beyond the erection of fortified posts gradually infringing upon it. This complex process started in 1730, when Abilay (Abulkhayr), khan of the Lesser Horde, expressed his wish that the Tsar be his suzerain, and the request was granted. For much of the eighteenth century, Russia received similar assurances of loyalty from other Kazakh leaders, and discovered that they were little more than expedient declarations designed to bolster the chieftains' positions in intertribal wars. Similar statements of allegiance were made to Manchu emperors of China after their conquest of Sinkiang in 1758.

Nevertheless, a firmer hold on the northwestern, northern and northeastern fringes of Kazakhstan began to take shape during the reign of Catherine the Great (ruled 1762–96), with creeping colonization by Russian peasants and implantation of military posts deeper in Kazakh territory, such as Akmolinsk and Turgai. The kindred Tatars of the Volga had since the fall of Kazan in 1552 been safely incorporated in the Russian empire, and their elites were now experiencing something of an economic and spiritual renaissance. Tatar traders spread out into Central Asia as well, and also represented Russian commercial interests there; the government, eager to protect the latter, saw in these Muslim subjects convenient proxies, and trade flourished. Moreover, in those parts of Kazakhstan that had by then come under a sufficient degree of Russian control, St. Petersburg deemed it practical to consolidate that control through the at first sight surprising device of tying the still only marginally Muslim Kazakhs more firmly to Islam; the idea was that this would entice the unruly nomads to a more sedate way of life, especially since it was the tsar's subjects, the Tatar mullahs, who spread among the Kazakhs as preceptors and even built mosques and madrasas. Equally remarkable was the concomitant reluctance of the Russian government to allow proselytizing activity by its Orthodox subjects. This policy of using Tatar elites, both mercantile and religious, as the Russian government's advanced infrastructure in Kazakhstan, devised in the 1770s, continued until 1860, thus until the eve of the final drive to conquer the core of Central Asia.

Somewhat curiously, Russia's interest in Central Asia proper, the area south of the Syr Darya, appeared even before her first involvement with Kazakhstan. In 1717–18 Peter the Great sent the aforementioned expedition of some 300 men under Colonel Bekovich-Cherkasskiy to Khiva; its mission was less to conquer than to reconnoiter and establish a contact, but it was as an enemy that the khan of Khiva Shirghazi (1715–28) met the troop and destroyed it. A similar attempt more than a century later, in 1839–40, led by General Perovskiy, foundered on logistical problems, for the khanate was well shielded from attack on most sides by inhospitable deserts. Aside from Central Asia itself, the goal of both these expeditions may have been to probe possible routes to India; this in turn remained more a daydream than a real plan, and was diametrically opposed to the methodical and realistic manner characteristic of Russian expansion.

We began our story by dividing the Russian conquest of Central Asia into two stages, 1730–1848 and 1864–84; the first stage could in turn be subdivided into two phases, of which the second occurred between 1822 and 1848, for that was when St. Petersburg resolved to eliminate the four Kazakh hordes altogether (a fourth, minor horde called Bükey's horde, had meanwhile formed to the west of the Lesser Horde between the Ural and Volga rivers): the Middle Horde was suppressed in 1822, the Lesser in 1824, Bükey's in 1845, and the Greater in 1848.

The suppression of the Kazakh hordes removed any ambivalence about Russia's dominance in the bulk of Kazakh territory, but it still left out its southern fringe. There were two reasons for that: logistical, for that area – primarily the middle and lower course of the Syr Darya – was rather remote and in parts separated from northern and central Kazakhstan by semi-arid stretches; and political, because it had by then come under the sway of the khanate of Khoqand. A conflict with Khoqand might have caused complications with Britain and China, which St. Petersburg wanted to avoid. Its acquisition thus required a different psychological, diplomatic, and military strategy. Nevertheless, by 1853 the Russians wrested Akmeshit from the Khoqandis. A year later they founded Vernyi – the eventual Kazakh capital Almaty – and pushed on to Bishkek, today the capital of Kyrgyzstan but then a Khoqandi frontier post. The strategy of these operations illustrates the vast resources at Russia's disposal: her giant pincers began to squeeze the remnant of Kazakhstan from west and east, the latter approach being realized from her Siberian frontier. The brief halt that followed was caused by external circumstances: the Crimean War, and the uprising led by Shaykh Shamil in the Caucasus. These hindrances disappeared with the advent of the 1860s, and the stage was set for the final assault: it began in 1864 with the fall of Chimkent and Aulie Ata (now Jambul), and culminated with the storming of Tashkent in June 1865.

Tashkent is of course the capital of Uzbekistan, and as such we associate it with that republic rather than with Kazakhstan. In 1865, however, the event was perceived more as the final step in the conquest of Kazakhstan. For the time being, accommodation with Khoqand, Bukhara, and Khiva, rather than their conquest, was viewed by the principal policy planners in St. Petersburg as preferable to any further push southward that might provoke Britain to action from India's northwest frontier. The clashes with Khoqandi forces did not yet mean war, and Tashkent was stormed almost against the wishes of the Russian government by the brash General Chernyaev.

Yet a mere three years later, in 1868, the Russians were at war with the emir of Bukhara, routing his forces in several battles, annexing a substantial part of the emirate's territory (including Samarkand), and allowing the rest to exist as a *de facto* Russian protectorate; five years later, in 1873, they defeated in a similar manner the khan of Khiva, annexing much of his territory, and leaving the rest as a protectorate; and by 1876 they did away with the khanate of Khoqand altogether, annexing all of its remaining area. Only the territory roughly corresponding to modern Turkmenistan remained untouched, but its turn came five years later when the Russians crushed Turkmen resistance at the battle of Göktepe in 1881.

The causes and goals of all these campaigns and conquests were complex and shifting, but two catalysts can be singled out: one was the unrealistic attempts by the local leaders, both secular and religious, to recover from the infidels what had been lost, thus provoking the Russians to actions they might not have taken so quickly (this was especially true of Bukhara); the other was the virtual collapse of government in the khanate of Khoqand, which began with the death of Madali Khan in 1842 and worsened in the 1850s and 1860s; the Russians, for several years endeavoring to establish a working relationship with a khan in Khoqand, finally threw up their hands and carried out the annexation. Yet another factor may have been the contradictory effect of the setback that Russia had suffered in the Crimean War: many Russians, especially the more fiery members of the military, sought psychological compensation through expansion elsewhere; in Central Asia this meant taking solace through thwarting the real or imagined designs of the world's principal colonial power and Russia's adversary, Great Britain. And finally there was of course the colonial motivation: to gain markets for the products of Russia's growing industry and acquire sources of raw materials for this industry.

The Russian conquest of Central Asia was completed by 1884 with the acquisition of Merv. This fertile oasis contained the ruins of the great pre-Islamic and early Islamic city, as well as a small settlement nearby which had the same name. However, it was not Merv's history but its proximity to Afghanistan and thus to British India that made the event of 1884 so important. Its fall to Russia and the subsequent Russian drive still farther south to Kushka on the Afghan border brought British fears for their colony to the verge of paranoia, and the mutual sparring of the two powers came close to war when in the early 1890s the Russians pushed south from their province of Fergana through the Pamirs to India's Kashmir border. Peace was rescued perhaps mainly because neither power had the intentions that the other had suspected, a circumstance that facilitated the work of the Pamir Boundary Commission in 1895. Its agreement, further strengthened by the 1907 Anglo-Russian Convention, bound the two partners to respect each other's zones of interest, and as both a symbol and effective buffer it created an elongated strip of territory between Pamir and Kashmir and attached it to Afghanistan (the "Afghan finger"), while linking up its eastern tip with China's Sinkiang province.

We may thus consider the year 1895 as the terminus by which the southern borders of Russian and then Soviet Central Asia – and now of the independent republics of Turkmenistan, Uzbekistan, and Tajikistan – had taken their definitive form. Russia's acquisition of a new, non-Russian, non-Slavic, non-Christian, Muslim territory of course had precedents bracketed by Ivan the Terrible's destruction of the khanates of Kazan in 1552, Astrakhan in 1556, and Catherine the Great's annexation of the khanate of Crimea in 1783. Those conquests, however, were not quite of the modern colonial type but had elements akin both to Spain's Reconquista and Russia's spread into the Siberian expanse; the conquest of Central Asia, on the other hand, bore all the hallmarks of nineteenth-century Europe's colonial expansion: the motivation of acquiring abundant and cheap sources of raw materials such as cotton for the Russian textile industry, and, inversely, of gaining a privileged position for Russia's commerce; the ease and rapidity of military operations in which handfuls of disciplined and well-armed troops of a modern European power overcame much larger native forces, and the resulting pacification and organization of the conquered territories along pragmatic lines so as to suit primarily the colonizer but also, up to a point, to benefit the colonized, were the chief elements of this expansion.

British India is the colony that is routinely mentioned as the antecedent, model, or counterpart to Russian Central Asia, but French North Africa presents an even closer parallel (although the initially tentative and protracted invasion of the Indian subcontinent does harbor certain analogies with Russia's initial probing of Kazakhstan). Chronologically, the French conquests bracket the Russian ones – Algeria in 1830, Tunisia in 1883, Morocco in 1912 – in contrast to the eighteenth-century inception of Britain's drive. Both the French and Russian conquests were government undertakings from the start, unlike the British arrival in India, which was at first a private enterprise of the East India Company; all three acquisitions were vast expanses of territory, but sizable colonization by settlers – both agricultural and urban – from the colonial powers occurred only in Central Asia and North Africa; finally, geographical realities must have been a powerful psychological as well as logistical factor: the contiguousness of Central Asia with Russia's own territories, and the relative proximity of North Africa to France, may have played a similar catalytic role in the evolving concept of those countries as indivisible parts of the fatherland, in contrast to India, whose remoteness beyond two oceans, a population vastly surpassing that of Britain, and a civilization too impressive to subordinate it to that of the conqueror, deterred any such contemplations.

The administrative structure devised by St. Petersburg for its new possessions went through several stages and modifications. The stages were the fall of Tashkent in 1865, the defeat and truncation of the emirate of Bukhara in 1868 and of the khanate of Khiva in 1873, the liquidation of the khanate of Khoqand in 1876, and the completion of the overall conquest with the fall of Merv in 1884 and penetration of the Pamirs by 1895. The result was the Governorate-General of Turkestan (Turkestanskoe General-Gubernatorstvo or General-Guberniya Turkestan), administered by a military governor residing in Tashkent and divided into five regions (*oblasts*) and two protectorates. The regions were Syrdarya (center Tashkent), Semireche (center Vernyi), Fergana (center Skobelev), Samarkand (center Samarkand), and Zakaspie (Transcaspia, center Ashgabad); the protectorates were the emirate of Bukhara and the khanate of Khiva.

Meanwhile, the organization of the steppes to the north – thus of the greater part of Kazakhstan – proceeded along lines that were somewhat distinct without, however, denying the many-faceted links with Turkestan. The distinctiveness resided, among other things, in their geographical and historical linkage with Russia proper and with Siberia. The result was that unlike the Governorate-General of Turkestan, which had a specific administrative and geographical unity, the territory inhabited by the Kazakhs consisted of three separate parts: the westernmost part, whose area corresponded to that of the Bükey and Lesser Hordes, was now the oblast of Uralsk, whose administrative center was the city of Uralsk and whose governor reported directly to the Ministry of Interior; its central part, more or less the former Middle Horde, consisted of the oblasts of Turgai and Akmolinsk; the governor of the Turgai oblast did not even reside there, but rather across the border in Orenburg, for he was at the same time governor of the Governorate-General of Orenburg and also reported to the Ministry of Interior; the oblasts of Akmolinsk and Semipalatinsk, on the other hand, formed a full-fledged Governorate-General, that of the Steppe, but their governor did not reside there either but across the border in the Siberian city of Omsk, which is thus also included in this governorate on some maps. The Semipalatinsk oblast covered some of the territory of the defunct Greater Horde, but the greater part of the latter now corresponded to the Turkestan oblast of Semireche and the eastern fringe of that of Syrdarya, both within the Governorate-General of Turkestan.

One final comment on the administrative borders of Central Asia: both the khanate of Khiva and the emirate of Bukhara lost important segments of their territories: those of Khiva were incorporated in the Syrdarya region, those of Bukhara in that of Samarkand, together with the precious city itself. On the other hand, the emirate's territory was extended farther east so as to include almost all of modern Tajikistan except eastern Badakhshan, which was incorporated in the Fergana region, and Khujand, which was divided between the Fergana and Samarkand regions.

The new political map of Central Asia thus reflected a blend of geographical, historical, and strategic factors used or created by the Russian conqueror. The native population played little or no active part in this process, which only marginally took account of a reality that in the Soviet period would play a paramount role, namely the ethnolinguistic one. Yet the life of the natives was immediately and increasingly affected by the new order. The break with the past brought about many radical departures, but two deserve special mention: the relative peace and order installed by the European conqueror in an area where internecine warfare and marauding had been endemic, and the surrender of the population's overall destiny to the discretion of a new and alien master who was an infidel.

Tashkent became the seat of the Russian governor and administration. The choice made sense on several counts. Its climate is salubrious and, although continental, without the extremes characteristic of places farther north or south; its location, at first sight somewhat eccentric, was quite central within the province of Turkestan; situated near the right bank of the Syr Darya, it also lay in an area where the worlds of historic Transoxania to the south and of the Kipchak steppe to the north met and overlapped; on the ethnolinguistic level, this was reflected in the Sart population of the city, which spoke Turki Turkic or Tajik Persian, and the Kazakh population of the countryside, which spoke Kipchak Turkic; this overlapping was also visible in the historic role of Tashkent as one of the crossroads of long-distance trade routes. The fact that its prominence had previously never equalled that of Bukhara or Samarkand may similarly be ascribed to this position in a transition zone: for although Tashkent benefited from the contact with the steppe nomads, it was also too exposed to their unpredictable incursions and tribal movements, and to occasional contests between the rulers of Transoxania and the Kazakhs and other nomads, to become a major metropolis. Once peace was solidly established by Russia, however, Tashkent quickly surpassed all other Central Asian cities. Much of this rise was of course due to the city's function as the first modern capital of Central Asia and seat of the colonial administration. The Russians built a quarter of their own alongside the native city, establishing a pattern that they would follow in a number of other places: a European city developed through a rational system of urban planning, presenting a sharp contrast to the traditional native quarters.

The second governor of the Turkestan Governorate-General was Konstantin Petrovich von Kaufman, a general descended from a Russified German Baltic family who had commanded the Russian troops in the crucial confrontation with Bukhara. He was an able officer and administrator, and his long tenure of office (1867–82) did much to put the colonial administration of Central Asia on a solid base. The system held firm until the entire edifice of the Russian empire collapsed in the Bolshevik Revolution of 1917. The prime motivation of the Russian conquest had been economic self-interest, and the evolution of the colony between 1868 and 1917 amply met that goal. The area became a supplier of raw materials for Russian industry and a consumer of Russian products, after the classical colonial pattern. We have already pointed to cotton as the most important commodity sent to Russia; its cultivation increased to the verge of becoming a monoculture, and the adverse effect of this one-sidedness was made worse by the concomitant decrease in the growing of cereals, which made Central Asia dependent on wheat imports from Russia. The other major aspect was the afore-mentioned colonization by agricultural settlers, mostly Russian and Ukrainian. This affected primarily Kazakhstan, but also the Semireche region of Turkestan, including portions of northern Kyrgyzstan. Some of the most fertile tracts of land were thus seized, with the doubly harmful effects of expropriating the nomads' grazing grounds and of hampering their seasonal movements in search of water and pasture land (thus a reverse process in comparison with the aforementioned desedentarization caused by the Mongols). Other forms of immigrant colonization existed too, and all over the two provinces; they were mostly of the professional urban type: civil service, transportation and communications, incipient industry, and modern education, staffed chiefly by and for the Russians. This arrangement led to the special demographic physiognomy of some cities where the European population, living in its own quarters, began to equal or even surpass the native one. Trade with Russia, formerly passing through the intermediary of Tatar merchants, was now taken over by the colonizers themselves. To a considerable extent the natives, essential to the base of the productive process, remained excluded on the executive and profit-taking level.

On the cultural and spiritual level, the Russians were fairly benevolent and tolerant colonizers. Although convinced of the superiority of their own civilization and religion, they had less of the condescending or downright contemptuous attitude toward the natives characteristic of most colonizers from Western Europe. Islam, the *sharia*, *waqf*, religious practices and education, and the general way of life were not interfered with unless in direct conflict with Russia's interests and with the exception of slavery, which the Russians suppressed in imitation of similar measures taken by other colonial powers in their possessions (and not long after the 1861 suppression of serfdom in Russia). Proselytism by the Orthodox Church, despite the participating priest's role at the storming of Tashkent, received no encouragement from the authorities. This attitude, however, was a result not only of Russian tolerance, but also of the changed intellectual and spiritual climate in Europe, and it presented a sharp contrast to the earlier, sixteenth-century conquest of Kazan, where forced conversion or expulsion of those who refused to convert, in addition to other forms of persecution, wrought havoc among the Tatar population; in the same manner, for example, the effects of the 1830 French landing at Algiers differed from those of the Spanish Reconquista, despite the participating French bishop's exuberant exclamation about Christianity's return to North Africa. Central Asia's natives, having lost their political and economic independence, thus retained their spiritual freedom, and most remained staunchly Muslim in their religion, culture, and way of life. This also meant, however, that the bulk of the population received little of the already vertiginous intellectual and scientific progress in which Russia had taken part since the time of Peter the Great.

Aside from the military occupation itself – about 40,000 troops are estimated to have been stationed in the two provinces, which had a population of about six million souls and an area of some 1,277,000 square kilometers (493,000 square miles) – the construction of railroads and of a telegraph network proved an effective means of controlling the colony. Especially the railroads facilitated this control and would later play a crucial role in the preservation of Turkestan as Russia's possession during the turbulent years of the Bolshevik Revolution. The first line, opened to traffic in September 1881, connected the Caspian port of Uzun Ada – to be shifted in 1894 to Krasnovodsk – with the Turkmen city of Kizil Arvat; the location of the earliest railroad line in this part of the colony, conquered last, may at first sight seem surprising, but the reason was its compatibility with the lively shipping traffic on the Caspian, linking it both with ports on the northern, Russian side of this sea and with Baku and thus Russia's Transcaucasus possessions. By 1898 this line was extended all the way to Tashkent, and in 1906 a line linking this city to Orenburg and thus to the rest of the empire – for example, on to Samara, Riazan, Moscow, and St. Petersburg – was completed. This network had great strategic, economic and psychological significance, emphasizing a structural feasibility of Central Asia's incorporation in the Russian empire that was impossible in the case of the overseas colonies of other European powers. Moreover, the construction of a branch from Merv to Kushka on the Afghan border, the southernmost point in Russian Turkestan and, for that matter, in the entire Russian empire, was dictated by the aforementioned strategic considerations, while that from Samarkand to Andijan served primarily economic interests. Another detail worth mentioning is the fact that this line, in its sector between Merv and Samarkand, passed through the emirate of Bukhara but skirted the city itself some twelve kilometers to the southeast; that was where Kagan or New Bukhara, a railroad station town populated mainly by Russian administrative personnel, developed and eventually played a role in the events leading to the collapse of the native regime.

Starting with General Romanovskiy (1865–67) and ending with General Kuropatkin (1914–17), eleven men served as governors-general of Turkestan. Central Asia experienced in the course of these decades an economic development that benefited, as we have said, the colonizer, and in certain basic respects harmed the native population, for example through loss of land to settlers, growth of detrimental monoculture, and dependence on food imports and finished products from Russia. On the positive side, the population drew some benefit from the *pax Russica* imposed on it by the colonizer, and from the contact with modern civilization as represented by Russia. True, most Central Asians continued to live as before; few were those who received education, and such education as there was continued to be of the traditional type based on the Koran and the classics of Arabo-Persian culture.

Nevertheless, a minority of Central Asians did become exposed to modern education. This happened through a variety of channels. One was a certain number of schools opened by the Russians for the natives, where teaching was done both in the vernacular and in Russian (the so-called *russko-tuzemnye shkoly* or "Russo-native schools"). Another was modern education propagated by the Muslims themselves; these reformers were often from other, older parts of the Russian empire, or were Central Asians who had lived or studied at Russian institutions. One such reformer, a Crimean Tatar named Ismail Bey Gasprinskiy (Gaspirali, 1851–1914), founded a movement known as *usul-i jadid*, "new method," because of the new type of education that was its main purpose. A certain number of *jadid* schools thus appeared also in the two provinces. Efforts to enlighten the people took other forms as well, such as the periodical press (for example the newspaper *Terjuman* published in the Crimean city of Bakhchesarai by Gasprinskiy from 1885 to 1914). Despite its incipient nature and often ephemeral duration, the effect of this press in forming the small but important group of those Central Asians who were increasingly aware of a need for modernization was considerable. Most of these new currents arrived by way of Russia and thanks to familiarity with the Russian language through which native intellectuals gained acquaintance with Western culture, but they were at the same time part of the general awakening to the need for reform that was gripping many Muslim countries, especially the Ottoman empire. While Russian cities such as Orenburg or St. Petersburg were where the select few from Central Asia would usually travel or study, some went to Istanbul, where they imbibed ideas not only of modernization but also of modern nationalism, mostly in its adapted forms of pan-Islamism or pan-Turkism. Abdarrauf Fitrat (1886–1938) thus spent some time in the Ottoman capital, and after returning to his native Bukhara he became one of the newly formed group of "Young Bukharans" who, like the "Young Turks" of the Ottoman empire, strove to reform their society. Reform became the leading motto of the Young Bukharans toward the end of the Tsarist period, and it began to surpass the parallel or competing mottos of pan-Islamism or pan-Turkism. It was no accident that the most articulate group appeared in Bukhara; in comparison with areas under direct administration from Tashkent, the emirate's backwardness became that much more evident, while its relative independence may have encouraged the Young Bukharans to consider reform rather than liberation from Russia as the most urgent goal. Fitrat's subsequent career and life epitomize the drama, ultimately tragic, that unfolded in Central Asia under Tsarist and then Soviet rule. The first act took place during the final years of the Tsarist regime, when Fitrat wrote his *Munazara* ("The Dispute"), a reformist essay urging his compatriots to awaken to the needs of modern times. Although he eventually became a major scholar and publisher of Chaghatay Turkic literature, he wrote the tract in Persian, a detail further stressing the initial reformist focus of this typically bilingual Bukharan who later became a major proponent of Turkic cultural renaissance. Politically, his main focus was reform, and for this reason he and most of his associates were at first not averse to cooperation and association with Russia.

Both the Russian administration and the emir of Bukhara looked warily on the various reformist currents in their territories, and never hesitated to intervene when they felt that the existing order was threatened. The native conservatives, especially the clerical class, gave support to the Russians in this matter. The Tsarist regime, however, had a more dangerous opponent than incipient nationalism to contend with: its own socialist dissidents, revolutionaries of various hues, whose numbers in Central Asia were swelling with deportees from Russia. Although mostly of the intellectual and professional class, these revolutionaries made rapid headway among the Russian workers and soldiers of the colony, while they virtually ignored and were ignored by the natives – whether their peers whom they barely knew or did not trust, or the peasants and such members of a marginal native working class as there were. This was a fateful evolution for Central Asia, for the drive, political skill and, eventually, the military means of these revolutionaries would in due course preserve the region as a Russian possession, thwarting the valiantly defended aspirations of the inexperienced and unarmed Muslims.

On the eve of the First World War and the upheavals that followed it, the two provinces of Central Asia were thus firmly incorporated in the Russian empire. The few native uprisings, usually fomented by such religious figures as the Naqshbandi *ishon* Madali (better remembered as Dukchi Ishon) of Fergana in 1898, were speedily put down by the Russians. Half a century of colonial rule had had effects not unlike those in other European colonies. Their possession flattered the Russians psychologically and benefited them economically; but perhaps the strongest and seemingly indissoluble tie was the presence of a by then quite entrenched Russian constituency, consisting of people of many walks of life, from professionals to workers and agriculturalists, who considered the colony their home and indeed had no other home elsewhere; again, the analogy with French settlers in North Africa is especially striking. Meanwhile, the native Muslim population, from the Kazakhs in the far north to the Turkmens and Tajiks in the deep south, had undergone a process that was as new, complex, uneven, and contradictory as the entire concept of a modern colony. Neither the colonizer nor perhaps even the colonized fully realized how temporary the arrangement was, in which again we can observe an analogy with other colonies, but especially with North Africa. The fact remains that by 1917, there had arisen in both provinces an elite of educated and politically sophisticated natives who proved themselves capable of putting up a brave fight for their people's rights. In the end they lost, but not even the heaviest hand of alien rule that followed could ultimately change the impermanence of that rule, as the events of 1991 have shown.

CHAPTER SIXTEEN

From Governorates-General to Union Republics

Among the symptoms of the second-class citizenship that the Muslims of Central Asia experienced in Tsarist Russia was their official status as *inorodtsy*, natives (literally, "alien-born"), and the fact that they were not required to perform military service. The latter aspect appeared to be an asset when the First World War broke out and their young men were spared shedding blood on the battlefields. In 1916, however, the imperial government took a step whose consequences proved detrimental to the Russians and disastrous for the natives: it issued a decree that large numbers of Central Asian Muslims be drafted for labor behind the battle lines – primarily that of digging trenches. The insulting nature of this order, compounded by still wilder rumors, provoked a number of uprisings in both provinces, directed against government representatives but also against civilians, especially the agricultural settlers. The authorities, taken by surprise, could not prevent serious casualties on the Russian side, but when they finally suppressed the revolts, the loss of life among the natives was staggeringly heavier and the suffering much worse. Especially hard hit were the Kyrgyz, because their attacks on the settlers in the neighborhood of the lake Issyk Kul were particularly violent and the resulting repression was that much harsher. Many fled across the border to Sinkiang, with further casualties wrought chiefly by the elements during the winter of 1916–17.

Kuropatkin, the governor-general of the Turkestan province, had the situation under control and was making plans for further exploitation of the colony now that more land had been vacated by the fleeing Kyrgyz, when the empire began to crack at the center. Although the attitude of the Provisional Government led by Kerenskiy after the February 1917 revolution was at best ambiguous with respect to Central Asian Muslims, the change did give the latter certain liberties they had not enjoyed before: they could form their own organizations, freely publish newspapers, and make demands. Thus on 4–8 April[1] the first congress of Turkestanian Muslims was held in Tashkent. It created the Türkistan Müslüman Merkezi Shurasi (Central Council of Turkestanian Muslims) and elected Mustafa Chokay as its president. On 8 April 1917 it passed the following resolution:

We, the Muslims of Turkestan, who after a subjugation of many years by Tsarist Russia find for the first time, thanks to the Revolution and to our struggle against Tsarist rule, the opportunity to present our demands: We consider it right to form an organization that will bring out our national voice and solve our main problems. This organization has the following goals:
1. To represent the interests of the Turkestanians before the Revolutionary authorities.
2. To prepare the ground for the autonomy of Turkestan.
3. To defend religious rights (the shariat courts, a central administration for religious affairs).
4. To solve the problem of land tenure.
5. To further the cultural development of Turkestan.
6. To examine all the laws that affect the Muslims of Turkestan.
The organization is called The Central Islamic Council of Turkestan. We want to emphasize that it does not have the function of a political party but has as its aim the unification of all the patriots of Turkestan concerned about the welfare of their fatherland.

The organization consisted of two wings: a conservative one led by Shir Ali Lapin, and a reformist one led by Münevver Qari. The conservatives then formed an organization of their own, the *Ulema Jemiyeti* (Association of the Ulema), and the reformists the *Shura-yi Islam* (Islamic Council). The statements and demands of the Central Islamic Council, addressed to no one in particular but implicitly to the Russian authorities in Tashkent and Petrograd, received little practical response from those quarters. The new contest for Turkestan between Muslims and Russians was only beginning.

It was the second Russian revolution of 1917, the Bolshevik one of October/November, that seemed to promise true liberation, for self-determination of all the subject peoples of the former Tsarist empire was one of its professed goals. This was explicitly stated in two proclamations which the new government, the Council of People's

---

[1] The question of exact dates for this period is troublesome because the Russian empire still used the Julian calendar, and a switch to the Gregorian system occurred only after the October/November Revolution. This has produced occasional inconsistencies in secondary sources, and I have made no attempt to ascertain whether specific dates had been "converted" or not.

Commissars, issued on 2 and 20 November 1917 respectively. The first proclamation was of a general nature and concerned all the non-Russian nationalities of Russia; the second proclamation addressed itself specifically to the Muslims, and read:[2]

> *To All Muslim Workers of Russia and the Orient*
> Comrades! Brothers!
> Great events are taking place in Russia. A bloody war that had been started for the sake of dividing up of foreign lands is drawing to a close. The rule of predators who had subjugated the nations of the world is collapsing. The old edifice of thraldom and serfdom is falling under the blows of the Russian revolution. The world of arbitrariness and oppression is living its last days. A new world, the world of workers who have liberated themselves, is being born. At the forefront of this world is the Workers' and Peasants' Government of Russia – the Council of People's Commissars.
>
> All Russia is studded with Revolutionary Councils of Workers', Soldiers', and Peasants' deputies. Power is in the hands of the people. The toiling masses of Russia speak with one voice about their wish to conclude an honest peace and to help the oppressed peoples of the world attain freedom.
>
> . . . In the face of these great events we are turning to you, the toiling and disinherited Muslims of Russia and the Orient.
>
> Muslims of Russia, Tatars of the Volga and the Crimea, Kyrgyz and Sarts of Siberia and Turkestan, Turks and Tatars of Transcaucasia, Chechens and mountain dwellers of the Caucasus, all you whose mosques and places of worship have been destroyed, whose beliefs and customs have been trampled on by the tsars and oppressors of Russia! From now on your beliefs and customs, your national and cultural institutions are being declared free and inviolable. Arrange your national life freely and without hindrance. This is your right. Know that your rights, just as the rights of all the peoples of Russia, are protected by the might of the Revolution and by its organs, the Councils of Workers', Soldiers', and Peasants' Deputies. Support then this Revolution and its executive organ, the Government!
>
> . . . Muslims of Russia! Muslims of the Orient! We expect your sympathy and support on this path toward a rebirth of the world!
> Signed: V. Ulyanov (Lenin), Chairman of the Council of Commissars; J. Dzhugashvili (Stalin), Commissar for Nationality Affairs.

The Bolshevik Revolution was replicated in Tashkent a few days after the events in Petrograd, and on 15 November 1917 the Third Regional Congress of the Soviets proclaimed the authority of the new regime over

---

[2] B. Hayit, *Sowjetrussische Orientpolitik am Beispiel Turkestans* (Köln-Berlin, 1962), pp. 217–18. The author cites two Soviet publications as the sources for the original Russian text: *Sobranie ukazov rasporyazheniy raboche-krestyanskogo pravitelstva* (Moscow, 1917–18), vol. 19 (Dec. 1917), no. 7, appendix 2; and Narodnyi komissariat po delam natsionalnostey, *Politika sovetskoy vlasti po natsionalnym delam za tri goda, 1917–1920* (Moscow, 1920).

Central Asia. This authority was to be expressed by the local government, the Turkestan Council of People's Commissars (Turkestanskiy Sovet Narodnykh Komissarov, usually shortened as *Turksovnarkom*). Concurrently with this congress, the Third Congress of Central Asian Muslims was meeting in Tashkent. Some of the participants demanded autonomy, but Shir Ali Lapin, who had presided over the conference, proposed to the Soviets that a Russian–Turkestanian coalition government be formed. These demands and proposals were rejected, and F. I. Kolesov, the chairman of the Turksovnarkom, issued the following statement:

> At the present time we cannot permit the admission of Muslims into the higher organs of the regional revolutionary authority, because the attitude of the native population toward the Soviet of Workers', Soldiers', and Peasants' Deputies is quite uncertain, and because the indigenous population lacks proletarian organizations which the [Bolshevik] faction could welcome into the organs of the higher government.

These events preceded by a few days the proclamation of the central government in Petrograd to the Muslims of Russia. Subsequent developments proved that it would be the spirit of the Tashkent statement, not that of the Petrograd proclamation, which would always determine the Soviet government's treatment of the Muslims of Russia. It is true, however, that the contradiction between the two attitudes was glossed over by a wording in the Petrograd proclamation that had far-reaching consequences: the appeal was addressed to all the *workers* (trudyashchiesya, perhaps more accurately translated as *toilers*) of the Muslim world, thus to its proletariat in Marxist terminology. Although it reiterated the right of nations to self-determination, its implicit exclusion of the bourgeoisie gave the Soviet regime a tactical advantage which it subsequently used to perfection: for in Central Asia – just as in other Muslim countries of the time – there was no native industrial working class, and most indigenous leaders came from the bourgeoisie or from the religious establishment.

Another significant feature of the Petrograd proclamation was its universality: it addressed itself to all Muslims, not just to those under Russian rule. It revealed how totally subordinated Central Asia was to the concept of a world revolution, and how automatic was the assumption that the men who now held power in Russia should be accepted as the unquestioned leaders of that revolution. To them, Turkestan was more a stepping stone than an area whose problems and wishes might be met for their own sake. Its role as an important pawn in a gigantic and deadly serious game came out quite clearly in a statement made by Stalin in 1919: "Turkestan, because of its geographical position, is a bridge connecting socialist Russia with the oppressed countries of the East, and in view of this the strengthening of the Soviet regime in Turkestan might have the greatest revolutionary significance for the entire Orient." This was the global view at the center of Communist power in Moscow (where it had moved from Petrograd), but there can be little doubt that it was not exempt from other considerations: the principal one being the psychologically natural tendency of those with power to force their views and wishes on those under their control, and the tendency to retain what has once been acquired. Moreover, the national pride in Russia's status as a great empire, although camouflaged behind thick layers of contradictory Marxist denials, may have played an important psychological role at all levels of Russian society, from humble Russian citizens to such aliens as Stalin once they had crossed the national divide to join or become the masters of this empire. Stalin was at the time the Commissar for Nationality Affairs, and subsequently he never ceased paying attention to the question of non-Russian nationalities of the Soviet Union even after the *Narkomnats* (short for Narodnyi Komissariat Natsionalnostey) had been abolished and he himself had become the most powerful man in Russia. With Stalin's rising power, the initially feasible debate of how seriously the right to self-determination should be taken was closed; only those with impeccable credentials had this right, and the foremost component of these credentials was unflinching loyalty to Moscow.

THE KHOQAND EXPERIMENT

At the inception of their rule in November 1917, the Bolsheviks of Tashkent hastened to establish firm ties with the government in Petrograd, and on 23 November they sent the following telegram: "The Sovnarkom considers the execution of your decrees to be its duty." The Sovnarkom and the Soviets – a rudimentary form of government and parliament – in Tashkent may have propagated revolutionary, progressive ideas, but they also represented almost exclusively the Russian and European minority in Turkestan. We have mentioned the attempt of Shir Ali Lapin to negotiate with the Russians to obtain a share in power. After the rebuttal by Kolesov, Muslim leaders decided to convoke a fourth congress in order to seek a solution. In December 1917 they thus met in Khoqand, which at the time remained outside the administrative

and military reach of revolutionary Tashkent. This congress was
marked not only by an alliance of the conservative Ulema Jemiyeti with
the progressive Shura-yi Islam, but also by the participation of non-
Muslims brought there by their anti-Bolshevik sentiments.

The congress elected a parliament, Khalq Shurasi (People's Council;
the word *shura* is a translation of the Russian *sovet*, "advice, council,"
usually spelled in English as soviet), which consisted of fifty-four
members: thirty-six of these were Muslims, while eighteen were
Russians or other non-Muslims. Shir Ali Lapin became president of this
parliament, which on 11 December 1917 nominated a committee of ten
members that was meant to function as a provisional government. This
parliament and government claimed to represent a territory and population identical with those claimed by the Soviet power in Tashkent:
1,524,000 square kilometers and 5,363,000 inhabitants. The following
resolution was adopted by the congress:

The Fourth Extraordinary Congress, expressing the will of the peoples of
Turkestan to self-determination in accordance with the principles proclaimed
by the Great Russian Revolution, declares Turkestan territory autonomous in
union with the Federal Democratic Republic of Russia. The elaboration of the
form of autonomy of Turkestan is entrusted to the Constituent Assembly of
Turkestan, which must be convened as soon as possible. The Congress solemnly
pledges herewith that the rights of national minorities will be fully safeguarded.

There thus developed in Turkestan a historic confrontation, from
December 1917 to February 1918, between the predominantly Muslim
regional government in Khoqand and the predominantly Russian one
in Tashkent. In terms of national self-determination, the former could
claim to be the more legitimate body; in the eyes of the Bolsheviks,
however, it was a bourgeois government that had to be eliminated: for
them, there was no compromise between the two, but the Muslims of
Khoqand had not yet fully grasped to which side of the contradiction
the central authorities in Moscow were leaning when in January 1918
the Khalq Shurasi made an indirect appeal to the Bolshevik government
that it honor its professed commitment to national self-determination.
As People's Commissar for Nationality Affairs, Stalin sent a sarcastic
reply to the appeal from Khoqand that the Tashkent Soviet be dissolved:

The [Tashkent] Soviets are autonomous in their internal affairs and they dis-
charge their duties by depending upon their actual resources. The native proletariat of Turkestan, therefore, should not appeal to the Central Soviet Power
with the request to dissolve the Turkestan Sovnarkom, which in their opinion is
depending upon the non-Muslim army elements, but should themselves dissolve it by force, if such force is available to the native proletariat and peasants.

Stalin of course knew that the only real force in Turkestan was the military force held by the Russians, and that there could be but one outcome from a confrontation between Tashkent and Khoqand. It was, in the last analysis, a confrontation between Moscow and Khoqand, except that the incipient civil war at first prevented direct intervention from the center. Even under those circumstances, the Muslims proved no match for the Russians of Tashkent: the government of Khoqand had virtually no army, little administrative apparatus, and negligible financial resources. The Tashkent government sent a small expeditionary corps that stormed Khoqand on 22 February 1918, arrested those members of the parliament who had not fled, and established Soviet rule in Fergana.

ALASH ORDA AND KYRGYZ (I.E. KAZAKH) AUTONOMOUS SOVIET SOCIALIST REPUBLIC (KAZSSR)

While the Muslims of the defunct Governorate-General of Turkestan were endeavoring to gain recognition of their rights first in Tashkent and then, having failed there, through the Khoqand experiment, the Kazakhs of the Governorate-General of the Steppe and of the other two provinces, Turgai and Uralsk, were making similar efforts on their part. These efforts crystallized in the formation of a movement that received the name "Alash Orda" after a traditional battle cry ("Alash!") of Kazakh nomads. The movement had at first a structure similar to that of various patriotic groups, but after its first general convention at Orenburg in July and August 1917, it assumed the role of the leading national party. By December 1917 this party formed a Kazakh government which then pleaded with Moscow for recognition in a manner similar to that of the slightly later but much briefer Khoqand government. It ultimately failed, and the reasons were again similar: with no real army at its disposal, and meager financial resources, it was no match for the Bolsheviks, who were determined to eliminate any rival to their power. As a national government controlling a sizable portion of Kazakh territory, the Alash Orda hardly even existed; as a movement, on the other hand, it managed to persist until March 1920 when the Kyrgyz (i.e. Kazakh) Revolutionary Committee (a body controlled by Russian Bolsheviks), after the definitive Red victory over the Whites, ordered its dissolution.

By then Moscow had its own plan for Kazakhstan and quickly proceeded to implement it. On 26 August 1920 Lenin and Kalinin signed a decree "On the creation of the Kyrgyz Autonomous Soviet Socialist

Republic." This became a reality in October of that year, when the Founding Convention of the Kazak Soviets gathered in Orenburg, and the Kyrgyz (i.e. Kazakh) Autonomous Soviet Socialist Republic was born. In some respects, the process and the results in Kazakhstan were analogous to those in Turkestan, where the Turkestan Autonomous Soviet Socialist Republic came into being at about the same time; in one special sense, however, the formation of the Kazakh ASSR was ahead of the rest of Central Asia, for unlike that of the Turkestan ASSR, it was based on the ethnolinguistic factor of a native nationality, the Kazakhs. This factor became the principle that in 1924 would lead to the formation of the other four republics of Central Asia, Uzbekistan, Kyrgyzstan, Turkmenistan and Tajikistan.

TURKESTAN AUTONOMOUS SOVIET SOCIALIST REPUBLIC (TASSR)

As we have seen, after the failure of the Khoqand experiment in February 1918, the Soviets of Tashkent were the only organized authority on the territory of Turkestan except for the still existing emirate of Bukhara and khanate of Khiva. Russian rule was on the whole secure, but distance from central Russia and temporary separation from it by the civil war did create certain special circumstances. One was that for a little longer, not only the Bolsheviks but also other Russian political factions had some share in power. Thus at the Fifth Congress of the Soviets of Turkestan, held in Tashkent in April 1918, from among the 263 delegates only 86 were Bolsheviks; the next strongest faction, the SRs (Socialist Revolutionaries), had 70 members, and there were minor groups; the 87 non-affiliated delegates (*bezpartiynye*) even outnumbered the Bolsheviks. It was only a matter of time before the latter would eliminate all the other parties and would assign the non-affiliates their permanently subordinate role, but the situation, even though temporary, had some significance for the Muslims.

With all their ruthless suppression of any Muslim attempts at genuine autonomy, the Bolsheviks did try, albeit inconsistently, to put an end to the mistreatment of the natives by the Russians, and they also began to recruit those Muslims whose class credentials made them worthier candidates for a share in power. Thus when a new Sovnarkom was appointed by the Congress, four out of the sixteen members of this regional government presided over by F. A. Kobozev were Muslims, as were ten out of the thirty-six members of the Central Executive

Committee (Tsentralnyi Ispolnitelnyi Komitet, usually abbreviated as *TsIK* or *Ispolkom*) elected by the Congress. The effort by Tashkent Bolsheviks to attract natives to their political process was a result of pressure from Moscow; left to themselves, they tended to display the same attitude as that of the other Russians of Turkestan: to maintain a fundamental separation between the rulers and the ruled, and to favor the strengthening of the Russian and European element at all levels. This attitude sometimes assumed even ideological, Marxist forms. Thus Tobolin, a prominent Bolshevik member of the Tashkent Sovnarkom, said in 1918: "From the Marxists' point of view, the Kyrgyz are weak. They have to die out anyway, so it is more important that the Revolution spend its resources on fighting its enemies on the front than on fighting the famine."

The famine that plagued Turkestan and Kazakhstan in those years, especially during the harsh winter of 1918 and 1919, hit the natives much harder than the Europeans, and the vast numbers of Muslim casualties were not altogether unwelcome: they could be replaced by Russian settlers. Estimates of how many natives died vary between one and three million people. G. Safarov, a Communist functionary in Semireche, stated at the Tenth Congress of the Russian Communist Party in 1921 that "since the establishment of Soviet power, Russian land ownership has increased in the Semireche province from 35% to 70%, while the number of the Kyrgyz who have perished is estimated at 35.5%."

Satisfaction with these developments seems to have been shared by some Bolshevik leaders in Moscow as well. G. L. Pyatakov wrote in 1921 that some two million (native) people had perished in Turkestan, and that plans had been made to carry out a transfer of one-and-a-half million Russians to the vacated lands and houses.

Nevertheless, the more ideologically attuned Bolshevik leadership in Moscow became concerned that this mistreatment of Turkestanian Muslims might compromise the plans for Central Asia as a stepping stone toward a revolution in the entire colonial world. Between 1918 and 1920 a contest thus developed between the Communist leaders at the center and the local ones in Tashkent. The Tashkent Soviets were aware that in the long run they would need Moscow's support to keep Turkestan Russian, but at the same time they demanded a great deal of autonomy for their way of running the province. Moscow eventually prevailed and forced the local group to treat the natives better and start a recruitment drive among them. At the same time, another contest began to take shape between Moscow and those Turkestanian Muslims who were joining the Communist Party while trying to retain their own views and goals as to the future of their country. Here too Moscow would emerge victorious. Both these parallel and rather contradictory contests marked the history of the Turkestan Autonomous Soviet Socialist Republic (TASSR).

The TASSR was established on 30 April 1918 at the end of the Fifth Regional Congress of the Soviets of Turkestan. In this the Tashkent communists followed the instructions brought from Moscow by P. A. Kobozev, who then became chairman of the aforementioned Central Executive Committee (TsIK). For almost a year, instructions that native leaders should be recruited into the Party, government and even army were ignored, because the civil war that separated Turkestan from Russia made that type of insubordination possible. The best that the Muslim leaders could do in the harsh winter of 1918/19 was to organize actions to alleviate the plight of their co-religionists who were dying of hunger. One such young leader was Turar Ryskulov or Riskul-uulu (1894–1938), a Kazakh or Kyrgyz from the Kazakh–Kyrgyz border area.

By the spring of 1919 the civil war had subsided, and Moscow began to act more decisively in Turkestan. A special commission, the Turkestanskaya Chrezvychaynaya Komissiya (Turkkomissiya) was sent to directly supervise the local Sovnarkom. Although only one of its members, Kobozev, managed to reach Tashkent at the time, the measures which he and his staff began to carry out brought important results. One of these was the formation, in April 1919, of a Muslim wing of the Communist Party, the Musulmanskoe byuro (*Musbyuro*). Soon the ranks of the party began to swell with such native leaders as T. Ryskulov and N. Khojaev (also spelled Khodzhaev; not to be confused with Fayzulla Khojaev, president of the Bukharan People's Republic). An unusual feature of this new policy was the neglect of the basic reservations which the Bolsheviks, whether in Tashkent or elsewhere, always had about the class identity of native recruits: these new members were genuine national leaders, and mostly came from the middle or upper classes. In its drive for *korenizatsiya*, a word which could be translated as "nativiza-tion," Moscow seemed to forget its own caveats and soon had to contend with a new problem in Turkestan: national communism.

Probably few of these native leaders were genuine converts to Communism, but they were no conservatives either. Most were descended from the reformist movement of the jadids, and modernization of Turkestan, social justice, and national liberation were their goals. The actions of Moscow in 1919 made them believe that they could reach these goals as national Communists, and this belief was at first encouraged by Lenin himself. Relations with the Muslims of Russia seemed to be generally improving. Hostilities between the Bolshevik government and the Kazakh and Bashkir groups had ceased; the Eighth Communist Party Congress launched a new drive of attracting Muslims into the Communist fold; and the government seemed ready to negotiate with Muslim leaders. The Bashkir Zeki Velidi (Togan) spent prolonged periods in Moscow, meeting with Lenin, Stalin, and other Bolsheviks. The question of the future status of Turkestan, Kazakhstan, Bashqurtistan, Tatarstan and other Muslim regions seemed open, and to contemporary observers and participants genuine autonomy or even independence may have seemed possible.

The Russians themselves appear to have been undecided at that time on one important point: whether Turkestan should become a politico-ethnic unit, or whether it should be divided up into smaller specific units. In fact, the question even transcended that of Turkestan in the administrative and political sense: many Muslim leaders viewed all of Central Asia in the broadest sense as Turkestan, including Kazakhstan, Bashqurtistan, and Tatarstan. This was implied in the discussions between Zeki Velidi and Lenin, for the Bashkir leader claimed to speak for such a comprehensive Turkestan. At the beginning of July 1919, Lenin asked Zeki Velidi to evaluate a project for the Muslim region that had been given to him by the Pan-Islamic propagandist Muhammad Barakatullah;[3] Zeki Velidi submitted instead a project of his own. According to Zeki Velidi, Lenin liked the proposals and incorporated most of them – though not all, and this is an important qualification: the army was one of the exceptions – into the instructions which were cabled to Tashkent on 12 July 1919. They caused consternation among the Bolsheviks of Turkestan. Indeed, even with the abovementioned exception, the new instructions went beyond the policy decided upon by the Eighth Party Congress and introduced by Kobozev in February of that year. Nevertheless, Moscow refused to replace the essentially Russian Red Army with a local one, or to relinquish the key government posts to Muslims, or to give Muslims a majority on the Turkkomissiya.

Even under these circumstances, Muslim nationalists in their new

[3] Muhammad Barakatullah (1859–1927) of Bhopal was one of the most colorful Muslim intellectuals who left India before the First World War to continue their Pan-Islamic, nationalist, or revolutionary activities. See J. M. Landau, *The Politics of Pan-Islam* (Oxford, 1990), pp. 195–97.

Communist garb seemed at first within reach of some of their goals. Led by Turar Ryskulov, they opposed the incipient division of Turkestan into separate nationalities but advocated a truly autonomous Turkestan republic that would have its own army, foreign affairs and finances. At the Fifth Regional Communist Party Congress held in Tashkent in January 1920, the Muslim members scored the greatest political victory they would ever attain within the Party framework. On 17 January the Congress adopted the following resolution:

In the interest of the international unity of workers and oppressed peoples, be it resolved that we shall oppose by means of communist agitation the strivings of Turkic nationals to divide themselves into various national groups such as Tatars, Kyrgyz, Kazakhs, Bashkirs, Uzbeks and others, and to establish small separate republics. Instead, with a view to forge the solidarity of all Turkic peoples who so far have not been included within the RSFSR (Russian Soviet Federative Socialist Republic), it is proposed to unify them within a Turkic Soviet Republic, and wherever it is not possible to achieve this, it is proposed to unite different Turkic nationalities in accordance with their territorial proximity.

The implications of this resolution were far-reaching: while not negating federal ties with Russia, the Muslim delegates envisioned a Turkic Soviet Republic of potentially vast size whose chief common denominator would be its Turkic identity. In addition to this resolution, the Ryskulov group also demanded a renaming of the Turkestan Autonomous Soviet Socialist Republic as the Turkic Republic, and of the Communist Party of Turkestan as the Communist Party of the Turkic Peoples; another demand was the dissolution of the Turkkommissiya on the grounds that it had violated the autonomy of Turkestan.

The demands of the nationalists may in retrospect appear unrealistic, but they were the result of a majority vote of the supreme political voice in the republic, the Communist Party of Turkestan, because that majority did reflect the ethnic composition of the area. It was at this point that the crucial factor of the Russian Communist Party, and of the Red Army, came into play. On 8 March 1920 Moscow gave its clear and decisive answer: the Communist Party of Turkestan had henceforward to be a part of the Communist Party of Russia with the status of a regional branch; there could be no question of a Turkic republic; as for the TASSR, the commissariats of defence, foreign affairs, railroads, finances, and postal services had to be under the jurisdiction of their federal counterparts.

This was the conclusion of the multidimensional struggle for Turkestan. In two stages, Moscow first neutralized the insubordinate Russian elements who had been loath to treat politically acceptable natives as equals; then, however, it fashioned the future of this former colony according to its own ideas and wishes, not to those of the Muslims. Moscow had played its cards well, but in the last analysis it was the irrefutable argument of having the Red Army at its disposal that made this victory possible.

THE KHOREZMIAN AND BUKHARAN PEOPLE'S SOVIET REPUBLICS

The TASSR (Turkestan Autonomous Soviet Socialist Republic), created in March 1920, lasted until October 1924, and in territorial terms it was a continuation of the Governorate-General of Turkestan. Territorial continuity also marked, in the same period, the People's Soviet Republics of Bukhara and Khorezm (Khwarazm). During the colonial period, both the emirs of Bukhara and the khans of Khiva had managed to impose upon their citizens the worst of the two worlds: the small but energetic groups of young Bukharans and Khivans knew that as Russia's vassals, their countries had joined the humiliated and exploited ranks of colonies; as subjects of semi-medieval autocrats, they themselves were deprived even of those marginal benefits that Russian colonialism did bring to the directly administered Governorate-General. The Revolution of October 1917 and the Bolsheviks' appeals to the Muslims of Russia offered them, they thought, a unique opportunity of liberating their countries both from decadent despotism and from colonialism. As a result, their conception of the struggle taking shape in Central Asia as well as their course of action between 1917 and 1920 had a different slant from those of their fellow Muslims elsewhere in the area.

The reformists at first did not aim at abolishing the two monarchies; all they wanted was a moderation of the despotism and some degree of modernization of the institutions and of education. The khan of Khiva and especially the emir of Bukhara with their conservative entourages proved tough and stubborn opponents, however. They persistently refused even these changes, so that the reformists were in the end driven both logistically and psychologically into the arms of the Russian revolutionaries as their indispensable allies. Thus while the Bolsheviks of Tashkent were extinguishing the poignant Khoqand experiment, the reformists of the two principalities were appealing to them for help in their struggle for freedom; and in the very same months of 1920, when Moscow was dashing the hopes of Muslim representatives in Tashkent for a truly independent republic of Turkestan, the Muslims of Bukhara saw their only hope in a Russian intervention against the ever more vicious despotism of the emir, who now thought himself freed from the restrictions that Tsarist suzerainty had imposed on him. The difficulty of the task was demonstrated not only by the inability of an indigenous effort to persuade the emir to accept reform, but also by the failure of the first military expedition that the Russians had undertaken against him in March 1920. The second campaign, which took place in September of that year, was better prepared, and it quickly prevailed. The emir fled, and the nationalists thought their dreams had come true when a People's Soviet Republic of Bukhara was established in October. Fayzulla Khojaev became prime minister and Abdarrauf Fitrat foreign minister. Although a few Russians also entered the government, the republic seemed to be what the patriots of Khoqand and Tashkent had striven for, an independent Muslim state. A similar process had already in February 1920 led to the establishment of the People's Soviet Republic of Khorezm (the territory's historic name prevailed over that of its recent capital, Khiva).

The national delimitation of 1924 put an end to the existence of these two republics and incorporated their territories into the newly formed republics of Uzbekistan, Turkmenistan, Kazakhstan, and Tajikistan. This measure revealed the illusory nature of the two republics' independence. Nevertheless, they did possess what might be called genuine autonomy, especially in the first two years of their existence, and gave a convincing demonstration of the vitality and potential that Central Asian Muslims had to govern themselves. Upon the abolition of the two republics, some of their leaders such as Khojaev and Fitrat, joined the political process and intellectual elites of the newly formed republics, especially Uzbekistan.

NATIONAL DELIMITATION

In the TASSR, the Muslim leaders had lost their bid for power by March 1920, but they did not surrender forthwith. Undaunted by the fact that their Russian comrades branded them as "bourgeois nationalists" or "deviationists," they took their case directly to Moscow in the hope that the central authorities would lend them a more sympathetic ear. In May 1920 their delegation, consisting of N. Khojaev, Bek-Ivanov, and T.

Ryskulov arrived in Moscow, bringing a petition which repeated their demands and contained complaints about the continuing suffering inflicted upon the native population by the local authorities and settlers. At the same time, unbeknown to the Muslim representatives, Sh. Z. Eliava and Ian E. Rudzutak had also arrived. These were members of the Turkestan Commission (neither was a Turkestanian; Eliava hailed from Georgia, Rudzutak from Russia's Baltic province) who were to give the central authorities their version of the story. The Politburo examined the situation on 25 May, and Lenin took a special interest in it. The decision was announced on 13 July: the Turkestan Commission was instructed to combat pan-Islamism and pan-Turkism, but also to organize the preparation of a map that would show the ethnic composition of Turkestan and to examine the question of whether a fusion (*sliyanie*) or delimitation (*razmezhevanie;* "demarcation" might be a better translation, but "delimitation" is the standard term used by Sovietologists) was the preferable solution. Thus began the process that would lead, by 1924, to the transformation of Turkestan into a region of five national units, early forms of the present republics of Kazakhstan, Kyrgyzstan, Uzbekistan, Turkmenistan, and Tajikistan.

One of the remarkable features of this process was that after the flurry of activities in the spring and summer of 1920, it lay dormant until the beginning of 1924. The two chief reasons for the delay were the complex situation in Central Asia itself, and the need felt by the Bolshevik leadership at the center to devise a broader form and name for their multinational empire than that of Russia; another factor was the Basmachi movement, a native uprising against the Soviets, the suppression of which took precedence over other measures in Central Asia. By the end of 1923 most of those problems had been solved or brought under control. The Union of Soviet Socialist Republics, formed in December 1922, offered both a fitting frame and name for new states to join it; the People's Republics of Bukhara and Khorezm were docile bodies ready to follow instructions from Moscow, and the Basmachis had ceased to be a threat. Thus, early in 1924, shortly after Lenin's death, Soviet leaders decided that the time had come for reshaping the borders within Central Asia along ethnolinguistic lines.

The first step was a meeting of the Central Committee of the Russian Communist Party in Moscow on 31 January 1924, where the decision was made to carry out a national delimitation (*natsionalnoe razmezhevanie*) of Central Asia. The aforementioned I. E. Rudzutak, a member of the Turkestan Commission, was entrusted with further study of the project.

An essential part of this "further study" was a transmission of the decision made in Moscow to the Communist Party organs of Central Asia: thus on 10 March 1924 the Central Committee of the Communist Party of Turkestan ASSR approved the project of delimitation; similar approvals were passed by the Party committees of the two People's Republics, Bukharan and Khorezmian. The next important step was again taken in Moscow, when on 11 May the Central Committee's Central Asian Bureau decided: (1) that an Uzbek Soviet Socialist Republic and a Turkmen Soviet Socialist Republic be formed; these two would then directly (*neposredstvenno*) enter the framework of the Union of Soviet Socialist Republics; (2) that a Tajik Autonomous Region (*oblast*) be formed; it would then enter the framework of the Uzbek SSR; (3) that a Kara-Kyrgyz (i.e., Kyrgyz in present terminology) Autonomous Region be formed, with the question deferred as to which framework it would enter; and (4) that those Kyrgyz (i.e. Kazakhs in present terminology) who inhabit the territory of the TASSR enter the framework of the already formed Kyrgyz (thus Kazakh) Autonomous SSR.

On 12 June 1924 the Central Committee of the Russian Communist Party accepted this project, and from then on it was primarily a question of implementation. The Central Territorial Commission and the Commission on National Delimitation, the two organs in charge of the project, met the formidable challenges of conducting ethnolinguistic surveys, distributing economic and financial assets, and checking a curious emergence of regional nationalism (e.g. Kazakh versus Uzbek: Tashkent was an Uzbek city, whereas its countryside was Kazakh), all within the amazingly short time of three months. On 25 September 1924 I. A. Zelenskiy, chairman of the Central Asian Bureau, presented a report to the Politburo on the final form of the project. The project was approved, and on 14 October it was the turn of the All-Russian Central Executive Committee of the Soviets to approve the delimitation draft; minor modifications were introduced at that point, and the decision was made that the Kara-Kyrgyz Autonomous Region would enter the framework of the Russian Soviet Federative Socialist Republic. This ruling was then given the final blessing at the plenary meeting of the Central Committee of the Russian Communist Party on 26 October 1924. The five republics of Central Asia, two in their definitive form, three in incipient forms, thus came into being.

CHAPTER SEVENTEEN

Soviet Central Asia

We have seen how in October 1924 the Turkic and Iranian Muslims of Central Asia attained nationhood and statehood through a unique historical process that was directed from Moscow and in which they themselves had little active participation. The identification of the languages and nationalities, their classification, and subsequent national delimitation resembled more the work of scientists studying animal or vegetable species and then assigning their location in a zoo or a botanical garden than a nation's internal rise toward self-determination. Nevertheless, the scientists, in this instance Russian linguists, anthropologists, and politicians, had done fairly competent work: one proof is that when the failed coup of August 1991 against Gorbachev's reforms brought about the collapse of the Soviet Union, Kazakhstan, Kyrgyzstan, Turkmenistan, and Uzbekistan have forcefully asserted their national identity as independent republics.

A frequent statement in the voluminous Sovietological and post-Sovietological literature produced in the West is that the borders created through national delimitation are "artificial," and minority pockets in many parts of Central Asia are mentioned as proof of that; moreover, incidents like the bloody fighting between the large Uzbek minority and Kyrgyz nationalists that occurred during June 1990 in the Osh region of Kyrgyzstan are adduced as portents of catastrophic upheavals in the future. The answer is that perfectly monoethnic and monolingual populations in a territory they consider their homeland and dominate politically are a rare occurrence in any part of the world, and that virtually every national state must devise a compromise on how to deal with one or more minorities. The related question of the official language versus dialects or minority languages is also sometimes mentioned as proof that the borders are "artificial": Uzbekistan, we are told, is really a mosaic of local Turkic idioms. Here too the dichotomy between the official or "correct" language and an assortment of regional or social dialects, besides minority languages, is not limited to Uzbekistan, and myriad examples could be cited, from the dialects of Germany and Britain to Ebonics and Spanish of the United States.

This is not to say that there cannot be cases where a minority ceases to be a minority, whether for reasons of sheer numbers or other circumstances such as the geopolitical ones. Kazakhstan displays both these aspects. Its large and fairly compact Slavic population, further swelled by two post-delimitation immigration waves, presents a perhaps intractable problem if the integrity of the republic's borders is identified with the identity and loyalty of its citizens. Tajikistan struggles with a somewhat contradictory problem: it even lacks the minimal cohesion offered by tribal formations and confederations, characteristic of Turkic nomads, that might help its people develop a sense of a national identity; at the same time, the one element that should cement Tajik society as a viable polity grounded in a politically defined territory, Persian language and civilization, is too vast and associated with other cultural and political centers to inject the necessary dose of patriotism in the minds and feelings of Tajik educated elites. Such places as Samarkand, Bukhara, or Shiraz are felt to be their historical and cultural centers, in comparison with which Tajikistan – even its capital, Dushanbe – may have difficulties shedding the stigma of provinciality or irrelevance.

The foundations of Soviet Central Asia's five republics were laid, as we have said, by October 1924. The framework that was the Union of Soviet Socialist Republics had been formed two years earlier, in December 1922, setting the stage for each of the non-Russian groups of the former Russian empire to find its niche in the new structure. The niche varied according to the label assigned to an ethnic group by the planners in Moscow, and some labels were modified or reshuffled in the course of time. This happened also in Central Asia, but by 1937 the process was completed, and the area acquired the political physiognomy that would last until the end of the Soviet regime. The hallmark of this political physiognomy was its ultimate uniformity. Each of the five republics acquired the status of a union republic – Uzbekistan and Turkmenistan as early as 1924, Tajikistan in 1929, Kazakhstan and Kyrgyzstan in 1936 – and a new constitution was adopted by the parliament of every republic in the spring of 1937 (to be replaced by yet another, the last Soviet, constitution in 1978). Each was called by its ethnic name in the adjectival form followed by the epithets "Soviet Socialist" qualifying the word "Republic": for example, Uzbek Sovet

Sotsialistik Respublikasi (UzSSR, this acronym having the advantage of serving also the republic's Russian name, Uzbekskaya Sovetskaya Sotsialisticheskaya Respublika). The form Uzbekiston, in Russian Uzbekistan, was used too, although in less official contexts. There were fifteen Union Republics in the Soviet Union, all modeled after the same pattern, except that the *prima inter pares* enjoyed a special status: the RSFSR, or Russian Soviet Federative Socialist Republic. The word "federative" expressed further internal federative structure, as this republic included sixteen "autonomous" republics, all forming a federation with the senior Russian partner. This usage was somewhat inaccurate or inconsistent, since some of the other Union republics also included "autonomous" republics such as the Karakalpak Autonomous Soviet Socialist Republic within the UzSSR, so that the latter should have contained that epithet too: Uzbek Soviet Federative Socialist Republic, UzSFSR. In Central Asia, Tajikistan was the only other republic to include a unit of this kind, though with a status still a notch lower: the Gorno-Badakhshan Autonomous Region (*Oblast*).

A Union republic had to meet certain conditions and enjoyed special rights, even if the latter were granted only theoretically. The most visible condition was that some of its borders run alongside a foreign country; of the five republics in question, Kazakhstan's and Kyrgyzstan's did so alongside China, Tajikistan's alongside China and Afghanistan, Uzbekistan's alongside Afghanistan, and Turkmenistan's alongside Afghanistan and Iran. Among the privileges of a Union republic, the most comprehensive – if it should indeed be considered a privilege and not an imposition – was a structure mirroring that of the Russian SFSR and, in certain respects, of the Soviet Union as a whole. Its most striking right, explicitly stated in the 1937 constitution, was that to leave the Soviet Union altogether and become an independent country. Additional symbols of each republic's "sovereignty" were its own flag, emblem, and national anthem. The term "sovereign," a loanword in Russian (*suverennyi*) and thence adopted also by the Central Asian languages (usually *suveren*) was used in the respective constitutions, rather than "independent" (*nezavisimyi* in Russian, *mustaqil* in Uzbek for example), a significant nuance. By "structure" we mean chiefly administrative, political and economic structure, but also the cultural and spiritual institutions and even the way of life, to the extent that the latter could be fashioned by Moscow.

A good example is the Uzbek SSR in its final Soviet form after the adoption of the third constitution in 1978, as it is described in the *Uzbek Sovet Entsiklopediyasi* (Uzbek Soviet Encyclopaedia, Tashkent 1980, vol. 14, pp. 490–91):

The Uzbek Soviet Socialist Republic is a socialist populist state (*sotsialistik umumkhalq davlat*) which expresses the will and interests of the republic's workers, agriculturists, and intellectuals (*ishchilar, dehqonlar, va ziyalilar*), and of the toilers (*mehnatkashlar*) of all nationalities (*millatlar*) and ethnic groups (*elatlar*). . . . The UzSSR is a sovereign state (*suveren davlat*) with equal rights (*teng huquqli*) within the framework of the Union of Soviet Socialist Republics, which firmly ties together all the nationalities and ethnic groups as a polity, the Soviet people, with the goal of together building communism (*kommunizm qurish uchun*). Its government functions on its own territory in an independent manner, <u>except for those questions that pertain to the highest organs of the USSR</u>; it has the right to freely leave the USSR (*öz erki bilan SSSRdan chiqish huquqini saqlaydi*). . . . The Uzbek SSR has the right to establish relations with foreign countries, to make treaties with them, to appoint diplomatic and consular representatives with them, to participate in the activities of international organizations. The sovereign rights of the Uzbek SSR are guaranteed by the USSR according to its own Constitution [that is, the Constitution of the Soviet Union]. . . . The highest governmental organ is the unicameral Supreme Soviet [Russian "sovet," literally, "council, advice" but here with the connotation of "parliament, congress"] of the Uzbek SSR (*Uzbekiston SSR Oliy Soveti*), elected for five years. . . . During the periods of recess, its work is done by the Presidium of the Supreme Soviet. The highest executive and administrative organ is the Council of Ministers of the Uzbek SSR (*Uzbekiston SSR Ministrlar Soveti*). The organs of local government are the Soviets of people's deputies from regions (*oblast*), districts (*raion*), towns (*shahar*), townships (*poselka*), villages (*qishloq*), and encampments (*ovul*), elected for two and a half years. Thirty-two deputies from Uzbekistan, and eleven deputies from Karakalpakistan are elected to the Soviet of Nationalities (*Millatlar Soveti*) of the Supreme Sovet of the USSR. . . . <u>The pivot (*özak*) of the republic's governmental and social organisms is the guiding and leading force of Soviet society, the Communist Party of the Soviet Union and one of its advance platoons (*avangard otryadlaridan biri*), the Communist Party of Uzbekistan.</u>

We have emphasized two clauses in the quoted summary, because they stand out for their special importance. The first states that the government of Uzbekistan functions on its territory <u>except in those matters that pertain to the whole USSR</u>; the principal matters in question were defense, finance, communications and transportation, and foreign affairs, all of which were centrally directed from Moscow. This alone shows how purely theoretical was Uzbekistan's freedom to leave the Soviet Union. The second clause, "<u>The pivot of the republic's governmental and social organisms is the guiding and leading force of</u>

Soviet society, the Communist Party of the Soviet Union. . .", is especially significant; it reveals the unique role of the Communist Party,
totally different from that of a political party in the Western sense: an
organism beyond and above the law and conventional government, it
was the real master of the country. The remark about its Uzbek branch
is revealing too: like a military platoon, it had to carry out the orders of
the high command at the center (hence the Russo-Uzbek term *otryad*,
rather uncommon outside of military parlance).

Aside from these specific aspects of integrated parallelism, there also
existed a less explicit but nevertheless pervasive and insidious integration. A doubling of functions was one such device: the fact that almost
every functionary in a top executive position, whether governmental,
political, or cultural, had a twin colleague, theoretically the number two
of that position but in fact performing the role of keeping an eye on his
partner. In most cases, the "number one" was an Uzbek, Kazakh, etc.,
according to the republic, "number two" being a Slav, usually a Russian
or a Ukrainian. Another device was the doubling of the basic institutions
or publications with Russian ones – or, rather, of the Russian ones with
the native ones. Thus the Communist Party of the RSFSR was paralleled by those of the republics, in addition to the existence, as the
supreme arbiter, of an All-Union party; the Academy of Sciences of the
Russian SFSR was paralleled by those of the other Union republics,
again in addition to the Academy of Sciences of the USSR; the Union
of Writers of the Russian SFSR, by those of the other republics (again,
besides the umbrella Union of Writers of the USSR). The literary
monthly *Novyi Mir*, published by the Union of Soviet Writers in Moscow,
had such counterparts as the bimonthly *Sharq Yulduzi* published by the
Union of Uzbek writers in Tashkent; the *Bolshaya Sovetskaya Entsiklopediya*,
the Great Soviet Encyclopedia, also had its counterparts in the encyclo-
pedias of the Union Republics, published to accompany the new constitutions of 1978 (besides the fourteen-volume Uzbek one, there is the
thirteen-volume *Qazaq Sovet Entsiklopediyasy*, the eight-volume *Türkmen
Sovet Entsiklopediyasy*, the eight-volume *Entsiklopediyai Sovetii Tojik*, and the
six-volume *Kyrgyz Sovet Entsiklopediyasy*).

The constitution naturally says nothing about religion, unless we take
the plausible view that Communism and the Communist Party assumed
the role of religion and of an organized religious hierarchy. We have
seen the central place that Islam had occupied in the life of the area's
Muslims, and the new regime made a sustained and massive effort to
eradicate it and to substitute "scientific atheism" and Communism for

it. It is true that the regime could not quite rid itself of its contradictions, for it did not dismantle the organized religious hierarchy altogether, and eventually allowed a drastically reduced church body to continue functioning as an obedient government agency. Thus in 1942 a "directorate of the Muslims of Central Asia and Kazakhstan" was established in Tashkent, and a reduced number of mosques was permitted to operate in the area. Two madrasas, Baraq Khan in Tashkent and Mir Arab in Bukhara, trained the small number of Muslim clergymen who would then enter a profession made ambiguous at best by the regime. Why did the Soviets allow even this marginal existence of organized Islam? For several reasons: one was simple imitation of the RSFSR, where the Orthodox Church was treated in a similar manner; another was the desire to court foreign Muslim countries, whose heads of state and official delegations to the Soviet Union routinely received a tour of Central Asia.

This integrated parallelism of Central Asia was buttressed by what must conventionally be considered remarkable progress, for the Soviets made efforts to modernize and develop the area and its society with unprecedented speed and energy. Once Soviet rule was established, reforms and creative innovation followed, some immediate, some gradual and appearing only after the Second World War.

Literacy became general within a few years among the school-age generation, and increased among the rest of the population through broad "campaigns to eradicate illiteracy." Education was restructured, expanded, and modernized along uniform Soviet lines, from the grade school level, where native attendance was made mandatory, to that of the university and academic research institutions, where it was facilitated and encouraged. The printed word gives another graphic example of the change. Where there had been few or no newspapers, periodicals, or printed books, after 1924 they quickly appeared in all the five languages, and the number and volume skyrocketed. Most remarkably, the end result of this linguistic-cultural revolution was the creation of six new literary languages (Uzbek, Kazakh, Kyrgyz, Turkmen, Tajik, and Karakalpak) in a society that had previously used Chaghatay Turkic and Farsi (Persian) for written expression.

The socio-economic restructuring broke the back of the old order and established a new one to the same degree it had done so in Russia. The means of production – agricultural and pastoral land and livestock, forests, mineral wealth, and industry – were nationalized or collectivized. The wealth of the religious establishment, especially considerable in Central Asia because of the Islamic institution of *waqf* (pious endowment), was confiscated, and its institutions – mosques, madrasas, khangahs – were closed, again except for the token cases of the aforementioned Baraq Khan madrasa in Tashkent and Mir Arab madrasa in Bukhara besides a scattering of mosques. Women were given equal rights and opportunity of education and employment, and the natives were not only welcomed but actively recruited to participate in the political and administrative process. The separation of Russians and natives, rulers and ruled, characteristic of the Tsarist and revolutionary eras, gave way to a theoretical equality tempered by a carefully monitored deference to the role played by the "Big Brother."

One of the characteristic results of Russian rule – Tsarist but especially Soviet – was population growth and urbanization. This was due partly to the law and order installed by the colonial power which presented a sharp contrast to the endemic warfare that used to plague the area; and to the introduction of modern medicine, however rudimentary it may have been (and remained) if judged by modern Western standards. Accurate figures with vital statistics prior to the Soviet period are lacking or of only limited use; before the conquest, censuses in the modern sense did not exist, and before the Soviet period, the administrative boundaries within Central Asia were too different from the present ones to allow accurate comparison. This changed with the National Delimitation of 1924. The first comprehensive census was taken in 1926 and was repeated in 1939, 1959, 1979, and 1989. In 1926, the total population was 13,671,000 souls; in 1989, it was 49,119,267. Some of this increase was due to the aforementioned influx of immigrants from other parts of the empire, chiefly from Russia and Ukraine, which reached massive proportions in Kazakhstan and to some extent also in Kyrgyzstan, and in administrative and industrial centers like Tashkent, Almaty, and Bishkek. The main reason for the growth has been, however, the high birthrate of the native population. Until recently, this phenomenon was viewed as a positive element in the development of Central Asia and was encouraged by the Soviet government.

These measures, goals, and accomplishments were based, however, on principles and methods which beyond certain limits undermined the system's positive achievements and ultimate justification. The total power enjoyed by the Communist elite created a new bureaucratic aristocracy in the supposedly classless society, a paradox underlined by the contradictory claim that Soviet rule was a rule of the working class. The interests of the workers never lost a place of importance in the policies of the government, but they became ever more subordinated to the paramount interests of the new class of Communist bureaucrats obsessed with the perpetuation of their own power and privileges, which could be assured only through the suppression of all attempts at any alternative methods, debates, or experiments, whether political, economic, or cultural (strikes, for example, were out of the question). It may be instructive to quote a Western journalist who in 1992 visited the Kazakh city of Karaganda, center of an extensive coalmining region. The place was still reeling from the unprecedented events of 1989: "In 1989 these fearful [coal mining] tunnels spat out their miners in a strike which was echoed across the Union. Its men were young, angry and organised. They demanded, and won, an independent trade union. After sixty years of servitude, the workers were on the march. But their model, they said, was the United States of America."[1]

On the all-Union level, this led to increasing stagnation and the development of an unnatural, hypocritical psychological climate; in the case of Central Asia, the "vertical" self-interest of the new Communist class was compounded by a "horizontal" self-interest, a pronounced Moscow-centered and Russo-centric chauvinism that continued the forced submission of the natives to the Russians despite the "international" equality claimed by the system. The word "international" (*internatsionalnyi* in Russian, introduced into Uzbek etc. as *internatsional*) had in this context a special significance: for its parameter was strictly circumscribed by the outside limits of the Soviet Union, so that the term applied exclusively to the mutual relationship of the ethnic conglomerate in that country, and it differed from the word *mezhdunarodnyi* (*khalqaro* in Uzbek), a synonym of *internatsionalnyi* but applied only to relations with *non*-Soviet countries and nationalities. *Internatsionalnyi* had a positive connotation, from the point of view of Soviet ideology, in a sense virtually the inverse of the word's original meaning: an effacement of ethnic differences in favor of a growing mutuality and eventual sameness. This sameness could not but be anchored in a Russian or Russified identity, a goal known as *sliyanie*, "fusion," with the eventual appearance of the legendary *sovetskiy chelovek*, the *homo sovieticus* who also found his way into Central Asian terminology (*sovet kishisi* in Uzbek for example). This may indeed have been the ultimate meaning of the perennial refrain of "together building Communism," otherwise puzzling for a society already ruled by a Communist government.[2]

---

[1] C. Thubron, *The Lost Heart of Asia* (Penguin Books, 1994), p. 340.

[2] Purists of Marxism-Leninism of course could retort that the role of the Communist Party was only to steer a socialist state under its stewardship toward the golden age of Communism.

The role of the Russian language and culture, and of the Russian people in general, as values and models to be adopted and ultimately to be identified with was overwhelming and beyond question or criticism. Russian was each republic's principal official language, and had the upper hand in the bilingual routine of public life and its "international" dimension; it also invaded the native languages in two ways: through the alphabet and through the vocabulary. A characteristic complement was the switch from the Roman to the Cyrillic alphabet ordered by Moscow in 1940. The Central Asians themselves had dropped the Arabic script and adopted the Roman one in 1928, a sensible move on several counts: like the Sogdian script in the case of classical Uighur for example, the structure of the Arabic script, viable in the case of a Semitic language, was ill-suited for both the Turkic and Iranian idioms of Central Asia, whereas Roman did meet such needs. A similar step was being taken in Turkey, and using the same alphabet would have enhanced the communication channels of the Central Asian and Anatolian Turks, besides bringing obvious practical dividends; and finally the Roman script is one more window to the world scene, so that its choice would have made sense in Central Asia no less than in Turkey. The last two reasons were of course the main arguments against it from Moscow's standpoint, and Moscow's wishes prevailed. The other measure was the lexical and phonetic intrusion of the Russian language into the native ones (thus mainly into the Turkic languages, but also into Tajik). Loanwords were no strangers in Central Asia, but they had entered the local languages through centuries-long processes of acculturation that responded to a natural need and bowed to the phonetic laws of the host idioms. Taking Kyrgyz as an example, the Arabic words *fatiha* (name of the opening sura in the Koran) became *bata*, *ramadan* (ninth month of the lunar calendar) became *yramazan*, the Persian word *hunar* (art, craft) became *önör*. Russian words and names, on the other hand, were introduced with all their tongue-twisting – that is, tongue-twisting for speakers of a Turkic or Iranian language – and graphic paraphernalia, and those that had been naturalized before the Soviet period were duly restored to their so totally alien phonetical shape (thus *iskusstvo* for fine art, despite the availability of the Kyrgyz *körköm önör*). A related feature was the substitution of imposed place names for native ones; thus *Przheval'sk*, a city that was so renamed to the detriment of the original and thoroughly Kyrgyz *Karakol*. This possibly deliberate tactlessness went beyond the question of language and was also symbolized by the case of the capital of Kyrgyzstan, Frunze: for Bishkek was renamed after Mikhail Vasilevich Frunze, the Bolshevik general born in Bishkek of Moldavian-Russian parents, who had led during the civil war the principal military operations that consolidated Soviet rule in Central Asia (even this measure might have been mitigated if the popular Kyrgyz pronunciation of the name, *Paranzo*, had been adopted). The Uzbek, Turkmen, etc. nations' foremost founding fathers, heroes, and contemporary leaders were Russians or Russified Soviet leaders, from Lenin to Stalin, Brezhnev and Gorbachev. The naming of the principal institutions after a Russian rather than an Uzbek, for example, could invade even what should have remained the natives' inviolable ground: thus the name of the Institute for Literature of the Uzbek Academy of Sciences had the epithetic label "Pushkin's" (*imeni Pushkina* in Russian, *Pushkin nomidagi* in Uzbek) – as if the Uzbeks had never had any great poets of their own. What indeed stood in the way of naming this institute, central to the nation's cultural dignity, after Mir Ali Shir Navai for example, the great Timurid poet of the fifteenth century? The fact that a more modern personality was deemed preferable? Then again, why not an Uzbek literary figure? The thought process of the Russian masters of Uzbekistan, or perhaps of those Uzbeks who were eager to ingratiate themselves with their masters, is an intriguing case of political psychopathology. Pushkin died in 1837 at the age of thirty-eight, humiliated by a system with which he had found it hard to compromise; a century later, the Uzbek poet Cholpan disappeared in the Gulag at a similar age and for similar reasons. This and his brave and beautiful verse induced some critics to call him "the Uzbek Pushkin." Cholpan was not a political figure, but compromise in his case would not have been just with a system but with a foreign invader. He was arrested in 1934, briefly released, then rearrested, and disappeared in the Gulag. When they first released Cholpan, the authorities must have hoped that he had been frightened into submission like most others, but he recited the following poem at a public appearance in a Tashkent theater: "Qolimda songgi tash qaldi, Yavimga atmaq istayman. Könglimdä songgi dard qaldi, Könglimdä songgi dard qaldi, Tiläkgä yetmaq istayman. . . ." ("The last stone is in my hand, I want to fling it at my foe. The last pain is in my heart, I want to reach my dream.")

The main goal of the repression may have been ultimate integration through a total abandonment of the national will to that of the Russians. The official versions of the republics' history and myriad statements and articles portrayed the Russian conquest not as a conquest but as a "voluntary unification (*dobrovolnoe prisoedinenie*) of the Uzbeks (or Kazakhs, Kyrgyz, etc.) with Russia," and its effects as positive, even though this "voluntary unification" had taken place in the days of the otherwise censured Tsarist regime; and the present was portrayed as a golden age in which the destinies of the two peoples were "forever" cemented in an association between a generous and wise senior partner and a grateful junior one. A perhaps not readily visible but important aspect of this doctrine is the fact that no other interpretation was allowed.

Those were the days when the Soviet government was posing as the champion of the oppressed colonial peoples of Africa and Asia and heaping abuse on the colonizers; and once the colonies had become independent in the 1950s and 1960s, the propaganda quickly switched to the thesis of neo-colonialism while using the resources of the Soviet empire for the deadly game of subversion so as to turn that part of the world into a Communist one. Yet at the same time its special brand of colonial exploitation of Central Asia not only went on unchecked, but in certain respects it reached monstrous proportions. The classic colonial pattern of hauling away raw materials in return for finished products acquired here a degree and forms never imposed by Western powers on their colonies. As we have said in the introductory chapter, Moscow turned Central Asia into a megafarm designed to produce ever greater quantities of cotton. To this end irrigation kept being expanded beyond the capacity of Central Asian rivers, the soil exhausted by monoculture kept being saturated with chemical fertilizers, the crops sprayed by clouds of pesticides and herbicides, and instead of fully mechanizing the production, cheap native labor was routinely used for harvesting the Uzbeks' *oq oltin*, "white gold," as the Soviet propaganda cruelly termed this special variant of "king cotton." A grim feature of this cheap labor was schoolchildren, driven to the insalubrious fields in the fall instead of studying in the classrooms. The policy of cotton monoculture became pronounced in the 1930s, but it was especially from the 1960s to the 1980s that it reached truly monstrous proportions. Meanwhile genuinely beneficial economic development of the area such as industrialization, modestly begun in the 1920s, remained stunted as Moscow chose to place capital investment elsewhere. Moreover, such industry as there was tended to be concentrated in urban areas where Russian and other European workforces, often imported for the purpose, outnumbered the natives.

Uzbekistan, Turkmenistan, Tajikistan, and up to a point Kazakhstan were the main producers of cotton. Kazakhstan and Kyrgyzstan were used in other ways to suit the rulers in Moscow. The nomadic herders of Kazakhstan had seen much of their grazing space reduced by the influx of Russian settlers in the Tsarist era, but in the early years of Soviet rule they still occupied considerable tracts in the country's center and east. At the end of the 1920s and beginning of the 1930s the Soviet government launched forced collectivization of their herds and imposed their own sedentarization. The nomads met this campaign with resistance, often destroying their livestock, and the ensuing famine in turn decimated the Kazakhs' population by at least one million souls. By the late 1930s, the percentage of the Kazakhs in their own republic fell to 29 percent. The vacated or sparsely populated territories became that much more inviting for further influx of Slavic settlers, which culminated in the celebrated "virgin land" campaign launched by Khrushchev in the late 1950s and early 1960s. The economic wisdom of this policy was questionable at best. The area seems to lack adequate rainfall for full-scale farming, whereas it was suited for a pastoral economy. There appeared ominous signs of soil erosion and desertification, but that did not bother the authorities any more than the many other forms of environmental degradation caused by ruthless exploitation such as strip mining.

The province of Semipalatinsk in eastern Kazakhstan was chosen as the area for Soviet nuclear experiments, but neither the testing nor the damage it caused to the health of the people were even mentionable before the dawn of *glasnost* and *perestroika*. The testing has ceased, but its consequences are still very much there, and the Kazakhs can point to it as yet another example of violence done to their country by the alien who had conquered it a century ago. Moreover, it appears that other parts of Central Asia were used as dumping grounds of toxic waste. One such site apparently was in the vicinity of Chirchik, a town some thirty kilometers to the northeast of Tashkent. According to the Uzbek writer Dada Khan Nuriy, the officials – Uzbek officials – tried to cover up the existence of this dump, and the eventual confession is worth quoting:

Now that we have *glasnost*, then so be it: the truth is, comrades, that in 1985, on instructions from higher authority, arsenic wastes were brought from the Ministry of Electronics Industry in the Moscow region and buried. . . . I had to obey orders."[3]

Whether it was cotton fields with which Moscow blanketed vast tracts of Central Asia, or kolkhozes where Slavic settlers were brought to grow maize, or dumping grounds for toxic waste, the policy had smooth sailing among the native politicians of Central Asia. The generation of

[3] J. Critchlow, *Nationalism in Uzbekistan* (Boulder, 1991), pp. 92–94. The author refers to an article published by Dada Khan Nuriy in the newspaper *Özbekistan adabiyati va sanati*, 15 December 1989.

Communist patriots of the 1920s and 1930s was now replaced by a new breed of *apparatchiks* whose main ambition was how to please their masters in Moscow and thereby attain their own positions of privilege and comfort. The price of this was total betrayal of the interests of their own countries and peoples.

Politicians were not the only elite in Central Asia, however. There arose a whole new generation of educated people, individuals who had benefited from the bright side of Soviet rule. They availed themselves of the expanded and free education vigorously promoted by the government, and came to occupy professions of their choice, but especially those most congenial to them such as journalism or teaching and research in the proliferating schools, universities, and academies. True, there was some degree of overlapping between them and the politicians. They had to be realists, and membership in the Communist Party or at least demonstration of loyalty to the regime was a prerequisite for any individual to function successfully. By the time the native scholars and writers were producing the voluminous literary and learned output of the post-Second World War decades, they knew what they could and could not dare. This had been driven home during the 1930s so forcefully that only occasional reminders were needed later on. The total submission and integration of each nation was achieved through a political process conceived, planned, and carried out by Moscow, and then guarded by means of an all-pervasive control and enforcement apparatus. The aforementioned Cholpan was only the most poignant example of all those who fell victim to the terror designed to stifle the least stirrings of independent patriotism. Thus Abdarrauf Fitrat, the reformist and scholar of the early decades of the century, disappeared in the Gulag by the end of the 1930s, as did several other prominent leaders; Fayzulla Khojaev, Fitrat's contemporary and prime minister of the Uzbek SSR in the early years, was one of those tried and executed in Moscow in 1938. Törekul Aitmatov, father of the renowned Kyrgyz writer Chingiz Aitmatov and a member of the Communist Party, also succumbed in the Gulag on the mere suspicion of harboring nationalist tendencies. The result was that the Uzbeks and other Central Asians learned to tread warily when questions of their national dignity, values, or even their people's material interests were concerned. Fitrat's fate warned those who might have wished to follow his example and overstep the confines of the Uzbek republic in their quest for a Central Asian cultural heritage symbolized by the Chaghatay language and literature; the example of Khojaev, who had verses from the Koran recited at the grave of his brother, made it clear that an act anchored in their spiritual values might later be cited as one of the crimes contributing to their doom in a Soviet courthouse; and Cholpan's and Törekul Aitmatov's fate, at the two poles of the spectrum and thus seemingly incompatible – one was a dissident, the other a member of the Communist Party – may have been linked by the Moscow-based dictator's determination to break the spirit of his subject peoples.

As we have already implied, however, our critical view of the imposition of things Russian on Central Asians does need qualifications. Contradiction marked Soviet national and linguistic policies, as it did, in fact, much of the philosophy underlying the entire system. It began at the very inception with the establishment of ethnolinguistic borders. Moscow could have chosen other ways to organize Central Asia, for example along economic or geographical lines. Such measures would have made Russian the only really viable language, with education, literacy, and publishing taking place exclusively through it, and with the Kipchak, Turki, and Tajik "dialects" receding into the well-meaning paternalism of anthropological studies. Yet not only did Moscow anchor the correctly identified principal nationalities in a firm linguistic base, but it proceeded forthwith to consolidate that base through the aforementioned campaigns of education and publishing. If ultimate Russification was the goal, the Delimitation of 1924 was the wrong move, and the subsequent policies of mass education and publishing in the newly codified languages made it a fatal one.[4] The contradictory nature of Communist Moscow's psyche may indeed have reached its climax in its nationalities policy. It brutally bore down on "chaghatayism," an intellectual current among the area's Turks wishing to conceive of Central Asia as a cultural unit, branding it as "bourgeois nationalism" and fearing it as a potent tool for unification and secession; yet at the same time it promoted the establishment of an Uzbek ethnolinguistic identity, allowing the natives to cultivate the identical national heritage under the officially sanctioned Uzbek (or "Old Uzbek," in the case of Chaghatay Turki language) label. Although there were times when Moscow invaded this last-named form of identity too and important aspects of national patrimony were pushed aside while those of Russia were prescribed as the monuments to admire and adopt, even then the system did not manage to abandon its own principles proclaiming the right to ethnolinguistic self-determination and development, as long as

---

[4] Fatal, that is, for the idea of Russification.

central authority and Communism remained unchallenged. Moscow at times tried to slander the Uzbek epic Alpamysh or the Kyrgyz epic Manas, but it never ceased publishing the translated works of Lenin, the Party's dailies, and the republics' literary magazines in those nations' own languages.

And the Central Asians remained keenly aware of their own identity. A generation or two after the sacrifice of such leaders as Fitrat and Cholpan, thus in the final stage of the Soviet system, their successors emerged as champions of the same values but able to survive both thanks to the lessons they had learned from the examples of their elders and to the system's own contradictions or recognition of the inevitable. We have mentioned Törekul Aitmatov's son, Chingiz Aitmatov (b. 1928), as an eloquent messenger of these values. His stories and novels became a celebration of the Kyrgyz and Kyrgyzstan, although most had first been written in Russian and the author, on the surface, seemed willing to give the Caesar in Moscow his due. These two aspects – their Russian versions and the apparent acceptance of the system – made it possible for Aitmatov to survive and, instead of remaining confined to his charming but little known homeland and language, become famous throughout the Soviet Union and, indeed, worldwide. Once more we cannot but marvel at the contradictory complexity of the system in its final decades and eschew simplistic definitions or explanations. Aitmatov, the son of a Communist murdered for his Kyrgyz patriotism, was in his early youth rescued by the solidarity of his clan (a social feature which the system had condemned as a "feudal relic" and marked it for extinction); once survival was assured, he could enter the Soviet system of education which at first enabled him to acquire a decent profession (he became a veterinarian); once he began to write, his talent was noticed and he was offered a study fellowship at the Gorkiy Institute of Literature in Moscow; the two years of training there enabled him to perfect his talent with a well-honed technique, and the subsequent employment as a correspondent of *Pravda* in Kyrgyzstan proved to be an excellent gate of entry into his ultimate profession as a writer. Like most of his successful compatriots, he joined the Communist Party, and charmed his Kyrgyz as well as Russian and other readers with beautiful short stories and novels, several of which were used as film scenarios. Yet even he was once forcefully reminded of the system's unforgiving strictures. When he published the novel *The White Ship* (it appeared first in Russian as *Belyi parokhod*, "The White Steamship," in 1970, and only later in Kyrgyz as *Ak keme*, "The White Ship"), the official establishment disapproved of the novel's tragic conclusion and ordered Aitmatov to rewrite it with the obligatory Soviet requirement of an Optimistic End. He did, and neither he nor his readers took that cosmetic change seriously – with the possible exception of the Party vigilantes still willing to fool themselves. Their discomfort was less readily removed when a whole novel turned out to be based on a theme that made them uncomfortable. An example of this was the Uzbek writer Pirimqul Qodirov's *Yulduzli tunlar* ("Starry Nights"), a historical novel about the great native of Andijan, Emperor Babur. Like Aitmatov's *White Steamship*, *Starry Nights* too was first hailed as a masterpiece by critics and readers, until "Party watchdogs" attacked it for its implicit nationalism. There is thus an analogy between the two writers, but there are also interesting differences. Both men, born in the same year (1928), received the critical part of their literary training at the Gorkiy Institute in Moscow, an example of the bright side of the system; Aitmatov was censored after the publication of the *White Ship* not for nationalism, but for pessimism – an example of where the system could be evenhanded (a Russian writer or artist would have run into the same trouble – as Shostakovich did for his opera *Lady Macbeth of the Mtsensk District*), whereas Qodirov was censored for nationalism (here, the system was Russo-centric; the great historical novels of Alexey Tolstoy glorifying Peter the Great met with acclaim from the highest quarters).

While discussing the activities and tragic fate of people like Fitrat, we could have also mentioned their important contemporary Sadriddin Ayni (1878–1954). Ayni initially belonged to the circle of Bukharan *jadids* and displayed other analogies with them, especially with Fitrat. His later fate could not, however, have been more different. Ayni not only survived the terror of the 1930s but had a smooth sailing throughout the rest of his life, ever more honored by the official establishment as represented by the local and all-Union Unions of Soviet writers. His career reached its apogee with the presidency of the newly created Academy of Sciences of the Tajik SSR in 1951, a post he held until his death. A glance at his early life in the emirate of Bukhara, at the years of his prime in Samarkand, and at the closing period in Dushanbe may help us gain an idea of the secret of his success and importance.

Ayni was born in Saktare, an agricultural village near Gijduvan,[5] a district town some forty kilometers to the northeast of Bukhara on the

---

[5] This was also the hometown of Abd al-Khaliq Ghijduvani, the important *khwaja*, in the "*uwaysī*" form, of Baha al-Din Naqshband (see p. 138).

road to Samarkand by the northern bank of the Zarafshan. Most people there were Tajiks, so that Farsi (Persian) was the boy's mother tongue. From an early age, however, he also knew Turki-speaking neighbors, and after he had moved to Bukhara at the age of eleven in order to attend the *madrasa*, he became bilingual and literate in both languages. The decade he spent at this Muslim combination of highschool and university (1890–1900; the madrasas were Mir Arab, 1889–91; Olimjon, 1892–93; Badalbek, 1894–96; Hoji Zohid, 1896–99; and Kukaldosh, 1899–1900) exposed him to the influence of two types of his society's educated elite: the conservative, chiefly clerical one with a basically medieval outlook; and those who had grasped the need for reform and were struggling to propagate it. Instruction at the madrasas was of the scholastic kind; some of the faculty and associates, however, passed over to the reformist camp, and it was through contact with them or their work, often in the midst of animated literary debates and parties in teachers' cells at the madrasas or in people's homes, that Ayni was initiated to the new ideas. In volumes 3 and 4 of his *Yoddoshtho* ("Memoirs"), Ayni tells about the effect the personality and writings of Ahmad Donish (1827–97) had on him in his formative years. Donish, a Bukharan scholar and civil servant who participated in several diplomatic missions sent by the emir to St. Petersburg, observed the intellectual revolution that had set Europe on the path of modernization and dominance, and became the earliest harbinger of the need for reform in his homeland. He could do so without suffering the emir's reprisal because the latter had at that stage not yet grasped the magnitude of a reformist's criticism. Like most Bukharan intellectuals, Donish wrote in Farsi; and like Ayni, he was later appropriated by the Republic of Tajikistan as a "Tajik." The Academy of Sciences of the Tajik SSR bore the honorific epithet "In the name of Donish" (*Donish nomidagi Akademiyai Ulumi Tojik*).

By the time he left school and began his career as a teacher, writer, scholar, and journalist, Ayni had wholly espoused the reformists' main goal, the new method [of education] (the *usul-i jadid*). Significantly, one of the first publications of this subsequently prodigiously productive writer and scholar was a textbook of readings for school-age children, *Yoshlar tarbiyasi* ("Youths' education," in Turki). This was the time when he and other members of the informal group of Young Bukharans still hoped that the Emir's rule could be reformed without being overthrown, and that Islamic society in general only needed to rid itself of alien accretions and adopt some of the modern trends offered by Western civilization to recover its former glory and shake off the West's tutelage.

Alim Khan's despotic rule, however, dashed these hopes, for it fiercely resisted the Young Bukharans' efforts, especially once the latter group had become bolder after the February 1917 revolution in St. Petersburg. The despot's rejection of reform was brutally demonstrated in the summer of that year, when he ordered his henchmen to round up a number of reformists and had them flogged; Ayni received 75 strokes, and may have survived only because Russian troops, quartered in the nearby railroad station enclave of Kagan, intervened and brought the victims to an infirmary there.[6] The intervention failed to save Ayni's younger brother, however, who perished in the subsequent repression. One can imagine the powerful effect this traumatic experience must have left on Ayni's psyche to the very end of his life.

The October Revolution occurred on the heels of the repression in Bukhara, and the Jadids, as we have already stated, hailed it as they would have hailed any Russian power that gave promise to rid them of the emir and allow them to strive for a modernization and self-determination of Turkestan. Their activities were now centered at Tashkent and Samarkand, until such time as they could move back to Bukhara once the Russian troops ousted the Emir. That time came, we have seen, in September 1920. Significantly, Ayni did not join them but stayed in Samarkand. This had a more than just logistical significance. Unlike Fitrat, Khojaev, and the other former Young Bukharans, he stopped short of actively participating in the political drama that was unfolding in Central Asia, but mostly stayed within the cultural parameter of the revolution. Moreover, he took the Bolshevik side, and followed this line to the end of his life. This ensured not only his survival but his growing prominence as a pampered favorite of the official cultural establishment both in Moscow and in Central Asia.

We might thus be tempted to write Sadriddin Ayni off as a collaborator, albeit a pardonable one. His case, however, is too complex and interesting, and his literary and scholarly contributions too valuable, to justify such a dismissal. On the literary level, his poems, short stories, and novels, written either in Farsi or Turki, became a powerful tool for giving these idioms – henceforward officially called Tajik and Uzbek – a firm literary base and thus a weapon against the danger of Russification (besides possessing an undeniable intrinsic value); this was compounded by the newly created periodical press where he often participated as a

---

[6] See the illustration no. 36 in *Kniga zhizni Sadriddina Ayni; The Book of Life of Sadriddin Aini* (Dushanbe, 1978) (a photograph showing his lacerated back).

contributor and editor. On the scholarly level, he published solid historical and literary studies, again in both these languages (the former chiefly
in Uzbek, the latter in Tajik). Admittedly, he did not openly come out
against the terror of the 1930s which destroyed a number of his former
comrades-at-arms and for a time dragged contemporary Central Asian
culture to an even lower level than that of Russia. To do that would have
been suicidal; what he managed to avoid, however, was the sycophantic
behavior of those of his compatriots who, in order to save their lives,
wallowed in the dust at the feet of the Moscow dictator. Ayni's success
was no doubt partly due to an early and then consistent espousal of the
mainstream line with his political and journalistic tracts published in
such newspapers as *Mehnatkashlar tovushi* ("Workers' Voice," 1918–22;
Uzbek) or *Shu"lai inqilob* ("Flame of the Revolution," 1919–21; Tajik),
and his subsequent avoidance of too closely associating with the
Chaghatay gurungi ("Chaghatay association"), founded in the 1920s by
Fitrat and other Turkestani patriots who could not foresee that their
patriotism, branded as nationalism, would later lead to their doom. It
may be that Ayni's separation from that group was not a simple case of
political opportunism. His mother tongue was, after all, Persian, and the
principal cultural heritage he adhered to was that of Iran in the broadest sense of the word. Fitrat, although he too grew up as a bilingual
Bukharan, ultimately identified with the Turkic dimension of Central
Asia, and there the two men parted company. Here too luck was on
Ayni's side: Moscow feared Turkic nationalism far more than Persian, or
Tajik, or Iranian nationalism in Central Asia, and the cultivation of the
region's Iranian heritage may in fact have been viewed as a welcome
antidote to the much more powerful and dangerous Turkic nationalism.
The creation of Tajikistan could be seen as an extension of this view: in
addition to partitioning Central Asia along separate Turkic languages,
the creation of an Iranian unit built yet another obstacle to the dream
of a unified Turkestan. Tajikistan, we have said, was the least natural of
the republics that came into being through the process of *razmezhevanie*,
and the chief reason for its creation would have been the Russian policy
of *divide et impera*. Once again, however, the reality was not that simple.
We have already expressed our reservations concerning a wholesale
adoption of this interpretation, and Ayni's life may serve here as an illustration of the contradictory nature of Soviet policy. He chose
Samarkand as his home, and no doubt would have ended his days there
if the nomination to the presidency of the newly established Tajik
Academy of Sciences had not mandated his presence in Dushanbe for

the final four years of his life. To him, Samarkand with its surroundings must have been an essentially Tajik city, as was probably Bukhara, whereas Dushanbe may have seemed but a paltry provincial town in comparison with those historic centers of Central Asian civilization. It is not known whether he ever uttered a word of disapproval at the time of the *razmezhevanie* or later, but he would surely have been delighted if Moscow had allotted Samarkand and Bukhara to Tajikistan as enclaves under the republic's jurisdiction. Moscow, in turn, should have been glad to possess this special form of gerrymander as a fail-safe barrier against an effective pan-Turkic front. It had the means to create it, yet it didn't. Sheer oversight may have been the cause, but then Moscow may also have drawn the line here and decided that these enclaves would cause too much confusion. (Another way would have been simply to attach the entire course of the Zarafshan to Tajikistan, treating the Uzbeks there as a minority; this would have dealt a still heavier blow to the goals of Pan-Turanism.)

It may be worthwhile to mention a few of Ayni's works. In 1920, he published in Turki *Bukhoro inqilobi tarikhi uchun materiallar*, "Materials on the history of the revolution of Bukhara," in other words, of the fall of the emirate and establishment of the People's Republic of Bukhara; in the following year came out his *Bukhoro Manghit amirligining tarikhi*, "History of the Manghit emirate of Bukhara," again in Turki. In 1926 Ayni published an anthology of Tajik (i.e. Persian) literature, *Namunahoi adabieti Tojik*, and in the 1930s and 1940s a number of studies of Persian and Chaghatay literary figures such as Firdawsi, Rudaki, Khujandi, Vasifi, and Navai. Meanwhile he never ceased writing chiefly political poetry, combining the time-honored Persian tradition of court poets with one of his principal activities, politically engaged journalism. An illustration of that is the quaint "Freedom March," a poem in Turki (*Marsh-i hurriyat*) and in Farsi (*Surud-i azadi*), composed in 1918, to be sung to the tune of the *Marseillaise*.

Writing poetry was of course an avocation of most educated Iranians, and writing scholarly and historical prose too had a long tradition. Belletristic prose, on the other hand, was all but non-existent, and here Ayni's contribution was fundamental, for with his short stories, novels, and a lengthy autobiography he laid the foundations of this genre in both Tajik and Uzbek literature. Almost without exception, the theme of these works was the Farsi and Turki-speaking society of Bukhara in the nineteenth and early twentieth centuries. In 1934 Ayni published what is considered his best novel, "Slaves," simultaneously in Tajik

(*Ghulomon*) and Uzbek (*Qullar*). The year of the publication was significant: Socialist Realism, the doctrine proclaimed at the 1932 convention of the Union of Soviet Writers in Moscow as the only ideological and thematic method permitted to Soviet authors, was in full swing, and Stalinist terror was beginning to flex its muscle. Yet Ayni managed to write a genuine work of literature, presenting a gripping picture of three generations of Bukharans before the transformations wrought by the Soviet regime. He demonstrated a similar ability with his impressive four-volume autobiography, which again he wrote both in Tajik (*Yoddoshtha*) and Uzbek (*Esdaliklar*). Published between 1949 and 1954, they cover his boyhood in Saktare (vol. 1), his school years in the madrasas of Bukhara (vol. 2), the society of Bukhara of those days (vol. 3), and the political and social ferment gripping the emirate in its last years (vol. 4). Only death, we are told, prevented Ayni from continuing or completing the memoirs. That would of course have meant employing all the paraphernalia of Socialist Realism for depicting the happiness of contemporary society, and it may have been this consideration rather than inexorable fate that thwarted the completion of the memoirs. Significantly, Ayni's scholarly and belletristic prose was entirely focused on pre-Soviet themes, and only marginally or apparently did he give some due to the Caesar in Moscow. Even a theme like the eighth-century uprising of al-Muqanna (*Isyëni Muqanna*, Stalinabad 1944; see pp. 65–6) could be interpreted in this ambiguous way: the somewhat socialist-like ideas reportedly harbored by the leader of Central Asians fighting against the Arab conqueror made this event one of the acceptable themes in Soviet historiography, but it could also be viewed as a patriotic rebellion against a foreign invader. Even more intriguing is Ayni's study of an episode from the time of the Mongol invasion. Timur-Malik, governor of Khujand, put up a heroic though ultimately vain resistance to Mongol detachments sent by Genghis Khan's sons Chaghatay and Ögedey. Ayni's *Qahramoni khalqi Tojik Temurmalik* ("Timur-Malik, hero of the Tajik people") also appeared during the war years, and symbolized, according to Soviet and satellite literary historians, "the hatred the author felt for the invaders of his homeland" (i.e. for the Germans invading Russia). The plausibility of a more nuanced interpretation is obvious. Sadriddin Ayni thus played an invaluable role in the reaffirmation of Central Asian cultural and linguistic identity, but in the complex and contradictory climate of Soviet national and colonial policy this role defies a simple definition. Above all, he took advantage of those aspects of Soviet rule that made it possible for Central Asians to successfully withstand the attempts of Russification. At the same time, his virtually double Tajik–Uzbek identity within the framework of Central Asia illustrates a case of ethnolinguistic complexity that may serve as a model for mutual respect and cooperation, but that also may need all the wisdom and tolerance of the region's statesmen and citizens if its people want to strive for a harmonious future.

Islam played an intriguing and complex role in this drama of one nation and civilization trying to force its will upon another. Like Orthodox Christianity in Russia, it was all but effaced from the surface of public and even private life until the Second World War, and officially propagated atheism came close to vie with Communism for the position of a new religion. What the government could not do, however, was to change the psychological substratum of a millennium-old lifestyle. Even the most avowed Communist Party members remained Muslim in certain basic respects, such as dietary preferences, marriages, burials, customs like circumcision. All that separated them from their Russian comrades. Mixed marriages between Muslims and Russians or other Europeans were rare, especially when the *bride* would have been a Muslim (a combination banned by Islamic law) – a fact that played a significant role in the resistance to linguistic and cultural Russification.

The role of Islam did not stop there, however. Driven underground,[7] its members continued to practice their religion in clandestine mosques, and some of them belonged to one or another of the aforementioned Sufi orders (*tariqas*) that had since the Middle Ages played a considerable social and political role in Central Asia. Moreover, an extremely potent force in religious life was veneration of local saints and pilgrimage to their shrines; those powerful and wealthy also often chose to be buried in the vicinity of a renowned saint's tomb. This last-named practice could be prevented by the Soviet government, but the pilgrimage itself, popular especially among the masses, weathered all attempts of the authorities to stamp it out. A few examples may be instructive.

One such site is the so-called Shah-i Zinda, "the Living King," in the northern outskirts of Samarkand. It is the putative tomb of Qutham ibn Abbas, a cousin of the Prophet Muhammad, who according to tradition fell there as a martyr for the faith in 676 at the vanguard of an Arab army. Eventually his tomb generated two classical features of Islamic

---

[7] Or "parallel Islam," a label favored by Sovietologists: parallel to the officially permitted religion controlled by the aforementioned Directorate of Muslims of Central Asia and Kazakhstan, itself controlled by the government.

holy sites: its vicinity became a favorite final resting place of the elite, and the faithful of all levels made frequent pilgrimages to it (in fact, the people of Samarkand came twice a week, on Thursdays and Sundays). A series of magnificent mausolea arose there in the Timurid period, and the site eventually also attracted the attention of cultural historians and tourists. The Soviet authorities encouraged the tourists but discouraged the pilgrims; when the present author visited the site in the final years of Soviet rule before *glasnost*, however, the pilgrims gave every sign of out-numbering the tourists – this despite the presence of an office, at the entrance to the site, of the local chapter of "The Atheist" (*Bezbozhnik*).

Another memorable site is the *mazar* of Shahimardan, situated in a small Uzbek enclave within Kyrgyzstan just south of the Uzbek cities of Fergana and Margilan. According to popular belief, Ali ibn Abi Talib, the Prophet Muhammad's cousin, son-in-law, the fourth caliph, and the first Shii Imam, is buried there, hence the name: for Shahimardan, lit-erally "The King (*Shah*) of men (*mardan*)" is one of his Persian titles. The fact that the story has no historical basis is irrelevant (Ali's real – or at least principal – tomb is in the Iraqi city of Najaf), and the legend has parallels in many other similar sites associated, in popular imagination, with the burial of revered saints (the most famous legendary tomb of Ali, the reader may recall, is Mazar-i Sharif in Afghanistan). In 1929, Hamza Hakimzade Niyazi (b. 1889), an Uzbek and a former *jadid* teacher and playwright who had joined the Bolshevik cause, agitated aginst the *mazar* and pilgrimage to it, but was murdered by "fanatical mullahs" – or so the official Soviet version said. The government destroyed the brick dome sheltering the tomb and punished the culprits, but the sanctuary was rebuilt a year later by the resilient natives; in 1940 it was demolished again and replaced with a monument commemorat-ing the Bolshevik martyr-saint and a "Museum of Atheism." The site was then developed as a "Culture Park" and renamed (together with the neighboring town) Hamzaabad, "Hamza city."[8] The murdered writer-propagandist thus entered the pantheon of Soviet hagiography, honored by countless recollections such as the *dastan* (legend, epic) "Shahimardan" composed in 1932 by his junior acquaintance and sub-sequent stalwart of official Uzbek letters, Hamid Alimjan (1909–44). It seems, however, that all the efforts to convert a Muslim shrine into a Bolshevik one, and a sanctuary of Islamic devotion into one of militant

---

[8] Khamzaabad in Cyrillic script if approached through Russian; in Uzbek Cyrillic it would be Hamzaobod.

atheism, failed on the popular level. The faithful continued to flock there throughout the Soviet period, and in 1978 a Soviet scholar decried the importance of pilgrimage to the place "under the cover of tourism," which included public prayers and sacrifices. The Uzbek writer K. Yashen even describes in his novel *Hamza* a Yasavi *zikr* performed there.[9] All the government could do was to curb such manifestations of the true purpose of the *ziyarats*, devotional visits, on the more explicit or intellectual level. In this latter respect they have been fairly successful: to foreign or less initiated observers and visitors, the genuine nature of the site became unknown, and Hamzaabad acquired a public identity as a shrine worshiping a Bolshevik saint. The cycle is closing in the post-Soviet period, however: according to the British journalist C. Thubron, local old-timers now assert that Niyazi was killed not by fanatical mullahs but by two brothers avenging their sister who had been dishonored by the womanizing Communist.[10]

From among the multitude of other *mazars* in Central Asia, the following deserve at least a brief mention: Khwaja Ahmad Yasavi's mausoleum in Yasi (Turkestan), Khwaja Baha al-Din Naqshband's shrine near Bukhara, and Najm al-Din Kubra's tomb near Urgench. These three Sufis, the reader may recall, founded the three great *tariqas* named after them in their Central Asian homeland. Their tombs subsequently gave rise to major shrines, *mazars* visited by the Muslim faithful down to our own day. As in the case of other such sites, the Soviet government tried different methods to combat these centers of enduring religious cults. Khwaja Ahmad Yasavi's mausoleum was declared an important architectural monument and the government financed its restoration, while transforming the *mazar* complex into a *dom otdykha* (lit. "house of rest") "something between an anti-religious museum and a culture park." The *mazar* of Baha al-Din Naqshband, less impressive architecturally, received no such attention, and the government may have long been successful in isolating the sanctuary. Once *glasnost* set in, however, the shrine reasserted its role, and "in 1987, during abortive demonstrations, it was to this forbidden tomb that the Bukhara protesters had marched, as if to the last symbol of purity in their city." As in its pre-modern past, the shrine of Baha al-Din Naqshband has again received veneration from the mighty and humble alike: in 1993 the

---

[9] Cited by Bennigsen, *Le soufi et le commissaire*, p. 213; two chapters of the novel appeared in *Nauka i religiya* (1982), nos. 5 and 7.   [10] *The Lost Heart of Asia*, pp. 242–43.

President of Uzbekistan, Islam Karimov, appropriated state funds for refurbishing it, and a project sign standing outside the shrine in that year listed Egypt and Saudi Arabia as other contributors to its renovation. In 1994, Mukhtar Abdullaev, an imam from the Naqshbandi shrine, was appointed *mufti* of Tashkent by the Uzbek government. Meanwhile the faithful of all hues now flock to it, as any visitor interested in the subject can witness. As for the tomb of Shaykh Najm al-Din Kubra near Old Urgench, it illustrates the characteristic vitality of such sites as *mazars* visited by large numbers of Muslim faithful even when the order they had founded has disappeared or has been absorbed by other orders.

One could almost say that a curious kind of compromise, even dual personality, had appeared in Central Asia during these final years of the Soviet Union. On the formal, official level, little seemed to have changed since the days of Stalin. This was illustrated by the national anthems the republics were forced to adopt with their new constitutions of 1978. We shall quote the Uzbek anthem as an example, and suggest that it and its Kazakh, Turkmen etc. counterparts could hardly have been taken seriously, though the Central Asians had to bow in contemptuous and temporary submission. We shall then quote excerpts from two poems. One is by the Uzbek poet Mirtemir Tursunov (b. 1910), published on New Year's day of 1970 in the daily *Sovet Ozbekistani*. The other is by the Turkmen poet Magtymguly (1732–90), published as part of his collected works in 1983. Both were genuine hymns to their peoples and countries – in fact, their real national anthems. Here it was the masters in Moscow who had bowed to the inevitable; they had the power to force absurd anthems down the throats of their subjects, but became helpless in the face of the resurgence of genuine national feelings. Finally, yet another qualification may be needed. The Russian chauvinism or nationalism characteristic of the Soviet period may have been more the work of the political system than of the Russian people themselves. What mattered most to the Bolshevik masters in Moscow was control of their multinational empire, and for that they needed a common denominator that could only be the Russian language and the Russified identity of the subject peoples. Diversity could mean difference, dissidence, or secession, and had therefore to be rendered harmless by vaccinating it with the Russian component. Lust for power or fear of losing it in the outer marches, an ominous breach in the masters' omnipotence that might then cause cracks at the center, was the motivation behind the "Russian" chauvinism of these dictators, as the ethnic background of the grimmest propagator of this policy, Joseph Stalin, shows. 1978 was the year of a new constitution of the Soviet Union and of all the Union republics. The waves of terror were by then long past, and Central Asians, like the rest of Soviet citizenry except for the rather new and on the whole marginal appearance of active dissidents, had accepted a *modus vivendi* with the system. The compromise had become mutual. Moscow learned to live with the fact that the main non-Russian nations were there to stay, allowed them to cultivate their cultural patrimony within the prescribed norms and limits, and appeared confident that the union welded through this compromise was there to stay, too. It never allowed Cholpan to be included in the wave of posthumous rehabilitations that accompanied Khrushchev's de-Stalinization campaign (Cholpan's name, for example, does not even appear in the otherwise remarkably daring Uzbek encyclopedia), but Fitrat and Khojaev did receive a partial pardon, and while Moscow could not resurrect Törekul Aitmatov, his son Chingis's writings became an apotheosis of the Kyrgyz people and homeland. The Uzbeks and other Central Asians must have seemed to justify Moscow's confidence when the republics' parliaments accepted new versions of the national anthems that accompanied the new constitutions. Here is the text of the Uzbek anthem:

> Salute to you, Russian people, our Great Brother! Greetings, our genius Lenin, dear one!
> You have shown us the road to freedom, The Uzbek has found glory in the Soviet homeland!
>
> The Party is the guide, dear Uzbekistan, You are a sun-bathed country, prosperous, developed!
> Your land is a treasure-trove, happiness is your lot, Fortune is your companion in the Soviet homeland!
>
> We did not see light in a sun-lit country, We lacked water alongside rivers.
> Dawn broke, Revolution, Lenin was the Guide, Peoples are thankful to Lenin the Guide!
>
> The garden of Communism – eternal springtime, Forever brotherhood – long live friendship!
> The flag of the Soviets is victorious, firmly implanted, The universe shines with light from this flag!

This anthem, which opens with a thunderous salute to the Russian people, mentions Uzbekistan only in the second stanza. As for the Uzbek people, their name appears in the somewhat condescending singular. It is an insult to the Uzbeks, and a display of the arrogant pretense of Communist ideology. The reversal of values and facts reaches its peak here: Instead of being a hymn to the Uzbek people, it is a hymn glorifying the Russians (while claiming to be the Uzbeks' anthem); instead of acknowledging the fact that Uzbekistan was conquered by Tsarist Russia and reconquered by Bolshevik Russia, it states that Russia's dictator showed the Uzbeks the road to freedom; instead of admitting that economic exploitation with colonial overtones has caused a catastrophic abuse of water resources, it states that the Revolution and Lenin provided the Uzbeks with water. The pretense is equally strident: terms like "eternal" and "universe" linked to Communism are symptomatic of this ideology's character as an intolerant, all-embracing religion.

The anthems of the other four Central Asian republics are identical in their central theme: glorification of Russia and Communism. These anthems could hardly have been taken seriously by the Central Asians, and they are relevant only as demonstrations of the special combination of hypocrisy and compromise characteristic of the system on the eve of its dissolution.

Few, if any, realized how doomed this compromise was destined to be. But the signs were there, and the aforementioned poems by Mirtemir and Magtymguly, rather than the official anthems, expressed the Central Asians' real feelings. First, the Uzbek poem entitled "Thou, Uzbekistan!":[11]

> I wished to speak about happiness,
> to sing a joyous ode,
> To think of tomorrow and today,
> To hold a fabulous feast;
> In my eyes thou appearst,
> Thou at last art the one, the eternal object of learning,
> Thou, Uzbekistan.
>
> Child of toil art thou, sound of heart,
> And the enviers are distraught and downcast,
> with every year;
> At every step art thou paradise, an Eden, a garden,
> Thy nights unending myriads of candelabra,
> Thou art despot to enemy, solace to friend,
> Danger afar, art thou a bower of calm,
> Thou, Uzbekistan.

---

[11] Quoted by Critchlow, *Nationalism in Uzbekistan*, pp. 22–24.

Thy hand holds the key to treasures of riches,
In thy garden and desert a happy year's song,
Left and right thy gold and thy silk;
How many the peoples enrapt in thy path,
Thou art fruit and wine and water and cake,
Thou art twin rivers of love,
Thou, Uzbekistan.

Thou art thine own machine builder, thine own livestock breeder,
Thine own scholar, thine own cultural worker.
Thou art volunteer soldier, noble guide,
A storehouse of cotton priceless, without peer,
Thy soul Lenin's child forever,
Thou, Uzbekistan!

Like Aitmatov and Qodirov, Mirtemir was a member of the Communist Party, and like all of his compatriots who did not wish to become needless martyrs, he was paying the dues to the Caesar in Moscow and his deputies in Central Asia. The ritual reference to Lenin (and, in the case of an Uzbek, to cotton) was a standard means of evading the ever-present danger of the Inquisition.

Here are a few excerpts from the Turkmen poem:

Between the Oxus River and the Caspian, over the desert blows the Turkmen's gale.
The rose-bud, the black pupil of my eye – The Turkmen's torrent descends from the black mountain.

God has raised him and placed him under His shadow, his herds and flocks range over the steppe.
Blossoms of many hues crowd his green summer pasture – the Turkmen's steppe drowns in basil's scent.

His fair maidens appear clad in red and green, spreading their ambergris-like fragrance.
Begs and elders are the lords of the land – guardians of the Turkmen's beautiful homeland.

He is a warrior's son, a warrior was his father; Goroghli is his brother, inebriated are his senses;
Should foes pursue him in mountains or plains – they could not take the Turkmen, the tiger's son, alive.

…Tribes are like brothers, clans are friends; their fate is not adverse, they are God's rays.
When warriors mount their horses, it is for battle – The Turkmen sets out against the foe!

He sets out in high spirits, his heart is not faint; he splits the
mountains, his road is not blocked.
My eye's glance and heart's pleasure seek no other scenes –
Magtymguly speaks the Turkmen's tongue![12]

The Soviet government obviously considered such expressions of
national feelings harmless, because the people who harbored them also
gave impression of accepting their national anthems and all the other
paraphernalia of Soviet patriotism imposed by Moscow. One can
suspect, however, that if this poem had been composed by a *living*
Turkmen, the Inquisition would not have spared him unless some kind
of homage to Lenin or Russia had been tagged on to it. Magtymguly
could "get away with it" because he was long dead, and his publishers
could too because official Soviet historiography endeavored to cast some
of his poems as a protest against "feudal" or "obscurantist Islamic" elements.

Things might indeed have continued in the same manner for yet
another generation if it hadn't been for the historical accident (or inev-
itability?) of Mikhail Gorbachev.

[12] W. Feldman, "Interpreting the poetry of Makhtumquli," in Jo-Ann Gross (ed.), *Muslims in Central
Asia: Expressions of identity and change* (Durham and London: Duke University Press, 1992), pp.
167–89 (includes the Turkmen text and English translation). The Turkmen text of the poem has
also been included in *Zindaginamah va barguzidah-i ashar-i Makhtumquli Firaghi* (Biography and selec-
tion of poems of Makhtumquli Firaghi, in Persian), ed. Abd al-Rahman Dihji (Tehran,
1373/1994), pp. 227–28 (Arabic script).

STOP

CHAPTER EIGHTEEN

Central Asia becomes independent

By the time Gorbachev became First Secretary of the Communist Party of the Soviet Union in 1985, people knew that his country had serious economic, social, and perhaps even military problems. The inherent flaws of the system had begun to sap its strength to a point where some of its leaders started wondering whether modifications were necessary, and if so, what kind and to what extent.

One problem was corruption among high officials. For some reason this corruption turned out to be especially rampant in Central Asia, and worst in Uzbekistan. Sharaf Rashidov (1917–83) was since 1959 First Secretary of the republic's Communist Party, and in 1961 Moscow showed its trust in this Uzbek by elevating him to membership in the system's highest political aristocracy, the CC CPSU (Central Committee of the Communist Party of the Soviet Union). He retained both posts until his death in 1983, and when he died he was buried with honors comparable only to those of his role models, Lenin and Stalin: his body was placed in a mausoleum built for that purpose on the Uzbek capital's main square.

Rashidov of course had to earn Moscow's trust, and there was ample opportunity to do that. His record as a perfect Party member was impeccable, and the rulers in the Soviet capital knew that they could count on his cooperation in their control of Uzbekistan as an obedient republic. He knew what they wanted above anything else: (Communist) law and order and stability in Uzbekistan, and as much cotton as possible from it. He was their man on both counts, and had no qualms if that meant a surrender of Uzbek national will and spiritual as well as material values to Moscow, and a catastrophic destruction of the country's environment and people's health.

The result was a curiously split personality and an elusive local ruling elite, characteristic of Central Asian leadership in the final decades of Soviet rule. Rashidov gained enormous power in Uzbekistan, by building up a political and bureaucratic-managerial infrastructure loyal to him and benefiting from this association. These people became the country's privileged class. Their privileges were many and fundamental, and sharply separated them from the common people, but also from their Russian masters: for a special feature that accompanied this process was the "Uzbekization" (or "Kazakhization," etc.) of the political and bureaucratic infrastructure of the Central Asian republics. At first sight this could be viewed as a reappearance of the aforementioned developments of the 1920s: "national communism" and "nativization" (*korenizatsiya*). On a closer look, however, we see a striking difference: champions of national Communism (like the Kazakh Ryskulov or Uzbek Khojaev) were true Central Asian patriots who took Moscow's manifesto of 1917 about self-determination seriously; and the representatives of the "native working class" were reluctantly recruited into the ranks of the Party membership and bureaucracy by the province's Russian directorate to satisfy Moscow's idea of "nativization." Rashidov and his peers and cohorts, on the other hand, were anything but patriots, and they came to their position of power and comfort by their own initiative and political virtuosity, though at the price of absolute subordination to Moscow and disregard of the true interests of their countries. The national Communists of the 1920s paid for their error with their lives or disappearance in the Gulag a decade later; they were joined by some of the recruits of the "nativization" years, who too had come to believe that a sincere dialogue with Moscow about the genuine interests of their native land and people was possible. Rashidov and his Uzbek clansmen made no such mistakes, and the rewards were great.

Rashidov's long rule of Uzbekistan (1959–83) coincided with several power shifts in Moscow, from Khrushchev to Brezhnev, Andropov, and Chernenko, and he had the good luck to die before the accession of Gorbachev. In his eagerness to serve his masters, he even outdid their demands: while the planners in Moscow set the price of cotton delivered by Uzbekistan below its international market value, Rashidov proposed to lower the price even further, and when Moscow stipulated how much cotton Uzbekistan should deliver, he promised an even larger quantity, and the ensuing figures and statistics showed that he had kept his word.

Especially in Brezhnev's time the empire basked in the sunlight of this "international" cooperation. *Mutatis mutandis*, the situation was similar in the other Central Asian republics. In neighboring Kazakhstan, Dinmukhamed Kunaev (b. 1911) had risen to a similar pinnacle of power and comfort and through similar methods. In 1964 he became First Secretary of the Communist Party of Kazakhstan, and in 1971 he also entered the Politburo of the CC CPSU, and held those posts until 1986. Like Rashidov in Uzbekistan, Kunaev in his republic gradually acquired enormous authority by building up a network of politicians and bureaucrats who owed their positions of power and comfort to him. And again, most of these people were "natives," in this instance Kazakhs. What is more, many belonged to the Horde of which Kunaev was a member, the Greater Horde (a social phenomenon that according to official theory had long been swept away by the new Soviet Order). One of the results was that while the Kazakhs still only had a plurality in the republic, they came to occupy the majority of seats in the republic's parliament, the Supreme Soviet. Like Kunaev himself, most of these deputies were of course members of the Communist Party, and the rest equally loyal non-affiliates. One can surmise that the Soviet government was fully aware of this surge of native power in Kazakhstan, but preferred to look the other way, because otherwise things were under its complete control, or seemed to be. Kunaev and his cohorts never failed to do Moscow's bidding and suffer its doings, even if it meant destroying the country's environment and people's health through nuclear tests in the area of Semipalatinsk, or, on a less lethal level, a continuation of the semi-colonial relationship fashioned to suit Russia rather than Kazakhstan. The Kazakh leaders of the final Soviet era were no nationalists or patriots, but within the parameter of the permissible they were thoroughly Kazakh: the family, the clan, the tribe, the Horde had traditionally been the avenues through which power and positions of comfort were distributed, and by the time Kunaev became the nation's number one Communist, these traditions had reasserted themselves despite the strictures imposed by Moscow. Russians and other non-Kazakh citizens of Kazakhstan were, in a sense, left out in the cold.

Moscow, we have said, appeared satisfied with this state of affairs, but by the time Brezhnev had died and his first successors lamely grappled with the unwieldy empire, doubts must have begun to creep into the minds of some people whose concern about the probity of their country and the survivability of the system surpassed the satisfaction they drew from their own power and comfort. These doubts encompassed a vast array of flaws, but problems in Central Asia were a special and ultimately contradictory part of them.

The doubts burst into the open only with the accession of Mikhail Gorbachev to the captainship of the Soviet Union. More lucid and honest than his predecessors, he realized that his country and political faith might lose the contest with the Western world and capitalism unless they reformed themselves. The ideological hostility and closure of the Soviet Union to the West was one of the chief causes of its growing stagnation. This stagnation included those aspects that must have mattered most especially to the military – the rapidly evolving electronic technology. President Reagan's "Star Wars" gave Gorbachev the necessary tool with which to persuade his peers that a "restructuring," *perestroika*, was necessary if they wanted their system to survive. This restructuring included an unprecedented openness and dismantling of at least a part of the ideological wall erected along the Soviet frontier. It might be interesting to compare the Ottoman and Soviet empires with respect to their stagnation and its causes, the remedies sought by their reformers, and the ultimate dissolution of these empires and of their ideologies.

The challenge was enormous, and Gorbachev's answer included a major contradiction: this statesman, a sincere Communist, wanted to save Communism by grafting a strong dose of humanism and openness onto it, something no one had tried before. The combination proved to be a utopian idea, and brought about the collapse of the whole system years, perhaps decades, before this process might otherwise have come to fruition.

The contradiction took on a special form in Central Asia, however. By the time Mikhail Gorbachev succeeded Konstantin Chernenko, it was no secret that something was wrong especially in the republic of Uzbekistan. People had discovered that the figures showing the quantity of cotton shipped to Russia did not quite tally with the actual quantity, and that this falsification had reached a vast scale and had especially mushroomed in the Brezhnev era. Moreover, those masterminding this deception had included some of the highest officials – Rashidov himself, and they had coopted people at the center like Brezhnev's son-in-law, Yuriy Churbanov. The scandal had generated investigations and firings and prison terms already under Andropov, but Gorbachev widened the clean-up by launching a massive campaign against "corruption." Corruption in this context is perhaps an inaccurate term, for it was spawned by a system and relationship which in themselves were corrupt. What was *rashidovshchina*, a term devised for the wily bureaucrats' gimmicks to line their pockets or promote their nephews, in comparison with the environmental blight spread by Moscow's policies in Central Asia? What was their petty pilfery in comparison with the grand larceny perpetrated by the center of the empire, as it dictated the below-the-market prices paid for the cotton and other commodities hauled away from the region?[1]

The Central Asians had to bow to Moscow's grand-scale dictates, but, as we have said, the fortunate elite was rewarded by access to positions of local power, prestige, handsome salaries and perks through a network of acquaintances and special relationships. These ties were intimately related to family, clan, locality, or tribal affiliations, in other words, to the native element of Soviet society. To his consternation, Gorbachev realized that the Soviet state was faced with what somehow looked like nationalism, yet virtually all of the indigenous actors were Communists professing unflinching loyalty to Moscow. We have already pointed out that in contrast to their predecessors of the 1920s, this new brand of national Communists were no nationalists, and that they were routinely sacrificing the interests of their countries in order to advance their own careers. They had learnt how to do it, and since the 1960s were playing this card with increasing virtuosity, often coopting Russians and other Europeans into their schemes but not quite letting them penetrate the periphery of their ethnic infrastructure. Rashidov and Kunaev were past masters in this game, but they were only the best noticed examples of a process that was spreading through the power structure of the Soviet empire in Central Asia. But there was worse. Gorbachev and his comrades in Moscow realized that their Uzbek comrades, however corrupt, were less alarming than those Central Asians who had somehow begun to reveal an independent national spirit, despite all the damnations of nationalism and admonitions that "internationalism" was the supreme form of patriotism incumbent on every Soviet citizen. This new nationalism was real and surging fast, but before *glasnost* it could manifest itself only indirectly and cautiously. Its standardbearers were the native intellectuals and professionals; their ranks were growing, and they ended up representing an alternative elite to that of the Communist politicians and bureaucrats. We have suggested that up to a point the two groups overlapped each other. Some of the politicians and bureaucrats were no doubt at times trying to defend not only their personal interests but also those of their countries; and the intellectuals and professionals had to play the Communist card just to be able to function. Mirtemir, the

---

[1] Many Russians would of course point out that the below-the-market pricing was mutual, and that in some respects Central Asia was more a burden than an asset to the Russian economy. Adequately documented studies of this question remain to be done; in my view, the environmental blight visited on Central Asia through wholesale abuse of natural resources, now fully revealed, is the most damning aspect of the relationship.

author of the poem "Thou, Uzbekistan!," was a member of the Communist Party, and he made sure to mention Lenin at the end of the eloquent hymn to his country as a safeguard against the Inquisition. The year was 1970, the Prague Spring of 1968 seemed to be safely tucked away in the dustbin of history, and Mirtemir went as far as an Uzbek could possibly go in that period. What he could not do was to challenge Moscow to cease the colonial exploitation of his country, to stop destroying its environment and people's health, to let the Uzbeks write the real history of their country. Had he done that, the KGB would have taken care of the rest. As it was, he was one of the many who had begun to rekindle the flame of the national spirit. Frontal attack had to wait for *glasnost* and *perestroika*.

That time came when in the core of Soviet society and state Gorbachev set in motion the unprecedented program of reforms that became famous as *perestroika* (restructuring; *qayta quruu* in Uzbek) and *glasnost* (openness [of expression and criticism]; *ochiqliq* in Uzbek). To be sure, criticism (and self-criticism, a particularly favorite device of the system) had been a standard feature of the Communist Party and Soviet state, but there was a sharp difference between the two phases. Before Gorbachev, criticism meant that the criticized were not living up to the demands and norms of Marxism-Leninism, and the remedy was even more Marxism-Leninism; those few who dared to propose different remedies quickly ended up in the Gulag. The two words so characteristic of the Gorbachev era had previously not been used as technical terms; their new use was a hint that something had changed. Most observers would undoubtedly agree on that, and even on the effects of that change, but what its causes, nature, and goals exactly meant is a matter of controversy.

For an explanation we should go back to the revolution's very nature, or even to its initiator's personality. The unprecedented element, absent from all earlier attempts at reform, was the aforementioned dose of humanism injected by Gorbachev into the system. The notorious coercive apparatus lost its former punch, and the spontaneous energies of human nature began to act all over the empire and in a variety of ways. In Russia, such heresies as proposals of a market economy, political pluralism, practice of religion, or workers' strikes were no longer a guarantee of a trip to Gulag; in Berlin, the Wall came down; in Czechoslovakia, the Prague Spring of 1968 had a victorious rebirth in the Velvet Revolution of 1989; and in Central Asia, the indigenous peoples reached for their national liberation for the first time since their defeat of 1917–18. Gorbachev's efforts to save Communism and the Soviet empire failed because the system itself was beyond redemption, and we should not succumb to the temptation to berate him for his failures in practically every direction, from fumbling attempts to revamp the Soviet economy to grasping that Communism was bankrupt to trying his hand at politics in post-Soviet Russia. Gorbachev's great merit rests in the fact that he had tried to humanize the Soviet system. This attempt unleashed forces that brought about the "evil empire's" collapse sooner and less bloodily than had been anticipated and, above all, removed the specter of a nuclear war.[2]

In Central Asia, neither the severity of the fight against "corruption," nor the subsequently inconclusive results of the liberation there, should mislead us into underestimating this liberation's genesis and victory. The repression may have succeeded where it was "justified" (and where, paradoxically, it may have mattered the least): purges of officials who were truly corrupt within the Soviet system by not being "honest" (although they almost by definition were "loyal" to the system), defrauding the state, creating networks of vested interests, fostering cults of personality (of party bosses) on a whole gamut of levels. Many of these people were punished, there were even some death sentences. The main object of the repression – bridling the resurgence of nationalism – proved a dismal failure, however. The Central Asians, no longer afraid of the "restructured" comrades in Moscow and of the defanged KGB, vigorously came forth defending their national heritage, reminding Russia of her colonial conquest, accusing her of maintaining a colonial domination, and sounding alarm at the destruction of the Central Asian environment and of people's health. This revolution charted its own course and timetable in Central Asia, and some of that has been paradoxical or contradictory.

The process was similar in all the five republics (with the partial exception of Tajikistan), and Kazakhstan presents perhaps the most graphic example. When in 1986 Gorbachev had fired the Kazakh Kunaev and replaced him with the Russian Kolbin, this satrap set about cleaning the house with all the energy and speed expected of him. People were arrested, fired, demoted, replaced with newcomers who often were neither members of the Great Horde nor even Kazakhs, "honesty"

---

[2] A fascinating illustration of this process is a documentary on Ronald Reagan and his presidency televised in February 1998. The American president's merit was equally great, and both statesmen, who from adversaries became friends, deserved the Nobel Peace prize (Gorbachev was awarded his in 1990).

began to be restored. What had not been expected, however, was the Kazakhs' reaction. In December 1986 great numbers of protesters, mainly young people, gathered on the main square of Almaty and staged demonstrations against Kolbin and what was viewed as an assault on their nationality. The Soviet state still wielded enough power (*glasnost* was only just starting) to carry out a crackdown on the demonstrators Some people were killed (as usual, official and unofficial figures differ), many others were arrested, and peace was restored. What Kolbin did not and probably could not do, however, was to pass beyond the identifiable and legally definable "corruption" or mass demonstrations and tackle the *fait accompli* of a largely "Kazakhized" legislature and political-bureaucratic infrastructure, and a Kazakh public no longer afraid of the KGB. Far from bowing to Gorbachev's demands of scaling down their ethnic resurgence, they accelerated it, and by 1989 Moscow surrendered: it recalled Gennadiy Kolbin and replaced him with the Kazakh Nursultan Nazarbaev, and stood by helpless as it watched the Kazakh Supreme Soviet pass a motion proclaiming Kazakh to be the official language of the republic. This motion was chiefly theoretical, for even its authors knew that in most situations of public life Russian would for the time being remain the only viable medium of communication, but its symbolic and long-range importance was undeniable.

Meanwhile *perestroika* and *glasnost* gained their own momentum at the center of the USSR and all over the empire, forging ahead far beyond what Gorbachev had wished or expected. By 1990, the destinies of Central Asia began to be fashioned more along the Baltic Sea or in Ukraine than on its home ground. Spearheaded by the three Baltic republics, the drive for independence burst forth among the non-Russian members of the Union with an intensity that baffled Gorbachev and carried the rest along. The process was consummated by the end of 1991, when all the five republics of Central Asia, almost against the will of their political elites, were fully independent states, left to their own devices how to fashion their future.

The first stage of this process occurred in 1989 and 1990 with the proclamation, by the legislature of each republic, of its respective idiom as the official language, and, by three of the five, of their sovereignty: Turkmenistan on 22 August, Tajikistan on 25 August, Kazakhstan on 25 October 1990.

The second stage came in March 1991, when a referendum was held throughout the Soviet Union whether to preserve its existing structure, to modify it, or to dissolve it. Each of the five Central Asian republics overwhelmigly voted to preserve the Soviet Union (97 percent on the average). Here we can see one of the aforementioned contradictions of the liberation process. We have mentioned the explicitly or implicitly defiant stance Central Asians of all hues – from Communist Party stalwarts to genuine patriots – had assumed against Moscow's crackdown. On that level they were victorious, despite the purges of "corrupt" officials, and they were united in this victory. When it came to the question of full-fledged independence, however, things became complicated. The intellectuals and independent professionals made no secret about their wish to see their countries fully independent. However, the Party professionals and government bureaucrats who had survived the purges – and they were, after all, the vast majority – knew they owed their privileges and security to the Soviet system, and did not want to rock the boat too much. Consequently they availed themselves of the still formidable control and propaganda apparatus of the state to ensure the outcome of the referendum. They had indeed kept their options open by the time the third and final stage of liberation dawned over Central Asia.

20 August 1991 was the day when in Moscow Russia and the other republics that had approved the Union's modified preservation were to sign the new pact. On the 19th, however, the notorious coup staged by a junta of generals and politicians proclaimed its seizure of power, dismissal of Gorbachev who was vacationing in the Crimea, and cancellation of the whole array of *perestroika* measures and *glasnost* freedoms. The rest is well known: Boris Yeltsin's and his supporters' triumphant defiance from the Russian Chamber of Deputies, Gorbachev's return, the collapse of the coup, and the rapid dissolution of the Soviet Union. In Central Asia, Kyrgyzstan and Uzbekistan declared independence on 31 August, Tajikistan on 9 September, Turkmenistan on 27 October, and Kazakhstan on 16 December. History has drawn the logical conclusion of a process conceived with the 1924 National Delimitation.

CHAPTER NINETEEN

Sinkiang as part of China

Sinkiang came under Chinese rule, as we have seen, in 1758 with the defeat of the Jungar Mongols. The arrangement was analogous to that with Outer Mongolia, for the region became a possession of the Manchu Dynasty rather than being integrated into the empire as one more province. This had two important effects: the native population, mostly Muslim and Turkic-speaking after the virtual extermination of the Mongol population in Jungaria, retained a considerable degree of self-rule at all but the highest levels, and no immigration from China proper was allowed.

The Manchus followed the natural configuration of the conquered territory by dividing its administration into Pei Lu and Nan Lu, the aforementioned division of the province into a northern and southern segment. The *amban* or lieutenant-governor of the former resided at Urumchi, that of the latter at Yarkand; both halves were under the governor-general whose residence, Kulja (Yi-ning or Ining in Chinese), was founded by the Manchus near the remnants of the historic city of Almaliq on the Ili river. Peace and prosperity marked the first decades of this benign colonial rule, and in fact continued for over a century despite increasing flare-ups of native unrest in Nan Lu, often fomented by spiritual or relational descendants of seventeenth-century Khwajas (events of 1825, 1830, 1846, and 1857). These disturbances received some support from the khanate of Khoqand, whose rulers, although on occasion opportunely recognizing a vague form of Chinese suzerainty, obtained special privileges in western Sinkiang all the way to the river and city of Aksu: trading advantages for its merchants and even the right to collect certain taxes were among these. On the whole, however, the khans of Khoqand did not entertain further ambitions to the east of the Tianshan mountains; their expansionist mood looked west and north, where it entangled them, as we have seen, in wars with the emir of Bukhara and, ultimately, with Russia.

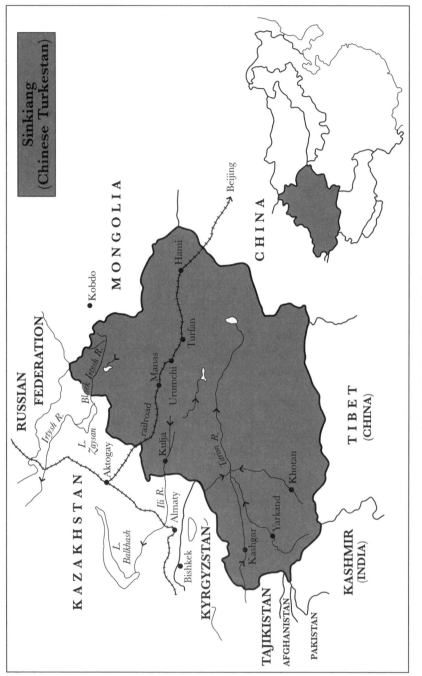

Map 7   Sinkiang (Chinese Turkestan)

A prominent participant in Khoqand's expeditions and politics was one Muhammad Yaqub Beg (1820–77), a native of Fergana. His career began promisingly when in 1851 he was appointed governor of the Syrdarya town of Akmeshit. He soon developed problems with Khudayar Khan, however – for reasons that are not clear but that may have stemmed from his inability to withstand the Russian onslaught on the town in 1853 – and had to flee to Bukhara. He was eventually pardoned and could return to Khoqand, and in 1865 the Khan sent him to Kashgar as aide to Buzruq or Buzurg Khan, a *khwaja* (Sufi shaykh of the Naqshbandi order. We have mentioned the sad end of the last khwajas to rule Kashgaria, the Aqtaghliq brothers Burhan at Kashgar and Jahan or Jan at Yarkand, in 1759; other descendants of Aqtaghliq and Qarataghliq khwajas had survived in the khanate of Khoqand and fomented – or tried to exploit – the aforementioned uprisings against Manchu rule in Kashgaria) who was launching yet another attempt at restoring theocracy in western Sinkiang. Unlike earlier such attempts, this time the Manchus did not quash it forthwith because of a rebellion that had erupted in 1862 among the Chinese Muslims of Kansu, thus creating a barrier between China proper and Sinkiang. Yaqub Beg proved a stronger personality than the khwaja he had come to serve, for by 1867 he had shoved him aside and established himself as the ruler of an Islamic state.

He at first professed to be a vassal of the khans of Khoqand, contenting himself with the title of "Ataliq Ghazi," but later he claimed full independence and changed his title to "Yaqub Beg Badawlat" ("Yaqub Beg, [Blessed] with [divine] auspiciousness"). The coins struck in the mint of Kashgar between 1867 and 1873 still bore the legend "Struck in the Mint of Khoqand" and the name of Malla Khan (1858–62), but then the legend was changed to "Struck in the Mint of Kashgar, the Capital" and bore the name of the Ottoman sultan Abdülaziz.

His realm, often referred to in the sources as Yettishahr ("Heptapolis," the seven cities being Kashgar, Khotan, Yarkand, Yangihisar, Aksu, Kucha, and Korla), lasted until 1877 and attracted considerable international attention, especially from Great Britain, Russia, and the Ottoman empire. The reason lay in the fact that by then the almost romantic "Great Game," the gigantic though perhaps overblown contest between Russia and Britain for the control of Inner Asia, was gaining momentum: the British conquered Punjab in 1849; the Russians, taking Tashkent in 1865 and Samarkand in 1868, were established in Transoxania and showed appetite for more; meanwhile, the collapse of Manchu rule in

Sinkiang created a power vacuum there that further exacerbated the sparring of the two colonial empires. Russia and Britain wished to avoid a conflict but felt that a war might have to be fought if either of them advanced too brashly into a territory like Sinkiang; a minor native ruler thus appeared as a welcome compromise, especially to the British, who quickly tried to strengthen him and gain his friendship.

Yaqub Beg himself also preferred the British alliance to a Russian one, no doubt because Russia, thanks to her geopolitical and logistical advantage, was a potentially far more dangerous friend. He received two British missions, of which the second, led by Douglas Forsyth in 1874, was especially memorable and established diplomatic relations between Kashgar and British India. Meanwhile Yaqub Beg, who had tried to give Russia the cold shoulder and even to dispute certain border posts, realized the peril of such intransigence and made concessions with far-reaching consequences for the whole province: renewal of Russia's right, gained as early as 1860, to have a consulate in Kashgar, and greater freedom for the Tsar's subjects to trade in the region. Another sign of Russia's position of strength was her occupation of the Ili area in response to Yaqub Beg's seizure of Urumchi in 1870; the ostensible reason was the Tsar's fear that his subjects, visiting Kulja and other places in the region, or even residing there, might suffer harm if fighting reached those quarters. By this clever move, the Russians acquired a strategically important area, a historic gateway to Sinkiang's Bei Lu and farther east which some observers have compared to the Khyber Pass between British India and Afghanistan. All in all, the Russians extracted from Yaqub Beg concessions superior to those won by the British, while treating him with a mixture of condescension and threats.

The most interesting, though perhaps the least effective, of the Kashgar ruler's foreign contacts were those with the Ottoman sultan. Yaqub Beg claimed to rule in the name of Islam, and such visitors as Forsyth do confirm the reality of this claim: the regime was rigorously Islamic, with the *sharia* and religious precepts being applied and enforced to the point where the Muslim population complained and fondly remembered the days of Chinese rule. Yaqub Beg was probably too well-informed and realistic to expect effective military help from the Ottomans, although some advisers and weapons were indeed sent to him from Turkey; the support he hoped for and received was moral, for the sultan enjoyed the prestige of being the leader of the Muslim world, whose letter of investiture did make a difference. Thus in 1873 the Kashgar ruler sent his nephew Sayyid Yaqub Khan Tora to Istanbul, and the envoy brought back a document calling Yaqub Beg *Amir al-Muminin*, "Commander of the Faithful." This once prestigious title, which used to be reserved for the Caliph, seems despite its subsequent inflation to have truly consolidated the new Islamic state when in 1874 the envoy returned via India, with Douglas Forsyth's mission, to Kashgar.

A mere three years later, however, Yaqub Beg was defeated by the Chinese general Tso Tsung-t'ang in two battles near Turfan and Urumchi, and died, probably of a stroke, in May 1877 at Korla, while retreating with the remainder of his troops toward Yarkand. This turn of events was probably more a result of the fragility of the Kashgar ruler's kingdom than of China's might, although the conquering general's ability and determination did play a catalytic role in the Chinese victory. Having acquitted himself well in his charge to quell the uprising of the Hui (Chinese-speaking) Muslims in Kansu, Tso Tsung-t'ang had methodically prepared the reconquest of Sinkiang against tremendous odds, such as doubts in government circles as to the wisdom of the whole enterprise, and an almost complete lack of funds, which had forced him to spend three years gathering his own resources before launching the operation.

The reconquest remained incomplete in one area, however: that of the Ili with the former capital of the province, Kulja, occupied since 1870 by Russia. The Russians refused to relinquish it, citing a variety of reasons, one being the expense they had incurred while occupying the area. When they finally did withdraw in 1881, after two series of negotiations in St. Petersburg and London, against payment of a large indemnity, they still retained its westernmost portion. The exact boundaries of this segment remained controversial, and the controversy resurfaced during the years of the Sino-Soviet split in the 1970s and 1980s when Chinese maps showed as China's territory an area extending all the way to Lake Balkhash.

Once the dispute with Russia was settled, Beijing imposed upon Sinkiang a system closer to that of a regular Chinese province rather than restoring its former status as a family possession of the Manchu (Ching) Dynasty. Four administrative segments were created in 1884, and their lieutenant-governors (*tao-tai*) reported to a governor-general who resided at Urumchi renamed in Chinese as Ti-hwa. Thus began the final chapter of Sinkiang under the rule of imperial China and lasted until the events of 1911–12 ushered in the republican era. Despite the aforementioned reorganization, the administration of the province bore some basic characteristics of the former period, such as greater independence of the governor-general and local self-rule by the Muslim population, especially in the Nan Lu segment. Relative contentment, peace, and order were the result.

Among the beneficiaries of this situation were European travelers, scholars, and archaeologists, who began to discover previously undreamt-of cultural treasures buried under the sands or hidden in the caves of Sinkiang. This was a truly romantic era of modern archaeology, a kind of scholarly mirror image of the political and colonial Great Game going on at the same time in the same general area. British, German, French, and Russian explorers vied with each other, making sensational discoveries and often endeavoring to haul what could be moved to the museums and libraries of their own countries. One of these scholars was Sir Aurel Stein (1862–1943), who for many years headed the Archaeology Service of British India. He undertook three prolonged expeditions between 1900 and 1916 to a number of points along the ancient Silk Road. His discoveries and studies were many, but the most sensational was the exploration of the grottoes of Tunhuang on the Kansu side of the trade route, with their riches of ancient manuscripts and Buddhist sculptures. Another famous site was that of the Turfan oasis, where a German team under A. Von Lecoq and A. Grünwedel found priceless linguistic documents. French scholars led by Paul Pelliot also made their contributions and took their share, especially at Tunhuang. The foundation of the Chinese republic in 1912 signaled an end to the relative freedom of archaeological exploration, although some of it, especially that of the "Mission Pelliot," did return in the 1920s and early 1930s. Much work had been accomplished, however, in the short period of the 1890s and the first two decades of the twentieth century, and the achievements of this branch of European Orientalism are truly admirable. The study of the thousands of documents brought to London, Berlin, Paris, and St. Petersburg continues to this day.

Meanwhile, during this final period of Manchu rule, the political Great Game abated somewhat, at least between its chief players, Britain and Russia. The two powers gradually edged toward mutual accommodation, a process initiated with the 1895 agreement and strengthened by the 1907 convention. This special truce allayed Britain's fear for the northwest frontier of the Raj; from then on, growing Russian presence in Sinkiang no longer met with noticeable British opposition. Russia's position of strength in Inner Asia secured her an influence in Sinkiang that far outstripped that of Britain. In contrast to the diminutive British consulate at Kashgar staffed by the isolated though remarkable George Macartney, Russia had large missions both at Kashgar and Kulja; a Russo-Asiatic Bank was founded in Kashgar, and a cart road was built between Irkeshtam at the Turkestan Governorate-General border and Kashgar; the Russian border post of Tashkurgan on the Sinkiang side of the Sarikol range, in the sensitive Pamir part of the Fergana *oblast*, controlled access to Chinese territory from that side. Indeed, Russia seemed poised to do in Eastern Turkestan what she had recently done in Western Turkestan – to conquer it and transform it into yet another Governorate-General of the Tsar's empire. Among the factors that deterred her from doing so may have been the complications that this would have caused with China, and, perhaps most importantly, the mutually felt need to improve relations with Britain, for both powers were becoming alarmed at the growing military might of Germany. The energy and ability of the first governor of the republican era, Yang Tseng-hsin, may also have had a share in keeping Sinkiang Chinese.

Thus began a new phase in the history of Sinkiang, its existence as a province of the Republic of China, which lasted from 1912 to 1943 – or, in theory, until 1949. It was characterized by the long tenure of the first three governors at Urumchi: Yang Tseng-hsin (1912–28), Chin Shu-jen (1928–33), and Sheng Shih-ts'ai (1933–43), and by the subsequent turmoil of national rebellions and short-lived regional governments until the People's Liberation Army re-established Beijing's rule in 1949, this time Communist rule.

The first of the three governors, Yang Tseng-hsin, was faced with for-midable challenges: Chinese military garrisons, infected by rebellious secret societies that had infiltrated here from China proper, showed signs of mutiny; the awakening Muslim separatism made its first attempts at self-rule in the Ili province, while erupting in revolt around the eastern Nan Lu city of Hami (Qomul). Yang Tseng-hsin originally hailed from the largely Muslim province of Yunnan in south-west China, and this background must have helped him regain control of a province increas-ingly disturbed by these Muslim currents. He subsequently steered the province along a course designed to develop it economically while con-solidating its Chinese orientation. Chinese was the only language per-mitted to be used in newspapers, at the expense of Turki and other native tongues.

It was during Yang's tenure of office that Russia experienced historic upheavals. In 1916, the First World War sent one of its distant echoes to Sinkiang in the form of the wave of mainly Kyrgyz and Kazakh refugees, some 300,000 souls, fleeing from reprisals following the collapse of the aforementioned uprising against Russian attempts to draft Muslim men for trench work on the fronts. Yang arranged a voluntary repatriation of most of them, in return for the colonial authorities' promise of amnesty. By then – 1917 – Russia had been shaken by the February Revolution, and soon entered the whirlwind of the October Revolution, Bolshevik seizure of power, and the civil war. After peace – Bolshevik peace – had been restored, Russian Turkestan was transformed into five republics of the newly formed Soviet Union. Mongolia joined this commotion only to emerge, by that same year of 1924, as a People's Republic and a virtual protectorate of the USSR. A similar development could have occurred in Chinese Turkestan but for the careful steerage of Yang, whose authority inspired enough confidence to persuade General Anenkov and his 7,000 White troops, who in 1920 retreated to Sinkiang, to let themselves be disarmed and interned, instead of acting like Ungern-Sternberg in Mongolia with, as a consequence, the Red Army entering the country and playing the role of the final arbiter.

For all his policy of benign Sinicization, however, Yang Tseng-hsin could not stem the continued growth of Muslim Turkic nationalism in Sinkiang. Spurred on by a conference of Turkic Muslims of Central Asia held at Tashkent in 1921, native renaissance became sophisticated enough to rise above local particularism and reach for a common denominator, which was the historic but long extinct name "Uighur." We shall never know how widely this concept would have been accepted by all the Turks of Sinkiang, had the province attained independence; we may suspect that the Kazakhs would have preferred to join their kinsmen across the border or agitated for their autonomy, and that the Kyrgyz would have done likewise. History, however, never put these questions to the test, and the main Muslim group of Sinkiang, the Turki-speaking urban dwellers and agriculturalists of Nan Lu, as well as their offshoot the Taranchis of Bei Lu, were – and still are – preoccupied, or at least some of their intellectual elite are, with how to fashion their newly formulated Uighur identity under the Chinese government's watchful eye.

Meanwhile Russian official presence, briefly interrupted in 1918, became further consolidated and expanded in its Soviet garb during the final years of Yang's office. Moscow now had five consulates in Sinkiang, and Yang allowed them to stay open even after 1927 when Chiang Kai-shek and his Kuomintang government in Nanjing suddenly assumed an anti-Soviet stance and severed diplomatic relations with Moscow. The significance of this measure could hardly be exaggerated, for it illustrates what was so special about Sinkiang – its distance from China proper in contrast to the proximity of Siberian and Central Asian Russia, with the relative – and at times nearly full – independence of its governors from the Chinese government, but with a seemingly inexorable growth of Russian influence.

During Yang's less capable successor Chin Shu-jen's governorate (1928–33), the problems that had until then been held in check re-emerged. Hami stirred again, and in 1933 at Kashgar Khoja Niyaz and his partisans proclaimed an Uighur Republic, demanding independence or at least autonomy; this attempt is usually referred to as the "First Revolution." Disorders multiplied in the east, where Dungans (Chinese Muslims) were making inroads from Kansu, and finally a mutiny of Russian mercenaries at Urumchi brought about Chin's downfall and his replacement by Sheng Shih-ts'ai, a professional soldier from Manchuria.

Sheng proved a remarkably able and relatively honest administrator. He restored order and, although he quashed the Kashgar experiment, he reversed Yang's policy of stifling the native ethnolinguistic renais-sance and allowed Uighur to flourish. In the early years of his tenure his reforms followed a "numbers" pattern popular in China: in 1933 he pro-claimed an "Eight Points" policy: interethnic equality, religious freedom, reform in land tenure, finances, administration, education, and the judi-ciary, and development of self-government; this was in 1936 modified to "Six Great Policies" which in fact expanded the earlier scope to include "anti-imperialism" and "cooperation with the Soviet Union." The two last-named clauses revealed his orientation, which became pro-Soviet to the extent that not Nanjing but Moscow was his sponsor and supporter. Russia's help was financial, but even more through technicians, setting in motion a program of industrialization, improved communications, and development of the oilfields of Karamai with a refinery near Urumchi. Following the Soviet line and receiving their help did not make Sheng a communist, however: his reforms stopped well short of the radical measures such as collectivization of agriculture and herding that had created havoc across the border; nor did he launch a dogmatic and all-pervasive indoctrination of his people, of the kind the Soviets were inflicting upon their subjects. Characteristically, there was no link between him and the Communist uprising led by Mao Tse-tung against the central government. Like several other Chinese warlords whose local rule replaced the collapsing authority of the center, Sheng was driven by lust for personal power, but the province that he ruled benefited in the main from his lucidity and relative honesty.

In 1941, however, Sheng made a mistake that would put an end to his fairly successful rule: expecting a defeat of Russia by Germany, he swerved to an anti-Soviet and anti-Communist stance and tried to patch up his relations with the government of Chiang Kai-shek (which had meanwhile moved to Chungking). This both deprived him of Soviet support and ended his independence from the central government. By 1943 Sheng also realized that Russia's defeat was neither imminent nor even likely, and he once more reversed his orientation. It did not work, and in 1944 the once so powerful satrap left Sinkiang for China.

One of the results of Sheng's 1941 turnabout was a shift from his relatively liberal policies, especially with respect to the Uighurs and other non-Chinese ethnic groups, to the far less tolerant attitude of the Kuomintang government. The change had the effect of spurring on the Muslims to again strive for self-rule, and in 1944 a group led by Saifuddin proclaimed autonomy at Kulja – the so-called "Second Revolution." The location of this attempt was significant: no longer limited to the Uighurs of Kashgaria, it also included the Kazakhs of the Ili region and showed that political ferment had reached the more cosmopolitan Bei Lu centers. The Kuomintang authorities, now installed at Urumchi, were unable to crush the secessionists and tried to resolve the crisis by forming a coalition government of the province that included also Turkic Muslims, and by promising liberal reforms with greater rights for the minorities. Its Chinese chairman, General Chang Chih-chung, did not go far enough for the natives, while going too far for the central government, so that in 1947 he was replaced as chairman by Masud Sabri, a conservative Uighur landowner. This seemingly viable compromise did not work either, and in December 1948 yet another attempt was made by replacing him with Burhan Shahidi, a Muslim of complex (possibly Tatar) background that included several years as a citizen of Russian Turkestan and as a member of the Russian Communist Party. These attempts, however, lost any relevance in the wake of the victory of the Communist side in China's civil war. On 17 December 1949 a Provisional People's Government was established at Urumchi.

China thus regained full control of her Inner Asian possession, and the subsequent process contained elements partly analogous to those present in Russia's Central Asia of the early 1920s. Recognizing Sinkiang's special ethnic physiognomy, Beijing gave it the status of an "autonomous region," with the name of the principal group as the determinant: Sinkiang Uighur Autonomous Region. This happened in

1955, but already in 1954 the Ili segment had been established as an autonomous sub-section with the name of its principal group as the determinant: Ili Kazakh Autonomous District. Several other autonomous districts, such as the Artush Kyrgyz Autonomous District, were established. This process may have been partly inspired by the *razmezhevanie* (delimitation) that in 1924 created the republics and autonomous regions of Soviet Central Asia, and the goal was no doubt similar: to give the minorities their due, while retaining control of the area. The subsequent composition of the regional government, parliament, and most institutions also followed the Soviet pattern of filling the nominally principal posts with the natives, while doubling them with Chinese officials so as to make the system fail-safe.

Sinkiang, the former Chinese Turkestan, has since then gone through a process that bears many other analogies with its western twin, the former Russian Turkestan. Like Moscow, Beijing has on the whole sincerely allowed the natives to assert their cultural identity, speak and use and teach their languages, and associate with the Chinese on a basis of personal equality. Economic development has been pursued vigorously, transportation and communications media expanded, education and the foundation of schools, including the University of Urumchi, supported. All of that had a price, of course. To begin with, Beijing imposed its Marxist system on the province, with collectivization and other measures of questionable economic soundness. The uncompromising hand of Communism could not but deprive the people of Sinkiang of those freedoms which by the standards of Western democracy are deemed indispensable. Like their brethren across the border, the Uighurs and other Muslims of Sinkiang lived in the 1960s their years of nightmare, some two decades after the nightmare in Soviet Central Asia: the Cultural Revolution hit the natives in a manner not unlike the terror launched by Stalin in the 1930s to break the native Muslims' national spirit. One of the targets was religion, and organized Islam was indeed put on the defensive; it lived the same marginal kind of existence, carefully monitored by the Chinese government, to which it had been relegated by the Soviet government.

Finally one salient feature must be emphasized: the role that the Chinese language has played as the common medium for the region's citizens, especially for its younger generations. Here too the analogy with Russian across the border is striking. All students learn Chinese at school and many become bilingual, especially those with greater professional ambition. Moreover, immigration from China proper has increased to the point where the Han (ethnic Chinese) element has come close to that of the Uighurs, if the Hui (Chinese-speaking Muslims) are also taken into account. According to the 1990 census, out of the total population of 15,156,883 inhabitants, 7,191,845 were Uighurs, thus less than one-half (47.45 percent) of the total population, the Han 5,695,409, and Hui 682,912, thus 6,378,321 citizens whose mother tongue is Chinese, or 42.09 percent of the total population. One can somewhat improve the native Turkic population's representation by combining the Uighurs with the Kazakhs: if we add the 1,106,271 or 7.30 percent to the Uighurs, we obtain 8,298,116 Turkic speakers (54.75 percent of the total population; the percentage will be still slightly higher if we add the Kyrgyz and Uzbeks of Sinkiang); moreover, the impact of the large eth-nolinguistic Chinese component might be considered somewhat less-ened if the religious criterion were applied and the Hui were added to the Turkic element: the figure would be over 8,981,028 Muslims, or 59.26 percent of the total population. On the other hand again, the significance of these figures is modified by the lopsided ratio in centers of political or economic power: thus the population of Urumchi, 1,217,316 strong, consisted of 934,851 (76.80 percent) Han Chinese, 161,643 (13.28 percent) Uighurs, and 83,001 (6.82 percent) Hui Chinese; taken together, the Chinese-speaking component in the provincial capital represented 83.62 percent. Another example is Karamai, a center of oil production. Its 210,064 inhabitants consisted of 161,097 (76.69 percent) Han Chinese, 30,895 (14.71 percent) Uighurs, and 4,997 (2.38 percent) Hui Chinese. It is true that the ratio changes in most agglomerations of Nan Lu, the now obsolete name for the more traditional southern part of Sinkiang. In Kashgar, the figures show 76.53 percent Uighurs, 21.98 percent Han, and only 0.46 percent Hui; in Khotan, 83.32 percent Uighurs, 16.13 percent Han, and 0.40 percent Hui; in Turfan, 71.82 percent Uighurs as against 20.25 percent Han. Even in Nan Lu, however, Aksu, a city that has occasionally been the residence of Chinese governors, still boasts a Han majority: 51.51 percent, as compared with 47.02 percent for the Uighurs; while the strategically located Hami has a Han majority of 66.11 percent as against 25.94 percent Uighurs. These statistics suggest that even if we admit that a certain proportion of these Chinese are temporary residents, Chinese presence in Sinkiang is anchored in a solid demographic base, with the conclusion that Eastern Turkestan is likely to remain Chinese Turkestan, unlike Western Turkestan which is no longer Russian.

CHAPTER TWENTY

Independent Central Asian Republics

We have chronicled the rush to independence that in the final stage of Gorbachev's *perestroika* seized all the Union republics, a torrent that ultimately carried the five Central Asian republics along. The dam really burst with the collapse of the attempted coup against the reforms and their proponent, but there had been two daring trailblazers: Lithuania on 11 March 1990, and Georgia on 9 April of that year. The rest took the plunge only after the August 1991 coup: Estonia and Latvia on the 20th (thus still while the drama was being played out in Moscow), Armenia on the 23rd, Ukraine and Belarus on the 24th, Moldova on the 27th, Azerbaijan on the 30th. The Central Asians were the last to jump on the bandwagon.

Thus on 31 August the Uzbek parliament proclaimed the existence of an independent Republic of Uzbekistan; the declaration was submitted to a popular vote which confirmed it in December of the same year, and which also elected Islam Karimov as the republic's president. Similar steps were taken in the other four republics. Meanwhile, those former Soviet public figures who had survived the upheavals, or who had surged forward to seize the leadership from the "old guard," succeeded in forging a special sequel to the USSR, the CIS (Commonwealth of Independent States, *Soyuz Nezavisimykh Gosudarstv* in Russian, *Mustaqil Davlatlar Hamdostligi* in Uzbek). Representatives of the participating members met on 21 December 1991 in the Kazakh capital Almaty to sign a treaty establishing the commonwealth.

The new commonwealth resembles the former Soviet Union no more than the British Commonwealth of Nations did the former British empire or the Union Française did the French one. This time the member states became truly independent, and their membership in the commonwealth resulted from a decision made by the indigenous leaders in Central Asia, not the Russian ones in Moscow. The difference between the old and new order is fundamental, and derives from the fact

275

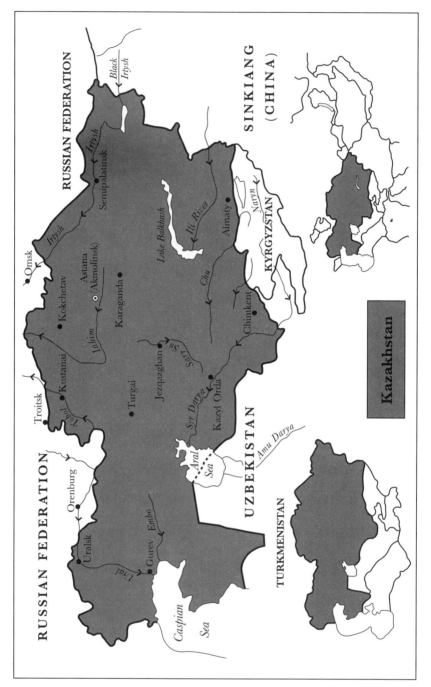

Map 8   Kazakhstan

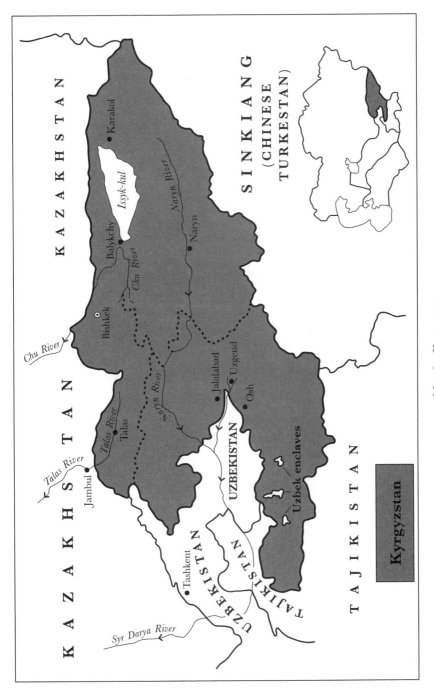

KAZAKHSTAN

KAZAKHSTAN

SINKIANG

(CHINESE TURKESTAN)

Karakol

Issyk-kul

Naryn River

Balykchy

Naryn

Chu River

Bishkek

Chu River

Naryn River

Jalalabad

Uzgend

Talas River

Osh

Talas

UZBEKISTAN

Talas River

Jambul

Uzbek enclaves

UZBEKISTAN

Tashkent

TAJIKISTAN

TAJIKISTAN

Syr Darya River

Kyrgyzstan

Map 9   Kyrgyzstan

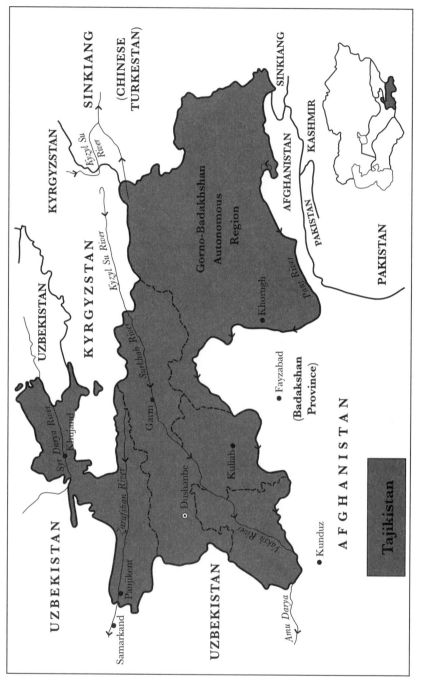

Map 10   Tajikistan

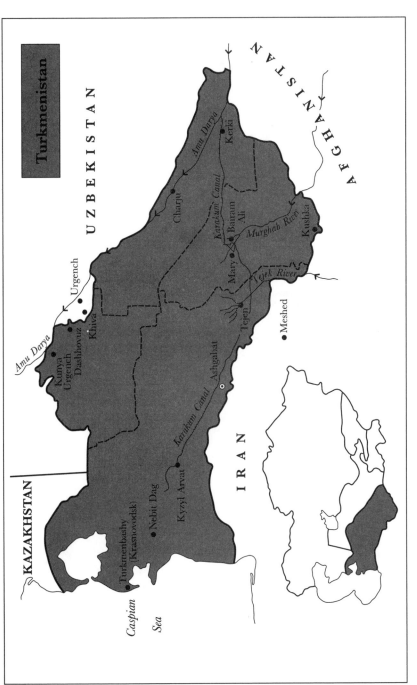

Map 11   Turkmenistan

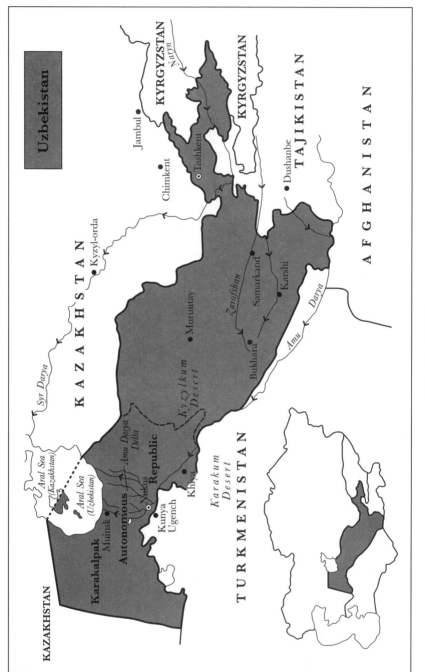

Map 12   Uzbekistan

that there is no central government or authority in Moscow ruling its subordinates in the republics.

Why did the Central Asians even bother to join the new commonwealth? For practical reasons. Obviously, decades of Moscow's rule, central economic planning and population movement had created bonds that, although not indissoluble (one of the favorite slogans of the former regime), were deemed worth keeping if modified in positive, mutually beneficial directions.

The legacy of the past of course includes problems and even scars of many kinds. One is the simple fact that much of the political leadership and bureaucratic infrastructure still is the same as before: the same Communist bureaucrats and their obedient staff are at the helm of the newly independent countries. Four out of the five republics have members of the former Communist elite as presidents: the Uzbek Islam Karimov, the Kazakh Nursultan Nazarbaev, the Turkmen Saparmurad Niyazov, and the Tajik Imomali Rakhmonov; Askar Akaev, President of Kyrgyzstan, is the only exception (he too appears to have been a member of the Party, but not as a career politician). Delegates of the recent Communist parties fill the parliaments, and offices are staffed by the same bureaucrats as before. Most of these people depended on the Soviet system for their careers, privileges, and livelihood, and we could be tempted to view their roles since 1991 with skepticism. The chief political parties in Uzbekistan and Turkmenistan are the Communist ones, except that they sport new names ("People's Democratic Party [of Uzbekistan"] and "Democratic Party of Turkmenistan"), while that of Tajikistan did not even bother to change its name (those of Kazakhstan and Kyrgyzstan, briefly banned, were revived under their old names without, however, regaining power as the ruling parties). Worse still, opposition parties and individuals championing a free political process have been mistreated by the government of Uzbekistan to a degree hardly compatible with true democracy; the situation has been similar in Turkmenistan, where moreover the personality cult, symptomatic of many former colonies now ruled by "strongman regimes," has reached almost pathological proportions: the President, Saparmurad Niyazov, has demanded and received an adulation comparable only to that enjoyed by Stalin (or by such present-day leaders as Saddam Hussein and Muammar Kadhafi), and like the great Soviet dictator, he found his civilian name incapable of expressing his greatness: he is now known as Turkmenbashy, "Chief of the Turkmens." In all fairness to Stalin, we have to admit that the "Russian" dictator could plead a sensible reason for assuming this name (which, incidentally, is based on the Russian loanword for steel, *stal'*). Jugashvili, his real name (especially when spelled in Russian which lacks the phoneme *j*, and circumvents the problem of transliterating it in foreign words by combining two letters, which in turn become three when transliterated from Russian into English: Dzhugashvili), would indeed have been unwieldy in the Russian-speaking society that had the misfortune of adopting him. Turkmenbashy has no such excuse, for Niyazov is a perfectly viable name in the society which he represents, and the only reservation that could be made concerns the Russian ending *-ov*. This import, introduced in the colonial era and reinforced under the Soviets, had the double purpose of creating distinctive fixed family names and facilitating their use in Russian. It has now begun to give way to genuine indigenous forms, especially the variants of *oghli*, "son of," in Turkic languages, and its synonym *zoda* in Tajik. And in all fairness to Turkmenbashy, it is not Stalin, Hussein, or Kadhafi whom he claims as his role models. His hero is Kemal Atatürk, the founder of modern Turkey, who had his good Turkish name Mustafa Kemal embellished by that of "Turk *par excellence.*" If Niyazov/Turkmenbashy does indeed decide to sincerely emulate his Turkish hero, he will secure for himself an honorable place in Turkmen and world history.

Meanwhile Tajikistan has gone through terrible convulsions – in fact a civil war – to the point where recovery of power by the experienced Communist Party and reinforcement of military control by CIS troops – chiefly Russian ones – appeared preferable to chaos or a takeover by Islamic fundamentalists. It is true that some observers consider the latter threat remote and the label wrong. (Until recently, one could share their skepticism with respect to a fundamentalist danger in Central Asia. The well-nigh complete victory of the Taliban in neighboring Afghanistan shows, however, that the danger may be real in Tajikistan.) Unlike the other four republics, this one has not developed a sense of nationhood, and in the prolonged near-anarchy Islamic radicals might have become the strongest among the contending forces, bringing about a process analogous to that in Afghanistan if it had not been for the troops of the CIS.

The totalitarian past of the Soviet period has thus been succeeded by the authoritarian regimes of present-day Uzbekistan and Turkmenistan, and although Kazakhstan and Kyrgyzstan came close to establishing genuine democracy – or so their Western well-wishers had hoped – in the last few years they too have shown a disturbing trend toward authoritarianism. Such reservations, however, could make us forget how radical and fundamental the break that occurred in 1991 was, and the fact that this break has deepened ever since. Three interrelated aspects stand out: the leaders and governments of the republics no longer obey Moscow but follow their own judgement; the interests of the republics, rather than those of a supranational empire (or indeed of Russia), are the decisive criteria for their policies; and the obligatory quasi-religious worship of the Communist doctrine and atheism has gone by the wayside. Islam Karimov, the President of Uzbekistan, is the same man who rose to power as a member of the Communist Party through the former Soviet apparatus, but the conditions under which he can act now are totally different from those imposed upon him before 1991. The age-old question of whether man fashions history or history fashions man at least here receives an answer: even those leaders of Central Asian republics who are the same as before have become different men now that the circumstances have changed.[1]

The transformations that have imposed themselves or have been carried out, initiated, or announced, are legion. Again, some could be derided as purely cosmetic changes or brazen deceptions, but even those are likely to eventually make their effect felt. The foremost is of course the very principle of human rights with guaranteed political and intellectual freedom. All the republics have between 1992 and 1996 adopted new constitutions which proclaim these principles. The economic front comes next; here, the double change from Moscow-controlled central planning to that determined by the republics, and the switch from a monolithic state-run economy to a market economy, lead the roster. Progress in both these respects – free citizens and free enterprise – has been slow and riddled with reverses, but then after seven decades of the old system successful change cannot happen overnight.

International relations can be viewed as the third giant step into a different present and a promising future. For the first time since their creation in 1924, Central Asian republics have been free to take their rightful place in the world community, and they have done so with a vengeance. All have become members of the United Nations and of other major international organizations, and have diplomatic relations with a

---

[1] This observation could apply even to political parties: the Communist Party of Tajikistan – despite the name – is no longer the organization subservient to its Moscow patron or bound by a rigid dogmatic ideology. Pragmatism, nationalism, and recognition of basic Western values are its hallmarks now, at least on the theoretical level. This is no doubt why its rule has been deemed preferable to the danger of a fundamentalist takeover.

growing number of foreign countries, including Western Europe, the Russian Federation, the United States, the People's Republic of China, the Islamic Republic of Iran, the Arab countries, and Israel. This combination alone reveals the magnitude of the novelty and the nature of their independence: treating Russia as a foreign country would have been anathema under the previous system; dealing directly with the United States would have been treasonous; contacts with China depended entirely on the vicissitudes of relations between Moscow and Beijing; friendship at the same time with the Arab countries, Iran, and Israel might have seemed impossible.

Russia may have become a foreign country, but her role in each of the five republics has been paramount and is likely to remain so for the foreseeable future. There are many reasons for that, some obvious, some discernible only on closer look. Comparison with "French" North Africa and "British" India may again be instructive here. The bureaucratic, intellectual, scientific, technological, economic, and logistical infrastructure, including publishing, is to a large degree Russian-trained and functions in Russian, just as it does in French and English in the latter two areas. In Central Asia too the former colonial power's language and legacy form a bond if not of unity, then at least of smoother communication and access to scientific and technological literature. On the other hand, the idea of a common Turkic language – a "modernized" form of Chaghatay, may yet gain favor and the dream of Turkistani nationalists of the 1920s could come true. More likely, however, is further consolidation of the separate forms of Turkic, with English making an inroad into the hitherto exclusive domain of Russian as the supranational language even in Central Asia.

Then there is the factor of minorities, primarily Russian and Ukrainian, living in the five republics. It is of course not limited to Central Asia, and the news media have profusely reported the degree to which this problem has caused tension between the three Baltic republics and Russia, for example. Similar questions have arisen at the time of decolonization in other parts of the world, especially in French North Africa. The intensity and nature of the problem varies with the republics, but one question, that of double citizenship, is universal. Should the Russians living in a republic have the right to be citizens of that republic, while also retaining Russian citizenship? In order to qualify for local citizenship, should they be required to fulfill certain conditions, the foremost being knowledge of the local (Uzbek, Kazakh, etc.) language? Since Russian presence has tended to concentrate in compact neighborhoods, whether urban (Uzbekistan, Turkmenistan, Tajikistan) or both urban and rural (Kazakhstan and Kyrgyzstan), several generations have been able to function without any attempt to learn the natives' language, a situation further reinforced by the Central Asians' own indispensable study of Russian. For the time being, compromise seems to be the answer, with the provision that the next generation of Russians will have mastered the language of the respective republic through obligatory inclusion in school curricula. A graver, almost unique problem is posed by the Russian and Ukrainian minority in Kazakhstan. Much of the republic's northern belt along Russia's European and Siberian frontier has become a *de facto* Russian territory because of the movement of settlers that began in the late eighteenth century and continued into the Khrushchev era. Both the predominance of the Slavic population in this belt, and its contiguity with Russia herself, beg the inevitable question of whether this part of Kazakhstan should not receive special treatment, or even be separated from the republic and join the Russian Federation. It led to a disagreement between the presidents of the two countries, Yeltsin and Nazarbaev, in 1992; the tension has since subsided without, however, having been quite resolved. The question resurfaced during the Russian electoral campaign of 1993, when such nationalists as Zhirinovskiy (and, in a more traditional vein, Solzhenitsyn), called for annexation of the Slavic-populated belt by Russia, and the Kazakh President retorted that such an act would resemble Hitler's annexation of the Sudeten region of former Czechoslovakia. One of the symptoms of the Kazakhs' nervousness about these northern territories is the transferral of the government's seat to Aqmola (Akmolinsk in Russian), for the ostensible reason that this city is less excentrically located than Almaty, but probably also because it symbolically stakes out Kazakh authority over the heavily Russian-populated northern belt of the republic. A glance at the map shows that Aqmola, though less excentric than Almaty, does not lie in the geographical center of the republic but rather near the Russian border. Places like Zhezkazgan should have been preferable if centrality was the goal. The Kazakh name means "white tomb," and the city grew up around a military fort built there in 1830 shortly after the Russian penetration into the area. In 1961 its name was changed to Tselinograd (a Russian word translatable as "Virgin Soil Town"), to celebrate the agricultural expansion campaign with the concomitant arrival of the last wave of Slavic settlers. This renaming was also forced on the Kazakhs (thus the entry "Tselinograd," not "Aqmola," in the *Qazaq Sovet Entsiklopediasy*). It was only with Kazakhstan's independence that the city recovered its Kazakh name. On 9 June 1998 the Fifth Turkic Summit was held there, and the next day, 10 June, was marked by a celebration inaugurating Astana as the new capital of Kazakhstan – for that is the new and presumably final name of this city. "Astana" simply means "capital city" in Kazakh and one must thus conclude that it has become the republic's *city par excellence.*

Nevertheless, the leading theme in relations between Central Asia and Russia is cooperation, not confrontation. This includes a whole gamut of economic and professional aspects, but two deserve to be singled out. One is the location of the former Soviet, and now Russian, missile-launching ground and space program center at Baikonur in Kazakhstan. Baikonur, situated in west-central Kazakhstan, was chosen in the Soviet era for strategic, logistical and climatic reasons, and it has retained most of these aspects to this day. Its continued use, against an initial payment of $1 billion and a lease fee of $115 million annually (both to be deducted from Kazakhstan's debt to Russia), is likely to be an asset or a liability – or both – for Kazakhstan.

The other aspect is defense. Before independence, the republics' military, from raw recruits to generals, were integrated in the Red Army. Now all five are striving to create their own armed forces, but it is a laborious and costly process, so that reliance on those of the CIS or of Russia has proved unavoidable. Our definition is deliberately vague or confusing, because the situation itself is fluid and incompletely reported. Thus when Islamic fundamentalists, drawing on help from the *mujahideen* of Afghanistan, seemed able to prevail in Tajikistan during 1992, it was the CIS troops commanded by General Piankov who saved the situation, to the great relief not only of the fundamentalists' Tajik opponents but also of Tajikistan's Uzbek and Turkmen neighbors and even of the other Central Asians, the Kyrgyz and Kazakhs; the CIS troops continue to guard the Tajik–Afghan border, thus in fact the Central Asian–Afghan border. A more recent agreement in 1993 between the Turkmen and Russian governments garrisons Turkmenistan's strategic points along the Afghan and Iranian borders with Russian armed forces, and entrusts the training of the Turkmen ones to Russian officers. We witness here one of history's paradoxical but not infrequent paraphrases of itself: the Tsarist empire's Turkestan was once guarded by Russian troops along these frontiers against a perceived threat from the British empire, with an undercurrent of a wish to push toward the Indian Ocean; this undercurrent resurfaced, or was perceived to do so, with the recent Soviet invasion of Afghanistan; today, Russia's troops guard the same frontier but within an entirely different and unexpected context.

The newly established international profile of the Central Asian republics is forcefully reflected in their relations with the United States. Diplomatic representation is only one part of the multifaceted and lively contacts; American business, academe, and foundations pursue the newly found opportunities for self-interest, research, and altruistic help abounding in this part of the world that was previously all but inaccessible to them. Moreover, the presence of the United Nations Organization in New York adds a further and unique dimension to Central Asian–American relations.

One of the riches of Central Asia is mineral wealth, and American companies have entered the competitive arena of developing its exploitation. The oil of Kazakhstan and natural gas of Turkmenistan lead this roster. The Kazakh President Nursultan Nazarbaev signed in March 1993, during one of his visits to Washington, a contract with the Chevron Oil Company to develop the oilfields of Tengiz in the Caspian confines of western Kazakhstan; James Baker, the former Secretary of State in the Bush administration, was one of the business leaders who at about the same time went to Turkmenistan to negotiate contracts with Saparmurad Niyazov, that republic's President, aiming at developing the especially rich gas deposits of Nebit Dag. While both Kazakhstan and Turkmenistan (and, across the Caspian, Azerbaijan) have already benefited from their deposits of oil and natural gas, it is no more than a preview of the expected boom. For reasons of both technology and policy, only their surface, literally and figuratively, had been "scratched" in the Tsarist and Soviet periods. The technology of their exploitation lagged far behind that applied by the industrial West; and Moscow preferred to give priority to developing deposits in territories more safely under its control, primarily those of the Russian Federation. On the other hand, the promising potential of the Caspian basin suffers from a serious drawback: the lack of direct access to adequate ports from which to export oil and natural gas to Europe, America, or Japan. In order to do so, construction of long and costly pipelines will be necessary, but still more problematic may be the fact that these conduits will have to pass through other countries and thus remain at the mercy of their governments' whims and demands (and even of world powers across the oceans).

A plan to build a pipeline through Turkmenistan to a Mediterranean port, or again to the Persian Gulf, has been discussed between the governments concerned, but it at first remained blocked by the US State Department because the pipeline would pass through Iran. The Turkmen government suddenly found itself thwarted by the presumptuous policies of both Russia and America. In 1993, Russia prevented the hard currency-starved Turkmenistan from exporting its natural gas to Western Europe at world prices (where it had been sold in the Soviet period with the income cashed in by Moscow) by simply choking off the pipeline conduit there, and forced the republic to sell the precious energy resource to impecunious members of the CIS such as Ukraine. America tried to subordinate the recently liberated republic's economic interests to her own strategies. Both superpowers, however, have been successfully defied in this case, for a new pipeline, whose construction had been financed by Iran, was opened on 29 December 1997 in a festive ceremony attended by the two presidents, Turkmenbashy and Khatami. It links Korpeje, a site in the natural gas deposit area of Nebit Dag, with Kurd Kul on the Iranian side of the border near Gurgan.[2] The initial difficulty shows, however, that there is no good substitute for unhindered, direct access to a port capable of accommodating ocean-going supertankers. In the case of oil, the only firm project so far is to build a 1,500-kilometers-long pipeline from Tengiz, Kazakhstan, to the Black Sea port of Novorossiysk just east of the Crimean peninsula. Aside from the fact that this project and its functioning will again depend on Russia's goodwill, another drawback is that supertankers that routinely haul oil from the Persian Gulf are likely to be barred from the relatively narrow and vulnerable straits of Bosphorus and the Dardanelles (the specter of a supertanker spilling its cargo into the Golden Horn...).

Thanks to its "central" position, Central Asia used to be the hub of world trade passing through the Silk Road network. The discovery of the maritime route between Atlantic Europe and the Orient at the dawn of the modern era turned this advantage of centrality in the Eurasian continent into the disadvantage of a landlocked area. With the end of the Cold War, we have heard much about the resurrected strategic and economic importance of a liberated Central Asia, often with references to the Silk Road and to the rediscovered advantages of the area's "central-

---

[2] S. LeVine, "Iran opens big gas pipeline to neighbor, defying US," *New York Times*, 30 December 1997; LeVine quotes Julia Nanay, an analyst with the Washington-based Petroleum Finance Company: "It's a victory for Iran over the United States, over Russia, and a victory for Turkmenistan as well, because it's the first to get its reserves to market through a non-Russian pipeline."

ity." Now, at the threshold of the third millennium, the drawbacks of barred access to maritime routes seem once more to haunt landlocked Central Asia whose centrality may become a liability rather than an asset. One potent compensation should be a modified intensification of trade and other relations with the area's immediate neighbors – Russia, China, the Indian subcontinent, Iran. When discussing the Silk Road trade of antiquity, it was axiomatic to say that it was a trade of high-priced and easily transportable commodities – such as silk or china or spices. Yet even this trade did not quite hold ground when forced to compete with maritime routes.

In the academic and philanthropic field, American universities and foundations have hosted a steady stream of individuals, delegations, and conferences invited or held to study a broad scale of matters ranging from the American way of democracy to business methods and techno-logical know-how. On the United States side, a question mark has been the fate of Radio Liberty, a Munich-based organization sponsored by the United States government that for many years has broadcast news and programs to the non-Russian republics of the former Soviet Union, thus also to those of Central Asia; there is an Uzbek, a Kazakh, a Kyrgyz, a Turkmen, and a Tajik desk. The creation of Radio Liberty was based on the premise that its broadcasts were the only channel through which peoples ruled by Moscow could obtain objective and meaningful news. The collapse of the Soviet Union and the liberation of the republics have made Radio Liberty obsolete, some argue, but its future nevertheless seems assured. Together with its sister organization, Radio Free Europe, whose broadcasts have served what were once the Soviet satellites in Eastern Europe, it has only been scaled down and moved from Munich to Prague. A somewhat analogous organization has been the govern-ment-sponsored IREX (International Research Exchange; located at first in New York, then in Princeton, and since 1992 in Washington), which has supported academic research by American scholars in Eastern Europe and the Soviet Union and vice versa. During the Soviet period, the participation of Central Asia, though not unheard of, was rare; after its liberation, the area joined the organization's activities with a ven-geance. In contrast to Radio Free Europe/Radio Liberty, IREX has not been scaled down but expanded since the events of 1991, and it now stands in the vanguard of the organizations sponsoring academic coop-eration between Central Asia and the United States.

The People's Republic of China occupies a place of special impor-tance among the Central Asian republics' neighbors. First of all, its long border with the area as a whole – specifically, with Kazakhstan, Kyrgyzstan, and Tajikistan – is second in length only to that between the Russian Federation and Kazakhstan, and it dwarfs that between Central Asia and its other two neighbors, Iran and Afghanistan. This relative proximity and her current economic growth enhances China's potential as Central Asia's major trading partner, a fact perhaps further strengthened by a geo-economic context reminiscent of the historic Silk Road network of antiquity and the Middle Ages. A number of agreements between each of the republics and the Chinese government relating to commerce, communications, transportation, financial credit, and tourism have been signed since 1992. This progress is especially significant when placed in the context of a potentially vexing problem, that of the Sinkiang Uighur Autonomous Region or Chinese Turkestan.

Chinese Turkestan presents a striking parallel, as we have seen, to Russian Turkestan, and the independence won by the Muslims of the latter area quite naturally revived the hopes of some of their Uighur kinsmen that they too might set up their own republic, an Uighuristan on a par with Kazakhstan, for example. The government of the People's Republic of China, however, shows no sign of willingness to give up the country's outlying ethnic areas, least of all Sinkiang. There are strategic, economic, political, historical, and demographic grounds for that; the last-named factor may in the long run be the most powerful one, for the Chinese minority in Sinkiang has risen to over 40 percent of the total population. The governments of the five Central Asian republics seem to have accepted this reality, and to have given priority to good relations with the Chinese government and overall cooperation with China. This was at least the tenor of the communiqués and agreements resulting from the official visit paid by the Chinese prime minister Li Peng to the republics of Central Asia in April 1994. One of the treaties signed confirms as definitive the 1,700–kilometer border between China (that is, Sinkiang) and Kazakhstan, laying to rest a problem that had been festering for several centuries, and was exacerbated during the Sino-Soviet dispute of the 1960s.

Relations between Central Asia and other countries are also gathering momentum. Those between the republics and other Muslim countries, ranging from economic development to religious proselytism, naturally occupy a special place. A perhaps surprising dose of pragmatism seems to dominate relations with Iran, especially in the case of its closest Central Asian neighbor, Turkmenistan. The two countries, whose past was plagued by a bloody Sunni–Shii conflict and by slave raids, and whose present leaders rose to power through the antithetical (or at least superficially so) doctrines of godless Communism and theocratic Islam, have now discovered a common ground for economic, technical, and even cultural cooperation. On the other hand, more distant Saudi Arabia has endeavored to further the spiritual renaissance of the Central Asians; besides assisting with such specific measures as distribution of the Koran, the Saudi government attempted to finance the foundation of an Islamic university in Uzbekistan's Fergana province, until the project was abandoned after the republic's Supreme Court ruled that religiously slanted education is unconstitutional. Islam as propagated by Saudi representatives and money has received in Uzbekistan the label of Wahhabism and its adepts are called Wahhabis, so named after the fundamentalist religious movement that toward the end of the eighteenth century brought the Saudi dynasty to power. It is these missionaries and their adepts who seem to worry the Uzbeks, rather than any threat from an ever more pragmatic Iran.

Quite naturally, relations between Central Asia's four Turkic republics and Turkey occupy a place of exceptional importance. They range from the romantic reminiscences of a common past in the Altai mountains and the Orkhon valley to hard-headed questions of improved air links, economic development, and a switch, by the Central Asian Turks, to a Roman alphabet based on the one used in Turkey. Above all, the volume of personal contacts, ranging from a tour of the Turkic republics by President Turgut Özal in 1992 and five "summits" of Turkic republics (Ankara 1992, Istanbul 1994, Bishkek 1995, Tashkent 1997, Astana 1998), to rising numbers of Turkish businessmen active in Central Asia and of young Central Asian Turks studying at Turkish universities, is tantamount to the dream of pan-Turkism that had inspired earlier generations of nationalists and frightened Moscow. The effects of this community of feeling and planning have been positive, and they promise even more for the future, if the present realism of Central Asian leaders holds fast; they have invariably emphasized the fact that the new trend should not be exclusionary or directed against any outsider – a somewhat contradictory claim, but a far cry from the calls for a Greater Turkestan voiced by some nationalists in the early decades of the twentieth century. It is significant that the word "Turkestan" appears to have lost its former political connotation, and is used only as a geographical or cultural concept. It is a sense of common ties and interests that appears almost to force itself upon them, based as it is on the reality of ethnolinguistic and cultural identity, geopolitics, history, and economics.

Cooperation is the rule now, and the economic union formed by Uzbekistan, Kazakhstan, and Kyrgyzstan in the first months of 1994 is only the most visible example of this evolution. This does not mean that the area is devoid of disputes, chiefly ethnic and economic. The most dramatic cases were those of Meskhetian Turks in Uzbekistan's Fergana province who were attacked by Uzbek "hooligans" in June 1989, and of a large Uzbek minority in the Osh region of Kyrgyzstan, which in 1990 became the target of bloody assaults by the Kyrgyz populace. The Meskhetians once lived in Soviet Armenia along the Turkish border, and were deported by Stalin during the war years; the recent trouble made most of them leave Uzbekistan and move to Russia. As for the Uzbek–Kyrgyz dispute, it remained localized; condemned by both countries' governments and citizenry, it was speedily resolved.

An obvious and potentially troublesome question is relations between Tajikistan and the four Turkic republics. So far it has been overshadowed by the civil war that erupted in 1992. The complexity of its causes, parties involved, goals pursued, conflicting reports and interpretations offered defies convincing conclusions, but one important consensus appears certain: that of the leaders of the other four Central Asian republics and of the Russian Federation regarding the need to prevent the possibility of a militant Islamic takeover. Their fears may have been unfounded or unjust, but there is no way of knowing that for sure; it may indeed be that their intervention has played a decisive role in the prevention of any such takeover, and at any rate it is likely to continue doing so for some time to come. The crisis has also deepened the perceived difference between the Tajiks and the Turks; why has this chaos occurred in Tajikistan, and not in the other republics of Central Asia? Is it just because of the proximity of Afghanistan, or have the Tajik Muslims been more receptive to inspiration from that quarter because of their Iranian identity? In the long run and in the context discussed here, however, there may yet surface a more intractable problem: that of the Tajik minorities (some Tajiks would say majorities) in such cities as Samarkand and Bukhara, or even of the entire Zarafshan valllley, and of the Uzbek minority in western Tajikistan.

Problems of an economic nature arising from the question of how to manage the distribution of vital water resources may also prove vexing. Turkmenistan's aforementioned Karakum canal has tapped the Amu Darya so heavily that it is blamed by the Uzbeks for the catastrophic desiccation of the Aral Sea and the plight of Uzbekistan's agricultural districts near the river's delta; the Turkmen government, however, has so far been reluctant to accept their neighbor's proposals to review the existing situation, a legacy of the Soviet era. Some have made the sensible proposal that the Karakum canal be eliminated altogether. Besides debilitating the Amu Darya, the canal also wastes much of the precious water because of primitive or mismanaged technology (most of its course lacks lining, hence considerable seepage or flooding in places where the water is not needed), a problem characteristic of many irrigation projects carried out in the Soviet period.

Each of the five republics now has a new constitution that guarantees the familiar political and human rights as understood in terms of Western democracy, and although, as we have pointed out, the innovation has so far had little practical application, the stage is set. Meanwhile all five republics are struggling to survive the economic crisis brought about by the transition from central planning and state ownership to market economy and privatization. The struggle and its prospective outcome are inevitably affected by similar processes in other parts of the former Soviet Union, particularly the Russian Federation, but there are grounds for optimism.

The area abounds in mineral and agricultural wealth; the value of Uzbekistan's gold, copper, and zinc deposits has been estimated at $3 trillion, and gold deposits in Kyrgyzstan appear promising; the aforementioned oil of Kazakhstan, natural gas of Turkmenistan, hydroelectric power of Tajikistan and Kyrgyzstan, and cotton of Uzbekistan, Turkmenistan, and Tajikistan are other examples. An abundant and well-trained labor force and an advantageous geo-economic position (here again, the Silk Road may not be just a romantic saga[3]) are the ideal complement to these natural assets. The problems, however, are also formidable. Aside from the birth pangs of a new system, the area faces two major challenges: ecological and demographic. The plight of the Aral Sea has become familiar to anyone following the news media, and it is only the most visible case of catastrophic abuse of water resources; the related ill effects of cotton monoculture propped up by chemical fertilizers and pesticides have attained similar notoriety. Total disregard of these dangers was one of the hallmarks of the Communist era (and not only in Central Asia; zones of pollution and moonscapes of man-made wasteland littered the rest of the empire and its satellites in Eastern Europe as well) and has become one of its worst legacies: for basic economic and psychological reasons, the solution of the problem will be

---

[3] See, however, our aforementioned qualifications.

slow and costly, and one of the problems will be who should sacrifice how much for the common good. We have already referred to Turkmenistan's reluctance to reduce the volume of water diverted from the Amu Darya into its Karakum canal. A conference on the Aral Sea held in Tashkent in September 1995 failed to elicit much commitment from any of the participants, but was enlivened by the Uzbek President Karimov's proposal that a once contemplated but then scrapped plan to divert the Siberian rivers Irtysh and Ob to Central Asia be revived.

The problem is made worse by the high birthrate of the Muslim population, especially that of Tajikistan and Uzbekistan. If unchecked, this too could bring disaster: rising numbers of young men deprived of prospects for decent employment easily fall prey to proponents of simplistic radical solutions. In Central Asia, the question of birth control has an absurd past and an intriguing future. The Soviet authorities, far from promoting birth control, used to encourage and reward high birthrates. A partial reversal occurred in the Brezhnev era, but the timid attempts to advocate planned parenthood had no effect where it was needed the most, among the tradition-bound rural population. In the future, acceptance and practice of birth control may be further stymied by a resurrected Islamic militancy. Advocates of a more rational approach at the July 1994 World Population Conference held in Cairo were frustrated by the uncompromising attitude of Roman Catholic and Islamic hierarchies and even by the negative stance from such quarters as the United States government (no doubt alert at that point to the voices of domestic fundamentalism). It is a paradox of our time that the problem of overpopulation, which in many parts of the world is approaching catastrophic proportions comparable only to those of the degradation of the environment (and related to it), receives the least attention from most governments.

An intriguing question is the routinely cited shortage of a qualified indigenous workforce. An inordinate proportion of managerial, technical, and skilled jobs is said to be occupied by "Europeans," chiefly Russians and Ukrainians, while the natives are spread over the broad spectrum of unskilled and service occupations. The reality is more complex. First of all, the available statistics as well as informal reports suggest that the Central Asians were by no means "shut out" from the better occupations. They admittedly had to overcome certain handicaps before acquiring the necessary education or training and becoming competitive: the traditions of rural life and ignorance of Russian kept many at a disadvantage in comparison with the mostly urban

Europeans. Those willing and able to buck the tradition had ample opportunity to acquire the necessary training and competitiveness, and many did. To name just a few examples: by training, the Kazakh President Nazarbaev is a mining engineer; the Kyrgyz President Akaev is a nuclear physicist; the renowned Kyrgyz writer Aitmatov is a veterinarian. The disparity is thus probably not a result of deliberate discrimination but of a force of inertia on both sides: tradition of a mostly rural population on the native side, convenience of an already qualified workforce on the mostly "European" employer's side, occupational preferences among the educated Central Asians all have played their specific roles. This is borne out by the fact that in the fields congenial to Central Asians, they became well represented (or sometimes even "over-represented"): in the humanities and social sciences of the academe, in politics and journalism.

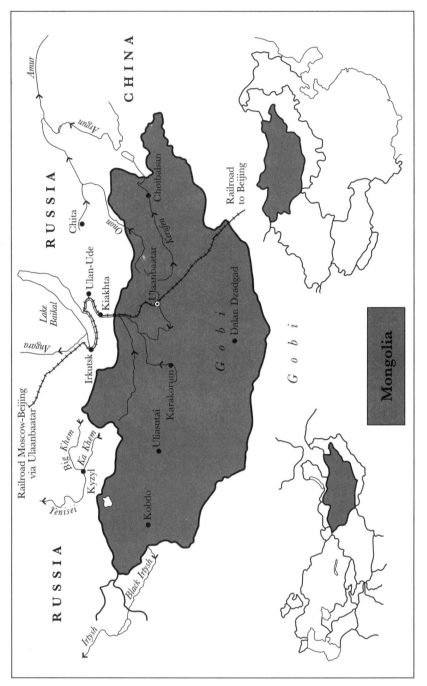

Map 13   Mongolia

CHAPTER TWENTY-ONE

The Republic of Mongolia

When the Uzbeks and other Central Asians declared independence in 1991, it was not only a liberation from Russian rule but also from a tyrannical ideology. The significance of the latter dimension is illustrated by the case of Mongolia. This Soviet satellite did not need to declare independence, for it had enjoyed the privilege of being independent since its creation in 1921, if only because it was Moscow's faithful ally not by force but by choice. It did need, however, the latter liberation, and it too attained it thanks to the bloodless revolution unwittingly unleashed by Mikhail Gorbachev.

The Communist system, which had initially wrought transformations beneficial to Mongolia, had begun to stagnate in a way similar to its evolution in the Soviet Union; and here the country's status as Russia's mirror image once more brought good dividends when first *glasnost* and *perestroika* jumped the border and spread to Mongolia as well, and then again when the collapse of Communism in Russia allowed the Mongols too to shed this straitjacket.

BRIEF HISTORY SINCE 1911

We have related in Chapter 13 how between 1691 and 1911 Mongolia was a personal dependency of the Manchu Dynasty ruling China. Toward the end of that period it also began to be called Outer Mongolia (an appellation somewhat resented by the Mongols themselves), in contrast to Inner Mongolia, the territory along its southeastern border inhabited by Mongols but administratively integrated into China. Emancipation from Manchu rule occurred in 1911 with that dynasty's collapse and replacement by the Republic of China. Chinese claims to suzerainty over Mongolia reappeared, however, by 1915, and in 1919 Beijing's troops reoccupied the country. They were driven out in 1921 at the end of a bizarre conflict that pitted three sides against each other:

the Chinese, White Russian troops led by a Baltic German, Baron Ungern-Sternberg who assumed the role of a Mongol patriot, and joint Soviet-Russian and Mongol troops whose native leaders espoused the Bolshevik cause. The Russo-Mongol forces won, and the new government proclaimed independence on 11 July 1921.

Although officially Mongolia has been a republic only since 1924, when the theocratic head of state, the "living Buddha" of Urga died, in practice the modern state was founded in 1921. The period from 1921 to 1991 can thus be considered that of the Mongolian People's Republic, a Communist state closely imitating its Soviet model, and the transformation of Mongol society during those years was radical. At the inception of this period the country was home to a confederation of tribal groups governed by a two-pronged aristocracy of lay tribal and Buddhist church leaders, and served by several types of commoners (*arat*) and semi-serfs (*shabit*). Property was concentrated in the hands of the elite, and consisted mainly of livestock and grazing rights, and only secondarily of land under cultivation; crafts and commerce led a marginal existence in the few towns that existed, or at the lamaseries. Lamaseries or monasteries of the Yellow Hat Buddhist church were the centers of economic power, spiritual and political authority, and cultural life. Both men and women could enter monastic life, and although celibacy was not as absolute as claimed by theory, it was important enough to contribute to a demographic decline which was so serious that some observers were predicting the extinction of the Mongols as a nation: only about 651,000 souls were estimated to people the country in 1925. This decline was not caused by monasticism alone; birthrate appears to have been generally low among Eurasian nomads. The advantage of the sedentary Chinese and Russians, for example, over their neighbors, the nomadic Mongols and Turks before the latter's sedentarization, is striking. Nevertheless, the rapid rate of this decline, specifically in this increasingly lamaistic society, has been partly attributed to the exceptionally widespread monasticism, and to the concomitant spread of syphilis.

Native cadres educated even with a minimum of modern methods were almost non-existent before 1921; those few who had such education obtained it mainly through Russian schools or preceptors across the border in Siberia. Among these were Sükhbaatar (1893–1923) and Choibalsan (1895–1952), the two founders of modern Mongolia.

Mongolia's official status as a state changed in the course of the seventy years between 1921 and 1991 through several stages, the least real but most curious milestone occurring in 1945. Until that year, the country, although a People's Republic, an explicitly sovereign state, officially remained under Chinese suzerainty: this was a contradiction verging on the absurd, for at the same time Mongolia's main supporter and *de facto* suzerain was the Soviet Union. In June 1940 the Great National Khural (parliament) adopted a new constitution, further consolidating the 1924 constitution's clause establishing Mongolia as a People's Republic; it did not renounce Chinese suzerainty, however, an act that only took place in 1945 through a plebiscite in which the Mongol people overwhelmingly approved its abrogation.

The political, economic, social, and cultural transformation of Mongolia was thus from 1921 on inspired and in many ways directed by the country's senior partner and protector, the Soviet Union. The sole native possessor of political authority, the Mongolian People's Revolutionary Party, following its model, the Communist Party of the Soviet Union, acted through a government and a variety of channels to effect the transformation. On the political level, the process, probably designed to ensure unflinching loyalty to the person or persons forming the Party's power center, displayed some of the aspects of the Soviet model, including show trials staged in the late 1930s by Choibalsan (often referred to as "the Mongol Stalin," while Sükhbaatar has been called "the Mongol Lenin") against selected "enemies of the people" (in fact, Choibalsan's potential rivals) in imitation of the trials staged by Stalin in Moscow.

On the social and cultural levels, the elimination of the lay and lamaistic aristocracy, and the suppression of religion led the roster. All lamaseries, including the earliest and most prestigious one, Erdene Zu at Kharkhorin (Qaraqorum) near the erstwhile "capital" of the Mongol empire, were closed, although Gandan, the Buddhist temple at Ulan Bator, was reopened, chiefly for propagandistic and touristic purposes. A massive campaign of education and indoctrination was mounted, aimed at spreading literacy, general education, devotion to Marxist-Leninist ideology propagated by the Party, and renouncement of the previously so pervasive Buddhist religion. In 1940, a new alphabet based on Cyrillic replaced the traditional Mongol script; this change was beneficial insofar as it equipped the Mongols with a system better suited to the phonetic structure of their language, but it also followed the double goal of further cementing their ties with the Soviet Union while creating yet another barrier between them and their past, and incidentally also between them and the non-Soviet modern Western world, which uses the Roman script. Significantly, a similar step occurred in

1940 in Soviet Central Asia, where all the five republics switched from the Arabic or Roman alphabet to Cyrillic; a related aspect of this process was the study of Russian, which became an integral part of education. Public health was improved by phasing out the traditional native or Tibetan medicine and replacing it with modern medicine made freely accessible, like education, to all citizens.

As in Kazakhstan, collectivization caused great hardships during its initial phase between 1930 and 1932, but unlike there it was suspended, and it then proceeded more cautiously while retaining some aspects specific to Mongolia. Thus even in 1959, a law promulgating the function of the *goskhoz* (state-owned livestock or agricultural enterprise, an approximate imitation of the Soviet *sovkhoz*) and the *negdel* (its cooperative counterpart, an imitation of the Soviet *kolkhoz*) as the obligatory establishments to which citizens engaged in herding or agriculture had to belong, allowed a family to own a certain number of beasts: up to fifty in the north, up to seventy-five in the Gobi. These steps were accompanied by further measures leading to specialization of herders according to the livestock species, improvement of the livestock's quality, and other factors; especially beneficial was the building of winter shelters stocked with fodder, a measure that reduced the ravages of weather, especially of *dzut*. The importance of the livestock economy for Mongolia is illustrated by the number of animals: by 1965, it reached 24 million (the role of herding in Mongolia is illustrated by this number, when we compare it with the number of inhabitants, which by that year had barely risen above 2 million). Agriculture, previously marginal, made great strides during this period. Its relative novelty is illustrated by the fact that in 1965, 70 percent of the harvest was produced by newly developed goskhozes and negdels. Cereals, fodder plants, potatoes, and legumes have been the principal crops.

Even newer than agriculture was industry. Planned and fostered centrally by the government, it drew chiefly on the two main local resources – livestock and mineral wealth. Its growth in turn stimulated the appearance of another new feature, urbanization. Besides Urga, Uliasutai, and Kobdo, there were virtually no towns before the period under discussion. Urga owed its prominence to the fact that the Jebtsundamba-qutuqtu, the chief lama, had resided there since 1779, and that in 1911 the last incumbent was proclaimed head of state; yet it was still little more than an agglomeration of yurts around the "Living Buddha's" residence and a few other official buildings when Mongolia became a People's Republic after the last lama's death in 1924. Renamed as Ulan Bator

(Ulaanbaatar in Mongolian, "Red Hero"), the Mongol capital has since then become a sprawling modern city and an industrial center; Choibalsan, Darkhan, and Erden are the other most prominent examples. Administrative structure and population increase have also contributed to the appearance of an urban center in each of the eighteen (eventually twenty-one) *aimags*, the administrative provinces of Mongolia. In 1949, Ulan Bator was linked to the Transsiberian railroad by a branch built from Ulan-Ude, and in 1955 this line was extended to link up with the Chinese network, thus producing the shortest rail connection between Moscow and Beijing.

Until the early 1960s, Mongolia's only diplomatic and economic partners were the Soviet Union and its satellites, and China. We have said that Mongolia was Russia's only willing satellite. This resulted from several factors, the foremost being the country's Chinese experience: the danger of being overwhelmed by China just as Inner Mongolia had been, first militarily and then demographically (this situation presented an analogy to that of northern Kazakhstan with respect to Russia, where the Kazakhs faced a similar danger from their Slavic neighbor; unlike there and elsewhere, however, Russia never invaded Mongolia against her will, and there had never been any influx of Russian settlers); another reason was a relatively fair economic cooperation and assistance, again in contrast to the Soviet Union's other dependencies and satellites, where the relationship often included a hefty dose of colonial exploitation; and finally, it was Soviet troops that helped the Mongol army repel a Japanese attempt to invade the eastern tip of the country in 1939.

Mongolia thus benefited from the new political and social order introduced in 1921, and from the support that saved her from absorption by China, but the price she paid was high. It included the familiar evils of an enforced monolithic ideology and the suppression of freedom. The harm that such systems can do by forcing the human spirit into artificial molds is well known, and it did not spare Mongolia either. Another development was the now commonly observed fact that beyond a certain point, the initially remarkable economic growth and social progress directed from a rigid center begin to lose their momentum and to give place to increasing contradictions, corruption, and stagnation. Many Mongol leaders seem to have been aware of these problems by the time Mikhail Gorbachev's reforms made it possible for the Soviet Union's satellites to launch their own reforms, and this led to the aforementioned changes that by 1992 had transformed Mongolia into a multiparty parliamentary democracy favoring free enterprise and a market economy.

In 1946, one year after the abrogation of Chinese suzerainty, Mongolia tried to become a member of the newly formed United Nations Organization. The attempt failed, chiefly due to the opposition of Western democracies led by the United States, on the grounds that the candidate was not a genuinely independent state. This could not but reinforce the isolation of Mongolia during the worst years of the Cold War, perpetuating the symbolism of the officially abandoned label of "Outer" that had made the country appear so remote to the rest of the world. The relative liberalization introduced by Khrushchev eased the tension between the West and the Soviet Union, and the success of a second attempt made by Mongolia in 1961 was one of the results and a harbinger of more changes to come. In 1963 Great Britain established diplomatic relations with Mongolia, the first Western democracy to do so, and was followed in this by France (1964) and other countries, the United States finally following suit. Only after 1991, however, did Mongolia's contacts with the wider world enter upon a broader avenue free from political or doctrinal inhibitions.

Summary and conclusion

We can summarize the transformations that took place in Inner Asia during the last decade in the following manner: the five Soviet republics of Central Asia have attained a double liberation – from colonial domination and from Communism; Mongolia, already independent, from Communism; Sinkiang, however, has experienced neither – except that Marxist-Leninist dogma has acquired a different ring in pragmatic China.

Mikhail Gorbachev's accession to power, we have suggested, greatly accelerated and modified a process that otherwise might still be the property of political scientists and Kremlinologists forecasting the future. A special feature of the Gorbachev years – 1985 to 1991 – were several cross-currents that clashed in Central Asia and created a unique political and cultural climate. This climate could be labeled "Central Asian Spring," for during those few years its citizens attained a degree of internal freedom unheard of before. This freedom has been considerably reduced since then – in other words, since the republics became independent.

Gorbachev's campaign against "corruption" in Central Asia was overshadowed, from a historian's vantage point, by yet another attempt to stave off nationalism there. It might have succeeded – for a time – if this statesman had had recourse to the formidable coercive apparatus of the Soviet state which was still in place at the time of his accession. *Glasnost* and *perestroika* declawed this apparatus, and the Central Asians, instead of withdrawing into a shell of sullen or sycophantic submission as they had been wont to do, counterattacked. By 1989 they had won the first and most critical round. In the short span of two to three years, they put Moscow on the defensive, accusing it of the evils of colonial conquest and exploitation, of destroying their countries' environment and people's health, of forcing on them a falsified version of their history.

A significant aspect of this counterattack was the fact that it was led mainly by the indigenous intellectuals – journalists, academicians, professionals. The politicians – professional Communists and government bureaucrats – mostly adopted a wait-and-see attitude, unsure of what the new climate of *glasnost* and *perestroika*, which now had also spread to Central Asia, would ultimately mean for their situation.

One of the novelties was that Central Asians were not only free to criticize Russia and Communist ideology, but also to demand democratic freedoms in their own republics. Political pluralism and a free press began to make their unprecedented appearance, just as they were doing in Russia and elsewhere in the expiring empire. An Uzbek movement called Birlik (Unity) was founded in November 1988. Led by Abdurahim Pulatov, a scientist, it was on the cutting edge of a campaign to make Uzbek the official language of the republic. The campaign was crowned with success when the Uzbek Supreme Soviet adopted a resolution to this effect on 21 October 1989. The movement demanded more, however: genuine democracy, and it did not hesitate to take on the Communist Party of Uzbekistan. Birlik stopped short of claiming the status of a political party, but that role was soon assumed by a group of intellectuals led by the poets Muhammad Salikh and Erkin Vahidov, who in April 1990 founded the Erk Democratic Party ("Erk" means "freedom" or "[people's] will," a favorite concept for naming political movements at the dawn of Central Asian independence). Erk gave every sign of offering the kind of constructive opposition to the ruling Democratic Party (as the Communist Party of Uzbekistan renamed itself after the collapse of the Soviet Union) that the country so desperately needed in order to become a healthy pluralistic democracy. Islam Karimov and the new political Democrats at first seemed to accept the new rules of the game, and Muhammad Salikh could even run for President in December 1991. He garnered 12 percent of the votes, against the 86 percent received by Karimov. How fair the election was is hard to say. What matters is the fact that Salikh could run without being excessively intimidated. Had that precious amount of freedom persisted, he might have done better next time, if the voters decided that new people should be given a chance to search for new solutions. Since 1992, however, those holding power have made their position virtually impregnable by means of decrees, legislation, and intimidation, and the initially promising alternatives have been pushed to the margin of political and public life. Erk is now withering as a party that has been refused official registration, and whose members have been under constant threat of prosecution and intermittent prison terms.

Genuine democrats thus soon ran into stiff resistance from the Uzbek political elite, but during the unique period of *glasnost* and its flickering afterglow in the first year of independence they could afford to take risks because of *glasnost* emanating from Moscow. This was the greatest irony: Moscow, which had just recently tried to once more cow the Uzbeks into a denationalized submission, now cast a protective shadow over those of their leaders who dared to challenge a system it had installed there in the first place.

The situation was similar in the other republics. In Turkmenistan a movement called Agzybirlik (Unity; a synonym of the Uzbek Birlik, except that Turkmen adds the word *agyz*, "mouth, voice," to the term based on the numeral *bir*, "one," augmented by the noun-forming suffix *-lik*; thus perhaps translatable as "Unison") made its appearance, and had a comparable agenda and subsequent fate. In Kazakhstan a similar movement chose the name Azat, "Free" (one could have expected rather its nominal derivation, *azattyk* = freedom; it is a synonym of *erk*, but in contrast to that genuinely Turkic word it has a Persian etymology), while the Kyrgyz simply called their analogous association "Kyrgyzstan." The Tajiks did not stay behind either, and one of their new parties took the suggestive name Rastokhez, "Renaissance." Moreover, these were not the only new associations or political parties. Others sprang up, and their number, type, ethnic coloring, effectiveness, and ultimate fate have varied from republic to republic. By and large, however, they belong to the same general political process which we have proposed to view as a Central Asian Spring, a phenomenon that celebrated its all too brief florescence between 1988 and 1992. Democracy, human rights, and economic recovery seemed to be within reach during those years. These hopes have dimmed since then. To a considerable extent this was inevitable, and similar retreats from the initial euphoria of liberation could be seen in most other parts of the defunct Soviet empire. Nevertheless, a disturbingly widening chasm between Central Asia and such countries as Russia, Poland, Hungary, or Georgia has made its appearance. On the Central Asian side there is a troubling evolution toward autocracy.

Liberated from the restrictive force of *glasnost* imposed upon them during the final years of membership in the Soviet Union, Islam Karimov and Saparmurad Niyazov, the presidents of Uzbekistan and Turkmenistan, have become virtual dictators, throwing the dissenters into jail, driving the opposition underground, or forcing those who escape into exile. Multiparty democracy and a free press have gone by the board, and when asked about these policies, the two leaders answer that Western-style democracy does not suit their societies or that their people are not ready for it. Law and order and stability are the path to prosperity and happiness, they say, and point to countries like China or those of Southeast Asia as examples of this alternative political philosophy.

While in Uzbekistan and Turkmenistan the screws have been tightened since 1992 or even earlier, things at first appeared brighter in Kazakhstan and Kyrgyzstan. Political pluralism, freedom of expression, and the public policies of presidents Nursultan Nazarbaev and Askar Akaev indicated that these two countries were on the "Western" (however reluctantly we use this term; "First World," obviously, would not work) side of the aforementioned chasm. In recent years, however, ominous changes have appeared there as well, and in 1998 we must reluctantly admit that Kazakhstan and Kyrgystan too may be moving toward excessive authoritarianism.

In all the five republics, the trend toward authoritarian rule has been compounded by the aforementioned feature of tribalism and localism. While in the Soviet period it may have performed the role of an often salutary bulwark against a mighty but baffled alien, it could now become a divisive force braking the desirable evolution toward democratic consensus, or even tearing a country asunder. Kyrgyzstan is one example. Askar Akaev may be its President, but he also represents both the republic's north and the tribe of Sary Bagysh; people from central areas (Jalalabad) and the south apparently feel shortchanged, and there have been rumors of demands for autonomy or even secession. Only time will tell whether such factionalisms can become fatally disruptive. Even countries with highly developed democratic traditions must live with their forms of factionalism – class, money, regions with differences of vested interest and agendas adversely affecting the unifying ideal.

In Tajikistan, civil war and guerrilla activities have been on the one hand spillovers from the religious war raging in neighboring Afghanistan, and on the other, a lingering conflict between the Communist clique still imbedded in the government and its various opponents. According to some observers, however, both religion and Communism play only a second fiddle in this multifaceted contest between regional and tribal factions led by warlords some of whom are little more than professional bandits taking hostages for ransom money. There is the north (Khujand) pitted against the south (Gulob) and center/east (Garm), aside from the ethnically centrifugal Badakhshan (the entire east of Tajikistan) and the large Uzbek minority along the border with Uzbekistan around the regional center of Tursunzod (besides an assertive pocket near Khujand). The fact remains that in the welter of contending currents, the Communists on the government side and Muslim clerics on that of the opposition have given the contest a distinctive tinge absent from the other Central Asian republics. The present government is headed by President Imamali Rakhmanov (b. 1952),[1] who rose as a Party *apparatchik* during the pre-*glasnost* years. In December 1992 (thus at the dawn of the post-*glasnost* period), as chairman of the Supreme Soviet, Rakhmanov virulently denounced the opposition highlighted by such leaders as Ali Akbar Turaevich Kahhorov, better known as Akbar Turajonzoda (or Turadzhonzoda, if we transliterate the name from Russian Cyrillic; b. 1954). Turajonzoda was in 1988 elected to head the Qoziyot, Muslim Spiritual Board of Tajikistan, hence his title *qozi* (more exactly *qozi kalon*, "The principal [lit. 'great'] judge") also prefixed – often with the capital Q – to his name. From the Islamic angle, Turajonzoda had impeccable credentials. His father, Ishoni Turajon, was a *murid* (disciple) of Said Qalandarshoh, a Naqshbandi *murshid* (Sufi master) who at the beginning of the twentieth century had come to Tajikistan from Afghanistan. Turajon eventually succeeded his master as leader of the local Naqshbandi dervishes, hence also the honorific title *ishon* ([his] eminence, lit. "they"). Turajonzoda (lit. "the offspring of Turajon") himself received excellent education in Islamic theology and jurisprudence: first at the Mir Arab madrasa in Bukhara, then at the Barak Khan madrasa in Tashkent, and finally at the University of Jordan in Amman, where he graduated with a degree in Islamic law. After his return he worked one year in the department of international relations of the Muslim Spiritual Board of Central Asia and Kazakhstan in Tashkent. His election to the Tajik *qoziyot* occurred in 1988, a year that happened to coincide with the fresh currents brought by *glasnost* and *perestroika*. Instead of remaining yet another (seemingly) docile Muslim cleric mindful of the strictures imposed by the system, Turajonzoda emerged as a vigorous leader of the Islamic community claiming its share of the public debate. Perhaps nobody could have then predicted the magnitude of the problems bound with his role

---

[1] Imamali Rakhmanov is the form of the name as it appears in Russian language media and as a result in most Western media. The Tajik form, Imomali Rahmonov (if we use E. Allworth's transliteration system), has also begun to appear in the media. The dilemma which form to use in a book like ours is obvious, and it affects most Central Asian names.

as the leading Islamic cleric, however. The Tajik intelligentsia – like that of the other Central Asian republics – turned out to be basically secular, and suspicious of the implications of an organized Islamic intervention in culture and politics. The international community, from Tashkent to Moscow to Washington, was no less wary, and has become ever more so since the victory of the Taliban in Afghanistan. The *qozi* himself endeavored to allay any fears, but could not quite escape the contradictions inherent in his cause. Although he paid homage to all the ideals of a democratic state, he did not distance himself from the idea of an eventual "Islamic Republic of Tajikistan." This placed him at loggerheads with secular nationalists no less than with nervous officials in the US State Department, a situation that has been adroitly exploited by the resilient post-Soviet Communist establishment headed by Imamali Rakhmanov, now President of the republic. This paradox has been illustrated by the following poignant incident: when in June 1996 a conference sponsored by private civil rights groups convened in Washington, D.C., Turajonzoda was invited as one of the star guests. The Tajik *qozi*, however, was refused a visa. He by then resided primarily in Tehran as a member of the far-flung diaspora of Tajik opposition leaders, some there, some in Moscow, some in the West. Meanwhile unrest oscillating between guerrilla ambushes to civil war continued to rage in Tajikistan. With none of the adversaries able to prevail by force, negotiations between the government and the opposition whose parties and factions ultimately organized themselves in a common front called "United Tajik Opposition" and led by another cleric, Said Abdullo Nuri (seconded by Turajonzoda as deputy leader), have finally come to a successful conclusion. Brokered by well-meaning outsiders and held in such capitals as Tehran, Moscow, or Islamabad, they were crowned with success on 27 June 1997, when in Moscow the Tajik President Imamali Rakhmanov and the United Tajik Opposition leader Said Abdullo Nuri signed the so-called Peace and National Reconciliation Accord.

In Uzbekistan, the most pressing problem may be the aforementioned environmental crisis. If Karimov and his presidential neighbors are right and their authoritarian rule will provide the necessary framework for the so desperately needed economic recovery and ecological salvation of Central Asia, history's verdict may yet concede them an honorable place. In order to succeed, however, they will need more than just a greater dose of personal integrity and law and order in the land. A whole infrastructure of efficient and reasonably honest officials, managers, engineeers, bankers, businessmen, entrepreneurs, agriculturalists, and other professionals, and, last but not least, responsible defenders of human rights and family planning will be needed, and there are indications that at present such people are in alarmingly short supply. Western journalists and businessmen write and speak about a world where the rules are too different, or are not observed, or simply do not exist, and astonishment, frustration, loss of invested capital is the more standard experience they bring back from their visits or attempts to do business in or with Central Asia. The infrastructure that does exist there is the aforementioned traditional one of family, clan, tribe, locality, or informal groups of vested interests that had come to dominate the indigenous political and bureaucratic process in the final decades of Soviet rule. How soon and well these people will learn the ropes of the capitalist entrepreneurial system remains to be seen. The collapse of the old system created a chaos whose most palpable effects are inflation, disappearance of the social safety net (with the recurring problem of salaries, wages and especially pensions grossly limping behind the deadlines), appearance of both street and organized crime, and a general slowdown or shutdown of economic activities with rising unemployment. One of the all-pervading aspects of the Soviet system was total economic integration. We have insisted on the evils of this system: Central Asia delivered cotton and other materials at below-the-market prices dictated by Moscow and received in return food and products such as energy supplies. It may have been shortchanged in the process, but at least the system saved the people from unpredictable and debilitating shortages by providing them with food and other necessities – these too at artificially low prices, as we have suggested. Now at the system's disintegration they repeatedly face such shortages, and the recurring crises create tensions between the authorities and their most articulate critics, the press and political opposition, aside from popular discontent and the refrain that "things used to be better." These tensions have now led to a tendency toward repression and stifling of any criticism. Yet it is precisely open debate, criticism, experimentation that their societies need in order to identify the problems of inefficiency and corruption, to search for better answers, to become competitive both on the domestic and international level, to mature into a civil society. This open debate, which appeared possible in the final years of *glasnost*, has now been either severely curtailed (Kazakhstan, Kyrgyzstan) or has completely ceased (Uzbekistan, Turkmenistan).

Nevertheless, there are grounds for hope that things may yet turn around in Central Asia. First of all, the repression has come nowhere near the extreme methods characteristic of the Stalinist past or of some current dictatorships around the world. There are no concentration camps, no death squads, no massacres, no systematic torture or routine disappearances of citizens, no man-made famines. There is no outrageous corruption by usurpers converting their countries' wealth into personal accounts in Swiss banks or real estate in Europe and America. There are no intolerant ideologies proclaimed by presumptuous leaders and forced upon the citizens. There are no claims and counterclaims between states claiming chunks of each other's territory or other assets and threatening war in case of non-compliance. As a general rule, in such basic respects as international relations, policies toward ethnic minorities, or intellectual freedom, the governments of Central Asia have displayed an undeniable dose of pragmatism, which is recognized even by many members of the opposition. In turn the opposition has refrained (with the partial exception of Tajikistan) from resorting to such terrorist methods as murdering officials and writers and tourists in downtown districts or slaughtering women and children in outlying villages. Islam has regained its glory but has not degenerated into fundamentalism or religious chauvinism, and nationalism has burst forth with a vengeance but has not turned into ethnic chauvinism. (The rash of often violent local disturbances caused by ethnic antagonisms has persuaded some observers that worse is to come. This may be so, but the relative fairness and firmness with which most clashes have been handled by the authorities could be an indication that saner forms of conflict resolution are just as likely.) Tolerance and compromise, not irredentism or interethnic strife predicted by various experts, have been the rule. Ethnic minorities are on the whole being treated fairly, and the governments have made efforts to assure the largest minority, the Russians, that they are safe and welcome to live as citizens in their republics (a demand that has been branded as "unfair" by many Russians is that as citizens of a Central Asian republic, they acquire a decent command of its principal language; one can sympathize with people confronted by such a challenge, but not necessarily agree that the demand is unfair). The once cherished dream of a Greater Turkestan has receded into oblivion as just that, a dream, and there is little evidence that it is being replaced by an aggressive and expansionist Uzbekistan expected by some observers. There is also little prospect of a Russia reconquering Central Asia in order to reconstitute her glorious empire. Most sides appear to be striving for realistic and mutually beneficial partnerships, dire predictions of post-Sovietologists notwithstanding.

It is in the domain of cultural liberation and education that Central Asians have benefited the most since the appearance of *glasnost* and attainment of independence. In sharp contrast to the Soviet period, the governments now abstain from ordering their citizens what to think or create. As long as they do not venture onto the political arena and challenge their leaders there, the intellectuals are free to cultivate their societies' cultural heritage or engage in their own scholarly or artistic pursuits as they wish. There is a staggering amount of work to do especially in the humanities and social sciences. It ranges from compiling objective and exhaustive histories of their countries, literatures, and cultures to producing school textbooks needed to replace the standard type that worshiped Lenin as the universal genius and benefactor of mankind and thanked Russians as the benefactors of Central Asians. Especially impressive, however, is the eagerness with which young Central Asians avail themselvers of the myriad educational opportunities at home and abroad that a mere decade ago were *terra incognita* or *prohibita* to them. Thousands are studying at various institutions in Turkey, Europe, and America, or are receiving professional training by international companies that do business with Central Asia. Their experience surely goes beyond the immediately utilitarian goals, for it helps them mature as citizens who will be the leaders of a new civil society.

As in Russia, here too religion has at last been allowed to come forth undisguised in all its glory, and Central Asians – from presidents to peasants – have emphatically reclaimed their Islamic heritage. Nothing could illustrate more graphically the magnitude of the revolution than the following example: Karimov, the former First Secretary of a militantly atheistic Communist Party, swore in January 1992 his presidential oath on the Koran, and instead of making trips to Moscow for political blessing, went on a *hajj* to Mecca. The sincerity of this opportunist's "conversion" may of course be no greater than his past profession of Communist faith. It does provide a framework, however, for a new climate in which others find their cultural and spiritual heritage truly fulfilling. An interesting parallel is the 1992 baptism of the former Soviet foreign minister Eduard Shevardnadze as Georgi in the Georgian Orthodox cathedral. Shevardnadze acquired a favorable image in the West at the time of his association with Mikhail Gorbachev and now as president of a promisingly democratic Georgia, but his past includes the positions of head of the Georgian KGB and First Secretary of the Communist Party of Georgia.

The proliferation of new or reopened mosques testifies to the participation of the masses. Here again it should be no surprise if this religious renaissance assumes a variety of forms depending on the intellectual level and social milieu of the participants. They range from the chiefly cultural appreciation by sophisticated secular urbanites to the somewhat contradictory programs of the young dynamic clergy (such as the aforementioned Turajonzoda) to the semi-pagan rites of the masses making pilgrimage to any of the countless burial sites of semi-legendary saints.

The leadership and the constituencies also meet on common ground when they venerate memories they had previously been forced to ignore, and disregard events they had previously been ordered to worship. An example is two sites in Turkmenistan, Göktepe and a nameless site by the railroad near Krasnovodsk. Göktepe was a fortress where in 1879 Turkmen defenders defeated a Russian army under General Lazarev, a major success of Central Asian resistance against colonial conquest. The Russians had their revenge two years later, when in 1881 another force, better prepared and led by the able General Skobelev, stormed the fortress and inflicted horrendous losses on the Turkmens. Soviet historiography played down this tragedy as a minor glitch in the otherwise "voluntary unification of the Turkmens with Russia," or better still, passed over it in silence. As for the nameless site near the Caspian, it witnessed a tragedy marking the still undecided pendulum swinging between the Reds and Whites in Azerbaijan and Turkmenistan: the execution of the "26 Baku commissars" on 20 September 1918. These Bosheviks fled Baku temporarily reconquered by the nationalists and boarded a steamer, hoping to reach Bolshevik-held Astrakhan. Instead, the captain steered the ship due east to Krasnovodsk, which was under the control of the Whites. The commissars – an assortment of Russians, Armenians, Georgians, and an Azerbaijani – were shot or bayoneted in a desolate location by the railroad, and they subsequently entered the pantheon of Soviet hagiography. The Turkmens were constantly reminded of the martyrdom that had taken place on their territory – in contrast to Göktepe which was better left unmentioned. With the arrival of *glasnost*, movements like Agzybirlik began to agitate for a commemoration of the real martyrdom. The still Communist leadership at first dragged its feet; once the Soviet empire fell and the Turkmen comrades became nationalists, however, they jumped on that bandwagon with gusto. The site, embellished with a newly errected memorial building, is now an important place of patriotic pilgrimage.

We are thus concluding this brief survey of the former Soviet Central Asia's past and present with a mixture of apprehension, hope, and an admission of the complexity and unpredictability of things to come. For the first time since colonial conquest in the nineteenth century, Central Asians are masters of their own house. Russians may be welcome and even encouraged to continue living in the independent republics, but no longer as a privileged minority. The Central Asian republics have many resources: agriculture, mineral deposits, a pleasant climate, historical monuments, natural beauty, position at the crossroads of the world, an able and plentiful administration and workforce. All these assets may turn this region into one of the world's choice places to live and do business with, and into one of the prime sites of archeology and tourism. This will happen, however, only if its leadership and citizens mature into a civil society that is mindful of its common interests, respectful of each other's rights, and aware of the need to preserve the environment not only through intelligent use and protection but also by admitting that unchecked population growth may ultimately exhaust and destroy it. If the oases of Uzbekistan gradually phase out some of the cotton production and return to growing a variety of fruits, melons and cereals less voracious of water, they may once again become the earthly paradise praised in the tenth century by the Arab traveler Ibn Hawqal. If the Uzbek hotel and other tourist industry infrastructure rises above the notorious Soviet standards to those of the developed world, international tourism will surely make Samarkand, Bukhara, and many other places prime targets of travel, and businessmen and technicians from abroad will enjoy their visits and assignments there. President Akaev has repeatedly stated his goal to turn Kyrgyzstan into a Central Asian Switzerland. It is a praiseworthy and realizable goal, for his country may even surpass Switzerland in natural beauty and historical interest. Again, however, the Kyrgyz need to learn much from the Swiss before they can compete with them. Akaev's Turkmen colleague Turkmenbashy (Saparmurad Niyazov) came out with an analogous ambition: to turn Turkmenistan into a Central Asian Kuwait, thanks to its fabulous deposits of natural gas and oil. Aside from the forgivable exaggeration, the ambition, before becoming a reality, will need a considerable dose of business acumen, international negotiations, and new pipelines to get these riches to the world market. Similar reservations can be made about Kazakhstan. At best, it will take a few years before Central Asian societies can begin to feel the benefits from these many assets, and things may keep getting worse before they get better.

Sinkiang, as in the past, so too at present displays striking analogies as well as marked differences when compared with the Muslim sister states to the west, and its future is both more and less predictable. The nationalist ferment that has boiled up across the border could be expected to well up in Sinkiang, and it did. Demands for more self-rule, street demonstrations and clashes between Uighur nationalists and organs of law and order in Urumchi and elsewhere have lately been reported. They have caused increasingly serious casualties and repression by the authorities. The parallel between Urumchi and Almaty of 1986 is striking, but so is the difference. The Kazakhs then stood at the threshold of *glasnost* and *perestroika*, which gave the contest a completely new slant and ultimately granted victory to the nationalists. No such thing seems to be occurring in Sinkiang. President Jiang Zemin is no Gorbachev, and no such counterpart is likely to succeed him anytime soon. The state's iron discipline apparatus remains intact and ready to act. On the other hand, if the Uighurs (and other minorities, including the Kazakhs) feel they have missed the millennium that has dawned over the Kazakhs and their other kinsmen across the border, they can seek solace by participating in China's economic miracle and expressing sympathy for their brethren across the border who are struggling to survive economic hardships. While they have been deprived of *glasnost*, they did not have to wait for a *perestroika* to embark on the road to prosperity, for China has devised her own methods to develop an efficient economy that has so far eluded Russia and her former dependencies. Moreover, Beijing's iron rule has not tried to curb the Uighurs' identity on the cultural level. The demands for more self-rule need not necessarily be the voice of the majority, which may opt for continuing political and economic integration in China while cherishing their cultural autonomy. This at least seems to be the implicit advice proffered by the Uighurs' Turkic kinsmen across the border. Kazakh and Kyrgyz governments have repeatedly expressed their recognition of the integrity of China's borders and Beijing's authority in Sinkiang. The agitation of Uighur nationalists in Almaty, Bishkek or elsewhere receives little support from the host countries.

Mongolia is enjoying her recently won freedom from a monolithic ideology, and pursuing the arduous ascent toward a pluralistic political system and a capitalist economy. As we have remarked earlier, there were almost no ethnic minorities in the country; this unusually monoethnic situation has now been brought close to 100 percent, because most of the Kazakhs who lived in the westernmost *aimag* have emigrated across the border to Kazakhstan. Meanwhile the Mongols across the border in China's Mongol Autonomous Region present a certain analogy to the Uighurs of Sinkiang, and here too Mongolia is as eager as Kazakhstan to maintain good relations with Beijing.

The destinies of the five Central Asian republics, Sinkiang, and Mongolia have throughout the past been intertwined, or run parallel courses, or collided, and as a result they have gathered enough common heritage to be viewed as a unique community. Their position in the heart of the Eurasian continent adds a special dimension to this uniqueness. In the past, it made them the crossroads or recipients of international trade, cultures, and religions. At present it makes them a landlocked area depending on their neighbors to export some of their possibly fabulous riches in return for no less promising material rewards. Some of these neighbors are world powers, some are countries beset by complex internal and international problems. This situation may further draw the Inner Asian states together or generate similar pragmatic policies. It makes economic and cultural cooperation between them desirable and feasible. It also makes realistic relations with the two giant neighbors, Russia and China, mandatory. The particular case of Sinkiang and Inner Mongolia only underscores this fact; here, China has become a special but most probably permanent member of the Inner Asian community. As for Russia, this former member has become a no less permanent partner. In Moscow they now like to call Kazakhstan and Central Asia their "near abroad," implying a relationship not unlike that of the United States with Mexico and Central America. The issues display remarkable analogies: security, economy, even the problem of narcotics flow from south to north.

There of course remains one unanswered question: the future role of Islam in Central Asia. As we have pointed out, the educated society there seems to be basically secular; some members of the intelligentsia even hold the conservative features of this religion responsible for their society's falling behind Russia and subsequent colonial status. As the economic and social conditions improve, more balanced views are likely to prevail and Islam will play a role similar to that of Christianity in the West – a spiritual heritage to be cherished by all those who feel inclined to do so, but which does not combat the accepted axiom of modern democracy: separation of church and state.

Appendix 1

DYNASTIC TABLES

This section is based chiefly on C. E. Bosworth, *The New Islamic Dynasties*, Edinburgh and New York 1996.

Samanids (Khurasan and Transoxania, 819–1005; Bukhara the capital; Bosworth, pp. 170–71)

(a) Saman Khuda
(b) Asad
(c) Asad's sons Nuh, Ahmad (= Ahmad I), Yahya, Ilyas
   1. Ahmad I (819–64) = 1st generation
   2. Nasr I (864–92), Ahmad I's son = 2nd generation
   3. Ismail I (892–907), Nasr I's brother
   4. Ahmad II (907–14), Ismail I's son = 3rd generation
   5. Nasr II (914–43), his cousin
   6. Nuh I (943–54), his son = 4th generation
   7. Abd al-Malik I (954–61), his son = 5th generation
   8. Mansur I (961–76), Abd al-Malik I's brother
   9. Nuh II (976–97), Mansur I's son = 6th generation
  10. Mansur II (997–99), his son = 7th generation
[11. Abd al-Malik II, 999–1000, his brother]
[12. Isma'il II, 1000–1005]

Qarakhanids (Semireche, Kashgaria, Fergana, Transoxania, tenth century – 1211; capitals Balasaghun, Kashgar, Uzgend, Samarkand; Bosworth, pp. 181–4)

(a) The beginnings:
x. Satuq Bughra Khan Abd al-Karim; the first major Turkic convert to Islam

x. sons Baytas Musa and Sulayman
   1. Ali (d. 998), Baytas Musa's son = 3rd generation
   2. Ahmad I Arslan Qara Khan (998–1015), his son = 4th generation
   3. Mansur Arslan Khan (1015–24), his brother
   4. Ahmad II Toghan Khan (1024–26), Sulayman's grandson and their second cousin = 4th generation
   5. Yusuf I Qadir Khan (1026–32), Ahmad II's brother
A split into an eastern and western branch

(b) Eastern branch (Balasaghun and Kashgar):
   1. Sulayman (1032–56), Yusuf I's son = 5th generation
   2. Muhammad I (1056–57), Sulayman's brother
   3. Ibrahim I (1057–59), Muhammad I's son = 6th generation
   4. Mahmud (1059–74), Ibrahim's uncle = 5th generation
   5. Umar (1074–75), Ibrahim's cousin = 6th generation
   6. Hasan (or Harun) (1075–1103), Umar's cousin
   7. Ahmad (or Harun) (1103–28), Hasan's son = 7th generation
   8. Ibrahim II (1128–58), his son = 8th generation
   9. Muhammad II (1158–?), his son = 9th generation
  10. Yusuf II (?–1211?), his son = 10th generation
  11. Muhammad III (d. 1211), his son = 11th generation
Occupation of Semireche and Ferghana by the Nayman Küchlüg

(c) Western branch (Samarkand):
   1. Muhammad Ayn al-Dawla (1041–52), the son of Ahmad I the son of Ali b. Musa = 5th generation
   2. Ibrahim I Böritigin Tamghach Khan (1052–68), his brother
   3. Nasr I (1068–80), Ibrahim I's son = 6th generation
   4. Khidr (1080–81), Nasr I's brother
   5. Ahmad I (1081?–89), his son = 7th generation
   6. Yaqub (1089–95), of the eastern branch, brother of its no. 6 (Hasan) = 6th generation
   7. Masud I (1095–97), Ahmad I's cousin = 7th generation
   8. Sulayman (1097), his cousin
   9. Mahmud I (1097–99), their uncle = 6th generation
  10. Jibrail (1099–1102), of the eastern branch, the son of its no. 5 (Umar) = 7th generation
  11. Muhammad II (1102–29), Sulayman's son = 8th generation
  11b. Nasr II (1129), Muhammad II's son = 9th generation
  12. Ahmad II (1129–30), his brother

13. Hasan (1130–32), of the eastern branch = 8th generation
14. Ibrahim II (1132), Muhammad II's brother = 8th generation
15. Mahmud II (1132–41), Ahmad II's brother = 9th generation
16. Ibrahim III (1141–56), his brother
17. Ali (1156–61), of the eastern branch, the son of no. 13 (Hasan) = 9th generation
18. Masud II (1161–78), his brother
19. Ibrahim IV (1178–1204), his nephew = 10th generation
20. Uthman (1204–12), his son = 11th generation
Occupation of Transoxania by the Khwarazmshah Muhammad

Ghaznavids (Khurasan, Afghanistan, Hindustan, 977–1186; Bosworth, pp. 296–9)

x. Sebüktigin (977–97)
  1. Ismail (997–98), his son
  2. Mahmud (998–1030), Ismail's brother
  3. Muhammad (1030–31 and 1041), Mahmud's son = 3rd generation
  4. Masud I (1031–41), his brother
  5. Mawdud (1041–50), his son = 4th generation
  6. Masud II (1050), his son = 5th generation
  7. Ali (1050), his uncle = 4th generation
  8. Abd al-Rashid (1050–53), his uncle = 3rd generation
  9. Farrukhzad (1053–59), Masud's son = 4th generation
  10. Ibrahim (1059–99), his brother
  11. Masud III (1099–1115), his son = 5th generation
  12. Shirzad (1115), his son = 6th generation
  13. Arslan Shah (1115–18), his brother
  14. Bahram Shah (1118–52), their brother
  15. Khusraw Shah (1152–60), his son = 7th generation
  16. Khusraw Malik (1160–86), his son = 8th generation
Ghurid (Afghan) conquest

Great Seljuks (Iran and Irak, 1038–1194; Bosworth pp. 185–8)

x. Seljuk
x. sons Arslan Israil, Mikail, Musa Yabghu, Yunus
  1. Tughril I (1038–63), Mikail's son
  2. Alp Arslan (1063–72), his son = 2nd generation
  3. Malik Shah I (1072–93), his son = 3rd generation

4. Mahmud I (1093–94), his son = 4th generation
5. Barkiyaruq (1094–1105), his brother
6. Malik Shah II (1105), his son = 5th generation
7. Muhammad I (1105–18), his uncle = 4th generation
8. Sanjar (1118–57), his brother
Takeover by the Khwarazmshahs

Khwarazmshahs (Khwarazm, later much of Central Asia and Iran; several dynasties, the earliest documented date being 898; the last Khwarazmshah perished in 1231; Bosworth, pp. 178–80)

(a) Semi-legendary Afrighids of Kath, possibly from the fourth century on; the first Shah with an Islamic name is the seventeenth, Abdallah b. T.r.k.s.batha, early ninth century; his successors were:

Mansur ibn Abdallah
Iraq ibn Mansur, reigning in 898
Muhammad ibn Iraq, reigning in 921
Abdallah ibn Ashkam, reigning c. 944
Ahmad ibn Muhammad, reigning in 967
Muhammad ibn Ahmad, died in 995
Mamunid conquest

(b) The Mamunids of Urgench, 995–1017

1. Mamun I ibn Muhammad, 995–97
2. Ali ibn Mamun, 997–1009
3. Mamun II ibn Mamun I, 1009–17
Ghaznavid conquest

(c) Ghaznavid governors with the title of Khwarazmshahs, 1017–41

1. Altuntash Hajib, Ghaznavid commander, 1017–32
2. Harun ibn Altuntash, similar function, later independent and assuming the title Khwarazmshah, 1032–34
3. Ismail ibn Khandan ibn Altuntash, 1034–41
Conquest of Khwarazm by the Oghuz Yabghu, Shah Malik ibn Ali of Jand, probably receiving the title Khwarazmshah from Masud of Ghazna.

(d) Anushtiginids, originally governors for the Seljuks with the title of Khwarazmshahs, eventually independent rulers in Khwarazm, Transoxania, and Iran (1077–1231)

1. Anushtigin Gharchai, 1077–97
2. Arslan Tigin Muhammad ibn Anushtigin, 1097–1127
3. Qizil Arslan Atsiz ibn Muhammad, 1127–56
4. Il Arslan ibn Atsiz, 1156–72
5. Tekish ibn Il Arslan, 1172–1200
6. Muhammad ibn Tekish, Ala al-Din, 1200–20
7. Mengübirti ibn Muhammad, Jalal al-Din, 1220–31
Mongol conquest

Qarakhitay (Semireche, Sinkiang, Transoxania, 1141–1211; not included in Bosworth's book because not an Islamic dynasty, but see his "Kara Khitay," *The Encyclopaedia of Islam*, vol. 4, pp. 580–3)

1. Yeh-lu Ta-shih (1124–43)
2. Kan-tien (1144–50)
3. I-lieh (1151–61)
4. Chieng-tien (1164–77)
5. Chih-lu-lu (1177–1211)
Destruction by the Nayman Küchlüg

Genghisids

(a) *Qaghans* or Great Khans, 1206–94; from 1235 official residence Qaraqorum, later (in Qubilay's time) Ta-tu (the future Beijing); Bosworth pp. 246–7

1. Genghis Khan (1206–27); sons Juchi, Chaghatay, Ögedey, and Toluy
2. Ögedey (1229–41) = 2nd generation
x. Töregene (Ögedey's widow; regent, 1241–46)
3. Güyük (1246–48), Ögedey's son = 3rd generation
x. Oghul Qaymish (Güyük's widow; regent, 1248–51)
4. Möngke (1251–59), Toluy's son and Güyük's cousin = 3rd generation
5. Qubilay (1260–94), Möngke's brother

(b) **Yüan** (China, 1260–1368); main residence Khanbaliq (Beijing); not included in Bosworth; see D. Morgan, *The Mongols*, tables on pp. 222–3.

1. Qubilay (1260–94), Toluy's son = 1st Yüan generation
2. Temür Oljeytü (1294–1307), his grandson = 3rd generation
3. Hai-shan (1307–11), Temür Oljetü's nephew = 4th generation
4. Ayurbarwada (1311–20), Hai-shan's brother = 4th generation
5. Shidebala (1320–23), Ayurbarwada's son = 5th generation
6. Yesün Temür (1323–28), Ayurbarwada's cousin = 5th generation

. . . .

11. Toghon Temür, a great-grandson of Hai-shan (1333–68; until 1370 in Mongolia) = 7th generation
Replaced by the native Chinese Ming dynasty (1368–1644)

(c) **Chaghatayids** (1227–1370 in Transoxania; until 1680 in Sinkiang; Bosworth, pp. 248–9)

x. Genghis Khan
  1. Chaghatay (1227–41)
  2. Qara Hülegü (1241–47 and again 1252), Chaghatay's grandson = 3rd Chaghatay generation
  3. Yesü Möngke (1247–52), Chaghatay's son = 2nd generation
x. Orqina Khatun, Qara Hülegü's widow (regent; 1252–61)
  4. Alughu (1261–66), Chaghatay's grandson and Qara Hülegü's cousin = 3rd generation
  5. Mubarak Shah (1266), Qara Hülegü's son = 4th generation
  6. Baraq (1266–71), his cousin
  7. Negübey (1271–72), Chaghatay's grandson and Alughu's cousin = 3rd generation
  8. Tuqa Temür (1272–91), Chaghatay's great-great-grandson = 5th generation
  9. Duva (1291–1306), Tuqa Temür's cousin
  10. Könchek (1306–1308), his son = 6th generation
  11. Taliqu (1308–1309), Duva's cousin once removed = 5th generation
  12. Kebek (1309, 1318–26), Könchek's brother = 6th generation
  13. Esen Buqa (1309–18), his brother
  14. Eljigidey (1318), his brother
  15. Duva Temür (1326), his brother
  16. Tarmashirin (1326), his brother
  17. Jangshi (1334), their nephew = 7th generation
  18. Buzan (1334–38), his cousin
  19. Yesün Temür (1338–42), Jangshi's brother
  20. Muhammad (1342–43), Könchek's grandson = 8th generation

21. Qazan (1343–46), Tuqa Timur's (no. 8)'s great-grandson = 8th generation

Confused situation, with puppet khans in Transoxania until 1357 and again later under Timur (Tamerlane; see that dynasty), but challenged by Tughluq Timur (1347–63), installed in Moghulistan and Altishahr. Tughluq Timur was a son of Imil Khwaja, the son of Duva (no. 9), thus 7th generation Genghisid.

Chaghatayid subsequent rule continued to the east of Transoxania, and was usually broken up into two or more concurrent reigns, covering two or three areas: Altishahr, Moghulistan, and Uighuristan. The following list does not claim to be complete or definitive, but only an attempt to bring out the more important names and dates:

Ilyas Khwaja, 1363–90; a son of Tughluq Timur
Khidr Khwaja, 1390–99; another son of Tughluq Timur
Sham'-i Jahan, 1399–1408, his son
Muhammad Khan, 1408–16, the latter's brother
Naqsh-i Jahan, 1416–18, a son of Sham'-i Jahan
Uways Khan, 1418–21 and 1425–28, a son of Shir Ali b. Khidr
Shir Muhammad, 1421–25, a son of Shah Jahan b. Khidr
Esen Buqa, 1428–62, a son of Uways Khan
Yunus Khan, 1462–81, another son of Uways Khan
Mahmud Khan, 1486–1508, a son of Yunus Khan
Mansur Khan, 1502–43, a grandson of Yunus; ruler of Moghulistan
Said (or Sayyid) Khan, 1514–32, a brother of Mansur; ruler of Altishahr
Abd al-Rashid, 1543–70, a son of Sayyid Khan

(d) **Golden Horde** and **White Horde** (Bosworth pp. 252–4)

Golden Horde (southern Russia, Ukraine, Kazakhstan, northern Khwarazm; principal headquarters Saray (eastern part of the Volga delta) and New Saray (near the eastern bank of the Volga not far from modern Volgograd)

x. Genghis Khan, d. 1227
x. Juchi, Genghis Khan's eldest son, died in 1227 three months before his father
  1. Batu (1227–55), Juchi's second son = 1st generation

2. Sartaq (1255–57), Batu's son = 2nd generation
3. Ulaghchi (1257), Sartaq's son = 3rd generation
4. Berke (1257–67), Batu's brother = 1st generation
5. Möngke Temür (1267–80), Batu's grandson = 3rd generation
6. Töde Möngke (1280–87), his brother = 3rd generation
7. Töle Buqa (1287–90), their nephew = 4th generation
8. Toqta (1290–1312), Möngke Temür's son = 4th generation
9. Özbeg (1312–41), Möngke Temür's grandson = 5th generation
10. Tini Beg (1341–42), Özbeg's son = 6th generation
11. Janibeg (1342–57), his brother
12. Berdi Beg (1357–59), Janibeg's son = 7th generation

Confused situation marked by internecine struggle, usurpations, and the first Russian victory in 1380; nominally, the Horde lasted until 1502

White Horde (eastern part of the Dasht-i Kipchak: Eastern Kazakhstan and western Siberia; headquarters shifting, often Sighnaq on the northern bank of the middle course of the Syr Darya)

    1. Orda, Juchi's eldest son and thus Batu's elder brother
. . . 8. Urus (1361–75)
. . . 11. Tokhtamish (1376–95), extended his rule over the Golden Horde but eliminated by Timur (Tamerlane)
. . . x. Shaykh Ahmad (1481–1502)

(e) **Ilkhanids** (Iran and Iraq, 1256–1335; Tabriz, Maragha and Sultaniya the main residences; Bosworth, pp. 250–1)

x. Toluy, Genghis Khan's youngest son
  1. Hülegü (1256–65), Toluy's third son
  2. Abaqa (1265–82), Hülegü's son = 2nd generation
  3. Tegüder Ahmad (1282–84), Abaqa's brother
  4. Arghun (1284–91), Abaqa's son, = 3rd generation
  5. Geykhatu (1291–95), Arghun's brother
  6. Baydu (1295), their uncle = 2nd generation
  7. Ghazan (1295–1304), Arghun's son = 4th generation
  8. Oljeytü (1304–17), Ghazan's brother
  9. Abu Said (1317–35), Oljeytü's son = 5th generation
x. struggle among various pretenders; the dynasty's replacement, in 1353, by several local ruling houses.

Timurid (non-Genghisid) interlude: **Timurids** (Samarkand, Herat; 1370–1507; Bosworth, pp. 270–2)

1. Timur (Temrlane; 1370–1405); sons Umar Shaykh, Jahangir, Miranshah, Shahrukh
2. Khalil Sultan (1405–1409), Timur's grandson through Miranshah = 3rd generation
3. Shah Rukh (1405–47) = 2nd generation
4. Ulugh Beg (1447–49), his son = 3rd generation
5. Abd al-Latif (1449–50), his son = 4th generation
6. Abdallah (1450–51), Shahrukh's grandson = 4th generation
7. Abu Said (1451–69), Timur's great-grandson through Miranshah – Sultan Muhammad = 4th generation
8. Ahmad (1469–94), his son = fifth generation
9. Mahmud (1494–1500), Ahmad's brother; succumbed to the Shaybanids.

The overlapping years of nos. 2 and 3, the rule of Khalil Sultan and Shah Rukh, stem both from the struggle for succession that followed Timur's death, and from the geopolitical dichotomy caused by the rise of Khurasan (capital Herat) seizing primacy from Transoxania (capital Samarkand). Shah Rukh preferred to stay in the Khurasanian city, and let his son Ulugh Beg rule Transoxania as a viceroy. Their immediate successors endeavored and mostly succeeded in unifying the empire and ruled from either city, but the split reappeared definitively after the death of the seventh ruler, Abu Said, in 1469. Khurasan and the rest of the empire in Iran was from then on ruled by the three following monarchs:

1. Yadigar Muhammad (1469–70), a great-grandson of Shahrukh = 5th generation
2. Husayn Bayqara (1470–1506), a great-great-grandson of Timur through Umar Shaykh – Bayqara – Mansur = 6th generation
3. Badi' al-Zaman (1506–1507), his son = 7th generation; suppressed by the Shaybanids

Timurid rule resumed, however, in India in 1526 and lasted until 1858, although the different area and circumstances have transformed its image, in Western perception, as that of the Great Mughals. Its founder, Zahir al-Din Babur, was a 6th generation Timurid through Miranshah

– Sultan Muhammad – Abu Said – Umar Shaykh. Agra was the dynasty's earliest capital, and the sixteenth and seventeenth centuries were its apogee. See Bosworth, pp. 331–4.

1. Babur (1526–30)
2. Humayun (1530–56), his son
3. Akbar (1556–1605), his son
4. Jahangir (1605–27), his son
5. Dawar Bakhsh (1627–28), his grandson
6. Shahjahan (1628–57), his brother
7. Dara Shikuh (1657–58), his son
8. Awrangzib (1658–1707), his brother

Genghisid restoration:
(f) **Abulkhayrid Shaybanids** (chiefly Bukhara, Samarkand, Tashkent, Balkh; 1500–1599; Bosworth, pp. 288–9)
x. Abu l-Khayr (1428–68), a descendant of Shiban, 5th son of Genghis Khan's eldest son Juchi
x. Shah Budaq, his son
1. Muhammad Shaybani (1500–10), Shah Budaq's son = 3rd generation, the founder of Shaybanid rule in Transoxania; two years of confusion and invasion by Safavid troops and Babur followed Muhammad's defeat and death
2. Köchkunju (1512–30), Muhammad's uncle = 2nd generation
3. Abu Said (1530–33), Muhammad's cousin = 3rd generation
4. Ubaydallah (1533–39), Muhammad's nephew = 4th generation; pivotal role since 1512
5. Abdallah I (1539–40), Abu Said's brother = 3rd generation
6. Abd al-Latif (1540–52), their brother = 3rd generation
7. Nawruz Ahmad "Baraq" (1552–56), their cousin = 3rd generation
8. Pir Muhammad I (1556–61), Ubaydallah's cousin = 4th generation
9. Iskander (1561–83), his brother = 4th generation
10. Abdallah II (1583–98), Iskander's son = 5th generation
11. Abd al-Mumin (1598), Abdallah II's son = 6th generation; succeeded by the Janids or Tuqay-Timurids

(g) **Janids** or **Ashtarkhanids** (or **Toqay-Timurids**: descendants of Toqay-Timur, Juchi's 13th son); Bukhara, 1599–1785; Bosworth, pp. 290–1)

x. Yar Muhammad
  1. Jani Muhammad (1599–1603)
  2. Baqi Muhammad (1603–1606), his son = 2nd generation
  3. Vali Muhammad (1606–12), Baqi Muhammad's brother
  4. Imam Quli (1612–42), their nephew = 3rd generation
  5. Nazr Muhammad (1642–45), his brother
  6. Abd al-Aziz (1645–81), Nazr Muhammad's son = 4th generation
  7. Subhan Quli (1681–1702), Abd al-Aziz's brother
  8. Ubaydallah I (1702–11), Subhan Quli's son = 5th generation
  9. Abu l-Fayz (1711–47), Ubaydallah's brother
 10. Abd al-Mu'min (1747), his son = 6th generation
 11. Ubaydallah II (1747–53), Abd al-Mu'min's brother
x. [Muhammad Rahim the Manghit, in the absence of Janid incumbency]
12. Abu l-Ghazi (1758–85), from a lateral branch
End of Genghisid rule in Transoxania

Manghits (emirs of Bukhara, 1785–1920; Bosworth, p. 292)
  1. Mir Masum Shah Murad (1785–1800)
  2. Haydar Töre (1800–26), his son = 2nd generation
  3. Husayn (1826), his son = 3rd generation
  4. Umar (1826–27), his brother
  5. Nasr Allah (1827–60), his brother
  6. Muzaffar al-Din (1860–86), his son = 4th generation
  7. Abd al-Ahad (1886–1910), his son = 5th generation
  8. Alim (1910–20), his son = 6th generation
Bolshevik conquest and establishment of the People's Republic of Bukhara

Ming (Khoqand, ca. 1710–1876; until 1789 data incomplete and dates approximate; after 1845 frequent confusion and intermittent reign of Khudayar Khan; Bosworth, p. 295)
  1. Shahrukh Biy (1710–21)
  2. Muhammad Rahim Biy (1721–40)
  3. Abd al-Rahim Biy (1740–60)
  4. Narbuta Biy (1769–89)
  5. Alim Biy, later assumed the title Alim Khan (1789–1810)
  6. Umar Khan (1810–22)
  7. Muhammad Ali (Madali) Khan (1822–42)

8. Shir Ali Khan (1842–45)
9. Murad Khan (7 days)
10. Khudayar Khan (1845–75, three times)
x. Nasr al-Din Khan (1875–76)

Khans of Khiva 1515–1919; Bosworth, pp. 290–1

(a) **Arabshahids** or **Yadigarid Shaybanids**, ca. 1515–1804. This was a Genghisid dynasty, tracing its lineage, like the neighboring Shaybanids, to Juchi through Shiban. Ethnolinguistically, they were thus Kipchak-Turkic speaking Turco-Mongols.

1. Ilbars I (1515–25)
2. Sultan Haji (1525–?)
3. Hasan Quli
4. Sufyan
5. Bujugha
6. Avnik
7. Qal (1539–46)
8. Aqatay, (1546)
9. Dust Muhammad (1546–58)
10. Haji Muhammad I (1558–1602)
11. Arab Muhammad I (1602–23)
12. Isfandiyar (1623–43)
13. Abu l-Ghazi I Bahadur (1643–63)
14. Anusha (1663–87)
15. Muhammad Awrang (1687–88)
16. Ishaq Agha Shah Niyaz (1688–1702)
17. Arab Muhammad II (1702–?)
18. Haji Muhammad II
19. Yadigar (1714)
20. Awrang (1714–15)
21. Shir Ghazi (1715–28)
22. Ilbars II (1728–40)
Occupation by Nadir Shah Afshar, shah of Iran, execution of Ilbars II, and brief rule of Nadir Shah's governor Tekir or Tahir Khan
23. Abu l-Ghazi II Muhammad (1742–45)
24. Ghaib (1745–70)

25. Abu l-Ghazi III (1770)
Confused situation, with leaders of the Qungrat tribe assuming the role
of *inaq* or majordomo similar to that of the *ataliq* played in Bukhara by
Manghit chieftains; Muhammad Amin (1770–90) and his son Avaz
(1790–1803) thus ruled in the name of puppet khans, but the latter's son
Iltüzer put an end to this practice and proclaimed himself khan.

(b) **Qungrats** or **Inaqids**, 1803–1919

1. Iltüzer, son of the inak Avaz (1803–1806)
2. Muhammad Rahim (1806–25)
3. Allah Quli (1825–42)
4. Rahim Quli (1842–45)
5. Muhammad Amin (1845–55)
6. Abdallah (1855)
7. Qutlugh Murad (1855–56)
8. Sayyid Muhammad (1856–65)
9. Sayyid Muhammad Rahim (1865–1919); Russian conquest in 1873,
truncation of the khanate's territory (the entire area on the right – northern – bank of the Amu Darya was detached from Khiva and added to
the Syr Darya *oblast* of the Governorate-General of Turkestan), continuation of his rule as the Tsar's vassal.
10. Abd al-Sayyid (1919)
Bolshevik revolution, establishment of the Khorezm People's Republic
in 1920

Yalavachids (Central Asia and China, thirteenth–fourteenth centuries; see T. T. Allsen, "Mahmud Yalavach, Mas'ud Beg, Ali Beg, Safaliq,
Bujir," *In the Service of the Khan: Eminent Personalities of the Early Mongol Yuan
Period*, ed. I. de Rachewiltz, Wiesbaden 1993, pp. 122–36)

In 1218, Genghis Khan sent three Muslim merchants to the
Khwarazmshah Muhammad with proposals of trade and friendship.
One of the three envoys was Mahmud Yalavach, a Khwarazmian who
appears to have entered Mongol service sometime between 1211 and
1218. It was the beginning of a glorious career in the service of
the Great Khans that ended only with Mahmud's natural death at
Beijing in 1254; what is more, his son Masud and three of his grandsons also held high posts in the Mongol empire, a true dynasty of admin-

istrators whose historical importance may have surpassed that of most khans.

1. Mahmud Yalavach, fl. 1218–54
2. Masud Beg, his son, fl. 1239–89
3. Abu Bakr, Masud Beg's son, fl. 1289–98
4. Satilmish, Abu Bakr's brother, fl. 1298–1302. Suyunich, another brother, fl. 1302–?

The **Khwajas of Kashgaria** (Isenbike Togan, table 29 and pp. 474–76 in *Encyclopaedia Iranica*, vol. 5; A. G. Schwarz, "The Khwajas of Eastern Turkestan," *Central Asiatic Journal*, 20 (1976): 266–96)

The term *khwaja* (also spelled *khvaja*, and its more popular form *khoja*) has a complex history, multifaceted connotation, and uncertain etymology. In the case under discussion here, it was an honorific title assumed by two branches of a family of Naqshbandi dervishes originally from Transoxania but who from the middle of the sixteenth to the middle of the eighteenth centuries wielded considerable spiritual, economic and political power in Kashgaria or Sinkiang's Altishahr portion ("Hexapolis" or region of six cities: Kashgar, Yarkand, Khotan, Aksu, Uch Turfan, and Kucha).

The two branches were descended from the Naqshbandi sufi Ahmad Kasani, better remembered as Makhdum-i Azam (an honorific title with Arabic etymology and Persian construction, meaning "The Great Master" (1462–1543).

(a) the **Afaqiya branch** (**Aqtaghliq** or **"White Mountain"** **Khwajas**)

1. Makhdum-i Azam's son Muhammad Amin called "Ishan-i Kalan" (an honorific title with Persian and Turki etymology, an approximate synonym of Makhdum-i Azam; d. 1597/8)
2. Muhammad Yusuf (d. ca. 1653)
3. Hidayat Allah commonly called Khwaja Afaq or Apaq (d. 1694; the name Afaqi or Afaqiya was coined after this Khwaja)
4. Khan Khwajam Yahya (d. 1696)
5. Hasan Bughra Khan (d. 1725)
6. Ahmad

7a. Qilich Burhan al-Din called "The Great Khwaja" (d. 1759)
7b. Khwaja Jahan Yahya called "The Little Khwaja" (d. 1779)

(b) the Ishaqiya branch (Qarataghliq or "Black Mountain" Khwajas)
1. Makhdum-i Azam's son Ishaq Vali (d. ca. 1605; the name Ishaqi or Ishaqiya started with him)
2. Khwaja Shadi (d. 1655)
3. Ubaydallah called Khwajam Padshah (d. 1684)
4. Danyal (d. 1736)
5a. Yusuf (d. ca 1755)
5b. Yaqub (d. ca 1755)

Appendix 2

Kazakhstan

Area: 2,717,300 square kilometers (1,049,150 square miles); Kazakhstan is the second largest republic of the former Soviet Union (and now of the CIS, Commonwealth of Independent States), after Russia, and also the largest of the seven units discussed in our book; its size can be visualized by comparison with Sinkiang (1,646,800 square kilometers), Mongolia (1,565,000 square kilometers), Turkey (780,000 square kilometers), Ukraine (603,700 square kilometers), France (551,000 square kilometers), and Uzbekistan (447,400 square kilometers). The country extends 1,900 kilometers from west to east and 1,300 kilometers from north to south.

Population (in 1995, according to the United Nations Food and Population Agency): 17,100,000; this makes Kazakhstan the fourth most populous republic of the CIS, after Russia, Ukraine, and Uzbekistan. Density per square kilometers: 6.2.

Ethnic composition (in 1994): Kazakh 44.3%, Russian 35.8%, Ukrainian 5.1%, German 3.6%, Uzbek 2.2%, Tatar 2.0%, Belarusian 1.1%. These ratios are rapidly changing, chiefly due to the higher birthrate of the Kazakh component but also to the emigration of the Europeans.

Official language: Kazakh, a Turkic language of the Kipchak group, written in the Cyrillic script; and Russian, which enjoys a special status as the "language of interethnic communication."

Religion: Islam, of the Sunni denomination. It gradually asserted itself among the Kazakhs since the late Middle Ages. In the Soviet period,

Kazakh Muslims were under the spiritual jurisdiction of the *mufti* (lit. jurisconsult, here head of the religious community) of Central Asia and Kazakhstan whose office was established at Tashkent in 1942; in 1990 a separate muftiate for Kazakhstan was created. The office of the present mufti, Haji Ratbek Nysanbay-uly, is in Almaty. Orthodox Christianity is the titular religion of the chiefly Russian Slavic minority.

Capital: Astana. Until late 1997 – or until June 1998, depending on inter-pretation – the capital was Almaty (formerly known as Alma-Ata), with 1,176,000 inhabitants (1993 estimate), situated excentrically in the southeastern corner of the country near the Kyrgyz border and the Kyrgyz capital Bishkek. Like many Central Asian cities, especially the capitals, Almaty became in the Soviet period a predominantly Slavic, chiefly Russian city: by 1970, Kazakhs constituted only 12.4% of the city's population; since then the trend has changed in their favor (22.5% in 1989), but the Slavic majority is still overwhelming and underscores the complexity of the republic's ethnic identity. On 6 July 1994 the parliament approved a project to transfer the role of capital to Akmola (Akmolinsk in Russian; on the other hand, the city is now also referred to in the media as Astana, which is also the generic Kazakh word for "capital"), situated farther north near the "Russian belt" of the republic, by the year 2000. This seems to have been primarily President Nursultan Nazarbaev's idea, whose vigorous support advanced the date of a preliminary inauguration to November 1997 (see "A Glittering new Kazakh capital, on the face of it," *The New York Times*, 9 November 1997), and the official inauguration took place on 10 June 1998.

Currency: the tenge (100 tein = 1 tenge), which on 15 November 1993 replaced the rouble.

Geopolitical situation: Kazakhstan borders European Russia on the west and Siberian Russia on the north and northeast; Turkmenistan, Uzbekistan, and Kyrgyzstan on the south; and China's Sinkiang Uighur Autonomous Region on the southeast. The Caspian and Aral Seas also delimit it on the southwest and south.

The republic's nineteen provinces (*oblys*) and provincial capitals (pro-ceeding from west to east and from north to south; the names are given in Kazakh, with their former – often Russian – counterparts in paren-theses):

Batys Qazaqstan (West Kazakhstan), capital Oral (Uralsk); Atyrau, capital Atyrau (Gurev); Mangghystau (Mangyshlak), capital Aqtau (Shevchenko); Aqtöbe, capital Aqtöbe (Aktiubinsk); Qostanay, capital Qostanay (Kustanai); Torghay (Turgai), capital Arqalyq; Qyzylorda, capital Qyzylorda (Kzyl-Orda); Soltustyk Qazaqstan (North Kazakhstan), capital Petropavl (Petropavlovsk); Kökshetau, capital Kökshetau (Kokchetav); Aqmola, capital Aqmola (Akmolinsk, in the final years of Soviet rule called Tselinograd; since June 1998 the official capital of the republic, and seemingly called just that, Astana, "Capital City"); Qaraghandy, capital Qaraghandy (Karaganda); Zhezqazghan, capital Zhezqazghan (Dzhezkazgan); Ongtüstik Qazaqstan (South Kazakhstan), capital Shymkent (Chimkent); Zhambyl, capital Zhambyl (Dzhambul); Pavlodar, capital Pavlodar; Semey, capital Semey (Semipalatinsk); Taldyqorghan, capital Taldyqorghan (Taldy-Kurgan); Shyghys Qazaqstan (East Kazakhstan), capital Öskemen (Ust-Kamenogorsk).

Kyrgyzstan

Area: 198,500 square kilometers (76,600 square miles).

Population: 4,476,400 (in 1994). Density per square kilometer: 22.6.

Ethnic composition (in 1993): Kyrgyz 56.5%, Russian 18.8%, Uzbek 12.9%, Ukrainian 2.1%, German 1.0%, besides smaller groups.

Official language: Kyrgyz, a Turkic language written in the Cyrillic script, is the official language; as in the other Central Asian republics, there is a plan to switch to the Roman script. Russian, however, has remained the indispensable vehicle of communication in the sectors of economics, science, technology and health care; moreover, on 15 June 1994 President Akaev decreed that it would be the official language in districts where Russian speakers form the majority.

Religion: Historically, the Kyrgyz are Sunni Muslims of the Hanafite school.

Capital: Bishkek (named Frunze between 1926 and 1991), with 627,800 inhabitants in 1991.

Currency: The som; it is the Kyrgyz term for rouble, and the som remains integrated in the rouble system. 1 som = 100 tyiyns.

Geopolitical situation: Kyrgyzstan borders Kazakhstan on the north and northwest, Uzbekistan on the west, Tajikistan on the south, and Sinkiang Uighur Autonomous Region on the east. The capital, Bishkek, is located excentrically in the valley of the Chu river near the Kazakh border.

The republic's six provinces (*oblast*) and provincial capitals (proceeding from west to east and north to south):

Talas, capital Talas; Chüy (Chu; capital Bishkek, also capital of the republic); Ysyk-Köl (Issyk-Kul), capital Karakol (Przhevalsk); Jalal-Abad, capital Jalal-Abad; Osh, capital Osh; Naryn, capital Naryn.

Tajikistan

Area: 143,100 squre kilometers (55,251 square miles); it is the smallest of the five Central Asian republics (after Kazakhstan, Turkmenistan, Uzbekistan and Kyrgyzstan).

Population (in 1994): 5,751,000. Density per square kilometer: 40.2.

Ethnic composition (according to the 1989 census): Tajik 62.3%, Uzbek 23.5%, Russian 7.6%; the rest consists of smaller groups that include Tatars, Germans, and Jews. Noteworthy is the large Uzbek minority, present chiefly in the mixed Tajik-Uzbek area along the Uzbek border and in the northwestern protrusion around the city of Khujand. Another special group is the Pamiris, inhabitants of the eastern half of the republic, the Gorno-Badakhshan Autonomous Region (63,700 square kilometers). They speak an Iranian dialect of their own but are included among the speakers of Tajik in the census.

Official language: Tajik, an Iranian idiom virtually identical to Persian, the language of Iran; it is written in the Cyrillic alphabet, although projects for increased use of the Arabic alphabet or of the Roman script have been proposed and partly implemented in the case of the former.

Religion: Historically, Tajiks are Sunni Muslims of the Hanafite school; the Pamiris, however, also differ in this respect by adhering to Shiite

Islam's Ismailite form, a denomination that recognizes the Agha Khan as its spiritual head.

Capital: Dushanbe (602,000 inhabitants according in 1990); it was called Stalinabad between 1929 and 1956.

Currency: the rouble. 1 rouble = 100 kopeks.

Geopolitical situation: Tajikistan's neighbors are, on the south, Afghanistan; on the east, China (more exactly, her Sinkiang Uighur Autonomous Region); on the north, Kyrgyzstan; and on the west, Uzbekistan. The republic's fairly rectangular shape is broken on the northwest by an extension in a northeasterly direction, encompassing the city of Khujand and protruding into the Ferghana valley. This extension, correctly expressing the ethnolinguistic distribution of the population (despite the abovementioned Uzbek minority), has nevertheless created an intricate gerrymander involving three republics – Tajikistan, Uzbekistan, and Kyrgyzstan

The republic's four provinces (*viloyat*) and one autonomous region (*viloyati avtonomi*):

Leninobod (Leninabad), capital Khujand; Dushanbe, capital Dushanbe; also capital of the republic, called Stalinabad between 1926 and 1961); Qurghonteppa (Kurgan-Tiube), capital Qurghonteppa; Khatlon (Kuliab), capital Kulob; and Viloyati Avtonomii Badakhshoni Kuhi (Gorno-Badakhshanskaya Avtonomnaya Oblast, "Mountain-Badakhshan AR"), capital Khorugh (Khorog).

Turkmenistan

Area: 488,100 square kilometers (188,456 square miles).

Population (in 1995): 4,483,300. Density per square kilometer: 8.7.

Ethnic composition (1993 estimate): Turkmen 73.3%, Russian 9.8%, Uzbek 9%, Kazakh 2.0%.

Official language: Turkmen, a Turkic language of the Oghuz group closely related to the Turkish of Turkey; it is written in the Cyrillic script, but there is a plan to switch to the Roman script.

Religion: Historically, the Turkmens are Sunni Muslims of the Hanafite school.

Capital: Ashgabat (its Turkmen form; Ashkhabad in Russian), 1993 estimate: 517,200 inhabitants.

Currency: until recently part of the rouble system; since 1993 now based on the manat; one manat = 100 tenge.

Geopolitical situation: The republic forms an approximate rectangle, with its axis lying northwest–southeast. On the west it borders the Caspian sea; on the northwest, Kazakhstan; on the north and northeast, Uzbekistan; on the southeast, Afghanistan; on the south and southwest, Iran.

Turkmenistan consits of five provinces (*welayat*); their names and those of their capitals, proceeding from west to east and north to south:

Balkan, capital Nebitdag; Dashhowuz, capital Dashhowuz (Tashauz); Ahal, capital Ashgabat (Ashkhabad, capital of the republic); Lebap, capital Charjew (Chardzhou); Mary, capital Mary.

Uzbekistan

Area: 447,400 square kilometers (172,740 square miles).

Population (in 1994): 22,098,000. density per square kilometer: 49.4. This makes Uzbekistan the most populous republic of Central Asia.

Ethnic composition: Uzbek, 79.5%, Russian 8.3%, Tajik 4.7%, Kazakh 4.1%, Tatar 2.4%, and smaller groups which include an ancient Jewish community (primarily in Bukhara). The Tajik component may be larger than the official figure indicates, for many citizens in the cities and countryside of the Zarafshan valley are bilingual and for practical reasons claim Uzbek identity.

Official language: Uzbek, a Turkic language closely related to the Uighur of Sinkiang and formerly known as Turki; it is written in the Cyrillic script. A switch to the Roman script was approved by the Parliament in 1994, to be carried out gradually. Meanwhile Russian has retained its place as a semi-official language, not unlike English in India and French in North Africa.

Religion: Historically, most Uzbeks are Sunni Muslims of the Hanafite school.

Capital: Tashkent (2,094,000 inhabitants according to a 1990 estimate).

Currency: the som.

Geopolitical situation: Uzbekistan lies in the heart of Central Asia, or Western or (formerly) Russian Turkestan. Moreover, its position is also central in historical and cultural terms: for the core of Uzbekistan, the Zerafshan valley with the cities of Samarkand and Bukhara, is the ancient Sogdia and the center of gravity of Central Asian civilization, both pre-Islamic and Islamic. Today, Uzbekistan's neighbors are, on the north and west, Kazakhstan; on the south, Turkmenistan and Afghanistan; on the southeast, Tajikistan; and on the northeast, Kyrgyzstan. Uzbekistan's capital, Tashkent, is situated excentrically in the country's northeastern protrusion near the Kazakh border.

Uzbekistan consists of twelve provinces and one autonomous republic. The provinces are, proceeding from east to west:

Andijon (Andizhan), capital Andijon; Namangan, capital Namangan; Farghona (Fergana), capital Farghona; Toshkent (Tashkent), capital Toshkent, also capital of the republic; Sirdaryo (Syrdarya), capital Guliston (Gulistan); Zhizzakh (Dzhizak), capital Zhizzakh; Samarqand (Samarkand), capital Samarqand; Qashqadaryo (Kashkadarya), capital Qarshi (Karshi); Surkhondaryo (Surkhandarya), capital Termiz (Termez); Nawoiy (Navoi), capital Navoiy; Bukhoro (Bukhara), capital Bukhoro; Khorazm (capital Urganch).

Karakalpakistan

Qoraqalpoghiston (Karakalpakistan) Avtonom Respublikasi (as part of the Republic of Uzbekistan): the only "autonomous republic" in Central Asia, it has an area of 165,600 square kilometers (37% of Uzbekistan as a whole) and a population of 1,214,000 (in 1989); the capital is Nukus (175,000 inhabitants).

Sinkiang
(Sinkiang Uighur Autonomous Region, Xinjiang Weiwuer Zeji Chu)

Area: 1,646,800 square kilometers (635,830 square miles); this makes it the largest of China's administrative units, and the second largest from among the seven principal units discussed in our book.

Population (1990 census): 15,156,883.

Ethnic composition: 7,191,845 Uighur, 5,200,000 Han Chinese, 900,000 Kazakh, 570,000 Hui (Muslim) Chinese, 117,000 Mongol, 113,000 Kyrgyz, besides several smaller groups.

Official languages: Chinese and Uighur, a Turkic language of the Turki group closely related to Uzbek; in specific minority enclaves, it is Chinese and the language of the respective group.

Capital: Urumchi, with 1,217,316 inhabitants in 1990, of whom 934,851 were Han Chinese, 161,643 Uighurs, 83,001 Hui (Muslim) Chinese, and 15,462 Kazakhs.

Geopolitical situation and administrative structure: Sinkiang has common borders with China's Kansu and Tsinghai provinces, and with Tibet (Tibet Autonomous Region); proceeding clockwise, its borders run along India (Kashmir), Pakistan, the tip of Afghanistan's narrow protrusion that separates Pakistan from Tajikistan, Tajikistan, Kyrgyzstan, Kazakhstan, Russia's Siberian border (specifically, along its Gorno-Altaisk Autonomous Region), and Mongolia.

The present political and administrative structure was inaugurated on 1 October 1955, when Sinkiang became one of the four "autonomous regions" (*ze ji chu*) of the People's Republic of China (Inner Mongolia, Tibet, and Ningsia are the other three).

The administrative structure of Sinkiang is complex, reflecting its ethnic and cultural diversity. The area inhabited by the titular national-ity, the Uighurs, is subdivided into six sub-regions (*di chu*): Kashgar, Aksu, Chuguchak, Altai, Hami, and Khotan. The territories inhabited by five other minorities enjoy the status of "autonomous districts" (*ze ji chou*): the Ili Kazakh Autonomous District, capital Kulja (Ining); the Chang-chi Hui (Chinese Muslim) Autonomous District, capital Chang-chi; the Kizil Su Kyrgyz Autonomous District, center Artux (Atu shih); the

Borotala Mongol Autonomous District, administrative district Boro (Polo); and the Bayan Gol Mongol Autonomous District, capital Korla (Ku-erh-le). Four municipalities (*shih*) have a special status of their own; one is Urumchi together with a county (*xien*) of the same name; the other three are Kashgar, Kulja, and Karamai.

Mongolia

Area: 1,565,000 square kilometers (604,250 square miles).

Population (according to the 1994 UNFPA estimate): 2,400,000. Density per square kilometer: 1.5.

Ethnic composition: Mongols, 90% of the population; the rest are Turks (chiefly Kazakhs, most of whom, however, have recently emigrated to Kazakhstan; some Tuvans).

Official language: Mongolian (based on the Khalkha branch of Eastern Mongolian), written in the Cyrillic script.

Religion: Lamaistic Buddhism, now revived after seventy years of obscurity under Communist rule (1921–91); Islam (Kazakhs).

Capital: Ulan Bator (Ulaanbaatar), with 619,000 residents in 1993.

Currency: the togrik. 1 togrik (togrog) = 100 möngö.

Geopolitical situation: Mongolia borders the Russian Federative Republic on the north (its Gorno-Altai Autonomous Region, the Tuvan Autonomous Republic, the Buriat Autonomous Republic, and the Chita Region), and China on the south (its Sinkiang Uighur Autonomous Region and Inner Mongolian Autonomous Region).

The republic is divided into twenty-one provinces (*aymag*), besides the capital which has an autonomous status. Listed alphabetically (with the provincial centers in parentheses unless their names are identical), they are:

Arhangay (Tsetserleg); Bayan Hongor; Bayan Ölgiy (Ölgiy); Bulgan; Darhan Uul (Darhan); Dornod (Choybalsan); Dornogov (Saynshand);

Dundgov (Mandalgov); Dzavhan (Uliastay); Gov Altay (Altay); Gov Sümber (Choyr); Hentiy (Öndorhaan); Hovd; Hövsgöl (Mörön); Ömnögöv (Dalandzadgad); Orhon (Erdenet); Övörhangay (Arvayheer); Selenge (Sühbaatar); Sühbaatar (Baruun urt); Töv (Dzuun mod); and Uvs (Ulaangom).

Select bibliography

BIBLIOGRAPHIES, ENCYCLOPEDIAS, MULTIVOLUME SURVEYS, SPECIAL REFERENCE MANUALS AND PERIODICALS

Bregel, Yu. *Bibliography of Islamic Central Asia* (Bloomington, 1995). 3 vols.

Encyclopaedia Iranica. 1985– (in progress) An ambitious multivolume project founded by E. Yarshater; its scope resolutely includes Western and Eastern Turkestan as areas of Iranian habitation, languages or culture. Especially relevant segments for our subject are Bukhara, in vol. 4, pp. 511–45; Central Asia, in vol. 5, pp. 159–242; and Chinese Turkestan, in vol. 5, pp. 461–84; as well as entries Archeology V, VII, Architecture IV, and Art VI, VIII.

The Encyclopaedia of Islam. 1960– (in progress). New edition of a basic reference work whose 1st edition appeared between 1913 and 1938.

The Encyclopedia of Religion, edited by M. Eliade, (New York, 1987). Articles "Islam: an overview," by Fazlur Rahman; "Islam in Central Asia," by A. Bennigsen and Fanny E. Bryan; "Islam in China," by M. Rossabi; "Shiism," by W. Madelung and S. H. Nasr; "Sunnah," by Marilyn Waldman; "Tariqah," by A. H. Johns; "Buddhism" by F. E. Reynolds, Ch. Hallisey, R. E. Emmerick, W. Heissig, and H. Guenther; "Shamanism," by M. Eliade and Anna-Leena Siikala.

Philologiae Turcicae Fundamenta (Wiesbaden, 1959–64). 2 vols; in German, French or English. An authoritative introduction to Turkic languages and literatures by an international consortium of scholars.

The Cambridge History of China. 1978– (in progress); but volume numbers do not correspond to the chronological sequence of publication. Especially relevant for our subject are vol. 3, part I, Cambridge, 1979 and vol. II, part 1, Cambridge, 1978.

The Cambridge History of Early Inner Asia (CHEIA), edited by D. Sinor, 1990. An excellent one-volume reference work on the nomadic populations of Inner Asia; this limitation excludes, however, the area's sedentary civilizations.

The Cambridge History of Iran. Vols. 4–7 (1975–91) cover the Islamic period from the Arab conquest to the present.

The Cambridge History of Islam. 1978. 4 volumes.

Barthold, W. (V.V. Bartold). *An Historical Geography of Iran* (Princeton, 1984); translation, with annotations by Yu. Bregel and C. E. Bosworth, of Barthold's *Istoricheskiy obzor Irana.*

Bosworth, C. E. *The New Islamic Dynasties: A Chronological and Genealogical Manual* (Edinburgh and New York, 1996).

Herrmann, K. *Historical and Commercial Atlas of China* (Cambridge, Mass., 1935).

An Historical Atlas of Islam. Published to accompany the *Encyclopaedia of Islam* (Leiden, 1981).

Lane-Poole, S. *The Mohammadan Dynasties* (London, 1894). A basic reference work, which V.V. Bartold translated into Russian with improved and expanded coverage for Central Asia: *Musulmanskie dinastii: Khronologicheskie i genealogicheskie tablitsy s istoricheskimi vvedeniyami* (St. Petersburg, 1899). Bartold's translation was also used by Turkish and Persian scholars for their translations and editions: Halil Edhem, *Düvel-i islamiye* (Istanbul, 1927; Turkish in Arabic script); and Sadiq Sajjadi, *Tarikh-i dawlatha-yi islami va khandanha-yi hukumatgar* (Tehran, 1375/1955–56).

Le Strange, G. *The Lands of the Eastern Caliphate: Mesopotamia, Persia, and Central Asia from the Moslem conquest to the Time of Timur.* A classic of historical geography published at Cambridge in 1905 and reissued by AMS Press, New York, in 1976 (Central Asia: Khurasan, pp. 382–432; The Oxus, pp. 433–45; Khwarizm, pp. 446–59; Sughd, pp. 460–73; The Provinces of the Jaxartes, pp. 474–89).

Sauvaget, J. *Introduction à l'histoire de l'orient musulman*; 2nd edn. revised by Cl. Cahen (Paris, 1961); and its English translation: *Jean Sauvaget's Introduction to the History of the Muslim East* (Los Angeles, 1965).

The Times Concise Atlas of World History. 5th edn. (London, 1994).

Wüstenfeld, H. A. *Wüstenfeld-Mahler'sche Vergleichungstabellen zur Muslimischen und Iranischen Zeitrechnung.* 3rd edn. by J. Mayr and B. Spuler (Wiesbaden, 1961).

Index Islamicus (Cambridge, 1958–).

Cahiers du Monde Russe et Soviétique (Paris, 1969–93); continued by *Cahiers du Monde Russe,* 1994–

Central Asia Monitor (Fairhaven, Vermont, 1992–).

Central Asian Review (London, 1953–68).

Central Asian Survey (Oxford, 1982–).

Central Asiatic Journal (Wiesbaden, 1955–).

Harvard Journal of Asiatic Studies (Cambridge, Mass., 1941–).

Journal of Asian History (Wiesbaden, 1966–).

Mongolian Studies (Bloomington, 1974–).

Papers on Far Eastern History (Canberra, 1970–).

Post-Soviet Geography (Silver Spring, MD, 1992–); continues *Soviet Geography*

Ural-Altaische Jahrbücher (Wiesbaden, 1928–).

Facts-on-File.

Keesing's Record of World Events.

Europa World Year Book (London, 1926–).

United Nations Organization. *Demographic Yearbook.*

PRINCIPAL SURVEYS OR INTRODUCTIONS

Akiner, Shirin. *Islamic Peoples of the Soviet Union*. 2nd edn. (London, 1986).

Barthold, W. (V.V. Bartold). *Turkestan Down to the Mongol Invasion*. 3rd edn. edited by C. E. Bosworth (London, 1968) (cited in our annotation as Barthold, *Turkestan*); a classic which covers the period from the arrival of Islam. The first edition of the original appeared as *Turkestan v epokhu mongolskago nashestviya* (St. Petersburg, 1900); it included in a separate volume a number of original sources in Arabic and Persian. The first English translation (published in 1928, and confusingly called "Second Edition") had been edited by the author himself assisted by H. A. R. Gibb; the second printing of this "Second Edition" appeared in 1957 with corrections and additions by V. Minorsky. In 1963, a new edition of the Russian original appeared as the first volume of a 10–volume edition of Barthold's works (V.V. Bartold, *Sochineniya*, Moscow, 1963–67). It has recently appeared in Persian and Arabic translations, and many of Barthold's other works have also been published in English, German, French, Turkish, Persian, and Arabic translations. While *Turkestan Down to the Mongol Invasion* remains this scholar's unsurpassed *magnum opus*, its very erudition and depth make it somewhat daunting reading for the non-specialist, who may at first prefer to reach for Bartold's briefer studies mentioned below in the general bibliography.

Bennigsen, A. and S. Enders Wimbush. *Muslims of the Soviet Empire: A Guide* (Bloomington, 1986).

Golden, P. B. *An Introduction to the History of the Turkic Peoples* (Wiesbaden, 1992). A thoroughly documented work with emphasis on the linguistic dimension of the subject.

Grousset, R. *The Empire of the Steppes: A History of Central Asia* (New Brunswick, 1970). Translation of a classic whose French original was first published in 1939 as *L'Empire des steppes*. Its chronological span starts with antiquity and ends with the eighteenth century.

Hambis, L., ed. *L'Asie Centrale: histoire et civilisation* (Paris, 1977).

Hambly, G., ed. *Central Asia* (New York, 1969). A cooperative effort of nine scholars, with the editor responsible for ten of its nineteen chapters. It first appeared in German translation as *Zentralasien* (Frankfurt, 1966).

Krader, L. *Peoples of Central Asia*. 3rd edn., (Bloomington and The Hague, 1971).

Sinor, D. *Introduction à l'étude de l'Eurasie Centrale* (Wiesbaden, 1963). A thorough bibliographic introduction.

Inner Asia: History, Civilization, Languages: A Syllabus (Bloomington, 1969). An abridgement of the above.

OTHER LITERATURE

Adshead, S. A. M. *Central Asia in World History*. (London, 1993).

Aini, Sadriddin. *See* Ayni.

Aitmatov, C. *The White Ship* (New York, 1972); a novel, also published in a different translation as *The White Steamship* (London, 1972). Translated from the Russian original *Belyi parokhod* (Moscow, 1968) (the Kyrgyz version, translated as *Ak keme* from the Russian original, appeared only later). The author, although writing mostly in Russian, became with this and other novels and short stories a famous champion of national values of the Kyrgyz and of other Central Asian Turks.

Akiner, Shirin, ed. *Mongolia Today* (London, 1991).

Algar, H. "A brief history of the Naqshbandi order," in *Naqshbandis: Cheminements et situation actuelle d'un ordre mystique musulman . . . Table Ronde de Sèvres, 1985* (Paris and Istanbul, 1990).

"The Naqshbandi order: a preliminary survey," *Studia Islamica* 54 (1976): 123–52.

Allsen, T. T. "Mahmud Yalavach, Mas'ud Beg, Ali Beg, Safaliq, Bujir," in *In the Service of the Khan: Eminent Personalities of the Early Mongol Yuan Period*, ed. I. de Rachewiltz (Wiesbaden, 1993), pp. 122–36.

"Mongol empire: an overview," *Encyclopedia of Asian History*, (New York and London, 1988), vol. 3, pp. 23–30.

Mongol Imperialism: The Policies of the Grand Qan Möngke in China, Russia, and the Islamic Lands, 1251–1259 (Berkeley, 1987).

"The rise of the Mongolian empire and Mongolian rule in North China," *Cambridge History of China*, vol. 6 (1994), pp. 321–413.

"Spiritual geography and political legitimacy in the eastern steppe," in *Ideology in the Formation of the Early States*, ed. H. J. M. Claessen. (Leiden, 1996), pp. 116–35.

"The Yüan dynasty and the Uighurs of Turfan in the 13th century," in *China Among Equals: the Middle Kingdom and its Neighbors, 10th-14th Centuries*, ed. M. Rossabi (Berkeley, 1983).

Allworth, E. A., ed. *Central Asia: 130 Years of Russian Dominance*. (Durham and London, 1994).

The Modern Uzbeks (Stanford, 1990).

Nationalities of the Soviet East: Publications and Writing Systems: A Bibliographical Directory and Transliteration Tables for Iranian and Turkic Language Publications, 1818–1945 (New York, 1971).

Uzbek Literary Politics. (London and The Hague, 1964).

Amanzholova, Dina Akhmetzhanovna. *Kazakhskiy avtonomizm i Rossiya: istoriya dvizheniya Alash* (Kazakh autonomism and Russia: a history of the Alash movement) (Moscow, 1994).

Asfendiyarov, Sandzhar Dzhafarovich (1889–1938). *Istoriya Kazakhstana* (History of Kazakhstan) (Alma-Ata, 1993). 2nd edn. (1st edn. published in 1935, but was subsequently suppressed, concurrently with the author's disappearance in the Gulag).

Aubin, Françoise. "Mongolie," and "Mongolie (République Populaire de)," *Encyclopaedia Universalis* (Paris, 1992), vol. 15, pp. 656–84.

Aubin, J. "Le khanat de Čagatai et le Khorasan (1334–1380)," *Turcica* 8 (1970): 16–60.

"Réseau pastoral et réseau caravanier: les grand'routes du Khorassan à l'époque mongole," *Le monde iranien et l'Islam* 1 (1971): 105–30.

Ayalon, D. "The Great Yasa of Chingiz Khan: a reexamination," *Studia Islamica*, nos. 32–3, 36, 38 (1971–73).

Ayni, Sadriddin (1878–1954). *Ēddoshtha* (Memoirs) (Dushanbe, 1949–54). 4 vols.; in Cyrillic script; two editions in the Arabic script have also been published: Stalinabad (Dushanbe) 1958–59; and Tehran 1983 (as *Yaddashtha*; edited by Saidi Sirjani); the author also wrote an Uzbek version of his memoirs: *Esdaliklar*, which was published in Tashkent, while several Russian editions of its Russian translation appeared in Moscow as *Vospominaniya*; finally an English translation of vol. 1 by J. Perry and Rachel Lehr has appeared as *The Sands of Oxus: Boyhood Reminiscences of Sadridding* [sic] *Aini* (Costa Mesa, 1998).

Bacon, Elizabeth. *Central Asians under Russian Rule: A Study in Culture Change*. 2nd edn. (Ithaca, 1980).

Bartold, V. V. (W. Barthold). *Four Studies on the History of Central Asia*; translated from the Russian by Vladimir and Tatiana Minorsky (Leiden, 1956–62). 3 vols. The four studies are: vol. 1, *A Short History of Turkestan*; and *History of Semireche*; vol. 2, *Ulugh Beg and his Time*; vol. 3, *Mir 'Ali Shir*; and *A History of the Turkman People*.

Histoire des Turcs d'Asie Centrale (Paris, 1948); French adaptation of Bartold's *Zwölf Vorlesungen über die Geschichte der Turken Mittelasiens*. Reprint Hildesheim, 1962. (based on lectures delivered at the University of Istanbul in 1926).

"O pogrebenii Timura" ("The burial of Timur"), in *Zapiski Vostochnogo otdeleniya Imperatorskogo Russkogo Arkheologicheskogo Obshchestva* 23 (1916): 1–32, and reprinted in his *Sochineniya*, vol. 2, pt. 2, pp. 423–54. The article's interest has been enhanced with the translation/updating by J. M. Rogers in *Iran: Journal of the British Institute of Persian Studies*, 12 (1974): 65–87.

Baskakov, N. A. *Altayskaya semya yazykov i ee izuchenie* (The Altaic family of languages and its study) (Moscow, 1981).

Vvedenie v izuchenie tyurkskikh yazykov (Introduction to the study of Turkic languages) (Moscow, 1969).

Batmaev, M. M. *Kalmyki v XVII–XVIII vv.* (The Kalmyks in the 17th–18th centuries) (Elista, 1992).

Bazin, L. *Les systèmes chronologiques dans le monde Turk ancien* (Budapest and Paris, 1991).

Bečka, J. "Literature and men of letters in Tajikistan," *Journal of Turkish Studies* (Harvard University), 18 (1994): 263–99.

Sadriddin Ayni: Father of Modern Tajik Culture (Naples, 1980).

"Traditional schools in the works of Sadriddin Ayni and other writers of Central Asia," *Archiv Orientální* 39 (1971): 284–321; 40 (1972): 130–63.

Becker, S. *Russia's Protectorates in Central Asia: Bukhara and Khiva, 1865–1924* (Cambridge, Mass., 1968).

Belenitskiy, A. M. et al. *Srednevekovyi gorod Sredney Azii* (The medieval city of Central Asia) (Leningrad, 1973).

Bennigsen, A. and S. Enders Wimbush. *Muslim National Communism in the Soviet Union: A Revolutionary Strategy for the Colonial World.* (Chicago and London, 1979).

Mystics and Commissars (Berkeley, 1987). Translation of their *Le soufi et le commissaire: les confréries musulmanes en USSR* (Paris, 1986).

Bennigsen, A. and Chantal Lemercier-Quelquejay. *La Presse et le mouvement national chez les musulmans de Russie avant 1920* (Paris and La Haye, 1964).

Benson, Linda. *The Ili Rebellion: The Moslem Challenge to Chinese Authority in Xinjiang, 1944–1949* (Armonk and London, 1990).

Blair, Sheila S. and J. M. Bloom *The Art and Architecture of Islam, 1250–1800* (New Haven, 1994). (Pelican History of Art).

Bodrogligeti, A. "Yasavi ideology in Muhammad Shaybani Khan's vision of an Uzbek Islamic empire," *Harvard Journal of Turkish Studies* 18 (1994): 41–56.

Bosworth, C. E. *The Ghaznavids* (Edinburgh, 1963).

The Later Ghaznavids (New York, 1977).

Boulger, D. Ch. *The Life of Yakoob Beg, Athalik Ghazi, and Badaulet, Ameer of Kashgar.* (London, 1878).

Boulnois, Lucette. *The Silk Road* (London, 1966). Translation of her *Route de la Soie.*

Boyle, J. A. *The Mongol World Empire, 1206–1370* (London, 1977).

"The seasonal residences of the Great Khan Ögedei," *Central Asiatic Journal* 16 (1972): 125–31.

Brandenburg, D. *Die Madrasa; Ursprung, Entwicklung, Ausbreitung und künstlerische Gestaltung der islamischen Moschee-Hochschule* (Graz, 1978).

Samarkand: Studien zur islamischen Baukunst in Uzbekistan (Zentralasien) (Berlin and Hessling, 1972).

Bregel, Yu. Excellent articles in the *Encyclopaedia Iranica*: see entries with his signature in the sections on "Bukhara" and "Central Asia."

"Khokand, Khanate of," *Encyclopedia of Asian History*, vol. 2, pp. 301–3.

Buell, P. D. "Sino-Khitan administration in Mongol Bukhara," *Journal of Asian History* 13/2 (1979): 121–51.

Burton, Audrey. *Bukharan Trade, 1558–1718* (Bloomington, 1993).

Caroe, O. *Soviet Empire: The Turks of Central Asia and Stalinism* (London, 1953).

Carrère d'Encausse, Hélène. *The End of the Soviet Empire: The Triumph of the Nations* (New York, 1993).

Islam and the Russian Empire: Reform and Revolution in Central Asia (Berkeley, 1988); translation of her *Réforme et révolution chez les Musulmans de l'Empire Russe: Bukhara 1867–1924*, 2nd edn. (Paris, 1981).

Castagné, J. *Les Basmatchis: le mouvement national des indigènes d'Asie Centrale* (Paris, 1925).

Central Asia: Its Strategic Importance and Future Prospects. Ed. H. Malik (New York, 1994).

Chalidze, Francheska. "Aral Sea crisis: a legacy of Soviet rule," *Central Asia Monitor* 1 (1992): 30–6.

"Plateau Usturt," *Central Asia Monitor* 3 (1992): 35–8.

Ch'en, Ch'ing-lung. *Çin ve bati kaynaklarina göre 1828 isyanlarindan Yakup Bey'e kadar*

Dogu Türkistan tarihi (A history of Eastern Turkestan from the uprisings of 1828 to Yakub Beg according to Chinese and western sources) (Tai-Pei, 1967).

Clark, L.V. "Introduction to the Uygur civil documents of East Turkestan (13th–14th cc.)." PhD dissertation, Indiana University 1975.

Clubb, O. E. *China and Russia: The "Great Game"* (New York, 1971).

Courant, M. *L'Asie Centrale aux XVIIe et XVIIIe siècles; empire Kalmouk ou empire Mantchou?* (Paris and Lyon, 1912).

Critchlow, J. *Nationalism in Uzbekistan: A Soviet Republic's Road to Sovereignty.* (Boulder, 1991).

Curtis, G. E. ed. *Kazakstan, Kyrgyzstan, Tajikistan, Turkmenistan and Uzbekistan: Country Studies* (Washington, D.C., 1997) (Area Handbook Series).

Dabbs, J. S. *History of the Discovery and Exploration of Chinese Turkestan* (The Hague, 1963).

Dale, S. F. *Indian Merchants and Eurasian Trade, 1600–1750* (Cambridge, 1994).
"Steppe humanism: the autobiographical writings of Zahir al-Din Muhammad Babur, 1483–1530," *International Journal of Middle East Studies* 22 (1990): 37–58.

Dawson, C., ed. *The Mongol Mission* (London and New York, 1955).

Deny, J. "Un soyurghal du timouride Chahruh en écriture ouigoure," *Journal Asiatique* (1957): 253–66.

DeWeese, D. *Islamization and Native Religion in the Golden Horde: Baba Tükles and Conversion to Islam in Historical and Epic Tradition* (University Park, Pennsylvania, 1994).

Dickson, M. B. "Uzbek dynastic theory in the sixteenth century," *Proceedings of the 15th International Congress of Orientalists* (Moscow, 1960), pp. 208–16.

Doerfer, G. *Türkische und mongolische Elemente im Neupersischen*, 4 vols. (Wiesbaden, 1963–75).

Donnelly, A. S. "Peter the Great and Central Asia," *Canadian Slavonic Papers* 17 (1975): 202–17.

Dreyer, June. *China's Forty Millions: Minority Nationalities and National Integration in the People's Republic of China* (Cambridge, Mass., 1976).

Dunnell, Ruth W. *The Great State of White and High: Budhism and State Formation in Eleventh-Century Xia* (Honolulu, 1996).

Eckmann, J. *Chagatay Manual* (Bloomington, 1966).

Egorov, V. L. *Istoricheskaya geografiya Zolotoy Ordy v XIII-XIV vv.* (Historical geography of the Golden Horde in the 13th–14th centuries) (Moscow, 1985).

Ettinghausen, R. and O. Grabar. *The Art and Architecture of Islam, 650–1250* (Harmondsworth and New York, 1987). (Pelican History of Art).

Feldman, W. "Interpreting the poetry of Makhtumquli," in *Muslims in Central Asia: Expression of Identity and Change*, ed. Jo-Ann Gross, (Durham and London, 1992), pp. 167–89.

Feschbach, M. and A. Friendly. *Ecocide in the USSR: Health and Nature Under Siege.* (New York, 1992).

Fierman, W., ed. *Central Asia: The Failed Transformation* (Boulder, 1991).

Language Planning and National Development: The Uzbek Experience. (Berlin and New York, 1991).

Fletcher, J. "China and Central Asia, 1368–1884," in *The Chinese World Order*, ed. J. K. Fairbank (Cambridge, 1968), pp. 206–24.

"The heyday of the Ch'ing order in Mongolia, Sinkiang, and Tibet," *Cambridge History of China*, vol. 10, pt. 1 (1978): 351–95.

"The Mongols: ecological and social perspectives," *Harvard Journal of Asiatic Studies* 46:1 (1986): 11–50.

Forbes, A. D. W. *Warlords and Muslims in Chinese Central Asia: A Political History of Sinkiang, 1911–1949* (Cambridge, 1986).

Forsyth, J. *A History of the Peoples of Siberia* (Cambridge, 1992).

Forsyth, T. D. *Report of a Mission to Yarkund in 1873* (Calcutta, 1875).

Frye, R. N. *Bukhara: The Medieval Achievement* (Norman, 1965).

The Heritage of Central Asia: from Antiquity to the Turkish Expansion (Princeton, 1996).

Fuchs, W. "Das Turfangebiet: seine äussere Geschichte bis in die T'angzeit," *Ostasiatische Zeitschrift*, n.s., 2 (1926): 124–66.

Gabain, Annemarie von. *Das Leben im uigurischen Königreich von Qočo (850–1250).* 2 vols. (Wiesbaden, 1973).

"Steppe und Stadt im Leben der ältesten Türken," *Der Islam* 29 (1949): 30–62.

Galuzo, G. *Turkistan – koloniya: ocherki istorii Turkestana ot zavoevaniya russkimi do revolyutsii 1917 goda* (The colony of Turkestan: an outline of the history of Turkestan from its conquest by the Russians to the 1917 revolution) (Moscow, 1929).

Geyer, Georgie Anne. *Waiting for Winter to End: An Extraordinary Journey through Soviet Central Asia* (Washington and London, 1994).

Gibb, H. A. R. *The Arab Conquests in Central Asia* (New York, 1923).

Giraud, R. *L'Empire des Turcs Célestes: les règnes d'Elterich, Qapghan et Bilgä (680–734)* (Paris, 1960).

Gleason, Gregory. *The Central Asian States: Discovering Independence* (Boulder, 1997).

Gohlman, W. E. *The Life of Ibn Sina* (Albany, 1974).

Golden, P. *Khazar Studies.* 2 vols. (Budapest, 1980).

"The migrations of the Oghuz," *Archivum Ottomanicum* 4 (1972): 45–84.

"Turkic languages," *Encyclopedia of Asian History*, vol. 4, pp. 152–55.

Goldstein, M. C. and Cynthia M. Beall. *The Changing World of Mongolia's Nomads* (Berkeley, 1994).

Golombek, Lisa. *The Timurid Shrine at Gazur Gah* (Toronto, 1969).

Golombek, Lisa and D. Wilber. *The Timurid Architecture of Iran and Turan.* 2 vols. (Princeton, 1988).

Gray, B., ed. *The Arts of the Book in Central Asia, 14th–16th Centuries* (London, 1979).

Grekov, B. D. and A.Yu. Yakubovskiy. *Zolotaya Orda i eë padenie* (Moscow, 1950). (The Golden Horde and its fall; the French translation, *La Horde d'Or: la domination tatare au XIIIe siècle de la mer Jaune a la mer Noire*, Paris 1939, is based on the first edition of the Russian original, *Zolotaya Orda.*)

Gross, Jo-Ann. "Khoja Ahrar: a study of the perceptions of religious power and prestige in the late Timurid period." PhD dissertation, New York University, 1982.

Gross, Jo-Ann, ed. *Muslims in Central Asia: Expressions of Identity and Change* (Durham and London, 1992).

Grousset, R. *Conqueror of the World* (New York, 1966). A biography of Genghis Khan translated from the French original, *Le conquérant du monde*, Paris 1944; the introduction to the translation, written by D. Sinor, includes a magnificent tribute to the great Frenchman.

Haarmann, U. "Staat und Religion in Transoxanien im frühen 16. Jahrhundert," *Zeitschrift der Deutschen Morgenländischen Gesellschaft* 124/2 (1974): 332–69.

Haghayeghi, M. *Islam and Politics in Central Asia* (New York, 1995).

Halkovic, S. A. *The Mongols of the West* (Bloomington, 1985).

Hamada, M. "Islamic saints and their mausoleums," *Acta Asiatica* 34 (1978): 79–98.

Hamilton, J. R. *Les Ouighours à l'époque des cinq dynasties d'après les documents chinois* (Paris, 1955).

"Toquz Oguz et On Uygur," *Journal Asiatique* (1962): 23–63.

Hartmann, M. *Chinesisch-Turkestan: Geschichte, Versetzung, Geistesleben und Wirtschaft* (Halle, 1908).

Ein Heiligenstaat in Islam; das Ende der Čaghataiden und die Herrschaft der Choǧas in Kasgarien (Berlin, 1905).

Hayit, B. *Basmatschi: nationaler Kampf Turkestans in den Jahren 1917 bis 1934* (Köln, 1992).

Sowjetrussische Orientpolitik am Beispiel Turkestans (Köln and Berlin, 1962).

Turkestan im XX. Jahrhundert (Darmstadt, 1956).

Turkestan zwischen Russland und China (Amsterdam, 1971).

"Zwei Gestalten in der modernen Literatur der Özbek-Türken Turkestans: Qadir und Čolpan," *Die Welt des Islams* 9 (1964): 225–36.

Hedin, S. *The Silk Road* (London, 1938).

Hillenbrand, R. *Islamic Architecture: Form, Function and Meaning* (New York, 1994).

Historical Monuments of Islam in the U.S.S.R. Tashkent, Moslem Religious Board of Central Asia and Kazakhstan, n.d.

Hobsbawm, E. *Nations and Nationalism since 1780.* 2nd edn. (Cambridge, 1992).

Holdsworth, Mary. *Turkestan in the Nineteenth Century* (London and Oxford, 1959).

Hookham, Hilda. *Timburlaine the Conqueror* (London, 1968).

Hopkirk, P. *The Great Game: The Struggle for Empire in Central Asia* (New York, 1994).

Howorth, H. H. *History of the Mongols, from the 9th to the 19th Centuries.* 4 vols. (London, 1876–80).

Hsu, I. C. Y. *The Ili Crisis: A Study of Sino-Russian Diplomacy, 1871 to 1881* (Oxford, 1965).

Ignatev, N. P. *Mission of N.P. Ignatev to Khiva and Bukhara in 1858* (Newtonville, Mass., 1984). (Translation of *Missiya v Khivu i Bukharu v 1858 godu fligel'-adyutanta polkovnika N. Ignat'eva.*)

Istoriya Kazakhskoy SSR. Alma-Ata 1979. 5 vols. The "official" history of Kazakhstan written by a consortium of scholars under the auspices of the Kazakh Academy of Sciences and published in Russian. Despite the compilers' general compliance with the guidelines imposed by the political system, it is a valuable resource and will remain so until superseded by similarly ambitious projects produced in the new freer climate. It is the best from among parallel histories published in the other republics: *Istoriya Kirgizskoy SSR, Istoriya Tadzhikskoy SSR, Istoriya Turkmenskoy SSR,* and *Istoriya Uzbekskoy SSR*. Each also appeared in the language of the respective republic; these versions, however, came out in smaller editions, and have been all but unavailable outside of their homeland. It remains to be seen how their successors produced in the independent republics will be received by the scholarly community previously accustomed to easier access through Russian and through the centrally organized book trade in Moscow. At this time (1998), the first harbinger of this type, *Uzbekiston tarihi* (History of Uzbekistan; Tashkent 1994; 5 vols.), is still a rare occurrence in library collections.

Jackson, P. "Dissolution of the Mongol empire," *Central Asiatic Journal* 22 (1978): 186–244.

Jackson, P. and D. Morgan. *The Mission of Friar William of Rubruck* (London, 1990).

Jisl, L. "Wie sahen die alten Türken aus?" *Ural-Altaische Jahrbücher* 40 (1968): 181–99.

Julien, S. "Relation d'un voyage officiel dans le pays des Ougours (de 981 à 983) par Wang yen-te," *Journal Asiatique* 4 (1847): 50–66.

Karimov, I. *Building the Future: Uzbekistan – its Own Model for Transition to a Market Economy* (Tashkent, 1993). The author is President of Uzbekistan, and his book can serve as an example of publications likely to document the political and economic evolution in the newly independent republics; the fact that it was also published in English translation is significant, as is its version in Uzbek: *Uzbekiston: milliy istiqlol, iqtisod, siёsat, mafkura; nutqlar, maqolalar, suhbatlar* (Tashkent, 1993).

Kazakhstan (Washington, D.C., International Monetary Fund, 1993) (*IMF Economic Reviews*; 1993: 5). An updated expansion of the 1992 edition, with the implicit intention to make this an annual publication. There are parallel publications on Kyrgyzstan, Tajikistan, Turkmenistan, and Uzbekistan.

Kazakhstan: The Transition to a Market Economy (Washington D.C., World Bank, 1993) (*A World Bank Country Study*). There are parellel publications, with slight variations in the subtitles, on Kyrgyzstan, Tajikistan, Turkmenistan, and Uzbekistan.

Khanykov, N. *Bokhara: Its Amir and its People* (London, 1845); translation of his *Opisanie bukharskogo khanstva* (St. Petersburg, 1843).

Khazanov, A. M. *After the USSR: Ethnicity, Nationalism, and Politics in the Commonwealth of Independent States* (Madison, 1995). A brilliant appraisal of the situation.

Nomads and the Outside Word. 2nd edn (Madison, 1994). (The Russian original appeared in Moscow in 1983; the first English translation was published by Cambridge University Press in 1984.)

"Underdevelopment and ethnic relations in Central Asia," in *Central Asia in Historical Perspective*, ed. Beatrice F. Manz (Boulder, 1994), pp. 144–63.

Khodarkovsky, M. *Where Two Worlds Met: The Russian State and the Kalmyk Nomads, 1600–1771* (Ithaca and London, 1992).

Kim, Ho-dong. "The Muslim rebellion and the Kashghar emirate in Chinese Central Asia, 1864–1877." PhD dissertation, Harvard University 1986.

Knobloch, E. *Beyond the Oxus: Archaeology, Art and Architecture of Central Asia* (London, 1972).

Kolstoe, P. *Russians in the Former Soviet Republics* (London, 1995). (Especially pp. 209–58, devoted to Central Asia.)

Kotov, K. F. *Mestnaya natsional'naya avtonomiya v Kitayskoy Narodnoy Respublike na primere Sin'tszyan-Uygurskoy Avtnomnoy Oblasti* (Local national autonomy in the People's Republic of China on the example of the Sinkiang Uighur Autonomous Region) (Moscow, 1959). See also its summary in *Central Asian Review* (London), 8 (1960): 441–57.

Kuropatkin, A. N. *Kashgaria: Historical-Geographical Sketch of the Country.* (Calcutta, 1882). Translation of his *Kashgariya: istoriko-geograficheskiy ocherk* (St. Petersburg, 1879).

Kyrgyzstan: The Transition to a Market Economy (Washington, D.C., World Bank, 1993) (*A World Bank Country Study*).

Landau, J. M. *Pan-Turkism: From Irredentism to Cooperation.* 2nd edn. (London, 1995).

The Politics of Pan-Islam (London, 1994).

Lattimore, O. *Pivot of Asia: Sinkiang and the Inner Asian frontiers of China and Russia.* (Boston, 1950).

Studies in Frontier History (Oxford 1962).

Lecoq, A. von. *Die buddhistische Spätantike in Mittelasien* 7 vols. (Berlin 1922–33).

Lewis, B. *The Arabs in History.* New edn. (Oxford, 1993).

Lewis, R. A. *Geographic Perspectives on Soviet Central Asia* (London, 1992).

Lindner, R. P. "What was a nomadic tribe?" *Comparative Studies in Society and History* 24 (1982): 689–711.

Liu, Mau-tsai. *Die chinesischen Nachrichten zur Geschichte der Ost-Türken (T'u-küe)* (Wiesbaden, 1958).

Lubin, Nancy. *Labour and Nationality in Soviet Central Asia* (Princeton, 1984).

McChesney, R.D. "The Amirs of Muslim Central Asia in the XVIIth Century," *Journal of Economic and Social History of the Orient*, 26 (1983): 33–70.

"Economic and Social Aspects of Public Architecture of Bukhara in the 1560s and 1570s," *Islamic Art* 2 (1987): 217–42.

Waqf in Central Asia: Four Hundred Years in the History of a Muslim Shrine (Princeton, 1991).

Central Asia: Foundations of Change (Princeton, 1996).

McNeill, W. H. *Plagues and Peoples* (New York, 1989).

Mackenzie, M. "Kaufman of Turkestan: an assessment of his administration (1867–1881)," *Slavic Review* 26 (1967): 265–85.

Mackerras, C. *The Uighur Empire According to the T'ang Dynastic Histories: A Study in Sino-Uighur Relations 744–840* (Canberra, 1972).

China's Minorities: Integration and Modernization in the 20th Century (Hongkong and New York, 1994).

Mair, Victor H. "Perso-Turkic bakhshi = Mandarin po-shih: learned doctor," *Journal of Turkish Studies* (Harvard University), 16 (1992): 117–27.

Maitra, K. M. *A Persian Embassy to China, Being an Extract from Zubdatul Tavarikh of Hafiz Abru* (New York, 1934).

Mano, E. "Moghulistan," *Acta Asiatica* (Tokyo), 34 (1978): 46–60.

Manz, Beatrice F., ed. *Central Asia in Historical Perspective* (Boulder 1994).

The Rise and Rule of Tamerlane (Cambridge, 1989).

Medlin, W. K. et al. *Education and Development in Central Asia: A Case Study on Social Change in Uzbekistan* (Leiden, 1971).

Menges, K. *The Turkic Languages and Peoples* (Wiesbaden, 1968).

Minorsky, V. "Tamim ibn Bahr's journey to the Uyghurs," *Bulletin of the School of Oriental and African Studies (BSOAS)* 12 (1947): 275–305.

Morgan, D. "The 'Great Yasa of Chingiz Khan' and Mongol law in the Ilkhanate," *BSOAS* 49/1 (1986): 163–76.

The Mongols (Oxford, 1986).

Moseley, G. *A Sino-Soviet Cultural Frontier: The Ili-Kazakh Autonomous Chou* (Cambridge, Mass., 1966).

Mukanov, M. S. *Kazakhskaya yurta: kniga-albom* (The Kazakh yurt: a picture book) (Alma-Ata, 1981).

Muradgea d'Ohsson, A. C. *Histoire des Mongols depuis Tchinguiz-Khan jusqu'à Timour Bey ou Tamerlan.* 4 vols. 2nd edn. (Amsterdam, 1852).

Nagel, T. *Timur der Eroberer und die islamische Welt des späten Mittelalters* (München, 1993).

Nalivkin, V. P. *Histoire du Khanat de Kokand* (Paris, 1889); (Translation of his *Kratkaya istoriya Kokandskogo khanstva* (Kazan, 1886)).

The Nationalities Question in the Post-Soviet States. Ed. Graham Smith (London & New York, 1995) (especially pp. 315–409 devoted to Central Asia).

New States, New Politics: Building the Post-Soviet Nations. Ed. Ian Bremmer and Ray Taras (Cambridge, 1997) (especially pp. 547–680 devoted to Central Asia).

Nurmukhammedov, N. *Mavzoley Khodzhi Akhmeda Yasevi* (The Mausoleum of Khoja Ahmad Yasavi) (Alma-Ata, 1980).

O'Kane, B. *Timurid Architecture in Khurasan* (Costa Mesa, 1987).

Olcott, Martha B. *The Kazakhs* (Stanford, 1987).

Onon, U. and Pritchatt, D. *Asia's First Modern Revolution: Mongolia Proclaims its Independence in 1911* (Leiden, 1989).

Palen (Pahlen), K. K. *Mission to Turkestan.* Ed. R. Pierce (London, 1964). The original, *Im Auftrag des Zaren in Turkestan,* was published five years later (Stuttgart, 1969). The author, a high Tsarist official of Baltic German descent, wrote this account after the 11 vols. of the official report had appeared in St. Petersburg: *Otchet po revizii Turkestanskogo kraya* (St. Petersburg, 1909–11).

Park, A. G. *Bolshevism in Turkestan, 1917–1927* (New York, 1957).

Pelliot, P. "Kao-tch'ang, Qočo, Houo-tcheou et Qara-khodja," *Journal Asiatique* (1912): 579–603.

Notes critiques d'histoire kalmouke 2 vols. (Paris, 1960). (Oeuvres posthumes de Paul Pelliot, 6.)

Notes sur l'histoire de la Horde d'Or (Paris, 1949). (Oeuvres posthumes, 2.)

Recherches sur les chrétiens d'Asie Centrale et d'Extrême-Orient (Paris, 1984).

Pierce, R. A. *Russian Central Asia, 1867–1917: A Study in Colonial Rule* (Berkeley, 1960).

Pipes, R. *The Formation of the Soviet Union: Communism and Nationalism* (Cambridge, Mass., 1964).

Pritsak, O. "Al-i Burhan," *Der Islam* 30 (1952): 81–96.

Pugachenkova, Galina A. and A. Khakimov. *The Art of Central Asia* (Leningrad, 1988).

Rachewiltz, I. de. *Papal Envoys to the Great Khans* (Stanford, 1971).

"Some remarks on the ideological foundations of Chinggis Khan's empire," *Papers on Far Eastern History* 7 (1973): 21–36.

"Yeh-lu Ch'u-ts'ai (1189–1243): Buddhist idealist and Confucian states-man," in *Confucian Personalities*, ed. A.F. Wright and D. Twitchett (Stanford, 1962), pp. 189–216.

Rashid, A. *The Resurgence of Central Asia: Islam or Nationalism?* (Karachi, 1994).

Ratchnevsky, P. *Genghis Khan: His Life and Legacy* (Oxford, 1991).

Richard, J. "La conversion de Berke et les débuts de l'islamisation de la Horde d'Or," *Revue des Etudes Islamiques* 35 (1967): 173–84.

Roemer, H.R. "Die Nachfolger Timurs – Abriss der Geschichte Zentral- und Vorderasiens im 15. Jahrhundert," in *Islamwissenschaftliche Abhandlungen*, ed. R. Grämlich (Wiesbaden, 1974), pp. 226–62.

"Neuere Veröffentlichungen zur Geschichte Timurs und seiner Nachfolger," *Central Asiatic Journal* 2 (1956): 219–32.

Rossabi, M. *China and Inner Asia from 1368 to the Present Day* (London, 1975).

"The 'decline' of the Central Asian caravan trade," in *The Rise of Merchant Empires: Long-Distance Trade in the Early Modern World, 1350–1750*, ed. James D. Tracy (Cambridge, 1990).

Khubilai Khan: His Life and Times (Berkeley, 1988).

Roux, J.-P. *La religion des Turcs et des Mongols* (Paris, 1985).

Rywkin, M. *Moscow's Lost Empire* (Armonk, NY, 1994).

Moscow's Muslim Challenge. 2nd edn. (New York, 1990).

Safargaliev, M. G. *Raspad Zolotoy Ordy* (Saransk, 1960).

Sanders, A. J. K. *Mongolia: Politics, Economics and Society* (London, 1987).

Saunders, J. J. *The History of the Mongol Conquests* (London, 1971).

Schuyler, E. *Turkistan: Notes of a Journey in Russian Turkistan, Khokand, Bukhara and Kuldja* 2 vols. (London, 1876).

Schwarz, H. G. "The Khwajas of Eastern Turkestan," *Central Asiatic Journal* 20 (1976): 266–96.

Semenov, A. A. "Kul'turnyi uroven' pervykh Sheybanidov" ("The cultural level of the first Shaybanids"). *Sovetskoe vostokovedenie* 3 (1956): 51–9.

Shaw, R. B. *The History of the Khojas of Eastern Turkestan, Summarized from the Tazkira-i-Kwajagan of Muhammad Sadiq Kashgari* (Calcutta, 1897).

Sinor, D. "Horse and pasture in Inner Asian history," *Oriens Extremus* 19 (1972): 171–84; reprinted in his *Inner Asia and its Contacts with Medieval Europe* (London, 1977).

Skrine, C. P. *Chinese Central Asia* (Boston and New York, 1926).

Skrine, C. P. and Nightingale, Pamela. *Macartney at Kashgar: New Light on British, Chinese and Russian Activities in Sinkiang, 1870–1918* (London, 1973).

Spuler, B. "Central Asia from the sixteenth century to the Russian conquest," *Cambridge History of Islam*, vol. 1 (1978): 468–494.

Die Goldene Horde. 2nd edn. (Wiesbaden, 1965).

History of the Mongols, Based on Eastern and Western Accounts of the 13th and 14th Centuries. Selected and translated by B. Spuler (Berkeley, 1972). English translation of his *Geschichte der Mongolen, nach östlichen und europäischen Zeugnissen des 13. und 14. Jahrhunderts* (Zürich, 1968).

Stein, M. A. *Innermost Asia* 4 vols. (Oxford, 1928). The final volume is an atlas of 47 maps on separate sheets (1: 500,000), "Maps of Chinese Turkestan and Kansu, from surveys made during the explorations of Sir A. Stein, 1900–1915, published by the Survey of India, 1918–1922."

"Innermost Asia: its geography as a factor in history," *The Geographical Journal* 65 (1925): 377–403, 473–501.

On Ancient Central Asian Tracks: Brief Narrative of Three Expeditions in Innermost Asia and North-Western China (London, 1933).

Ruins of Desert Cathay: Personal Narrative of Explorations in Central Asia and Westernmost China. 2 vols. (London, 1912).

Serindia. 5 vols. (Oxford, 1921).

Subtelny, Eva M. "Art and politics in early 16th century Central Asia," *Central Asiatic Journal* 27 (1983): 121–49.

"Babur's rival relations: a study of kingship and conflict in 15th–16th century Central Asia," *Der Islam* 66 (1989): 102–48.

"The cult of holy places: religious practices among Soviet Muslims," *Middle East Journal* 43 (1989): 593–604.

"The symbiosis of Turk and Tajik," in *Central Asia in Historical Perspective*, ed. Beatrice F. Manz (Boulder, 1994), pp. 45–61.

"A Timurid educational and charitable foundation: the Ikhlasiyya complex of Ali Shir Nava'i in 15th century Herat," *Journal of the American Oriental Society* 111 (1991): 38–91.

"The vaqfiya of Mir 'Ali Sir Nava'i as apologia," *Journal of Turkish Studies* (Harvard University), 15 (1991): 257–86.

Thubron, C. *The Lost Heart of Asia* (London, 1994).

Togan, Z. V. *Bugünkü Türkili (Türkistan) ve yakin tarihi* (Recent history of present-day Turkili [Turkestan]) (Istanbul, 1942–47). The awkward title obscures the brilliance and scope of this book.

Trimingham, J. S. *The Sufi Orders in Islam* (Oxford, 1971).

Tryjarski, E. "Origins of royal sovereignty and doctrinal legitimacy of the ruler according to Yusuf Khass Hajib of Balasagun," *Proceedings of the 34th Permanent International Altaistic Conference, Berlin 1991* (Wiesbaden, 1993), pp. 283–93.

Turkmenbashy, S. *Saparmurat Niyazov: Speeches.* 2 vols. (Alma Ata and New York, 1994). The author is President of Turkmenistan, and the purpose of the publication is similar to that of the President of Uzbekistan I. Karimov. *Uzbekistan: An Agenda for Economic Reform* (Washington, D.C., World Bank, 1993).

Vaidyanath, R. *The Formation of the Soviet Central Asian Republics: A Study in Soviet Nationalities Policy, 1917–1936* (New Delhi, 1967).

Valikhanov, Ch. *Sobranie Sochineniy.* 5 vols. (Alma-Ata, 1984–85).

Vambéry, A. *Travels in Central Asia . . . in 1863* (London, 1964).

Vasary, I. "History and legend in Berke Khan's conversion to Islam," *Proceedings of the 30th Permanent International Altaistic Conference, Bloomington 1987* (Bloomington, 1990), pp. 23–52.

Vladimirtsov, B. *Le régime social des Mongols: le féodalisme nomade* (Paris, 1948). Translation of his *Obshchestvennyi stroy Mongolov* (Leningrad, 1934).

Wheeler, G. *The Modern History of Soviet Central Asia* (New York, 1964). *The Peoples of Soviet Central Asia: A Background Book* (London, 1966).

Whiting, A. S. and Sheng Shih-ts'ai. *Sinkiang: Pawn or Pivot?* (East Lansing, 1958).

Witfogel, K. A. and Feng Chia-sheng. *History of Chinese Society: Liao, 907–1125* (Philadelphia, 1949) (*Transactions of the American Philosophical Society*, n.s. 36).

Woods, John E. *The Timurid Dynasty* (Bloomington, 1990) (Indiana University Papers on Inner Asia, no. 14).

Yule, H. *Cathay and the Way Thither.* Rev. edn. H. Cordier. 4 vols. (London, 1913–14).

Zhou, Xiuan. "Cultural interaction between Uyghurs, Chinese and Sogdians in the 8th to 13th centuries." PhD dissertation, Columbia Universtiy, 1994.

Zlatkin, I. R. *Istoriya Dzhungarskogo khanstva, 1635–1758* (History of the Jungar khanate). 2nd edn. (Moscow, 1983).

SELECTED SAMPLES OF PRIMARY SOURCES AND ANCILLARY MATERIALS

Abu l-Ghazi Bahadur Khan (1603–63). [*Shajara-i Turk*; Turki] *Histoire des Mongols et des Tatares*; Turki text and French translation published by P.I. Desmaisons (St. Petersburg, 1871–74).

Babur, Zahir al-Din Muhammad (1483–1530). *Baburname* [Turki] *Baburnamah: Chaghatay Turkish text with Abdul-Rahim Khankhanan's Persian translation.* Turkish transcription, Persian edition and English translation by W. M. Thackston (Harvard University, Department of Near Eastern Languages and Civilizations, 1993). 3 vols. This valuable new presentation does not entirely supersede the facsimile edition and translation published by Annette S. Beveridge (London, 1905–22).

Bayhaqi, Abu l-Fazl Muhammad (995–1077). *Tarikh-i Bayhaqi* [Persian]. The best edition is by Ali Akbar Fayyaz as *Tarikh-i Mas'udi* (Meshed, 1350/1972); Russian translation by A. K. Arends as *Istoriya Masuda*, 2nd edn. (Moscow, 1969).

Bertels, E. E. *Iz arkhiva sheykhov Dzhuybari* (From the archive of the Juybar shaykhs) (Moscow and Leningrad, 1938).

Bretschneider, E. *Medieval Researches from Eastern Asiatic Sources*. 2 vols. (London, 1888).

Bukhari, Mir Abd al-Karim (fl. 1804–30). *Histoire de l'Asie Centrale . . .* [Persian] *publiée, traduite et annotée par Ch. Schefer* (Paris, 1876).

Bukharskiy vakf XIII v.: faksimile, izdanie teksta, perevod s arabskogo i persidskogo, vvedenie i kommentariy A.K. Arendsa, A.B. Khalilova, O.D. Chekhovich (The Bukharan waqf from the 13th century. . .) (Moscow, 1979) (*Pismennye pamyatniki Vostoka*, 52).

Carpini, John Plano (d. 1252). [*Historia Mongalorum*. Latin] *History of the Mongols*; a new edition of the Latin original accompanied by an Italian translation and notes: *Storia dei Mongoli . . .* Spoleto 1989. English translation on pp. 3–76 of Dawson, *The Mongol Mission*.

Ch'ang Ch'un (1148–1227). [Account of his journey; Chinese]; translations in Bretschneider, *Medieval researchers . . .*, vol. 1, pp. 35–108; A. Waley, *Travels of an Alchemist: the Journey of the Taoist, Ch'ang-Ch'un, from China to the Hindukush at the Summons of Chingiz Khan, Recorded by his Disciple Li Chih-Ch'ang* (London, 1931); and Jeannette Mirsky, *The Great Chinese Travelers* (Chicago, 1964), pp. 115–171.

Chavannes, E. *Documents sur les Tou-kiue (Turcs) occidentaux* [Chinese, in French translation] (St. Petersburg, 1903).

Chekhovich, Olga D. *Bukharskie dokumenty XIV veka* (Bukharan documents from the 14th century; Persian or Arabic with Russian translation and annotation) (Tashkent, 1965).

Samarkandskie dokumenty XV-XVI vv. (Samarkand documents from the 15th–16th centuries; Persian or Arabic with Russian translation and annotation) (Moscow, 1974).

Churas, Shah Mahmud ibn Fazil (d. 1696). [*Tarikh*; Persian] *Khronika. . .* (Moscow, 1976). *Kriticheskiy tekst, perevod, kommentarii, issledovanie i ukazateli O.F. Akimushkina* (*Pismennye Pamyatniki Vostoka*, 45). Edition and translation by Akimushkin.

Clavijo, Ruy Gonzales de (d. 1412). [*Embajada a Tamorlan*; Spanish] *Embassy to Tamerlane, 1403–1406*; translated by G. Le Strange (London, 1928); edition and study by F. Lopez Estrada (Madrid, 1943).

Dawson, C., ed. *The Mongol Mission* (London and New York, 1955).

Donish, A. (1826–97). [*Tarikh-i saltanat-i manghitiya*; Persian] *Traktat Akhmada Donisha "Istoriya mangitskoy dinastii."* Russian translation by I. A. Nadzhafova (Dushanbe, 1967).

Gardizi (11th century). [*Zayn al-akhbar*. Persian] *Tarikh-i Gardizi*. Ed. A. Habibi (Tehran, 1363/1984).

Partial translation by P. Martinez, "Gardizi's two chapters on the Turks," *Archivum Eurasiae Medii Aevi* 2 (1982): 109–217.

Hafiz-i Tanish Bukhari (16th century). [*Sharafnamah-i shahi*, also called *Abdallah-nama*; Persian]. Edited and translated by M. A. Salakhetdinova 2 vols. (Moscow, 1983).

Hamilton, J. R. *Manuscrits ouigours du IXe-Xe siècle de Touen- Houang; textes établis, traduits et commentés* 2 vols. (Paris, 1986).

Hamilton, J. R. and Shimin Geng. "L'Inscription ouigoure de la stèle commemorative des iduq qut de Qotcho," *Turcica* 13 (1981): 10–54.

Haydar Dughlat (1499–1551). *Tarikh-i Rashidi.* See *Tarikh-i Rashidi.*

Hsüan-tsang (596–664). [*Si-yu-ki*; Chinese] *Buddhist records of the Western world.* Translated from the Chinese of Hiuen Tsiang (AD 629) by S. Beal. 2 vols. (London, 1884). Mirsky, *The Great Chinese Travelers*, pp. 29–114.

Hudud al-'Alam. "The Regions of the World." A Persian geography, 372 AH/982 AD, translated by V. Minorsky (London, 1937). (GMS 11); see also Minorsky's "Addenda to the Hudud al-Alam," *BSOAS* 17 (1955): 250–70.

Ibn Arabshah (1392–1450). *Aja'ib al-maqdur fi akhbar Timur* [Arabic]. Ed. A. Himsi (Beirut, 1986); English translation of this account of Timur's career by J. H. Sanders as *Tamerlane* (London, 1936).

Ibn Battuta (fl. 1304–68). [*Rihla*; Arabic] Edited and translated by C. Defrémery and B. R. Sanguinetti as *Voyages d'Ibn Battuta*, 4 vols. (Paris, 1854); English translation by H. A. R. Gibb as *The Travels of Ibn Battuta.* 4 vols. (Cambridge, 1971–95).

Ibn Fadlan (fl. 921–22). [*Rihla*; Arabic] Edited and translated into German by Z. V. Togan as *Ibn Fadlans Reisebericht* (Leipzig, 1939).

Ibn Hawqal (fl. 943–73). *Kitab surat al-ard* [Arabic]. 3rd edn. by J. H. Kramers (Leiden, 1938); translated into French by G. Wiet as *Configuration de la terre.* 2 vols. (Paris and Beirut, 1964).

Jenkinson, P. (fl. 16th century; d. 1611). Account of his journey in *Early Voyages and Travels to Russia and Persia* (London, 1886).

Juvayni, Ata-Malik (1226–83). *Tarikh-i jahan-gusha* [Persian]. Ed. M. Qazvini. 3 vols. (London and Leiden, 1912–37). English translation by J. A. Boyle, *The History of the World Conqueror.* 2 vols. (Cambridge, Mass., 1958).

Juzjani, Minhaj Siraj (1193–1260). *Tabaqat-i Nasiri* [Persian]. 2nd edn., 2 vols. (Kabul, 1342–43/1963–64); English translation by H. G. Raverty, 2 vols. (London, 1881). (*Bibliotheca Indica* 78).

Kashghari, Mahmud (fl. 1072). *Divanu lugat-it-Türk* [Arabic/Turkic]. Edited and published by B. Atalay. 6 vols. (Ankara, 1939–57). Translated by R. Dankoff and J. Kelly as *Compendium of the Turkic Dialects*, 3 vols. (Cambridge, Mass., 1982–85), vol. 1., parts 1–3 (1982–85).

Khadr, M. "Deux actes de waqf d'un Qarahanide d'Asie Centrale," *Journal Asiatique* (1967): 305–34.

Khunji, Fazl Allah ibn Ruzbihan (1455–1521). *Mihmannama-i Bukhara* [Persian]. Ed. M. Sutudah (Tehran, 1976); ed. and translated into Russian by A. K.

Arends (Moscow, 1976). German abridgement by Ursula Ott, *Transoxanien und Turkestan zu Beginn des 16. Jahrhunderts: das Mihman-nama-yi Buhara* (Freiburg, 1974).

Khvand Amir (1475–1536). *Habib-i siyar* [Persian]. Edited by D. Siyaqi, 2nd edn. 4 vols. (Tehran, 1353/1974). English translation by W. M.Thackston (Cambridge, Mass., 1994– (in progress)).

Kurat, A. N. *Topkapi Sarayi Müzesi Arsivindeki Altin Ordu, Kirim ve Türkistan hanlarina ait yarlik ve bitikler* (*Yarliks* and *bitiks* issued by the khans of the Golden Horde, the Crimea and Turkestan in the archive of the Topkapi Palace Museum) (Istanbul, 1940).

Markov, A. *Inventarnyi katalog musul'manskikh monet Imperatorskogo Ermitazha* (Inventory catalog of Muslim coins in the Imperial Hermitage) (St. Petersburg, 1896).

Mirza Muhammad Haydar Dughlat (1499–1551). *Tarikh-i Rashidi*. See *Tarikh-i Rashidi*.

Munis Khwarazmi (1778–1829). *Firdaws al-iqbal: history of Khorezm*, ed. Yu. Bregel [Turki] (Leiden, 1988). (Also noteworthy is the editor's introduction on pp. 1–60.)

Narshakhi (d. 959). *Tarikh-i Bukhara* [Persian]; editions Ch. Schefer (Paris, 1892), and M. Razavi (Tehran, 1351/1972); English translation by R. Frye as *The History of Bukhara* (Cambridge, Mass., 1954).

Nasawi, Muhammad b. Ahmad (d. 1260). *Sirat Jalal al-Din*. Arabic text edited and translated into French by O. Houdas 2 vols. (Paris, 1891–95).

Nava'i, Mir Ali Shir (1441–1501). *Muhakamat al-lughatayn* [Turki] *Muhakamat al-lughatain* . . . Edited and translated by R. Devereux (Leiden, 1966).

Polo, Marco (1254–1323). *The book of Ser Marco Polo, the Venetian, concerning the kingdoms and marvels of the East* . . . translated and edited by H. Yule. 2 vols. (London, 1871). See also H. Cordier, *Ser Marco Polo: notes and addenda to Sir Henry Yule's edition* (London, 1920).

Rashid al-Din (1247–1318). *Jami' al-tavarikh* [Persian]. After several partial editions and translations of this important source, a full critical edition prepared by Muhammad Rawshan has now been published (Tehran, 1995); from among the partial translations, one example: *The Successors of Genghis Khan*, translated by J. A. Boyle (New York and London, 1971).

Riza Quli Khan (1800–71). *Relation de l'ambassade au Kharezm de Riza Qouly Khan* [Persian], traduite et annotée par Ch. Schefer (Paris, 1979).

Rubruck, William (Willem van Ruysbroeck) (1210–70). *The Journey of William of Rubruck* [Latin]; published by A. van den Wyngaert, Sinica Franciscana, vol. 1: *Itinera et relationes Fratrum Minorum saec. XIII et XIV*, (Quaracchi-Firenze, 1929); English translation ("by a Nun of Stanbrook Abbey") in Ch. Dawson, *The Mongol Mission*, pp. 87–220.

Sagang Sechen (b. 1604). *Erdeni-yin tobci*; [Mongolian] *Geschichte der Ostmongolen und ihres Fürstenhauses* . . . *übersetzt, mit dem Originaltexte* . . . *herausgegeben von I.J. Schmidt* (St. Petersburg and Leipzig, 1829; reprint The Hague 1961); English translation by J. R. Krueger, *A History of the Eastern Mongols to 1662* (Bloomington, 1964).

Salih, Muhammad (1455–1535). *Shaybani-name* [Turki]. Edition and German translation by H. Vambéry (Vienna, 1885).

Schiltberger, J. (b. 1380). [Reisebuch] *Als Sklave im Osmanischen Reich und bei den Tataren, 1394–1427*. Translated from Middle German by Ulrich Schlemmer (Stuttgart, 1983).

Schlegel, G. *Die chinesische Inschrift auf dem uigurischen Denkmal in Kara Balghasun* (Helsinki, 1896). (MSFOu 9).

The Secret History of the Mongols. [Mongolian: *Manghol un niuca tobca'an*; Chinese: *Yuan-ch'ao-pi-shi*] There are several editions and translations into German, Russian, French and English; the three English translations are by I. de Rachewiltz, in *Papers on Far Eastern History*, vols. 4–5, 10, 13, 16, 18, 21, 23, 26, 30, 31, and 33 (Canberra, 1971–86); F. Cleaves, as *The Secret History of the Mongols* (Cambridge, Mass., 1982), and U. Onon, as *The History and the Life of Ginggis Khan* (Leiden, 1990).

Seyfi Chelebi. [Ottoman Turkish] *L'Ouvrage de Seyfi Çelebi, historien Ottoman du XVIe siècle*; edited, critique, translation and commentary by J. Matuz (Paris, 1968).

Tarikh-i Rashidi [Persian]. By Mirza Muhammad Haydar Dughlat (1499–1551). English translation by N. Elias and E. Denison Ross as *Tarikh-i Rashidi: a History of the Moghuls of Central Asia* (London, 1898); ed. and trans. as Mirza Haydar Dughlat, *Tarikh-i-Rashidi: a History of the Khan of Moghulistan*, by W. M. Thackston, Harvard University Dept. of Near Eastern Languages and Civilizations, 1996, vol. 1 (Persian text), vol. 2 (English translation).

Tekin, T. *A Grammar of Orkhon Turkic* (Bloomington, 1968). Includes texts and translations of the Orkhon inscriptions, pp. 231–95.

Thackston, W. M. *A Century of Princes: Sources on Timurid History and Art*, selected and translated by W. M. Thackston (Cambridge, Mass., 1989).

Türkische Turfantexte. Texts with various degrees of analysis and translation published in 10 vols. by the Academy of Sciences, Berlin; vols. 1–5 were published and equipped with an index by W. Bang and Annemarie von Gabain (Berlin, 1929–31).

Umari, Ibn Fadl Allah (1301–49). *Masalik al-absar fi mamalik al-amsar* [Arabic]. Edited and translated by K. Lech as *Das Mongolische Weltreich: Al Umari's Darstellung der mongolischen Reiche in seinem Werk Masalik* (Wiesbaden, 1968).

Vali, Mahmud ibn Amir (17th century). *Bahr al-asrar fi manaqib al- akhyar* [Persian]. Russian translation of the geographical part by B. A. Akhmedov, *More tayn otnositelno doblestey blagorodnykh* (Tashkent, 1977).

Yazdi, Sharaf al-Din Ali (d. 1454). *Zafarname* [Persian]. Ed. M. Abbasi. 2 vols. (Tehran, 1336/1957). French translation (somewhat abridged) by A. L. M. Pétis de la Croix (1698–1751), *Histoire de Timur-Bec*. 4 vols. (Paris, 1722); and an English translation of the French abridgment as *The History of Timur-Bec, known by the name of Tamerlaine the Great, Emperor of the Moguls and Tatars*. 2 vols. (London, 1722).

Yusuf Khass Hajib (11th century). Qutadghu Bilig [Turkic]. Edited by R. R. Arat (Ankara, 1979); English translation by R. Dankoff, *Wisdom of Royal Glory* (Chicago, 1983).

Index